SPECIAL CHARACTERS

Bullet	Ctrl+Shift+8
Double quotation mark, opening	Ctrl+Shift+[
Double quotation mark, closing	Ctrl+Shift+]
Single quotation mark, opening	Ctrl+[
Single quotation mark, closing	Ctrl+]
Copyright mark	Ctrl+Shift+O (letter O)
Ellipses	Alt+0133
Em dash	Alt+0151
En dash	Alt+0150
Line break	Shift+Enter
Soft hyphen	Ctrl+hyphen
Paragraph mark	Ctrl+Shift+7
Registration mark	Ctrl+Shift+G
Section mark	Ctrl+Shift+6
Trademark symbol	Alt+0153

SPACING CONTROLS

Em space	Ctrl+Shift+M
En space	Ctrl+Shift+N
Nonbreaking space	Ctrl+Spacebar
Thin space	Ctrl+Shift+T
Kern apart .04 em	Ctrl+Keypad Plus
Kern apart .01 em	Ctrl+Shift+Keypad Plus
Kern together .04 em	Ctrl+Keypad Minus
Kern together .01 em	Ctrl+Shift+Keypad Minus
Clear manual kerning	Ctrl+Shift+0 (zero)

FOR EVERY KIND OF COMPUTER USER, THERE IS A SYBEX BOOK.

All computer users learn in their own way. Some need straightforward and methodical explanations. Others are just too busy for this approach. But no matter what camp you fall into, SYBEX has a book that can help you get the most out of your computer and computer software while learning at your own pace.

Beginners generally want to start at the beginning. The **ABC's** series, with its step-by-step lessons in plain language, helps you build basic skills quickly. Or you might try our **Quick & Easy** series, the friendly, full-color guide.

The **Mastering** and **Understanding** series will tell you everything you need to know about a subject. They're perfect for intermediate and advanced computer users, yet they don't make the mistake of leaving beginners behind.

If you're a busy person and are already comfortable with computers, you can choose from two SYBEX series—**Up & Running** and **Running Start**. The **Up & Running** series gets you started in just 20 lessons. Or you can get two books in one, a step-by-step tutorial and an alphabetical reference, with our **Running Start** series.

Everyone who uses computer software can also use a computer software reference. SYBEX offers the gamut—from portable **Instant References** to comprehensive **Encyclopedias, Desktop References**, and **Bibles**.

SYBEX even offers special titles on subjects that don't neatly fit a category—like **Tips & Tricks**, the **Shareware Treasure Chests**, and a wide range of books for Macintosh computers and software.

SYBEX books are written by authors who are expert in their subjects. In fact, many make their living as professionals, consultants or teachers in the field of computer software. And their manuscripts are thoroughly reviewed by our technical and editorial staff for accuracy and ease-of-use.

So when you want answers about computers or any popular software package, just help yourself to SYBEX.

For a complete catalog of our publications, please write:

SYBEX Inc.
2021 Challenger Drive
Alameda, CA 94501
Tel: (510) 523-8233/(800) 227-2346 Telex: 336311
Fax: (510) 523-2373

SYBEX is committed to using natural resources wisely to preserve and improve our environment. As a leader in the computer book publishing industry, we are aware that over 40% of America's solid waste is paper. This is why we have been printing the text of books like this one on recycled paper since 1982.

This year our use of recycled paper will result in the saving of more than 15,300 trees. We will lower air pollution effluents by 54,000 pounds, save 6,300,000 gallons of water, and reduce landfill by 2,700 cubic yards.

In choosing a SYBEX book you are not only making a choice for the best in skills and information, you are also choosing to enhance the quality of life for all of us.

mASTERING PAGEMAKER 5.0
FOR WINDOWS

MASTERING PAGEMAKER® 5.0 FOR WINDOWS™

Rebecca Bridges Altman
Rick Altman

SYBEX® San Francisco ■ Paris ■ Düsseldorf ■ Soest

Acquisitions Editor: Dianne King
Developmental Editor: Kenyon Brown
Editor: Savitha Varadan
Technical Editor: Dean Denno
Book Design and Chapter Art: Claudia Smelser
Screen Graphics: John Corrigan
Page Layout and Typesetting: Len Gilbert
Proofreader/Production Coordinator: Catherine Mahoney
Indexer: Matthew Spence
Cover Designer: Archer Design
Cover Photo Art Direction: Ingalls + Associates
Cover Photographer: Michael Lamotte

To our darling daughter, Erica,
who completely ruined our writing schedule by being born two weeks early

*a*CKNOWLEDGMENTS

Getting this book out on time with a newborn in the household was not an easy task, and we could not have done it without the help and patience of others. At SYBEX, we would like to thank our editors, Ken Brown and Savitha Varadan. Our technical editor, Dean Denno, was probably the finest we've ever worked with. We would also like to thank our contacts at Aldus, Freda Cook and Dan Keller; the Aldus technical support staff was extremely responsive and helpful also.

Finally, we'd like to thank Sandy Baker, a color meister at BCA Desktop Designs in Walnut Creek, for her help with the color chapter.

CONTENTS AT A GLANCE

Part III   *Working with Graphics*   359

C H a P T e R S

Part IV   *Managing Your Projects*   535

C H a P T e R S

Appendices

t ABLE OF CONTENTS

Part II Working with Text

C H a P T e R   5

Using the Story Editor   *155*

C H a P T e R   7

Going in Style   249

C H a P T e R   9

Advanced Text Formatting Techniques   **333**

Part III   Working with Graphics

C H a P T e R   10

Using the Graphics Tools   **361**

C H a P T e R   11

C H a P T e R 12

Working with Color 463

C H a P T e R   13

Using the Table Editor   **497**

Part IV   Managing Your Projects

C H a P T e R   14

Cloning Your Publications   537

C H a P T e R   15

Working with Monster Projects   573

C H a P T e R   16

The PageMaker Cookbook   617

Appendices

A P P e N d i X A

Installing PageMaker 5.0   653

A P P e N d i X B

Working with Fonts   667

A P P e N d i X C

Creating Print Files for Remote Printing   677

A P P e N d i X D

Aldus Additions   683

Index   691

*i*NTRODUCTION

Don't look now, but you're about to enter a war. The battles are not fought with guns and tanks, but with dialog boxes and floating palettes. In the short history of electronic publishing, the landscape has never been as competitive as it is today, and as a PageMaker user or prospective user, you'll get a front-line view of it all.

The choice of desktop publisher used to be so easy: You purchased Aldus PageMaker for short publications or Ventura Publisher for long documents. Today, PageMaker and Ventura barely compete; PageMaker now does battle with QuarkXPress, freshly ported to Windows, and this battle takes place a bunker away from the battle that Ventura Publisher and FrameMaker wage against each other.

And in its battle with QuarkXPress, PageMaker's primary weapon is obvious: Version 5.0. With this release, PageMaker joins the ranks of modern-day software, capable of using new typeface technology, sharing graphics, producing better color output, and providing instant access to formatting options in a control palette. Generally, the reaction to this news is either "Hallelujah!" or "It's about time." Your choice. Either way, Version 5.0 represents a significant and major new release of Aldus' flagship product.

HOW TO USE THIS BOOK

Mastering PageMaker for Windows is both a tutorial and a reference guide. If you are a PageMaker neophyte, you can start at the beginning of the book and read through to the end; each chapter builds on the material covered in the preceding chapter, and the instructions are clear and easy to follow. As a beginner, you will probably be interested in the Hands-On Practice section at the end of most chapters. This section is a tutorial, with easy step-by-step exercises that you can follow at your computer. The Hands-On Practice exercises are an ideal way to practice the techniques covered in the chapter, before you tackle your own projects. Pictures of the screen are provided at key points so that you can check to make sure you are on the right track, and the companion disk at the back of this book contains files for you to use in these exercises.

If you already have some experience with PageMaker, this book makes an excellent reference guide. Perhaps you are now ready to learn a new feature, such as paragraph styles. You can look in the table of contents or index and turn directly to this topic. It's not necessary to have read or gone through the exercises in the preceding chapters; each chapter stands on its own. Furthermore, the Fast Track section at the beginning of each chapter provides you with a quick reference to the chapter's main points. In this command summary, you will find the basic steps for doing a task, along with the page number on which the topic is discussed in greater detail. The Fast Track lets you locate the topics you are interested in and go directly to those discussions. It's also a great reference tool when you need to review a command.

NEW FEATURES IN PAGEMAKER 5

This book was written for the latest version of PageMaker, which contains an abundance of new features, as listed below.

- A control palette that offers handy access to text formatting options as well as commands for manipulating graphic objects

- Over 20 Additions that increase the functionality of the program

- Ability to have multiple files open

- A rotation tool

- OLE support

- Advanced color support

- A Multiple Paste option for creating several evenly spaced copies of an object

- The ability to create custom lines

Version
5.0
These are just the most noteworthy new features in PageMaker 5.0. There are dozens more that you will discover as you explore the program and read this book. All new features are marked with a 5.0 icon in the margin next to the appropriate paragraph (as shown here). If you are upgrading from Version 4.0 to Version 5.0, you will find these sections very useful.

HOW THIS BOOK IS ORGANIZED

This book is divided into four parts and has four appendices. The chapters in each part are briefly described below.

PART I: GETTING STARTED

Part I introduces the basic procedures for creating publications in Page-Maker. This part is the foundation upon which the book is built.

In Chapter 1, you will learn how to interact with PageMaker. This chapter describes how to start the program, and shows you how to use the mouse and give commands.

Chapter 2 provides new PageMaker users with a quick tour of the publishing process. As you follow the steps in this chapter, you will go through the mechanics and maneuvers inherent in building a publication in PageMaker.

Chapter 3 covers two important parts of the desktop publishing process: specifying the layout of your page and printing your publication.

PART II: WORKING WITH TEXT

Text is the primary ingredient in most publications, and Part II will demonstrate the variety of ways you can place and format text.

In Chapter 4, you will learn how to use PageMaker's text tool to correct typing errors, move text to another location on the page, and change the size and style of the type.

Chapter 5 describes how to use PageMaker's built-in word processor, the Story Editor. This editor has many of the same capabilities as a word processing program, including finding and replacing text and checking spelling.

Chapter 6 explains the many different ways you can format paragraphs: centering, justification, indentation, hyphenation, spacing, and so on. In the Hands-On Practice section, you will format paragraphs in a three-panel brochure.

Chapter 7 shows you how to automate the formatting process by using the *style* feature. With styles, changing a paragraph's format is only a few mouse clicks away.

Chapter 8 demonstrates another way to place text on the page: by importing it from a file you created in your word processor. You will also learn how to link your publication to an external text file so that when you change the text file, the publication automatically reflects this change.

Chapter 9 describes the different ways you can adjust the spacing between letters and words in PageMaker. You will also learn how to rotate and skew text as well as create drop caps.

PART III: WORKING WITH GRAPHICS

In Part III, you will learn how to add numerous graphic elements (lines, boxes, drawings, color, and so on) to your publications. Graphic elements contribute variety and visual interest to a page. There are two ways to add graphics to a page: by drawing them in PageMaker or by importing them from an external graphics program. Chapter 10 shows you how to create graphics with PageMaker's built-in drawing tools. Chapter 11 explains how to import external images. Chapter 12 shows you how to add color to your publications and print color separations.

Chapter 13 discusses the Table Editor, a stand-alone program included with PageMaker. With the Table Editor, you can create a wide variety of columnar material such as financial reports, forms, calendars, schedules, and price lists.

PART IV: MANAGING YOUR PROJECTS

Part IV presents strategies for managing different types of publishing projects. Chapter 14 describes how to clone a publication that you will be using over and over again, such as a monthly newsletter. Chapter 15 shows you how to manage "monster" (large) projects, such as a book. You will learn how to create a table of contents and an index. Chapter 16 is what we call "The PageMaker Cookbook." In this chapter, we give you recipes for a variety of projects, from business cards and resumes to menus and invitations.

APPENDICES

While the appendices are at the back of the book, don't wait until you have finished Chapters 1 through 16 before you read them. Appendix A takes you through the steps of installing PageMaker, so if you haven't yet run the ALDSETUP program, follow the steps in this appendix.

Appendix B discusses many different aspects of using fonts in Page-Maker. It discusses the difference between Type 1 and TrueType fonts, and covers issues such as font installation and downloading.

Appendix C explains the process of printing documents on remote Post-Script printers and high-resolution typesetting devices. If professional quality is your goal, read this appendix to see how you can achieve it.

Finally, Appendix D summarizes all of the Aldus Additions that come with PageMaker 5.0.

Part

O N e

I

Part I is dedicated to the novice PageMaker user. The three chapters in this section will introduce you to desktop publishing concepts and the basic procedures for creating publications in PageMaker. Even if you have been using PageMaker for a while, you still might want to read through these chapters because you will undoubtedly pick up a few shortcuts and fill in some gaps in your knowledge about the software.

GETTING STARTED

Interacting
with
PageMaker

*f*ast tracks

HENEVER YOU BUY A NEW electronic toy, whether it's a VCR, a microwave oven, or a PC with Page-Maker, the first thing you have to do after plugging it in is determine what you have to do to make it work. You need to know what all the buttons mean, how to give instructions, and how to read or understand the electronic display. This chapter gives you the information you need to begin working with PageMaker. You will start the program, learn how to use the menus, and learn the significance of what you see in the PageMaker window.

If you are experienced with other Windows applications or Macintosh software, you may find that you are already familiar with much of the information presented here. You may want to skim over the material, looking at the section headings to see if any of the topics are new to you.

STARTING PAGEMAKER

If you haven't yet installed PageMaker on your hard disk, you should turn to Appendix A for instructions and return here when you are finished. You also must have Microsoft Windows 3.1 installed on your computer before you can load PageMaker.

Follow these steps to start PageMaker:

1. In the Windows Program Manager, check to see if your Aldus group is open. If you see a window titled Aldus that contains the PageMaker 5.0 icon, as shown in Figure 1.1, proceed to step 4. Otherwise, continue with the next step.

2. Move the mouse pointer to the Aldus group icon (or whichever group PageMaker is in).

3. Click the left mouse button twice quickly. This is called *double-clicking*.

You will see a window containing the group's program icons. Your screen should look similar to Figure 1.1. If you got a menu instead of the window, you didn't click the button correctly. Press Esc and try again.

FIGURE 1.1: *The PageMaker 5.0 icon in the Aldus program group*

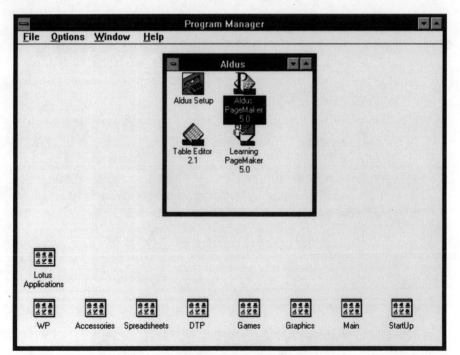

4. Move the mouse pointer to the PageMaker 5.0 icon.

5. Double-click the left mouse button to load the PageMaker program.

After 30 seconds or so, you will see the menu bar at the top of the screen.

USING THE MENUS

You use the menu bar to give PageMaker instructions on how to lay out your pages. As shown in Figure 1.2, the menu bar contains eight different options:

→ File: Use this menu to manipulate your files. You can create, open, close, save, export, and import files. The menu also contains commands for printing.

→ Edit: This menu contains options for cutting and pasting text and graphics.

→ Utilities: This menu is the gateway to the Aldus Additions. It also contains Story Editor commands (to perform searches, replacements, and spell checking), and options for creating tables of contents and indices.

→ Layout: Use this menu to view the page at different levels of magnification. For example, you can see the entire page at once with one option, or you can zoom a section of a page to twice its actual size with another. You can also choose to insert and delete pages. This menu also contains items that can be turned on and off, such as rulers and guides.

→ Type: The options on this menu allow you to specify the size and alignment of your text. Almost everything related to text is

FIGURE 1.2: *The menu bar*

on the Type menu, including fonts, sizes, alignment, type styles, spacing, and indentations. You will probably use this menu more than any other.

➤ Element: This menu contains options that affect graphic elements.

➤ Window: Use this menu to control what you see in your window. For example, you can turn on and off the display of a toolbox, color palette, control palette, and a style palette.

➤ Help: Use this menu to display an index of different topics on which online information is available. You can also press F1 at any time for help.

Version
5.0

If you are converting from version 4.0 to 5.0, you will notice that the Options and Page menus have been replaced with the Utilities and Layout menus, and that the commands on these menus have been shuffled around a bit. In addition, some of the options formerly on the Edit menu have been moved to other menus. For example, the table of contents and index commands are on the Utilities menu and the Preferences option is on the File menu.

OF MICE AND MENUS

How you work with the PageMaker menus depends on whether you want to use the mouse or the keyboard. Some people (namely, those who know how to type) prefer keeping their hands on the keyboard as much as possible. However, if you flunked Typing 1A in high school, you will love the mouse and will only resort to the keyboard when there is no alternative.

The Pull-Down Menus

To use the mouse in the menu bar, move the mouse pointer to the option you want to select, and then click the left mouse button once. You will see a *pull-down menu*, which displays options on a vertical list, directly below the option on the menu bar. For practice, let's look at some of the pull-down menus, without actually choosing any of the options (like going window shopping).

1. Place the mouse pointer on File in the menu bar.

2. Click the left mouse button. The File pull-down menu is displayed.

3. Place the mouse pointer on Type in the menu bar.

4. Click the left mouse button. The File pull-down menu disappears, and the Type pull-down menu is displayed.

5. Pull down the Utilities menu.

6. Pull down the File menu.

Now take a closer look at the File pull-down menu, which is shown in Figure 1.3. Notice that some of the options are in a different color or shade than the others. The options that are currently unavailable are dimmed (in a faint type). For example, Close and Save are dimmed because you can't close or save a file when you haven't created one yet. However, New and Open are currently available. If you try to choose an unavailable option, your request will be ignored.

Many of the options are followed by ellipses (for example, *Open…*, and *Save as…*). The three dots indicate that a dialog box will appear when you select the option. A *dialog box* is a fill-in-the-blank form that prompts you to supply further information. Later in this chapter, you'll learn how to fill in dialog boxes.

Cascading Menus

Some of the options on the menus have a right-pointing triangle next to them. For example, in the Element pull-down menu, the Line and Fill options have this symbol, which indicates that a *cascading menu* will appear

FIGURE 1.3: *Dimmed options are currently unavailable*

when you select the option. A cascading menu displays a list of additional choices. You can experiment with one now:

1. Pull down the Element menu.

2. Place the mouse pointer on the Fill option.

3. Click the left mouse button.

A cascading menu pops out to the right of the option, as shown in Figure 1.4. This particular menu displays the types of patterns that can fill the boxes and circles you draw. The currently selected option has a check mark next to it. Thus, None is the *default*, or automatic, setting for the Fill option.

4. To choose a different fill (for example, a 10% shade), click on that option.

5. If you would like additional practice, or just want to explore a bit, continue and select the other options that have cascading menus (but be sure to reset them to their original settings before continuing).

FIGURE 1.4: *The Fill cascading menu*

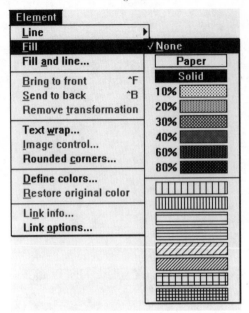

Toggle Options

On the Window and Layout menus, some of the options are checked. The check mark indicates that the option is turned on. Some options are *toggles*, which means that the same command turns an option both on and off. You will learn later exactly what these options are turning on and off, but for now, let's get accustomed to identifying the current setting (on or off) of an option, and learn how to change it.

1. Pull down the Layout menu and choose Guides and Rulers. As you can see by the check marks on this cascading menu, Rulers, Guides, Snap to Guides, and Scroll Bars are all turned on.

2. With the mouse pointer on Snap to Guides, click once. This action turns off the option.

3. Pull down the Layout menu again and choose Guides and Rulers. Notice that the Snap to Guides option is no longer checked.

4. While the Layout menu is still displayed, turn on the Snap to Rulers option.

5. Return the options to their defaults: Turn on Snap to Guides and turn off Snap to Rulers.

 ! *W* ARNiNG

If you make any changes to PageMaker settings when no publication is open, you will change the program's default settings for any new publications you create. As you play with the settings in this chapter, make sure you return to the original settings before continuing.

USING THE KEYBOARD

For those who would rather not shift their hands from the keyboard to the mouse, PageMaker offers two ways to give commands from the keyboard. First, you can access the menu with the F10 or Alt keys, and then type the underlined letter of each desired option. To see if you prefer this method, try the following example:

1. Press F10. The first option on the menu bar, File, is highlighted to let you know you have accessed that menu. Notice that each option has one letter underlined. For example, the *m* in *Element* is underlined.

2. Press **M** to pull down the Element menu. Each of the items on the pull-down menu also has a single underlined letter.

3. Press **F** to choose Fill. The Fill cascading menu pops out.

4. Press the arrow keys to highlight different options, and then highlight None and press Enter. If a cascading menu does not contain items with underlined letters, you must use the arrow keys or the mouse to select an option.

Although the mouse may be more fun to use, expert typists can probably issue commands faster with the keyboard. A fast typist can beat a fast mouser any day.

A second way to give commands with the keyboard is with keyboard shortcuts. These shortcuts usually consist of pressing the Ctrl (Control) key in conjunction with one other key. For example, instead of opening a file by pulling down the File menu and choosing Open, you can hold down Ctrl and press O.

Many PageMaker commands can be issued with keyboard shortcuts. How do you know what all these key combinations are? Just refer to the menus.

Pull down a menu now, such as the File menu, and you will see that some of the options have codes next to them. On the File menu, ^N is next to New and ^O is next to Open. The ^ symbol is an abbreviation for the Ctrl key.

The keyboard shortcuts appear on the menu to help you memorize them. As you issue commands from a menu, keep an eye on these codes; maybe the next time you give the command, you can save time by using the keyboard shortcut. Don't expend a lot of effort trying to memorize them—just learn them as you go. We will remind you of the keyboard shortcuts throughout the book.

CONVERSING WITH DIALOG BOXES

Sometimes when you pull down a menu and make a choice, that's all you have to do. When you instructed PageMaker to turn on the Snap to Rulers option, there was nothing more to the discussion. But to carry out many functions, PageMaker needs further direction, and so it presents you with a dialog box and asks you to fill in a few blanks.

As mentioned earlier, a menu option that has three dots after it displays a dialog box when you select it. A dialog box is the equivalent of a waitress asking you questions after you have given her your order: "Do you want soup or salad?"; "How would you like your steak prepared?"; "Would you prefer rice or baked potato?".

Dialog boxes ask you similar questions—not about food, obviously, but about the particular command you have selected. For example, if you choose the Open command on the File menu, a dialog box asks you for the name of a file to open.

There are several types of options in a dialog box, which are labeled in Figure 1.5 and described in Table 1.1. Some options require you to type in numbers or text (*text boxes*), and others have you choose from a list (*list boxes* and *drop-down lists*) or turn a setting on or off (*option buttons* and *check boxes*). Sometimes there are dialog boxes within dialog boxes.

With few exceptions, almost every dialog box has two *command buttons*, labeled OK and Cancel. You click on OK when you are finished filling in the box; click on the Cancel button if you decide to cancel the command you issued. You don't have to memorize the official names of all these types of options, but you should recognize them when you see them.

FIGURE 1.5: *The Page Setup dialog box*

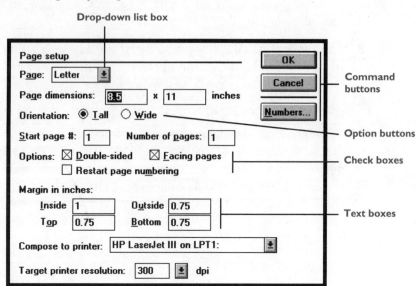

TABLE 1.1: *Dialog Box Options*

Option Type	Description
Drop-down list box	A vertical list of choices that is displayed when you click on the arrow.
Text boxes	Rectangles into which you type information.
Option buttons	A set of two or three circles that represent mutually exclusive options (only one option can be selected).
Check boxes	Squares that represent nonexclusive options (turn on or off as many as you like).
List box	A list of choices from which you can select one item.
Command buttons	Boxed words that carry out a command (OK), cancel the command (Cancel), or open another dialog box (Numbers…).

To practice using a dialog box, let's create a new file.

1. Pull down the File menu.

2. Choose New. The Page Setup dialog box appears (the one shown in Figure 1.5).

This dialog box lets you define your page size and layout. These options will be defined in more detail in Chapter 3. For now, we'll concentrate on the techniques to use to fill in a dialog box.

3. The first option in the dialog box, Page, has a downward-pointing arrow to the right of the current choice, Letter. Click on this arrow. A drop-down list of page sizes is displayed.

4. Click on Legal. Now Legal appears next to Page.

5. Orientation has two option buttons: Tall and Wide. Right now the dot is next to Tall. Click on the circle next to Wide (or even the word itself) to specify a horizontal page orientation, (also known as *landscape*). The dot jumps to Wide.

You type in values for many options in this dialog box: the Page Dimensions, Start Page #, Number of Pages, and the margins near the bottom of the box. In order to enter a new value, you must first select, or highlight, the current value. Probably the easiest way to highlight it is to double-click on it. Or, instead of highlighting the value, you can click to the right of the value and then delete it with the Backspace key.

6. To highlight the 1 in the Number of Pages field, double-click on the 1.

7. To replace 1 with a new number, type **2**.

8. The Double-Sided and Facing Pages options have check boxes next to them. Click on the box next to Facing Pages. The X disappears as the option is turned off.

Think of the check boxes as on/off switches. Click on the description or check box, and the option turns on or off, depending on its current state. If an X appears in the box, the option is turned on.

9. Click on the OK command button to accept all the choices you have entered. A page appears with the dimensions you specified.

Using the Keyboard with Dialog Boxes

You can also use the keyboard to choose dialog box options, as follows:

➤ Use the Tab key to move between the options in a dialog box.

➤ To go directly to an option, press Alt and type the underlined letter. For example, to choose the Wide option in the Page Setup dialog box, hold down Alt and press W.

➤ Press Enter instead of clicking on the OK button.

➤ Press Esc instead of clicking on the Cancel button.

Note that even if you are an avid mouser, it often makes more sense to press Enter than to click on OK. As instructors, we frequently observe students typing in a value, taking a hand off the keyboard, reaching for the mouse, moving the pointer to OK, and clicking the mouse button. The basic rule of thumb to follow is if you have your hands on the keyboard, press Enter; if you are selecting options with the mouse, click on OK.

UNDERSTANDING THE PAGEMAKER WINDOW

Before you go any further, you should understand the PageMaker window. As you read this section, refer to Figure 1.6, which points out the important areas.

Some of the areas of the screen are identical in all Windows applications; others are unique to PageMaker. As in other Windows applications, you can click on the document window maximize button to enlarge the area you have available for your page. You will see that we did this for most of the figures in this book.

The current page or page spread appears in the middle of the window. (A *page spread* consists of two pages side by side in a double-sided publication.) The dashed lines inside the page are your *margin guides*, which separate the body of the page from the margins. Although PageMaker will let you type in the margin area, usually your text and graphics will go inside the rectangle formed by the margin guides.

The margins, along with the page size and orientation (tall or wide), are specified when you create the publication. However, you can later change the page layout by using the Page Setup command on the File menu.

FIGURE 1.6:   *The PageMaker window*

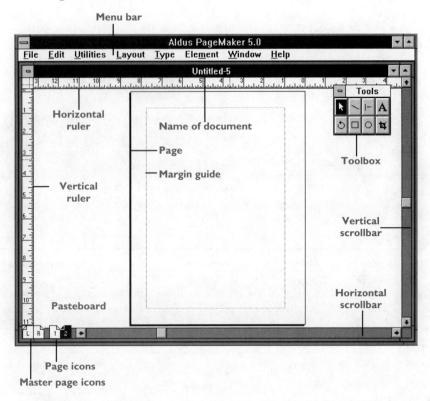

The empty area surrounding the page is called the *pasteboard*. The pasteboard is a temporary storage spot where you can place objects before you paste them onto the page. The pasteboard is actually bigger than the PageMaker window. You can use the scroll bars to view nonvisible parts of the pasteboard. You will practice scrolling later in this chapter.

The name of your publication appears in the *document window title bar*. Because you haven't assigned a name to the file you just created, the title bar displays *Untitled-1*.

WORKING WITH THE TOOLBOX

The *toolbox* appears in the upper-right corner of the window. Just as graphic designers have a box of tools, containing rulers, T-squares, exacto knives, blue pens, and so on, PageMaker users have a toolbox that rests on top of the pasteboard. The PageMaker tools let you create or modify text and graphics on the page. Table 1.2 describes each of these tools.

To practice using the toolbox, let's draw a box with the rectangle tool.

1. Click on the rectangle tool. The pointer turns into a crossbar when you move it onto the pasteboard or page.

2. Place the crossbar somewhere in the upper-left corner of the page. The exact position is not important in this example.

TABLE 1.2: *The Tools in the Toolbox*

Icon	Name	Function	Keyboard Shortcut
	Pointer tool	Selects objects on the page or pasteboard.	F9
	Line tool	Draws lines in any direction.	Shift+F2
	Rule tool	Draws lines restricted to 45-degree angles.	Shift+F3
	Text tool	Enters, edits, and selects text.	Shift+F4
	Rotation tool	Rotates text or graphics.	Shift+F5
	Rectangle tool	Draws rectangles and squares.	Shift+F6
	Oval tool	Draws circles and ellipses.	Shift+F7
	Cropping tool	Crops (trims) a graphic.	Shift+F8

3. Click and hold down the left mouse button. Do not release the button until you have finished drawing the box. If you let go of the button too soon, you will need to start over.

4. Drag the mouse in the direction you want to draw the box: down and to the right. As you move the mouse, a box forms in that direction.

5. Release the mouse button.

6. Since you don't want to draw any more boxes, click on the pointer tool. Your screen should look similar to Figure 1.7.

The technique you used to draw the box is called *click-and-drag*. You will use this technique frequently in PageMaker.

FIGURE 1.7:   *A rectangle drawn with the rectangle tool*

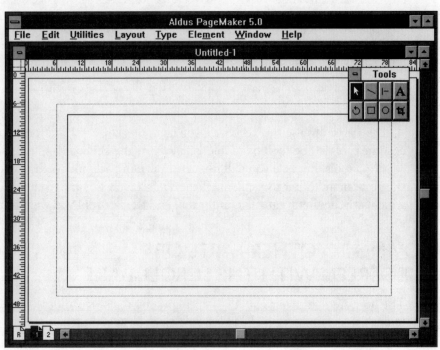

MOVING AND REMOVING THE TOOLBOX

If the toolbox ever gets in your way, you can easily move it elsewhere on the screen. You move the toolbox the same way you move any window. To see how this works, we'll move the toolbox to the lower-right corner of the screen.

1. Place the mouse pointer on the window's title bar, anywhere in the word *Tools*.

2. Click and hold down the left mouse button, and then drag the mouse down. As you move the mouse, an outline of the toolbox moves in the same direction.

3. Release the mouse button. The toolbox moves into the location you specified.

4. Repeat the procedure to move the toolbox back to its original position.

An alternative to moving the toolbox is getting rid of it altogether. Sometimes you will find that no matter where you move the toolbox, it keeps getting in the way. As long as you don't need to change tools, why not clean up your screen and just turn it off? To remove it, choose the Toolbox option on the Window menu or press Ctrl+6. Later, when you need to change tools, turn the Toolbox option back on using the same command you used to turn it off.

If you prefer to use the keyboard, you can press key combinations to access the tools in the toolbox. Table 1.2 also lists the keyboard shortcuts for selecting tools. Because you will frequently switch back and forth between the pointer and other tools, PageMaker offers a function key toggle, F9, which switches between the pointer tool and the last tool you were using.

MOVING TO OTHER PARTS OF THE SCREEN WITH THE SCROLL BARS

The horizontal and vertical *scroll bars* allow you to use the mouse to see different parts of the page and pasteboard. Right now, you can see the entire page on the screen, but if you were zoomed in on part of the page, you would need a way to scroll the screen. The scroll bar offers one way of repositioning what you see on the screen. Table 1.3 describes how to use the

TABLE 1.3: *Using the Scroll Bar*

Direction of Scrolling	Action
Down	Click on down arrow in vertical scroll bar.
Down one screen	Click on vertical scroll bar underneath the scroll box.
Up	Click on up arrow in vertical scroll bar.
Up one screen	Click on vertical scroll bar above the scroll box.
Right	Click on right arrow in horizontal scroll bar.
Right one screen	Click on horizontal scroll bar to the right of the scroll box.
Left	Click on left arrow in horizontal scroll bar.
Left one screen	Click on horizontal scroll bar to the left of the scroll box.
Top of pasteboard	Click and drag scroll box to top of vertical scroll bar.
Left edge of pasteboard	Click and drag scroll box to left end of horizontal scroll bar.

scroll bar, and Figure 1.8 points out the different parts of the horizontal and vertical scroll bars.

You should practice using the scroll bars until you feel comfortable with the mechanics of scrolling. This process can be a bit confusing at first because the screen scrolls in the opposite direction of the scroll arrows. For example, when you click on the down arrow, the screen shifts up. But keep in mind that the scroll arrows let you view something that exists in the direction of the arrow. In other words, clicking down shows you what's down there. This becomes easy with practice.

If your page disappears, it has probably scrolled off the screen, leaving you with just the pasteboard. To get your page back on the screen, you can scroll the screen in the opposite direction. However, an easier way is to use the command to fit the page in the window: Choose View from the Layout menu and choose Fit in Window, or press Ctrl+W.

FIGURE 1.8:   *Elements of the scroll bars*

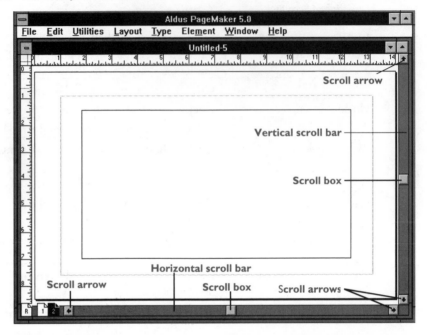

VIEWING THE PAGE

While we are on the subject of page views, let's review some of the other view options. As we discuss these options, you might want to choose the View option on the Layout menu.

The Fit in Window option lets you see the entire page or page spread inside your document window, as shown in the example in Figure 1.9. Notice that you can't read most of the text in this view.

The Fit in Window view is the default. It gives you an overall feel of the page layout. However, you can't see much detail unless you have one of those fancy oversized display monitors. To read small type or to precisely position an object on the page, you need to choose one of the other view magnifications.

FIGURE 1.9:   *The Fit in Window view*

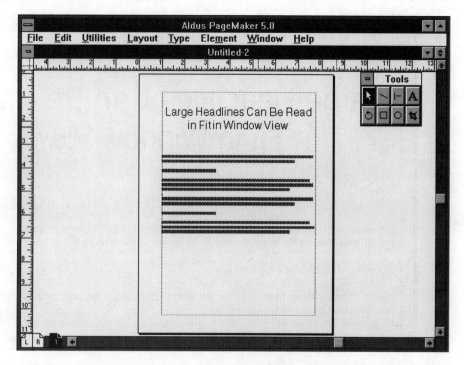

The Actual Size option displays the elements on your page at their actual printed size. Use this or the 75% Size option to read small type. Figure 1.10 shows the same document that appears in Figure 1.9, but in the Actual Size view. The right mouse button toggles between the Actual Size and Fit in Window views.

To see your page larger than life, use the 200% Size or 400% Size option. With these superzoomed views, it is easy to make sure two objects are aligned with each other. We recommend that you use the Actual Size, 200%, or 400% view for precise positioning.

Version
5.0   If you are interested in seeing more of the pasteboard, use the Show Pasteboard or the 25% Size option. These views are helpful if you tucked something away on the pasteboard, and you don't see it on your screen. Show Pasteboard is a new menu option in version 5.0; however, the

FIGURE 1.10: *The Actual Size view*

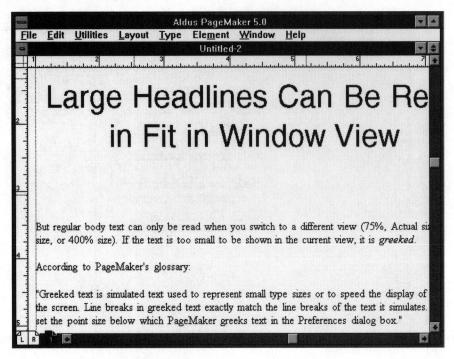

keyboard shortcut, Ctrl+Shift+W, was available in previous versions. Figure 1.11 gives an example of Show Pasteboard view.

As you can see on the View cascading menu, each of the page views has a Ctrl+key shortcut. These key combinations are listed in Table 1.4. Since most of these codes are mnemonic, they are fairly easy to memorize. Starting with the Show Pasteboard view, practice using each of the keyboard commands in Table 1.4. See how you gradually zoom in with each view.

Version
5.0

The view commands apply only to the current page or page spread. To set all pages in the publication to the same view, hold down Alt, press Ctrl as you display the menu, and select the view.

FIGURE 1.11:   *The Show Pasteboard view*

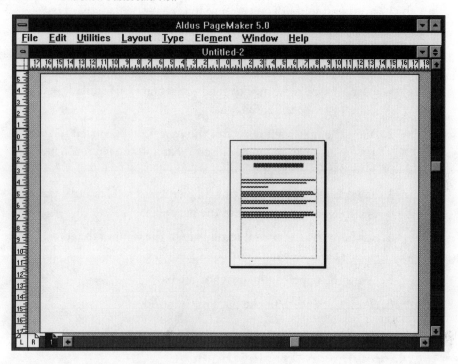

TABLE 1.4:   *Keyboard Commands for Page Views*

View	Key Combination
Show Pasteboard	Ctrl+Shift+W
25% Size	Ctrl+0 (zero)
Fit in Window	Ctrl+W
50% Size	Ctrl+5
75% Size	Ctrl+7
Actual Size	Ctrl+1
200% Size	Ctrl+2
400% Size	Ctrl+4

After you give a page view command, you will most likely need to move the page around so that you can zero in on a particular area. That's where the scroll bars come in handy. Let's practice using the scroll bars to see each of the four corners of the page in 200% view.

1. To switch to 200% view, press Ctrl+2. The section of the page you see right now depends on where you scrolled the last time you used the scroll bars.

2. View the upper-left corner of the page. You may need to click on the up arrow in the vertical scroll bar and the left arrow in the horizontal scroll bar.

3. Click on the down arrow in the vertical scroll bar until you can see the lower-left corner of the page.

4. Click in the horizontal scroll bar (to the right of the scroll box) to see the lower-right corner of the page.

5. View the upper-right corner of the page.

6. Press Ctrl+W to fit the page in the window.

Version
5.0

Magnifying an Area of the Page

Each of the standard page views centers the current work area in the document window. Frequently, though, you'll want to zoom in on a particular area of the page. The magnifying tool lets you do just that. Just hold down Ctrl and the Spacebar as you click the mouse on the area on which you want to zoom in. Each time you do this, the area is magnified to the next largest view. For example, if you are currently in Actual Size view, you will switch to 200% Size view.

To zoom out, use the reducing tool. This tool requires some dexterity: you must hold down Ctrl, Alt, and the Spacebar as you click the mouse. Each time you do this, the area is reduced to the next smallest view.

 **Note**

When you press Ctrl+Spacebar, you will see the magnifying tool—a magnifying glass with a + inside it. The reducing tool is similar except it has a – sign.

MOVING THE PAGE WITH THE GRABBER HAND

The *grabber hand* is another way to move the page around the screen. With it, you can grab and move the screen in any direction. While the scroll bars are restricted to horizontal and vertical movement, the grabber hand lets you move diagonally as well. The grabber hand requires teamwork between keyboard and mouse, as follows:

- ➤ Hold down the Alt key and keep it down through the entire procedure.

- ➤ Click and hold down the left mouse button. A pudgy little hand appears, as shown here in the margin. This is the grabber hand.

- ➤ Drag the mouse in the direction you want to move the page. As you move the mouse, the hand and the page move in that direction.

- ➤ When you have finished moving the page, release the Alt key and the mouse button.

Before pressing the left mouse button, you need to position the pointer on the screen. Place the pointer on the opposite side of the direction you want to move. For example, if you want to move the page to the right (so that you can see what's on the left), you should click on the left side of the screen and drag to the right. In the larger view magnifications (200% and 400%), you may need to repeat the process several times until you see what you want to view.

Now, let's use the grabber hand to move the page in Actual Size view.

1. To switch to Actual Size view, press Ctrl+1.

2. Place the mouse pointer in the lower-right corner of the screen.

3. Hold down the Alt key.

4. Click and hold down the left mouse button. The grabber hand appears.

5. Drag the mouse up and to the left.

6. Release the Alt key and the mouse button. You should now see the lower-right corner of the page.

DISPLAYING OTHER PAGES

To the left of the horizontal scroll bar are the page icons. A page number appears for each page in a publication. Since you specified that your document has two pages (by setting the Number of Pages field in the Page Setup dialog box to 2), the numbers 1 and 2 appear inside the page icons. You can move between pages by clicking on the appropriate number. Alternatively, you can press F12 to move to the next page and F11 to display the previous page. The Go to Page option on the Layout menu, or Ctrl+G, lets you specify a particular page to display.

PageMaker offers a way to view the pages in your publication one at a time. Each page or page spread is displayed for 2 seconds, allowing you to glance at the overall layout. (It's not enough time to study any details on the page, however.) To cycle through the pages in your publication, display the Layout menu and hold down Shift as you choose Go to Page. To stop the cycling, press any key or a mouse button.

Next to the numbered page icons are the master page icons. The master pages contain elements that appear on each page of the document, for example, chapter titles or vertical rules between columns. The L refers to the left-hand pages and the R refers to the right-hand pages in double-sided publications. Chapter 14 discusses master pages in detail.

SUMMARY

In this chapter, you learned how to interact (or *interface* as they say in the computer world) with PageMaker. You used both the mouse and the keyboard to make selections from the menus and to fill in dialog boxes. You also explored the PageMaker window, familiarizing yourself with the important parts of the screen (the toolbox, scroll bars, page icons, and so on), and experimented with several techniques for scrolling the screen.

In the next chapter, you will take a quick tour of the PageMaker publishing process.

QuickStart

fast tracks

THIS SECTION BREEZES THROUGH
the mechanics and the maneuvers inherent in building a publication in
PageMaker. We won't stop to explain everything fully, and we leave out
many details and considerations that we consider to be incidental. (They
are all to be covered in later chapters, we promise.)

Our goal here is to give you an overview of document production with
PageMaker, eschewing for the moment all of the details that get in the way.
Who knows, maybe you'll get everything you need out of this chapter and
save the rest of the book for a rainy day. On the other hand, if you already
know how to build a publication and you would rather read about the
specific features of the program, perhaps you would rather pass over this
chapter.

THE PUBLISHING RECIPE

The process of creating a PageMaker document is similar to following a
recipe from your favorite cookbook. To bake a pie, for example, you need
a number of ingredients (flour, cherries, sugar, etc.) and various utensils
(bowls, spoons, rolling pin, pie dish, and so on). Creating a PageMaker
document also requires certain ingredients and special utensils.

THE INGREDIENTS

In the beginning, the publishing gods created alphanumeric characters and geometric figures. When you get right down to it, those two heavenly bodies represent the essence of any publishing project. Sure, there is design, inspiration, structure, logic, and no small amount of sweat, but the basic ingredients for the publishing recipe are text and graphics.

Text

There are several ways to include text in a PageMaker document, and we might as well start using the correct terminology; PageMaker calls documents *publications*, and so we will, too. Each publication can comprise one or more stories. A *story* is a continuous block of text that PageMaker recognizes as a single unit. For example, each article in a newsletter might be a separate story. A story can be as short as a single headline or as long as a chapter in a book.

You can use one of four methods to include a story in a publication:

➤ Type it directly onto the page or pasteboard while in PageMaker.

➤ Type it into the Story Editor, a simple word processor that appears in its own window.

➤ Produce a text file in a word processor or text editor and import it into PageMaker.

➤ Type text in another program, copy the text to Windows' Clipboard, and then paste the text from the Clipboard into PageMaker.

The method you choose depends on the situation, and most of the time your choice will be immediately apparent to you. Let's look at several scenarios.

If all you need to do is create a few headlines or captions, simply type the text onto the page or pasteboard. This technique is explained in Chapter 4.

To type more than a few lines, use either the Story Editor or your word processor. The Story Editor is convenient because it's available inside Page-Maker. However, your word processor contains more extensive editing capabilities. You probably will feel more comfortable composing longer stories in your word processor. This is not to say that the Story Editor is worthless. On the contrary, it is quite useful for typing short blocks of text, making revisions, checking spelling, searching for and replacing text, and a few other things you will learn about in Chapter 5.

If the document already exists in a word processing program, you will want to import the file into PageMaker. Importing text files is discussed in Chapter 8.

To bring in part of a word processed document, the Clipboard's cut-and-paste method is your fastest route.

Regardless of where the text came from, once the story is in a publication, you can edit it directly on the page or in the Story Editor.

Graphics

The second basic ingredient, graphic elements, is usually a part of every publication, even if only in minimal form (such as lines above or below headlines). Graphic elements can be incorporated into publications in the following ways:

➤ Simple geometric figures, such as rectangles, circles, and lines, can be drawn from within PageMaker.

➤ Shades and rules can be added to text through various Page-Maker formatting commands.

➤ More complex graphics can be produced in external drawing or paint programs and imported into PageMaker.

➤ Many types of graphics can be brought across the Clipboard into PageMaker.

Version
5.0
You cannot edit an imported graphics file as you can a text file. To make actual changes to an image, you must return to the program that produced it. However, you can modify the way PageMaker presents a graphic by sizing or cropping it. In version 5.0, you can also rotate, skew, or flip the image.

To summarize, text and graphics can be created inside PageMaker or produced outside and then imported. Either way, it is within the confines of a PageMaker publication that the stew begins to simmer.

THE APPLIANCES

The PageMaker soup kitchen has more utensils than the Galloping Gourmet and Julia Child combined. In fact, some say that there are too many utensils, inviting well-meaning but inexperienced users to overuse them on their way to producing grossly overblown documents. That's where a few well-conceived recipes come in very handy.

Too numerous to list in their entirety, some of PageMaker's more significant tools include the following:

- ➤ Automatic flow of text across all the pages of a document
- ➤ Weaving and threading of multiple text files across one document
- ➤ Newsletter-style flow of text across columns
- ➤ Formatting and spacing of any portion of a paragraph, sentence, or word
- ➤ Global formatting of text and headlines
- ➤ Powerful header and footer controls, including automatic page numbering
- ➤ Generation of tables of contents and indexes
- ➤ Different ways of wrapping text around a graphic
- ➤ Typography tools to control the precise placement of each character on the page
- ➤ A Table Editor to help lay out columnar data

These are some of the slicers, the dicers, the skillets, and the casserole dishes of PageMaker. It is with these tools that you shape the two primary ingredients into a document.

THE RECIPE

Here comes the hard part (or the easy part, depending on your point of view), the part that comes from your own thoughts and feelings. We won't pretend to teach you the art of publishing because we don't believe any book can, or should even try. We do believe that there is a philosophy associated with using PageMaker. But you cannot practice instinct and you cannot learn feelings; they must come to you over time.

Nonetheless, having an understanding of how the ingredients and utensils are used together is absolutely crucial. Developing a sense of the appropriate use of PageMaker's power is equally important, and with these gray areas between technical skill and publishing instinct we will attempt to assist you.

To continue our culinary analogies, remember back to your high school or college days when you finally got a date with that person of your dreams. You offered to make dinner, despite a long history of burnt toast. Now what menu did you choose that evening? Did you go for it with beef Wellington in a wine and mushroom sauce, with stir-fried vegetables sauteed in garlic, butter, and cilantro, or did you play it safe with lemon chicken, salad, and French bread?

If you chose the former, you may be in for a few desktop disasters as a publisher. But if you recognized your limitations back then, maybe you will do so with your publications and stick with the stuff that you *know* you can produce effectively.

Unless you are a professional designer or have a natural sense of illustration and typography, leave the rule-breaking to the experts. At least for now, concentrate on simple recipes that don't get in the way of the intended message of the text. Without exception, the content of your document reigns supreme over its form. It's easy to forget that as you learn a program as rich in fancy features as PageMaker, but try to stay aware of your first reason for wanting to publish something, which is to get across a certain message.

CREATING A PUBLICATION

Figure 2.1 is the publication that you are about to produce. It is a simple page, yet it will provide you with an opportunity to learn the basics of building a PageMaker document.

You are now going to follow the publishing recipe just described to create the document shown in Figure 2.1. Before you start, you need to make sure you have all the necessary ingredients at your fingertips. In this publication, you will import the main story from a Word for Windows file, and the shuttle graphic from a file stored in Windows Metafile Format. The box around the graphic was created with a PageMaker drawing tool and the caption underneath the shuttle was typed right in PageMaker.

This publication requires two files from the companion disk included with this book: TRAVEL.DOC and SHUTTLE.WMF. You will need to install this disk (see the companion disk instruction page at the back of this book for details) before you continue with this hands-on exercise.

SETTING UP THE PAGE

Follow these steps to create the publication:

1. Pull down the File menu and choose New. The Page Setup dialog box appears.

2. Since this publication is single sided, turn off the Double-Sided option—just click on the option to turn off the check box.

3. Set 1-inch left and right margins, and 0.75-inch top and bottom margins.

4. Check the name of the printer in the Compose to Printer field. If this is not the printer you want to print to, click on the field and select the appropriate device.

5. Choose OK to close the dialog box.

FIGURE 2.1: *The publication you will create in this chapter*

Vacation Travel

The Adventure Begins

This trip really began in September last year when Gerry won first prize in a raffle at the fashion show which Rush-Presbyterian-St. Luke's Medical Center holds every year. The prize was two round trip tickets to Hong Kong on United Airlines, and then ten nights in the Hong Kong Hyatt Hotel. Analyzing our good fortune, we concluded that we wanted to do more than spend ten days in Hong Kong. However, United, having just gotten its routes and equipment from Pan American, had not yet received authority to fly to other destinations or between points in the Far East.

On February 10, United acquired this authority, and on February 11 Debbie began putting our trip together. We left on March 2 and returned on March 26. We entered seven countries, traveled over 25,000 miles on four airlines, made over 500 Kodachrome slides, almost 200 Kodacolor prints, and 5 1/2 hours of color and sound videotape.

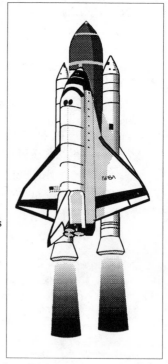

Chicago to Tokyo

11:03 P.M. Chicago time. 39,000 feet somewhere over the Western Pacific, we are 8 hours and 42 minutes out of Los Angeles with about two more hours to go to Tokyo. We were about an hour and ten minutes late out of Los Angeles.

Travel Log

So far, it's been a long and interesting day and I guess it's just about half over. We did the following:

♦ Arose at 5:30 A.M.

♦ Left the house at 7:00 A.M.

♦ Arrived in Los Angeles at 12:35 P.M.

♦ Arrived in Tokyo at 11:46 P.M.

♦ 11:31 P.M. Tuesday, March 4

Preferred vehicle for vacation travel

The time to define your page layout is when you are creating the file. By giving careful thought to your layout up front, you will save yourself extra work in the future. This is the time to determine page dimensions, orientation (Tall versus Wide), margins, and whether the document will be double or single sided.

IMPORTING THE TEXT

Once you have defined the page setup for your new publication, the next step is typically to import text from a word processing file. The text for this publication comes from a Word for Windows file called TRAVEL.DOC. (If you did not install the Word for Windows 2.0 Import filter during installation, you will need to do so before continuing. Also install the Windows Metafile Import filter, which you will need later in this chapter. See Appendix A for details.)

To bring in text from an external file, use the Place option on the File menu. This command actually has two parts to it. First, you select the file to import. Second, you place the text on the page by indicating where you want the text to begin. PageMaker offers several techniques for flowing text (automatically, manually, and semiautomatically), but we'll leave the details for Chapter 8.

TRAVEL.DOC is stored in C:\PM5PUBS. Follow these steps to place this file:

1. Pull down the File menu and choose Place. The Place Document dialog box is shown in Figure 2.2. Determine what your current path is by looking next to the word *Path*. Unless you have changed the defaults, your current path is probably C:\PM5.

2. If you aren't on drive C, click on the Drives field, and choose [-c-].

3. To go back to the root directory, double-click on [..] in the Directories list until the path is C:\.

4. Scroll the Directories list until you see [pm5pubs], and then double-click on this directory name. The list box on the left now displays the files in the C:\PM5PUBS directory.

5. Scroll the list of files and locate the file TRAVEL.DOC. Double-click on this file name, or click once and choose OK.

Notice that your mouse pointer has changed shape. Its new form is called a *text gun*. You place text simply by positioning the text gun where you want the text to begin and clicking the mouse button.

6. Place the text gun on the page, below the top margin and inside the left margin. Click the mouse button, and the text will flow onto the page.

7. To read the text, switch to Actual Size view by clicking the right mouse button.

FIGURE 2.2: *The Place Document dialog box*

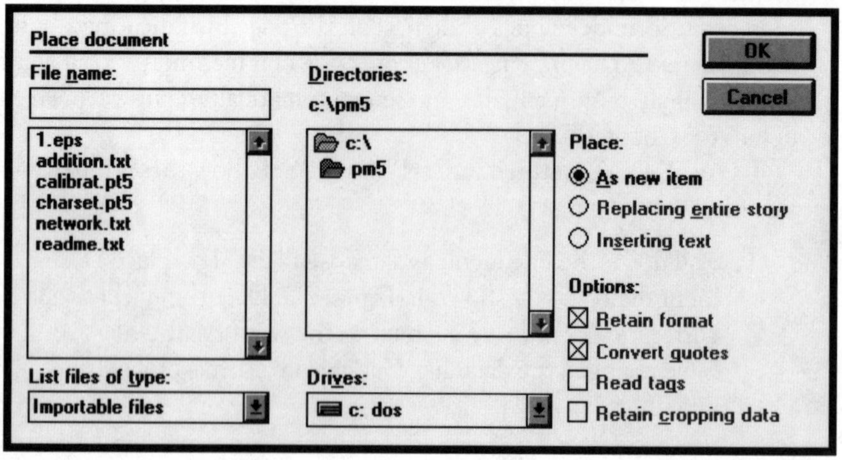

SAVING YOUR WORK

Save your file to disk about every 15 minutes, or when you complete an important task. It doesn't take very long to save your work, but it could take a long time to recreate something. Always save your most recent work before you leave your computer unattended.

The File pull-down menu offers both the Save and Save As options. The first time you save a file, you can choose either of these options. PageMaker first prompts you for a file name and then saves the file to the disk.

Do not type an extension for the file name. PageMaker automatically assigns the extension .PM5.

If you continue working on the document and make changes, you should resave the document. The Save option saves the file with the same name you gave it previously. The Save As option lets you assign a new name to the file. Thus, if you want to replace the previously saved version with the new version, choose Save (or press Ctrl+S). If you want to keep the original file and create a different file from the new version, choose Save As.

Follow these steps to save the publication you just created:

1. Pull down the File menu.

2. Choose Save As.

3. Type the name **QUICK**.

4. Click on OK or press Enter. The path and file name now appear as the window title.

If you take a look at the Save Publication As dialog box, you can see exactly where the file will be saved. The path (right below the word Directories) indicates the drive and subdirectory in which the file will be saved. For example, in Figure 2.3, the current path is C:\PM5PUBS. But what if you don't want to save your file here? Just use the Drives and Directories boxes to change the path.

FIGURE 2.3: *The Save Publication As dialog box*

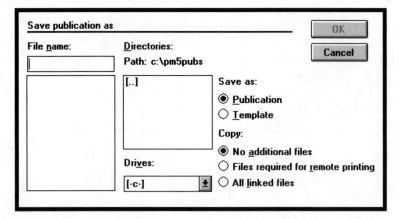

To change to a different drive, display the Drives drop-down list and click on the desired drive letter. If you have never navigated a Directories list, here is a summary of how it works:

- Each subdirectory is enclosed in square brackets.

- The first item, [..], refers to the parent directory. Choose this item to go back to the previous directory.

- If you have a lot of subdirectories, you may need to use the scroll bar.

- Double-click on a subdirectory name to switch to that subdirectory. The list of files will then reflect the files in that path.

Keep your eye on the path to see exactly where you are. Once you have navigated to the appropriate directory, click in the File Name field and type the name.

FORMATTING TEXT

PageMaker offers two sets of formatting commands: one for characters and one for paragraphs. Character formatting refers to the font, size, and type style of selected text. The formatting options that affect paragraphs include alignment, indents, vertical spacing, and hyphenation.

The Type Specifications dialog box, shown in Figure 2.4, contains all the options for formatting characters. You can display this box by pressing Ctrl+T or by choosing Type Specs from the Type menu. Many of the options in this dialog box are highly specialized and not used as often as Font, Size, and Type Style; the other options are covered in Chapter 9.

FIGURE 2.4:   *The Type Specifications dialog box*

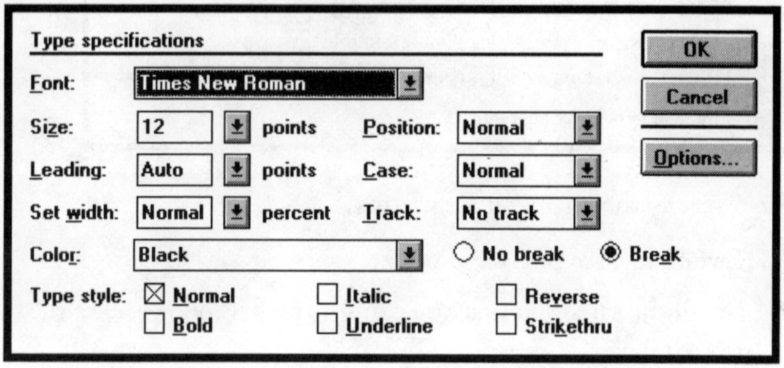

The Paragraph Specifications dialog box is shown in Figure 2.5. To display this box, either press Ctrl+M or choose Paragraph from the Type menu. This dialog box has a lot of options, but in this chapter we'll just be looking at indents, alignment, paragraph space, and rules. Most of the other options are described in Chapter 6.

FORMATTING THE MAIN HEADING

The main heading of this page (Vacation Travel) should be formatted with the following type specifications: 36 points, Arial font, with the bold type style. The paragraph should be right-aligned, have a half-inch of space after, and a two-point rule (line) below it.

FIGURE 2.5: *The Paragraph Specifications dialog box*

Paragraph specifications

Indents: Paragraph space: OK

Left   [0]   inches   Before [0]   inches   Cancel

First   [0]   inches   After   [0]   inches   Rules...

Right   [0]   inches   Spacing...

Alignment: [Left   ▼]   Dictionary: [English(American) ▼]

Options:

☐ Keep lines together   ☐ Keep with next   [0] lines

☐ Column break before   ☐ Widow control   [0] lines

☐ Page break before   ☐ Orphan control   [0] lines

☐ Include in table of contents

First, specify the character formatting:

1. Switch to 75% Size view.

2. Scroll the screen so that you can see the first line of text, Vacation Travel.

3. Choose the text tool.

4. Click and drag across the text you want to format: Vacation Travel.

5. Pull down the Type menu and choose Type Specs.

6. Click in the Font field and scroll to the top of the list. Click on Arial.

7. Click in the Size field and type **36** (you can also choose the size from the drop-down list, if you prefer).

8. Click on Bold for the Type Style.

9. Choose OK to close the dialog box.

The characters in the heading are now formatted as 36-point Arial bold. Now, specify the paragraph formatting:

1. Make sure the heading is still selected, or that the cursor is in the paragraph.

2. Pull down the Type menu and choose Paragraph.

3. Click in the Alignment field and choose Right.

4. Double-click in the After field and type **0.5i** (Note: The *i* stands for inches. If your default measurement is inches, you don't need to type the *i*.)

5. Choose the Rules command button.

6. Turn on the Rule below Paragraph check box.

7. Click on the Line Style field, and choose 2pt.

8. Close the dialog boxes.

When specifying paragraph formatting for a single paragraph, it is not necessary to select all the text in the paragraph; the cursor just needs to be somewhere in the paragraph. To format several consecutive paragraphs, you need to select at least some of the text in each paragraph.

The paragraph is now aligned on the right, has a half-inch of space after it, and a 2-point rule below it. Your heading should look similar to the one in Figure 2.6.

FORMATTING THE SUBHEADS

The three subheadings on the page should all be formatted the same way: 14-point Times New Roman bold italic with 16 points of space before the

FIGURE 2.6: *The formatted main heading*

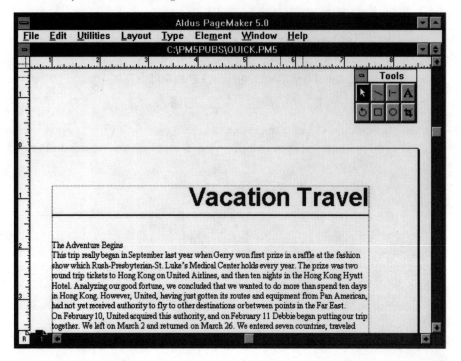

paragraph and 8 points of space after. Follow these steps to format the first subhead:

1. Select the subhead *The Adventure Begins*.

2. Press Ctrl+T to display the Type Specifications dialog box.

3. Make sure the Font is set to Times New Roman.

4. Change the size to 14 points.

5. Turn on Bold and Italic.

6. Choose OK to close the dialog box.

The only paragraph specifications you need to change are the space before and after. This time you will enter the measurements in points. You will frequently enter your vertical measurements in points since this is how type is measured.

1. Make sure the subhead is still selected or that the cursor is in the paragraph.

2. Press Ctrl+M to display the Paragraph Specifications dialog box.

3. In the Before field, type **0p16** (this is how you enter 16 points).

4. In the After field, type **0p8** (8 points).

5. Choose OK to close the dialog box.

The first subhead is formatted appropriately, and your next task is to format the other two subheads with the same specifications. Just select the subhead (*Chicago to Tokyo* and then *Travel Log*) and issue the commands listed above. Your formatted headings should look similar to those in Figure 2.7.

FIGURE 2.7:   *The formatted subheadings*

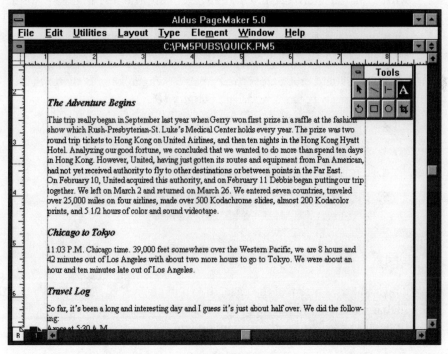

In a long document with dozens of subheads, it would be tedious to format each paragraph over and over again. A faster way is to use PageMaker *styles*. With this feature, you format one paragraph, assign a style name to it, and then apply the style to similar paragraphs. This technique is described in Chapter 7.

FORMATTING THE BODY TEXT

The paragraphs of body text should all be 12-point Times New Roman with a quarter-inch first-line indent. Actually, the text is already formatted with the correct font and size because the Word for Windows document was formatted this way. Therefore, the only formatting that needs to be done on body text is the first-line indent.

1. Click and drag across the first two paragraphs of body text (*This trip really began…* and *On February 10…*).

2. Press Ctrl+M to display the Paragraph Specifications dialog box.

3. In the First field, type **0.25i**.

4. Choose OK to close the dialog box.

5. Repeat steps 2 through 4 for the other two paragraphs of body text (*11:03 P.M.…* and *So far, it's been…*).

FORMATTING THE LIST

The list at the bottom of the page, shown in Figure 2.8, is indented a quarter-inch on the left and has 12 points of space before each paragraph. Each line is also preceded with a square bullet.

1. Select all five paragraphs in the list, beginning with ***Arose at 5:30 A.M.***

FIGURE 2.8: *An indented list with square bullets*

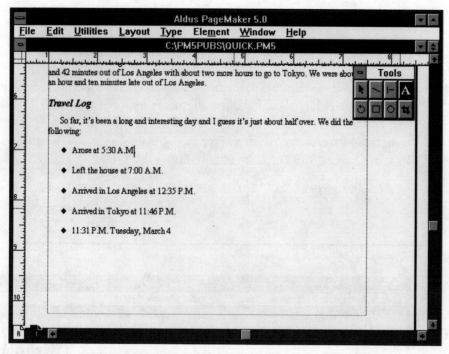

2. Press Ctrl+M to display the Paragraph Specifications dialog box.

3. In the Left field type **0.25i**.

4. In the Before field, type **0p12** (12 points).

5. Choose OK.

The diamond-shaped bullets you see in Figure 2.8 were inserted with the Bullets and Numbering Addition.

1. Click on the line *Arose at 5:30 A.M.*

2. Choose Utilities ➤ Aldus Additions ➤ Bullets and Numbering.

3. For the Bullet, click on the diamond.

4. For the Range, enter 5 in the For _ Paragraphs from Cursor field.

5. Choose OK.

6. Press Ctrl+S to save.

Your list should now match the one in Figure 2.8.

CREATING THE DROP CAP

Version
5.0

As you can see in Figure 2.9, the first paragraph of body text begins with a *drop cap*—an enlarged capital letter that is set into the paragraph. Page-Maker 5.0 offers an easy way to create this effect: with the Drop Cap addition. Before you create the drop cap, though, you should remove the first-line indent (drop caps are almost always flush-left).

I. Click anywhere in the paragraph that begins *This trip really began....*

FIGURE 2.9: *The enlarged T is a drop cap*

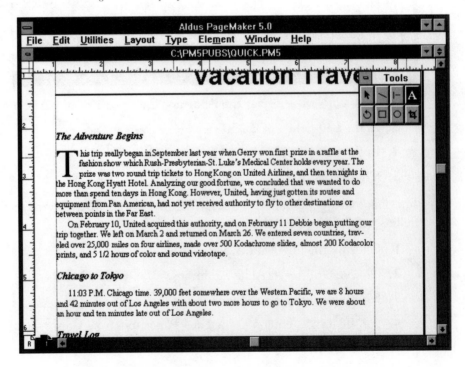

2. Press Ctrl+M to display the Paragraph Specifications dialog box and enter 0 in the First field. Choose OK.

3. Pull down the Utilities menu and choose Aldus Additions.

4. Choose Drop Cap.

5. Click on OK to create a drop cap that is three lines tall.

After a moment, the letter T will become a drop cap, as shown in Figure 2.9.

ADDING GRAPHIC ELEMENTS

So far the page has only two graphic elements: the rule under the main heading and the diamond-shaped bullets in the list. In this section, you will add two more: the shuttle graphic and the box surrounding it. You will import the graphic from a file and draw the box in PageMaker with the rectangle tool.

IMPORTING A GRAPHIC FILE

To import a graphic file, you use the same command as you do to import a text file: the Place option on the File menu. As when importing a text file, you will need to indicate the name of the file to import as well as its location. For specifics on importing graphics, see Chapter 11.

The graphic you are importing, SHUTTLE.WMF, is in Windows Metafile format, one of the most common graphic formats. (If you did not install the Windows Metafile filter during installation, you will need to do so before continuing. See Appendix A for details.) Follow the steps below to import this file. You will place the graphic on the pasteboard before moving it into position.

1. Switch to Fit in Window view.

2. Pull down the File menu and choose Place. Your path should still be set to C:\PM5PUBS.

3. Double-click on SHUTTLE.WMF. The mouse pointer now displays as a *graphics gun*.

4. Place the graphics gun at the top-left corner of the pasteboard, and click. The shuttle appears on the pasteboard in its full size, as shown in Figure 2.10.

Your next step is to move the shuttle onto the page, and to tell PageMaker to flow the text around the graphic.

1. Place the mouse pointer inside the shuttle—anywhere is fine. Just make sure you are not on one of the eight selection handles. (These handles are the small black squares.)

FIGURE 2.10: *The shuttle graphic is temporarily placed on the pasteboard*

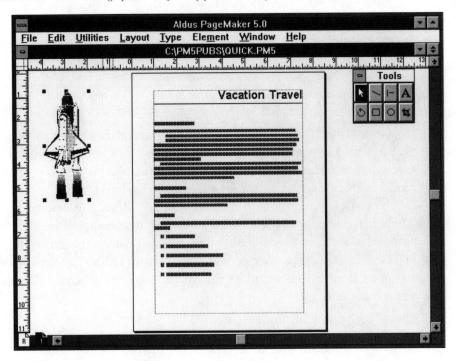

2. Drag the shuttle to the approximate position shown in Figure 2.11. When you release the mouse button, you'll see that the text flows behind the graphic, instead of around it as we want.

3. Pull down the Element menu and choose Text Wrap. Currently, the first Wrap Option is selected—text does not wrap around the graphic.

4. For the Wrap Option, click on the middle example—the one that shows text wrapping around the sides of a rectangular graphic.

5. Choose OK. The text now wraps around the shuttle.

FIGURE 2.11:   *The shuttle graphic after it has been placed on the page*

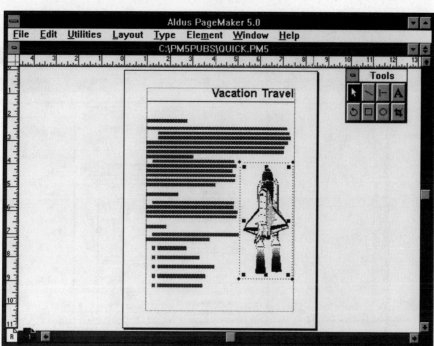

DRAWING A BOX

The shuttle graphic would look nice if it were framed with a rectangular box. The box in Figure 2.12 has a hairline thickness. *Hairlines* are very thin lines, less than a half-point thick. Use the rectangle tool to draw this box:

1. Click on the rectangle tool. When you move the pointer onto the page or pasteboard, it turns into a *crossbar*.

2. Without clicking the button, move the crossbar around the page. Notice that lines in the horizontal and vertical rulers indicate where the crossbar is on the page. Use these lines as a guide to positioning the box as you draw.

3. Place the crossbar at the upper-left corner of the box (see Figure 2.12 for location).

FIGURE 2.12: *The shuttle graphic is enclosed in a rectangular box*

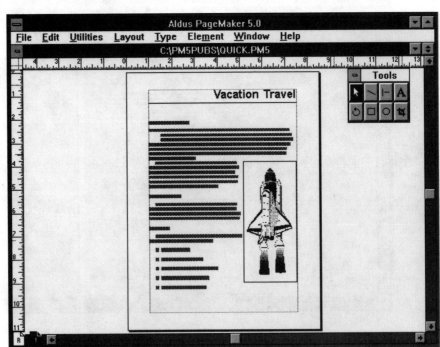

4. Click and drag the mouse to the right and down until the box matches the one shown in Figure 2.12.

5. Release the mouse button.

6. Pull down the Element menu and choose Line.

7. From the list of line styles, choose Hairline.

MOVING AND RESIZING GRAPHICS

Once you have drawn or imported a graphic, it's likely that you'll have to move or resize it. To move a graphic, just drag it to the new location using the pointer tool. To resize a graphic, select the object with the pointer tool and then drag one of the eight selection handles that surround the object. When you are resizing imported images, you may want the graphic to maintain its original proportions; to do this, hold down Shift as you drag a handle.

If necessary, move and/or resize the shuttle and box until they match Figure 2.12.

TYPING TEXT IN PAGEMAKER

To type text in PageMaker, select the text tool, and click on the page or pasteboard where you want to type the text. Instead of just clicking, you can drag a *text box* the approximate width and length of the text you will be typing. PageMaker will then word-wrap inside this area.

The shuttle graphic needs a caption. Type and format this text on the pasteboard and then move it into position. The final caption is shown in Figure 2.13.

1. Choose the text tool.

2. On the pasteboard, click and drag a text box that's about two and a half inches wide (the length doesn't matter). When you release the mouse button, the box disappears, but never fear—PageMaker will remember the size of box you drew.

FIGURE 2.13: *The caption was typed with the text tool*

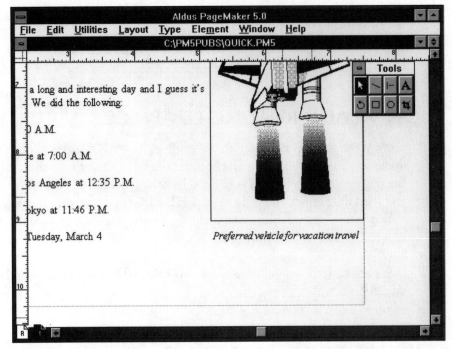

3. Switch to Actual Size view, and type Preferred vehicle for vacation travel.

4. Select the text and set it to 11-point Times New Roman italic.

MOVING A TEXT BLOCK

Moving a text block is similar to moving a graphic object: With the pointer tool, select the block and drag it to the new location.

Follow these steps to move the caption from the pasteboard to underneath the shuttle:

1. Switch to Fit in Window view.

2. Choose the pointer tool and click on the caption you just typed. Boundaries, called *window shades*, appear above and below the text block. The window shades indicate the block is selected.

3. With the pointer inside the window shades, click and hold down the mouse button. A four-headed arrow appears inside the block.

4. Drag the mouse until the block is centered under the graphic (see Figure 2.13).

5. Press Ctrl+S to save.

MANAGING YOUR FILES

This section explains basic file operations, including printing, closing, and opening publications. Saving was covered earlier in the chapter. All the options for file handling are on the File pull-down menu.

PRINTING A FILE

Chapter 3 covers PageMaker's printing options in detail. In the following steps, you will print your publication without specifying any special options. We are assuming that your printer has been set up in Windows.

1. Make sure your printer is turned on, switched online, and has paper.

2. Pull down the File menu.

3. Choose Print. The Print Document dialog box appears.

4. Click on the OK button or press Enter.

After a moment of flashing messages, the page will print. It should look something like Figure 2.1.

CLOSING A FILE

When you are finished working with a file, you will want to close it. The process of closing a file removes it from the screen and the computer's temporary memory. Fortunately, if you have made any changes since you last saved your file, PageMaker will warn you and ask if you want to save it.

PageMaker offers several ways to close a file:

➤ Pull down the File menu and choose Close.

➤ Click on the document window's Control-menu box and choose Close.

➤ Double-click on the document window's Control-menu box.

 **!** **WARNING**

> When you are closing a file with the **Control-menu box,**
> be careful that you don't click on the wrong box. The top
> box controls your **PageMaker application; the second**
> box controls your document window. If you close the ap-
> plication window, you will exit your publication *and* the
> PageMaker program.

Now you should close your QUICK publication:

1. Pull down the File menu.

2. Choose Close.

OPENING A FILE

To work with a publication you have previously created and saved, use the Open option on the File pull-down menu (or press Ctrl+O). The Open Publication dialog box is similar to the Save Publication As dialog box.

You type the name of the publication you want to work with in the File Name field, or select the name from the list. The names of your publications are listed alphabetically. If the file you want to open is not shown, use the scroll bar to view additional names. Once you have found the name, double-click on it to open the file.

If you still can't locate a file on the list, it might be stored in another drive or subdirectory. As in the Save Publication As dialog box, the current path is indicated under the word Directories. To change the path, you can navigate the Drives and/or Directories lists, just as when you are saving your work.

Follow these steps to open your QUICK publication:

1. Pull down the File menu.

2. Choose Open.

3. In the list of files, double-click on QUICK.PM5.

After a moment, the travel page will reappear, in the same view in which it was saved.

OPENING MULTIPLE PUBLICATIONS

Version
5.0
Version 5.0 of PageMaker lets you open more than one publication at a time. The maximum number of documents you can have open at once is limited only by the amount of memory in your computer. This ability to have multiple files open makes it easy to transfer text and graphics between publications.

To switch to another open publication, pull down the Window menu and select the name of the file. If you want to save all the files you currently have open, hold down Shift as you pull down the File menu. You will then see an option called Save All in place of the Save option. You will also see Close All instead of Close.

REVERTING TO THE ORIGINAL FILE

If you ever want to abandon all the changes you've made to a publication and retrieve the original file, use the Revert option on the File menu. This command will reopen the current file without saving any changes you have made since you last saved. You will be asked:

    Revert to last-saved version?

If you choose OK, the original file will be reopened; if you choose Cancel, the command will be canceled.

GETTING HELP

PageMaker has a comprehensive on-line Help facility that provides you with instant information about any command, as well as explanations of many different topics.

USING THE HELP INDEX

One way to use the Help feature is to select a command or topic from a table of contents. Let's use the Help feature to print a list of keyboard shortcuts.

1. Press F1 or pull down the Help menu and select Contents. You will see the Help window shown in Figure 2.14.

The Help window has its own menu, and it can be moved, sized, or scrolled like any other window.

2. Move the pointer to an option on the list. As you position the pointer, it changes to a hand with a pointing finger.

3. Click on Shortcuts. The bottom of the window displays icons representing different categories of shortcuts.

4. Click on the icon labeled File Tool.

FIGURE 2.14: *The Help window*

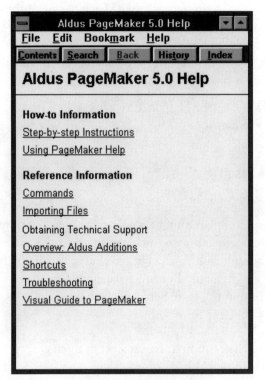

5. Read over the list of keyboard shortcuts and see how many you have learned already.

6. Pull down Help's File menu and choose Print Topic. After a moment, this Help topic, the list of file commands and tool keyboard shortcuts, is printed.

Underneath the menu is a series of buttons. Use the Contents option to go back to the initial table of contents. Back displays the Help window you just looked at. Use the Search option to specify which command or topic you want to find out about. History lists the help topics you have recently looked at; by double-clicking on an item, you can go back to one of these topics. When you click on the Index button, a second help window displays an alphabetical list of specific PageMaker features; click on a feature and the primary help window will display the help topic. Feel free to explore the Help window more if you like.

7. When you are ready to exit the Help facility, choose Exit from the Help window's File menu.

GETTING INFORMATION ABOUT DIALOG BOX OPTIONS

Occasionally, you will need an explanation of one or more of the options in a dialog box. To see a Help window with information about the current dialog box, hold down Shift and click on the background of the dialog box (not on an option) with the *right* mouse button. For example, here's how you can get help on an option in the Page Setup dialog box:

1. Pull down the File menu and choose Page Setup.

2. Hold down Shift and click the right mouse button in an empty area of the dialog box.

3. Read this screen. From here, you can proceed to see Help information about any other related topics that interest you.

4. Choose Exit from the Help window's File menu to leave the Help system.

5. At this point, you would normally finish filling in the Page Setup dialog box. But since you were just practicing, choose Cancel.

SUMMARY

After this quick tour, you should have a better sense of the process of producing a publication in PageMaker. Here is the recipe:

- ➤ Create a file.
- ➤ Add your basic ingredients: text and graphics.
- ➤ Spice it with up some formatting.
- ➤ Save and print the publication.

In the next chapter, you will learn more about setting up your page layout and printing your documents.

Page Setup
and
Printing

fast tracks

To insert a page:

Move to the desired location in your publication and choose Layout ➤ Insert Pages.

To change the page order of your publication:

Use the Sort Pages Addition. Click on the page or pages you want to move, and drag the mouse cursor to the desired new position. Then click on OK and PageMaker automatically sorts all the pages.

To automatically create signatures for your print shop:

Use the Build Booklet Addition. Choose the signature size, the binding method, and the pages from your publication to include, then click OK.

To create proof copies on a different printer from your target:

Choose File ➤ Print and then click on Print To to choose a different printer.

To print a non-contiguous page range:

Enter it in the Print dialog box next to Ranges. Use commas to separate each group of pages, such as: 1,3-7,10,13,15-20.

To cancel a print job before it has printed:

Switch to Print Manager, highlight the job in progress, and click on the Delete button.

HIS CHAPTER COVERS WHAT could arguably be the two most important parts of the desktop publishing process: determining the layout of your page and printing your publication. To the uninitiated, these two don't seem to have much to do with one another; in fact, they have everything to do with each other: Page-Maker needs to know your printer just as it needs to know the size of your page and its margins. Defining the page layout and setting up your printer should be done in the initial stages of publication production. When you are ready to print your publication, you can browse several printing options, but PageMaker wants to know the type of printer you use at the outset.

SETTING UP THE PAGE LAYOUT

You should give careful thought to your page setup when you are creating a publication. *Before you add any text or graphics to the page*, make the following important decisions:

- ➤ Paper size of the final document
- ➤ Margin settings

➤ Whether you want the page orientation to be tall or wide (Page-Maker insists on these grade-school terms while the rest of the publishing community uses Portrait and Landscape.)

➤ Whether the final printed document will be double- or single-sided

➤ How many columns your publication will have

Most of the page layout options are set from the Page Setup dialog box that appears when you select New on the File menu. This dialog box is shown in Figure 3.1. If you want to change any of these settings after you have created the publication, choosing Page Setup from the File menu presents you with the same dialog box. Column Guides is an option on the Layout menu, not on the Page Setup dialog box. It is not part of the page setup so that you can set a different number of guides on each page.

If PageMaker offers a way to change settings after the fact, then why are we lecturing you on the importance of determining your page setup before you create the document? After-the-fact changes to your page configuration carry a potentially high price tag, as many of the elements on your

FIGURE 3.1: *The Page Setup dialog box*

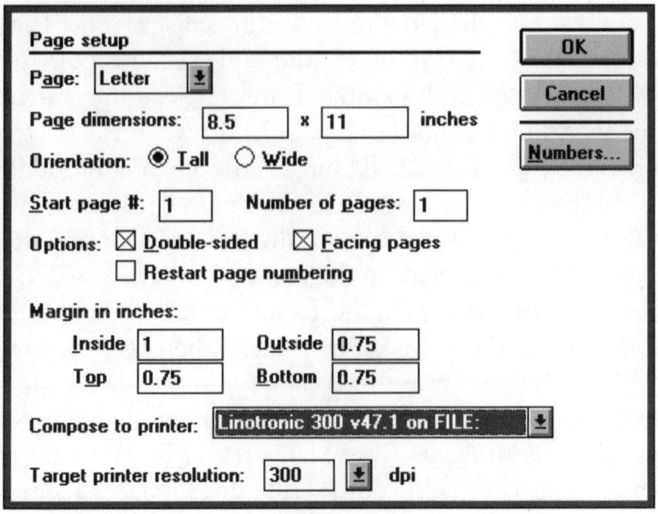

pages might have to be manually resized and/or repositioned. In a short one- or two-page document, this repositioning takes only a few minutes. But if you have a long publication, you're in for a long, tedious task.

Most of the options in the Page Setup dialog box are fairly straightforward, but for some, there are special considerations.

CHOOSING A PAGE SIZE

Version
5.0

PageMaker 5.0 provides a choice of seven industry-standard page sizes (up from three choices in version 4.0): Letter, Legal, Tabloid, A3, A4, A5, and B5. Furthermore, by choosing Custom, you can create a page of any size imaginable (although feet, yards, and miles are probably out as units of measurement). To create a page 7 by 9 inches in dimension, you would choose Custom, enter in the dimensions, and print the page on standard letter-size paper. By using PageMaker's *printer marks* (a fancy name for *crop marks*), you can tell your printer exactly where to cut the paper to achieve the desired size. Figure 3.2 shows crop marks around a 7-by-9-inch page printed on letter-size paper. You can turn printer marks on and off from the Print dialog box, covered later in this chapter.

SETTING THE ORIENTATION

You should be aware of how the Orientation setting impacts other Page-Maker options. First of all, when you select the Wide (Landscape) orientation, the two page dimension values switch. For example, if the current page dimensions are 8.5 by 11, they become 11 by 8.5 when you choose Wide. Thus, when the page is switched from a vertical to a horizontal orientation, the width becomes the length and the length becomes the width.

Version
5.0

New to version 5.0, PageMaker automatically changes the print orientation to match your page orientation. In the past, you were required to conscientiously change the orientation in the Target Printer dialog box. As a result, a lot of well-intended PageMaker users found their landscape brochures printing out with their lower thirds cut off.

Most PageMaker users will not have to worry about font handling with landscape print jobs, as both Adobe Type Manager and TrueType automatically reorient their font outlines. If you are still using bitmapped fonts, you

FIGURE 3.2: *Crop marks indicate the page size*

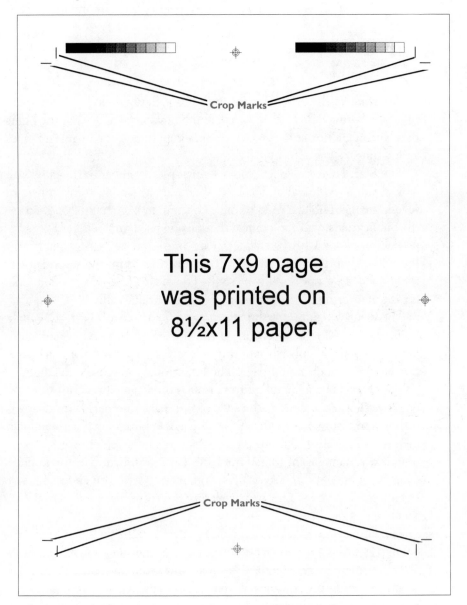

will need to produce or acquire landscape fonts, or better yet, throw them out in favor of ATM or TrueType. See Appendix B for information about using fonts.

NUMBERING PAGES

Unlike some of the other options in the Page Setup dialog box, the two page numbering fields (Start Page # and Number of Pages) and the Numbers button are not crucial to your page setup; they can easily be changed at any time.

The Start Page # field indicates the first page number in the publication. This option is useful when you have split a lengthy publishing project into several smaller publications. To have continuous page numbering across the publications, you can change the starting page number. Let's say you're producing a book with 10 chapters, each one stored as its own publication. If the first chapter has 17 pages, you would enter 18 for the second chapter's Start Page # option. If you use the book feature, as described in Chapter 15, the starting page number is changed automatically.

The value you enter for the Start Page # field controls both the numbers that appear inside the page icons at the bottom of the window and, more importantly, the numbers that print on each page when you specify page numbering on your master page. The latter topic is discussed in Chapter 14.

The Numbers command button displays the Page Numbering dialog box, where you can change the style of your page numbers. This dialog box is shown in Figure 3.3. By default, your pages are numbered with arabic numerals (1, 2, 3, etc.). But if the publication is a preface, foreword, appendix, or index, you may want roman numerals (such as i, ii, and iii) or alphabetic characters (A, B, C, and so on). The numbering style you choose here does not affect what you see in the page icons; the icons always display arabic numbers.

The Number of Pages option is straightforward. Just enter the total number of pages that your publication will have. Sometimes you will know exactly how many pages you need, such as when you are creating a two-page brochure. Other times, you won't be sure how many pages your publication will have until it is finished. This is often the case with longer documents such as manuals and books.

FIGURE 3.3: *The Page Numbering dialog box*

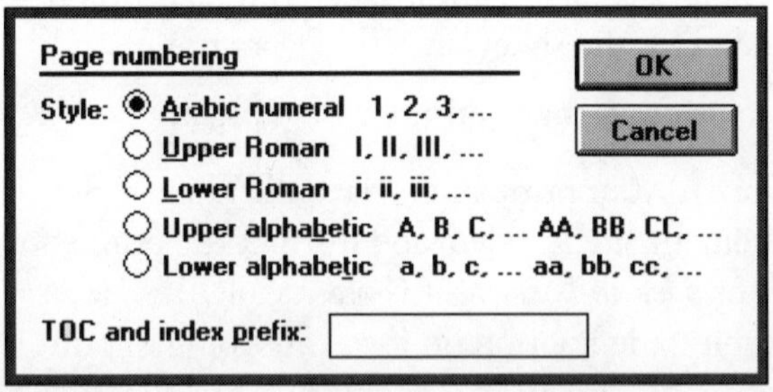

If you aren't sure how many pages your publication will have, don't worry; you can use the Insert Pages or Remove Pages option on the Layout pull-down menu to add or delete pages as necessary. In addition, Page-Maker can automatically insert pages when you import text, as you will see in Chapter 8. This capability, called *autoflow,* is invaluable when you are inserting a word processed document and don't know how many PageMaker pages it will need. Just leave Number of Pages set at 1, and PageMaker will create new pages as needed when the text is imported.

CREATING DOUBLE-SIDED PUBLICATIONS

If your final publication will be printed on both sides of the page, leave the Double-Sided check box alone, because its default setting is on. You will need to create double-sided publications when the pages are going to be bound together in some way: in a three-ring binder, spiral-bound, *perfect-bound* (glued at the spine), or folded and *saddle-stitched* (stapled once or twice in the fold).

Bear in mind that turning the Double-Sided option on does not magically transform your printer into a duplex printer, capable of printing on both sides. With most laser printers, you'll still need to send the paper through twice, or create a set of originals and take a trip to your print shop. To produce double-sided originals on a non-duplex printer, follow these steps:

I. In the Print dialog box tell PageMaker to print only the odd-numbered pages.

2. Flip these printed pages over and reinsert them into the printer. (Be prepared for a bit of trial and error to determine in which direction you should place the sheets into the paper tray.)

3. Tell PageMaker to print all the even-numbered pages.

If you leave this dirty work to your print shop, leave the Double-Sided option on, print the document single-sided, and instruct the print shop to print it double-sided (or *back-to-back*, as it is often called).

So why leave the Double-Sided option on if you are going to print it single-sided? For one very good reason: In a double-sided publication, the pages on the right and left sides might not be laid out the same way. For example, you would likely need different margins to accommodate the binding. With the Double-Sided option on, you can set up your right and left pages differently.

In conjunction with the Double-Sided option, you may want to use the Facing Pages option, which is also turned on by default. This option shows you the left and right pages that appear side by side in a double-sided publication. The two facing pages create what is called a *page spread*. Figure 3.4 shows a page spread, where the inside margins are wide enough to accommodate the binding, and the page numbers are set on the outside of the respective pages.

! WARNING

As you begin to design your double-sided publication, keep in mind how facing pages will look when seen as one. Your tendency as a PageMaker user will probably be to think of each page one by one. Your readers—who could care less how the publication looked on a Page-Maker screen—will react to what is put in front of their two eyes. They will react to the interplay between two facing pages, even if you have forgotten to consider that.

FIGURE 3.4:   *A page spread*

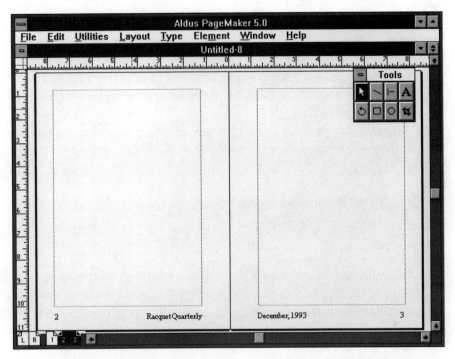

Here are a few things to note as you create double-sided publications with facing pages:

- → Even-numbered pages are displayed on the left, and odd-numbered pages are on the right.

- → By default, Page 1 is not part of a page spread, since it is an odd-numbered page and begins on the right. But through Page Setup, you can make the first page of your publication part of a spread by assigning an even page number to it.

- → You can only turn on the Facing Pages option if you have turned on the Double-Sided option.

- → You should make your inside margins large enough to accommodate your binding method. Setting margins is discussed in the next section.

SETTING MARGINS

The margins you set in the Page Setup dialog box define the white space around the edges of the page. As mentioned in Chapter 1, these margins are marked with dotted lines, called margin guides. Although you can place text and graphics outside the margins, most of your elements will be confined to the body of the page. That's why you set margins—to define the work area of the page.

In the dialog box area titled Margin in Inches, the following margins and default values are listed (assuming the Double-Sided option is on):

Inside	1 inch
Outside	0.75 inch
Top	0.75 inch
Bottom	0.75 inch

The most common elements that influence top and bottom margins are headers and footers, because you need to allow more space for them. Professional designers use a complex grid, closely linked to the size of the text, to determine top and bottom margins. For a more complete discussion of setting vertical spacing, see Chapter 6.

Inside and Outside Margins

The Inside and Outside settings apply to double-sided publications only. Pages are bound together at the inside margins in a double-sided publication, as previously shown in Figure 3.4. The inside margin is on the right side of a left-hand page and on the left side of a right-hand page. The outside margin is the space on the outer edges of the page spread. It's the left margin on a left-hand page, and the right margin on a right-hand page.

Depending on your binding method, you may want the inside margin to be slightly larger than the outside margin in order to accommodate the binding. If you forget to specify a larger inside margin, the text will be too close to the binding (undesirable), or the edge of the text might actually get cut off (disastrous).

A single-sided publication does not have inside and outside margins. It simply has the normal garden-variety left and right margins that you are accustomed to setting in your word processor. If you turn off the Double-Sided option, you see the Left and Right options listed instead of Inside and Outside.

Units of Measurement

PageMaker's default measurement system is inches, but yours might not be. You can choose one of the other available measurement systems by selecting the Preferences option under the File menu. For example, if you're from outside the United States, you might prefer entering your measurements in millimeters. Those involved in graphic design and/or typesetting would prefer the pica/point system. (There are about 6 picas to an inch and 72 points to an inch.) Once you change the default, you can enter the value in your preferred measuring system when a dialog box prompts you for a measurement (for margins, indentations, spacing, and so on).

If it's easier for you to enter inches for some measurements and picas for others, you can override the default system and specify a different system on the spot. For example, if your default system is in inches, but you want to specify a 3-pica indent, type 3p. The abbreviations to use to specify the measurement systems are as follows:

SYSTEM	ABBREVIATION
Inches	**i** after the value
Millimeters	**m** after the value
Picas	**p** after the value
Points	**p** before the value
Picas and points	**p** between the values

! **WARNING**

**You should be aware that PageMaker's designation for
points is not the standard syntax among Windows applications. Most other Windows applications accept, say,
12pt as the designation for 12 points. If you enter that in
PageMaker, it will see only the *p* after the 12 and enter
the value as 12 picas.**

What is also a bit unfortunate is that after you enter the value, PageMaker
converts it to the default measuring system. For example, if you enter 3p for
the top margin, and then return to the Page Setup dialog box, you will see
that the value is converted to 0.5 ($^{1}/_{2}$ inch). Looking on the bright side, it's
an easy way to convert values into the default unit of measurement.

CHANGING THE DEFAULT PAGE SETUP

If you find that you are frequently changing the page setup to the same values and options, you may want to modify your default page setup. Follow
these general steps to change the default settings:

1. If any publications are open, close them. (This first step is
   crucial to creating a new default setting in PageMaker.)

2. Pull down the File menu and choose Page Setup.

3. Adjust the dialog box settings to reflect the options you use
   most frequently.

4. Click on the OK button.

From this point on, any new publication you create will automatically have
this page setup. As with the original default settings, you can change your
new defaults whenever necessary. This procedure works for many Page-
Maker options, so remember this rule of thumb: When you change a setting *while a file is open*, you are changing that publication only. When you
make a change while no files are open, you are changing the program's

defaults. Thus, the key to resetting a PageMaker default is to not have any files open when you make the change.

MANIPULATING PAGES

If PageMaker is anything, it is flexible. In fact, it has earned its reputation in the graphics arts community by being the page-layout program that best lets you manipulate objects on the page. This flexibility extends beyond objects on the page—PageMaker also lets you freely manipulate pages in a publication.

INSERTING PAGES

The Insert Pages command under the Layout menu is about as simple as can be. The dialog box prompts you for the number of pages you want to insert and the positioning of the new pages (either before or after the current page). If yours is a double-sided document, PageMaker's default choice is to insert two pages; in a single-sided document, the default is one page. In either case, you can override the default and enter any number you want. The Insert Pages command is especially useful in two scenarios:

- ➤ When your free-form six-page publication suddenly needs to be seven pages. With the flip of one electronic switch, you can add an extra page.

- ➤ When a long publication with an autoflowed text file needs ancillary text inserted into a specific place. If, between pages 17 and 18, you decide to place a full-page image or sidebar article, this is easily accomplished with Insert Pages. The text automatically flows around the new page.

REMOVING PAGES

This is a straightforward command with an easy-to-operate dialog box. You can select any range of pages to remove, but they must be contiguous.

When you remove a page, all elements on the page vanish also. (Don't worry, Undo covers page removal if you do it accidentally.)

! **WARNING**

As with the Insert Pages command, the one caveat here also relates to autoflowed text. If you remove, say, page 14 from a 20-page publication with one long text file, PageMaker does not reflow the text. Instead, the text that was on the removed page is cut and the text file restitched together as if it never knew anything about the missing page of text.

MOVING PAGES WITH THE SORT PAGES ADDITION

Version
5.0

The Sort Pages Addition is a very handy tool for seeing the forest for the trees when working with multipage publications. As Figure 3.5 shows, this Addition provides you with instant thumbnails of all the pages in your publication. As you can also see, the Addition accurately depicts double-sided documents, and even provides an adequate account of a document's terrain.

But the main attraction of the Sort Pages Addition is inherent in its name: It will quickly move pages, and all elements, to different places in a publication. As with inserting and removing pages, resorting pages changes the flow of a multipage text file.

Sorting pages is a matter of clicking and dragging: You select the page or pages to move by clicking on them or by dragging around them. Once you've selected them, click, hold, and move the mouse to the desired new location. (A separate select step isn't needed to move a single page. Just drag and drop it where you want it.) If your publication is double-sided, then PageMaker shows you pages in pairs and treats its page spread as a single entity. (The Options button at the bottom of the window lets you override that and select pages one by one.) When you reorder pages, the Addition resorts the thumbnails for each page and shows you the original

FIGURE 3.5: *The new Sort Pages Addition makes page reordering a snap*

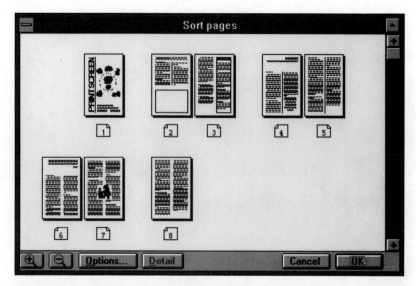

page number, with dotted lines around it, next to the new page number. Figure 3.6 shows the result of moving Pages 4 and 5 in between Pages 2 and 3. If you click OK, then the pages are actually sorted. To move a page to the end, you must drag it just to the right of the last page. Further out in the empty area won't work.

 ! WARNING

Undo does not extend to page sorting, so save before invoking the command, lest you be sorry if you change your mind.

For those who really want to entangle themselves, the Addition allows you to select noncontiguous pages. In other words, you could select Pages 1, 3, 6, and 9–12, and move them all to the back of the publication. Do the selection by holding down the Shift key as you click on each page or drag around a group.

FIGURE 3.6: *The Sort Pages Addition shows where the pages came from and where they are going to.*

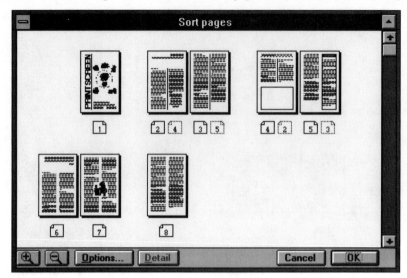

BUILDING A BOOKLET

Version
5.0

For some, the Build Booklet Addition will be worth the price of admission all by itself. In fact, perhaps many thousands of PageMaker users will rejoice over this new feature. While its value extends to many sects of commercial and professional printing, it got its name thanks to the largest group of users likely to take advantage of it: those who create $5\frac{1}{2}$-by-$8\frac{1}{2}$-inch booklets on $8\frac{1}{2}$-by-11-inch paper. According to a survey performed by a magazine servicing the electronic publishing industry, that is one of the most common projects being performed on the desktop. Right on its heels are $8\frac{1}{2}$-by-11-inch newsletters being produced on 11-by-17-inch paper. The Build Booklet Addition automates the part of these jobs that is most irritating—pagination.

Let's take the example of a monthly church newsletter, a little four-page publication of $5\frac{1}{2}$-by-$8\frac{1}{2}$-inch pages. The most efficient way to produce this project is with one single $8\frac{1}{2}$-by-11-inch piece of paper turned sideways. That way, two of the pages would be on one side, and two on the other. Folded once, this one sheet produces four distinct sides. Figure 3.7 shows you what the inside two pages look like, and if you thought about it

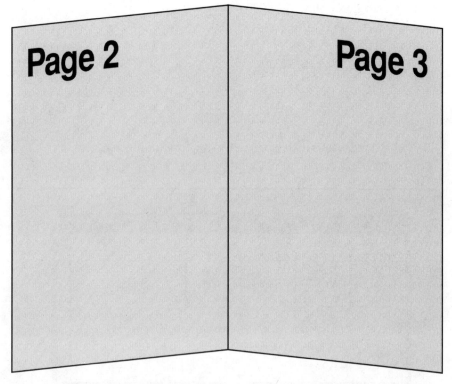

for a moment, you would probably figure out that Page 4 needs to be placed on the left half of the reverse side of the page, with Page 1 going on the right half. Imagine folding the page in Figure 3.7 and you'll see how it works.

This is not terribly hard to figure out with one sheet. Now imagine doing it with two sheets for an eight-page letter, three sheets for 12 pages, four sheets for 16 pages…or 40 sheets for 160 pages. In print shop terms, the sheets are called "signatures," and the complicated process of making everything come out right is called "pagination."

Version 5.0's Build Booklet Addition paginates your document automatically. It creates the right size sheet on which to place the pages, and it calculates where every page must go.

Let's assume you purchased a laser printer capable of printing 11-by-17-inch sheets of paper. You could save quite a lot of time and paper by structuring your publication so that two pages print on each sheet, in their proper order. Here are the steps you would take:

1. Create a new publication, consisting of four letter-sized pages.

2. On each page, create a distinct shape—circles and rectangles will do fine—and a line of type, Page 1 through Page 4, for each page. When you use the Sort Pages Addition to show thumbnails, your little publication might look like Figure 3.8.

FIGURE 3.8: *A thumbnail sketch of a four-page document*

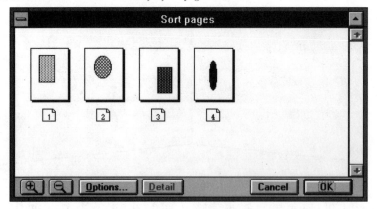

3. Save the publication as BOOKLET.PM5. Pretend this is the four-page newsletter you are producing for your company.

4. Pull down Utilities, choose Aldus Additions, and then Build Booklet. You are presented with a dialog box similar to the one shown in Figure 3.9.

5. Click on Page 1, hold the Shift key down, and click on Page 4 so that all pages are highlighted.

Your newsletter is to be saddle-stiched, a fancy phrase that means "stapled twice, down the middle."

FIGURE 3.9: *The Build Booklet dialog box*

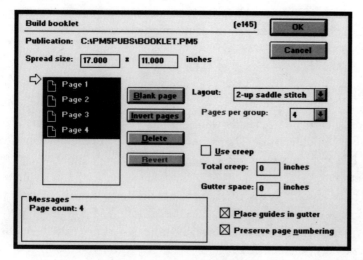

6. In order for two 8½-by-11-inch pages to fit on one sheet, the sheet must be turned sideways. Therefore, the size of the sheet—PageMaker calls it the "Spread Size"—must be 17-by-11. This size was automatically specified when you chose the Layout. At Layout, choose *2-up saddle stitch*.

Click OK to paginate your newsletter. PageMaker will first notify you that it is closing down your original publication and give you a chance to save changes. Then it will begin calculating the correct pagination and produce for you a new publication with all the pages properly placed on two sheets of 11-by-17-inch paper.

Experiment on your own with this powerful feature. If you produce projects in which you must calculate correct pagination, you will love using Build Booklet.

PRINTING FROM PAGEMAKER

Version
5.0
Perhaps the most significant changes in all of version 5.0 can be found in PageMaker's print engine, now a multitiered collection of dialog boxes with a bevy of switches, options, and controls buried therein. The print

functions are now more involved and more complex. Version 5.0 goes a long way toward providing more print capabilities, but you must take the good with the bad—the Version 5.0 print engine represents the ultimate electronic jig-saw puzzle.

CHOOSING A TARGET PRINTER

As mentioned earlier, PageMaker wants you to choose a printer when you begin work on a publication. Therefore, it makes you choose one when you perform a File ➤ New, and it allows you to change the printer through File ➤ Page Setup.

It used to be absolutely essential to choose the correct printer before you began adding text to the page. Today, in the age of ATM and TrueType, this is not as important as it used to be, as these two font-rendering engines use the same outline typefaces, regardless of the printer you use. If you didn't choose your target printer until you were ready to print, ATM or TrueType would ensure that you received correct output. If, however, you use bitmapped fonts (like fonts from Bitstream Fontware), proprietary fonts (such as LaserMaster's LXO format), or internal fonts (like the Univers and CG Times outlines in HP Series III printers), you must choose your printer first. If you don't, not only will you not get correct output, the fonts you intend to use probably won't even show up in the various font dialog boxes and lists. In light of all this, we maintain that the best habit you could get into would be to choose your target printer as you begin work on a publication.

Follow these steps to check your current target printer:

1. Pull down the File menu.

2. Choose Page Setup.

3. Look at the bottom of the dialog box, next to Compose To Printer. This is your current target printer.

If you installed more than one printer in Windows, you will have several choices in the printer list. Figure 3.10 shows three printers listed. To select a different printer, click on its name.

FIGURE 3.10: *A list of printers installed in Windows*

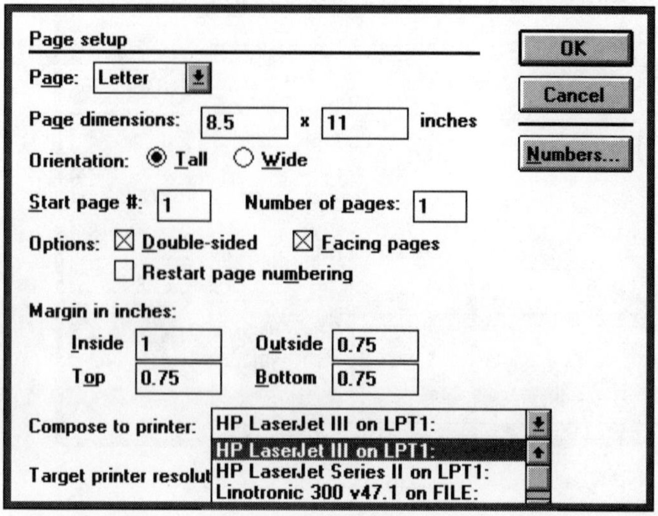

PageMaker shows you the name of the printer and the port to which it is connected. In Figure 3.10, the two HP printers share the LPT1 port via a printer switch box, while the Linotronic 300 has no port at all. When you print to the "Linotronic 300 v.47.1 on FILE," a small dialog box appears prompting you to issue a file name. The typical use for a printer connected to FILE is the creation of a PostScript print file, which is then given to a service bureau for high-resolution printing on film. See Appendix C for further information.

Version 4.0 used to provide a gateway to your printer options when you chose the target printer—a source of both flexibility and confusion for users. Now all printer controls and options are found in the series of dialog boxes under File ➤ Print.

BASIC PRINTING

Figure 3.11 shows the first-level dialog box under File ➤ Print, and for most jobs, this is the only place you would have to go to print your publications. Here is a tour of the options in this top-level dialog box.

FIGURE 3.11: *The Print Document dialog box*

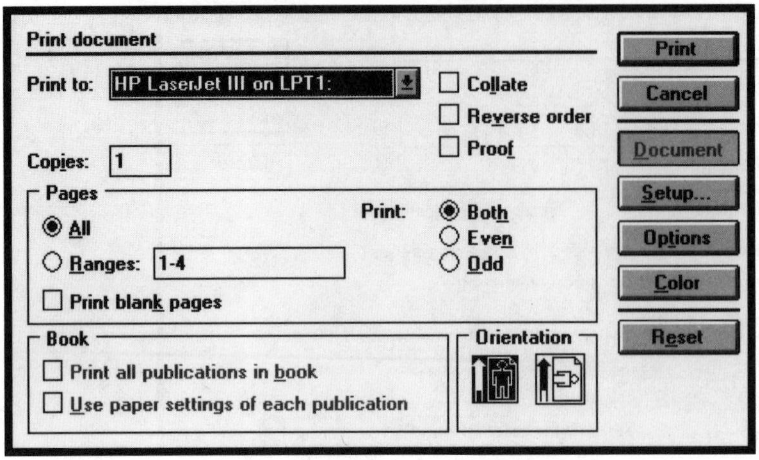

Print To

In case you haven't had enough time to choose your printer, you get one more chance before clicking on the Print button. Unlike in Page Setup, however, changing printers here does not instruct PageMaker to recompose the publication for the new printer; if you are using special fonts that won't print on the printer you designate here, that's just the way it goes. While this sounds dangerous, PageMaker's handling of last-minute printer-switching performs an important service: It lets you proof a document on your laser printer while it is intended ultimately for an off-site imagesetter.

The scenario would typically go something like this: Your eight-page sales catalog is a nice glossy affair, replete with four-color TIFF images and detailed EPS graphics. You are composing it for the Linotronic imagesetter at a neighborhood service bureau, from which you expect to receive film negatives produced at 2540 dots per inch. Those you will take directly to your print shop.

The Lino is a $15,000 piece of equipment, not the type of hardware you would normally find on someone's desktop. But you have to proof your work before sending it out, so you turn to your little desktop laser printer—let's say it's an HP III.

While you intend to print proofs on your HP III, you definitely do not want to recompose your publication for the HP III—it is carefully crafted with the Lino 300 in mind. Your target printer stays the same, but you tell PageMaker at print time to output the job to the HP III. The result: All line breaks, character widths, letter spacing, kerning, and other nuances determined by the target printer remain intact. Your HP III serves as a proofing device, and that's all. Because this particular HP III does not have PostScript capability, your EPS graphics do not print—you expect that, and are not alarmed by it.

To make the proofing process even more expeditious, you could click on the box labelled "Proof," and all imported graphics would print as rectangles with Xs in them. If you wanted to proof all aspects of the job, text and graphics (including EPS graphics), you would need to output to a PostScript laser printer.

Collating Multiple Copies

The other two boxes at the top of the dialog box enable you to print a publication in reverse order and to automatically collate print jobs of more than one copy. Automatically-collated copies might sound good, but wait until you see what it does to your print times. Let's take the case of a two-page flier, of which you want to make 4 copies. Uncollated, PageMaker's process looks like this:

ACTIVITY	TIME REQUIRED
Image 1st page	30 seconds
Make 2nd copy	1 second
Make 3rd copy	1 second
Make 4th copy	1 second
Image 2nd page	45 seconds
Make 2nd copy	1 second
Make 3rd copy	1 second
Make 4th copy	1 second
Total time:	1 minute, 21 seconds

If you saddle PageMaker with the job of collating the thing, here is the process it undertakes:

ACTIVITY	TIME REQUIRED
Image 1st page	30 seconds
Image 2nd page	45 seconds
Image 1st page again	30 seconds
Image 2nd page again	45 seconds
Image 1st page again	30 seconds
Image 2nd page again	45 seconds
Image 1st page again	30 seconds
Image 2nd page again	45 seconds
Total time:	5 minutes

Printing a Range of Pages

Version
5.0

All of the options here are self-explanatory, but as Figure 3.12 shows, you can select any range of pages to print, including non-contiguous ones (this is new to Version 5.0). The comma separates non-contiguous page ranges. We find it most unfortunate that while PageMaker allows you to print all pages or a selected range, it lacks a control that allows you to print the current page. This is arguably the most frequently-used print control of all.

While we are picking nits, we wonder if the default for the Print Blank Pages field shouldn't be on instead of off, given the importance of maintaining correct pagination across a long publication. You'll need to remember to check that box if you have intentionally added blank pages to your publication.

FIGURE 3.12: *Version 5.0 supports flexible page ranges.*

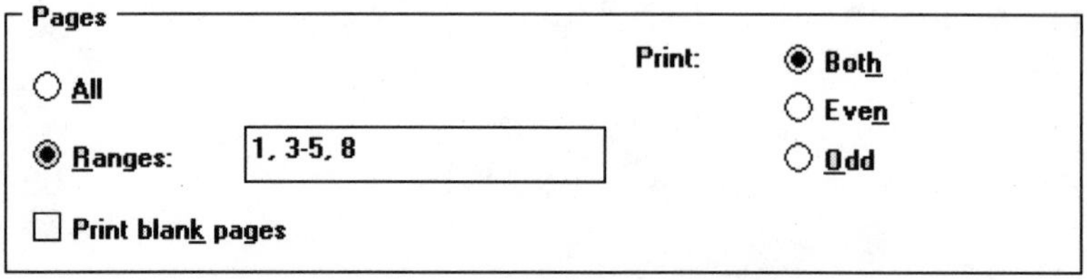

Book

When more than one publication is combined into a single project, Page-Maker makes available the Book options in the lower portion of the Print Document dialog box. Checking Print All Publications in Book tells Page-Maker to find the other publications that make up the book and print them all. See Chapter 15 for details on using the Book Feature.

Setting the Page Orientation

This setting only has to be changed if you actually intend to print a page in the wrong orientation. Otherwise, as discussed earlier, PageMaker automatically sets this field according to the one in Page Setup.

Along the right side of the Print Document dialog box in Figure 3.11 are seven command buttons. The top two begin the print job or cancel it altogether, while the bottom one returns all settings in the current dialog box to their defaults. The four in the middle contain all of the features, both new and old, of the PageMaker print engine. The first one, Document, is grayed out because it is already opened (when you choose File ➤ Print, PageMaker always takes you to this dialog box). The operation of the other three vary greatly depending upon the printer you have chosen. Some functions appear in different areas for different printers, and the Setup button even changes its name, showing up as Paper when you choose a PostScript printer. We sympathize with your plight in making heads or tails of this; it is just as hard for us as authors.

The following sections explore these buttons and how they function with HP LaserJet and PostScript printers. You can skip over the section that is not pertinent to you.

HP LASERJET OPTIONS

As Figure 3.13 shows, the Setup button is your gateway to the Printer section of the Windows Control Panel. Practically every Windows application that supports printing offers access to Printer Setup in some form or another. Most applications place Printer Setup directly on the File menu and again in the Print dialog box; PageMaker offers the latter, but not the former.

FIGURE 3.13: *The Setup and Options dialog boxes for an HP LaserJet III printer*

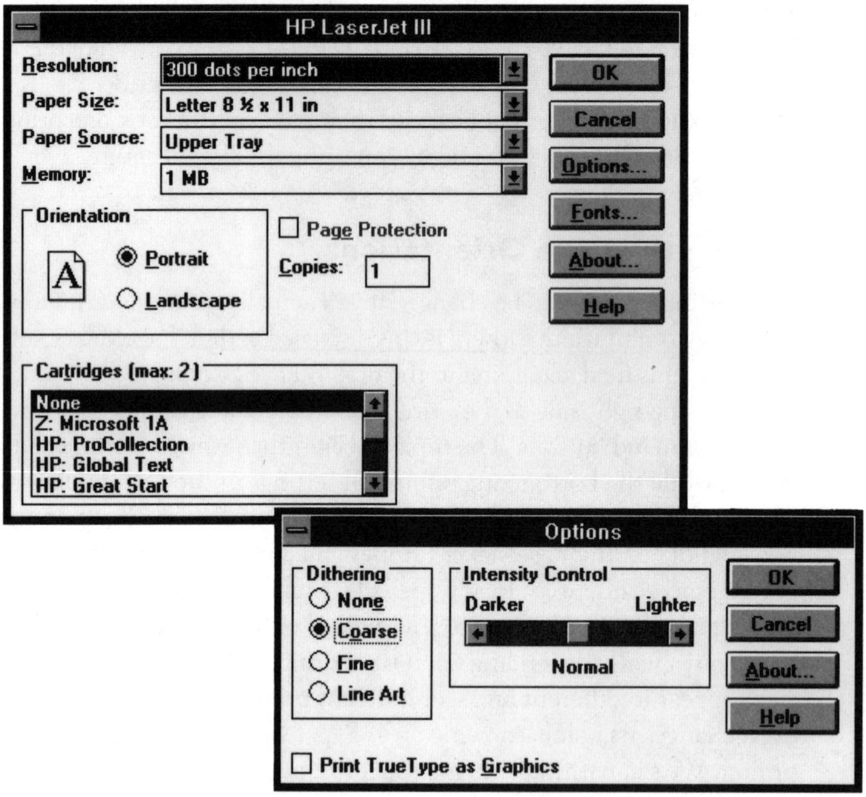

Changing the Resolution

The Resolution option refers to the number of dots per inch (dpi) at which your publication—or just its graphics—will be printed. The higher the resolution, the higher the quality. Also, on HP LaserJets, the higher the resolution, the longer the print job takes. For rough drafts on LaserJets, you may want to save time by printing at a lower resolution (for example, at 75 dpi). Also, if you don't have enough printer memory to print a complex graphic, you might succeed by dropping the resolution.

Setting the Paper Size

The Paper Size setting does not have to be the same as the Page dimensions in the Page Setup dialog box. As mentioned earlier, a page can be smaller than the paper on which it is printed. The *page size* refers to the dimension of the page in your final publication. The *paper size*, on the other hand, is the physical size of the paper in the printer. Therefore, if you are printing a 5-by-7-inch page on an $8\frac{1}{2}$-by-11-inch piece of paper, choose Letter for the Paper Size option.

Choosing the Paper Source

Your printer may have several different ways you can feed paper. For example, a laser printer has one or more trays, and can also be fed manually. The Paper Source option lets PageMaker know which feeding mechanism you are using.

Indicating Printer Memory

It would be nice if the Memory switch magically added more memory to your printer. Alas, it only tells Windows how much memory is available, so it can determine the best way to send a job. If Windows knows that your printer has, say 4MB of on-board RAM, it can then send data to it in big gulps. If your printer has the standard 1MB of RAM, then Windows spoonfeeds the data in bite-size pieces.

The HP LaserJet III, IIID, and IIIP printers come standard with 1MB of RAM, which can be expanded to 5MB, while the hefty LaserJet IIISi printer can be expanded up to 17MB. If you don't know how much memory is installed in your printer, you can run a self-test printout using your printer's control panel.

There are some jobs, with graphics so heavy and complex, that they might not print out at all on printers with minimal RAM, no matter how slowly Windows spools the data. If you expect to work with large TIFF images, scanned photos, and other bitmapped data, count on being frustrated by a 1MB laser printer.

Orientation

Here is yet one more place where you can change the orientation of a publication. For applications that do not have an orientation setting, this is the only place to set it. For applications like PageMaker that have orientation settings seemingly at every street corner, you can ignore this one.

Cartridges

HP's extensive third-party cartridge support is controlled here. If you own an external cartridge, all you have to do is plug it into your printer and then select it from this list.

Dithering Options

The Options sub-dialog box shown in Figure 3.13 is found by clicking on the Options... button in Setup. It is *not* the same as the Options button on PageMaker's main Print dialog box (sigh). You probably won't need to adjust these settings often, but you should know about the Dithering controls that are available for printers.

Dithering is the process by which a black-and-white output device can give the appearance of gray. The setting you choose controls the look of your printed graphics. We could speak until we were gray in the face— the best way to adjust these settings is to experiment. The *None* setting prints graphics in black and white with no gray shading. Select *Coarse* for a graphics resolution of 300 dpi or more. Choose *Fine* for images that require a smooth and realistic appearance; this setting provides soft contrasts between various shades of gray and is particularly good for color images being printed in black and white. Choose the *Line Art* setting when working with clip art or other images that are made up of mostly black lines on white background, or vice-versa.

The Intensity Control slider bar lets you increase or decrease the darkness of your graphics. Click on the left arrow to lighten the graphic; click on the right arrow to darken.

Remember, the Printer Setup dialog boxes shown in Figure 3.13 belong to Windows, not PageMaker. You can reach them from most Windows applications, or directly through the Windows Control Panel.

Scaling and Other Sizing Options

Backing out to the main Print Document dialog box, the Options button presents you with the dialog box shown in Figure 3.14. With the Scale controls, you can scale a document to any percentage, or click on the Reduce to Fit button if you want to shrink a publication down to a smaller page size. This works well for bringing a tabloid-size page down to $8\frac{1}{2}$ by 11 inches for proofing purposes. You could also choose to print your tabloid publication at full size, using more than one letter-sized page for each actual page. Click on Tile to achieve this. Finally, you could shrink down every page and print them on one sheet using Thumbnails.

Using Crop Marks

The Printer's Marks and Page Information buttons are for printing crop marks, color registration marks, and other information your print shop might need, like names of process colors used or CMYK values. For more about printing in color, and for an exploration of the Color button, see Chapter 12.

FIGURE 3.14: *The Options dialog box for HP LaserJet printers*

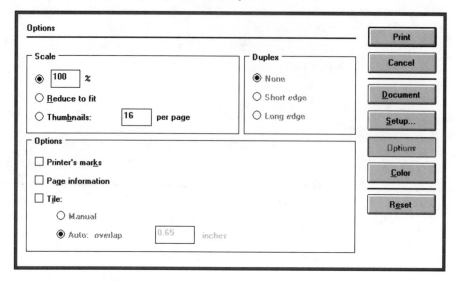

Duplex Options

If your printer can print on both sides of the page, then the Duplex options will be available in this dialog box. The Short Edge and Long Edge choices take page orientation one step further. With duplex printing, you must consider more than just how the page goes into the printer (tall or wide), but also how the page, with images on both sides, is to be incorporated into the document you are producing. Chapter 7 of the PageMaker 5.0 User Manual gives a good visual description of duplex printing dynamics.

POSTSCRIPT PRINTER OPTIONS

The options for PostScript printers are largely the same as those for HP LaserJet printers, but for reasons known only to the PageMaker developers, many of them are found in different places. If you use both types of printers, as we do, you'll get lost more than once, especially if you try to find your way to Printer Setup for PostScript printers (you can't). Figure 3.15 shows the dialog box for the so-called Paper option under the main Print screen. When a PostScript printer is selected, the Paper button takes the place of the Setup button that is there for other printers.

FIGURE 3.15: *The Paper dialog box for PostScript printers*

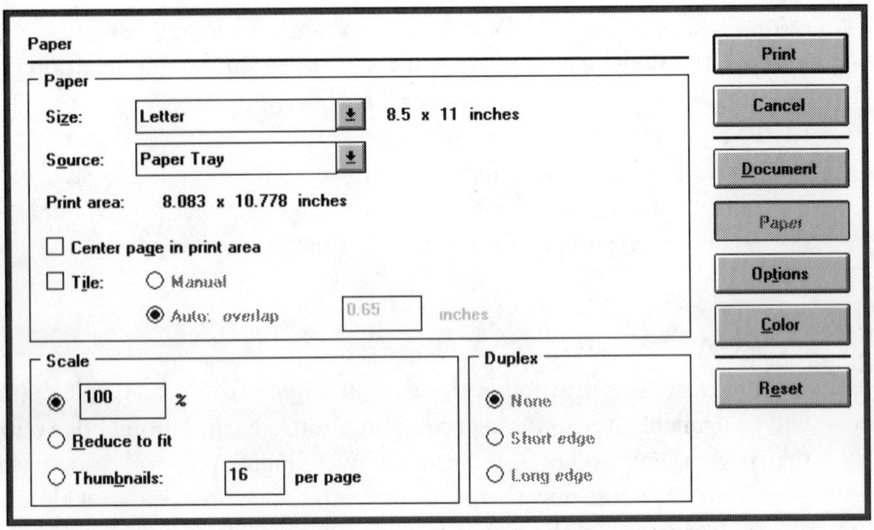

Paper		
Paper		
Size: Letter ▼ 8.5 x 11 inches		**Print**
Source: Paper Tray ▼		**Cancel**
Print area: 8.083 x 10.778 inches		**Document**
☐ Center page in print area		**Paper**
☐ Tile: ○ Manual		**Options**
● Auto: overlap [0.65] inches		**Color**
Scale	**Duplex**	**Reset**
● [100] %	● None	
○ Reduce to fit	○ Short edge	
○ Thumbnails: [16] per page	○ Long edge	

Setting the Paper Size

The Size setting does not have to be the same as the Page Dimensions in the Page Setup dialog box. As mentioned earlier, a page can be smaller than the paper on which it is printed. The *page size* refers to the dimension of the page in your final publication. The *paper size*, on the other hand, is the physical size of the paper in the printer. Therefore, if you are printing a 5-by-7-inch page on an $8\frac{1}{2}$-by-11-inch piece of paper, choose Letter for the Size option.

The Windows Control Panel offers more page sizes than listed here, including the all-important Letter Extra size—a 9-by-12 size that accommodates a full $8\frac{1}{2}$-by-11 page, with crop marks. This dialog box supercedes the Windows Control Panel.

Choosing the Paper Source

Your printer may have several different ways you can feed paper. For example, a laser printer has one or more trays, and can also be fed manually. The Source option lets PageMaker know which feeding mechanism you are using.

Scaling and Other Sizing Options

With the Scale controls, you can scale a document to any percentage, or click on the Reduce to Fit button if you want to shrink a publication down to a smaller page size. This works well for bringing a tabloid-size page down to $8\frac{1}{2}$ by 11 inches for proofing purposes. You could also choose to print your tabloid publication at full size, using more than one letter-sized page for each actual page. Click on Tile to achieve this. Finally, you could shrink down every page and print them on one sheet using Thumbnails.

Duplex Options

If your printer can print on both sides of the page, then the Duplex options will be available in this dialog box. The Short Edge and Long Edge choices take page orientation one step further. With duplex printing, you must consider more than just how the page goes into the printer (tall or wide), but also how the page, with images on both sides, is to be incorporated into the document you are producing. Chapter 7 of the PageMaker 5.0 User Manual gives a good visual description of duplex printing dynamics.

Printing TIFF Images

Figure 3.16 shows the Options dialog box for PostScript printers. The Graphics options address the handling of imported TIFF images. After the Normal setting—which prints TIFF images, well, normally—the Optimized setting is for images that were scanned at a resolution higher than the current printer can support. For instance, if you scan an image at 400 dpi and then print it on a 300-dpi laser printer, PageMaker works overtime to process a lot of image information that won't go to use. Clicking on Optimize insures against this happening. Low TIFF Resolution prints TIFF images at 72 dpi for fast draft printing, and Omit TIFF Files replaces all TIFF images with rectangles containing Xs for very fast draft printing.

FIGURE 3.16: *The Options dialog box for PostScript printers*

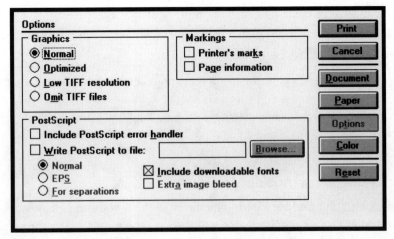

PostScript Error Handling

The PostScript options are for those who are sending output to a service bureau or who are incorporating pages from PageMaker into other documents. The first option, Include PostScript Error Handler, could be useful if your printer or service bureau fails to print your publication. With the error handler added to the print file, your printer will issue you a report of the failure. Beware though, that the report it returns is not along the lines of: "You know that headline you set? Well, it ran off the page. Please make it smaller." No, PostScript messages look more like the programming language that they are. Usually "undefined error line 37—limitcheck" is more like it.

Creating PostScript Files

Click on Normal to create a standard PostScript file, but choose EPS when you want to create an "encapsulated PostScript file." In so doing, you are taking a PostScript snapshot of one of your pages that can then be imported into another PageMaker document, or even a document from another application altogether. Your snapshot—your encapsulated graphic—can be sized and shaped to any dimension in the document that will house it. PostScript files can be more than one page, but EPS files must be created

from only one page. See Appendix C for additional details on creating Post-
Script files.

Creating Color Separations

Version
5.0 If you click on For Separations, you can create a special type of file that is
designed to be used in professional color separation utilities. PageMaker 5.0
can print color separations internally, so you might never need to use this
option.

Including Downloadable Fonts

By checking the Include Downloadable Fonts box, you can be confident
that the PostScript output device will have all the fonts used in the publication. However, be aware that the PostScript file will be significantly larger.
If you know the target printer has the fonts already, leave this option
unchecked.

Using Crop Marks

The Printer's Marks and Page Information buttons are for printing crop
marks, color registration marks, and other information your print shop
might need, like names of process colors used or CMYK values.

USING PRINT MANAGER

After you click on Print in the Print dialog box, PageMaker sends the document to Microsoft Windows for printing. More specifically, the Windows
Print Manager program handles the printing of your PageMaker documents.

As you've seen, several messages appear when you give the Print command. While these messages are displayed, the publication is in the process
of being sent to Print Manager. If you change your mind about printing this
document while the dialog box is displayed, you can click on Cancel. But
what if you want to discontinue printing after the dialog box has disap-
peared and before the document is finished printing? Because PageMaker's

role in the printing process is completed, you need to take this issue up with Print Manager.

Print Manager takes print jobs from Windows applications and places them in a print queue. A *print job* is a single print request you make in Page-Maker or any other Windows application. For example, if you tell PageMaker to print all the pages in a publication, that request becomes a print job in Print Manager. The program can handle multiple print requests from any number of Windows applications.

Each print job is lined up in a *print queue* and printed in the order it was requested. Let's say, for example, that you want to print title pages from two different publications. PageMaker cannot handle this in one request, so you must issue two Print commands. The first title page would become the first print job in the queue, and the second one takes its place behind the other in the queue.

Most laser printers can take advantage of Print Manager, but not all. High-speed printers that receive image data directly from the application to their video ports bypass Print Manager. If you use any of the LaserMaster products, you would be bypassing Print Manager (and the installation of the software probably turned it off for you). Other printers or software drivers supply their own print buffer for you to use instead of Print Manager.

Canceling a Print Job

Here are the basic steps for printing and then canceling a print job. To stop a document from printing, you must delete the print job from the Print Manager queue.

1. Pull down the File menu and choose Print.

2. Click on the OK button.

3. Read the screen messages that appear. They might make more sense now that you know that the file is being sent to Print Manager.

4. After the messages disappear (in other words, once the file has been sent to Print Manager), press Ctrl+Esc to bring up your Task List. (If you can see the Print Manager icon at the bottom

of your screen, you can double-click on it instead of going through the Task List.)

5. Double-click on Print Manager. The Print Manager window should look similar to Figure 3.17. The queue contains only one print job, the name of your PageMaker publication.

6. Click on the print job to highlight the line.

7. Click on the Delete button.

8. Click on the OK button to confirm that you want to remove the job from the queue.

9. To exit from Print Manager, pull down the Options menu and choose Exit.

Other Print Manager Functions

Besides deleting a print job, you can use Print Manager for other print-related tasks, such as the following:

➤ See how much of a print job has been sent to the printer. The percentage appears next to the document name in the queue.

FIGURE 3.17: *The Print Manager window*

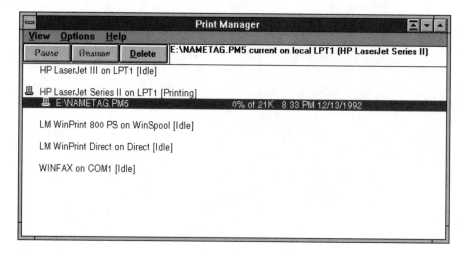

➤ Change the order in which print jobs are printed. (Use the
Options pull-down menu.)

➤ Resume printing after pausing. For example, Print Manager
pauses the printer when you run out of paper. Click on the Resume button to continue printing.

For additional information about Print Manager, use its Help feature or
refer to the chapter on printing in your Microsoft Windows *User's Guide*.

SUMMARY

Setting up your page and your printer are two important initial steps to producing a publication. If you take the time and effort to do these steps properly—before you begin placing text and graphics on the page—you will
avoid potentially tedious extra work as you build your publication.

This chapter concludes Part 1 of the book. In Part 2, you are going to
learn more about one of the publishing recipe's key ingredients—text.

part

Part II will demonstrate the variety of ways you can place and format text in your publications. Because text is such an integral part of publishing, this is the longest section in the book. There are three chapters devoted to getting text onto the page: by typing it with the text tool, placing it from PageMaker's Story Editor, or importing it from an external file. The other chapters concentrate on enhancing the appearance of your text.

WORKING WITH TEXT

Using the Text Tool

*f*ast tracks

To select text: 116

There are a number of ways to select text in PageMaker:

- ➤ Click and drag across the text.
- ➤ Click at the beginning of the text, place the I-beam at the end of the text, and press Shift as you click.
- ➤ Double-click to select a word.
- ➤ Triple-click to select a paragraph.

To assign type characteristics (font, size, type style): 116

Select the text to be formatted. Pull down the Type menu and choose Type Specifications (or press Ctrl+T). Make the desired changes to Font, Size, and/or Type Style. Choose OK. Alternatively, you can specify these characteristics in the control palette.

To insert special spacing: 125

Press Ctrl+Shift+M to insert an em space. Press Ctrl+Shift+N to insert an en space. Press Ctrl+Shift+T to insert a thin space.

HIS CHAPTER DESCRIBES HOW TO
use PageMaker's text tool to work with text. Regardless of which method
you used to place the text—through the text tool, the Story Editor, the
Windows Clipboard, or importing a word processor document—you can
use the text tool to correct and format it.

Using this tool, you can insert new text, delete unwanted characters,
and cut and paste. You can also change fonts, adjust type sizes, and add type
styles such as boldface and italic. There are quite a few other formatting options that you can specify while you are using the text tool, and these are
covered in Chapters 6 through 9.

WORKING WITH THE TEXT TOOL

To activate the text tool while you are working on a publication, click on
the A in the toolbox. When the text tool is active, you will notice two
changes on your screen:

- The A in the toolbox is reversed (white on black).
- The mouse pointer turns into an I-beam when you move it onto
  the page or pasteboard.

Before you can type with the text tool, you need to place the I-beam where
you want to type.

MOVING THE CURSOR

To position the I-beam, move it to where you want to begin entering text and click the left mouse button. You will see a blinking vertical bar, called the *insertion point*—PageMaker's fancy name for a cursor. The location of the insertion point indicates where text will appear as you type. Once you have an insertion point, you can slide the mouse to move the I-beam out of the way. From here on, we will refer to the insertion point as your cursor.

When you click inside the margin guides, the cursor appears just to the right of the left margin guide, regardless of where you clicked.

To move the cursor in existing text, you can use the keyboard. The arrow keys move the cursor (not the I-beam) one character or line at a time. Table 4.1 lists other keyboard controls for moving the cursor. These keystrokes may be the same ones used in your word processor.

TABLE 4.1: *Keystrokes for Moving the Cursor*

Movement of Cursor	Keystroke
Right one word	Ctrl+→
Left one word	Ctrl+←
Beginning of line	Home
End of line	End
Next sentence	Ctrl+End
Previous sentence	Ctrl+Home
Next paragraph	Ctrl+↓
Previous paragraph	Ctrl+↑
Next screen	PgDn
Previous screen	PgUp
Beginning of story	Ctrl+PgUp
End of story	Ctrl+PgDn

SELECTING TEXT

After you've entered text with the text tool, many of the changes you might make to it, such as formatting and rearranging, require that you first select the text to be affected .

PageMaker offers several ways to select text while you are using the text tool:

→ Click and drag across the text.

→ Click at the beginning of the text, place the I-beam at the end of the text, and press Shift as you click.

→ Place the I-beam on a word and double-click to select the word.

→ Place the I-beam on a paragraph and triple-click to select the entire paragraph.

→ Hold down Shift as you press the arrow keys. The Shift key will also extend the selection of any of the key combinations listed in Table 4.1.

! **WARNING**

Once text is selected, don't type anything! If you do, you'll replace the selected text with whatever you type.

FORMATTING CHARACTERS

The three primary qualities you can assign to characters are font, size, and type style. The following sections define these formatting options.

USING FONTS

PageMaker defines the word *font* differently from the rest of the world. In PageMaker, a font refers to a specific typeface, such as Helvetica, Times

Roman, Courier, and Line Printer. It does *not* refer to a character's size or style (bold, italic, and so on).

There are two basic types of fonts: serif and sans serif. *Serif* fonts have tiny decorative tails at the ends of the strokes of each character. *Sans serif* fonts do not have these decorative touches.

Figure 4.1 compares a serif font (Times New Roman) with a sans serif font (Arial). Times New Roman is commonly used for body text, Arial for headlines or subheads. However, this is not written in stone. In fact, many books use serif fonts for all type: body text, headlines, and subheads. Whatever you do, do not mix two different serif (or sans serif) fonts on a page. Instead of providing variety, it will look unprofessional.

FIGURE 4.1: *Serif and sans serif fonts*

This is a serif font (Times New Roman).

This is a sans serif font (Arial).

The spacing of a particular font is either proportional or fixed. In a *fixed-space font,* each character is assigned the same amount of space, regardless of how thin or fat the character is. In a *proportional font,* the space each character occupies depends on the size of the character. For example, a lowercase *i* or *t* takes up much less space than an uppercase M or W. Figure 4.2 compares a fixed-space font (Courier) with a proportional font (Times New Roman). Proportional fonts are used most often in professional publications.

FIGURE 4.2: *Fixed-space and proportional fonts*

```
Courier is a fixed-space font.
```

Times New Roman is a proportional font.

To see which fonts you have, pull down the Type menu and choose Font. The cascading menu lists the fonts available on your target printer. The one that has a check mark is the currently selected font. If you have more fonts than can fit on a single list, the font names will display in multiple columns.

 **OTe**

Windows 3.1 comes with four fonts: Arial, Times New Roman, Courier New, and Wingdings. Arial is a sans serif font similar to Helvetica, and Times New Roman is a serif font. Courier New is a fixed-space font. Wingdings is a font made up of special symbols, such as checkmarks, bullets, pointing fingers, and circled numbers.

SELECTING SIZES

Character sizes are measured in *points*. The larger the point size in a particular font, the larger the character. There are about 72 points to an inch. Body text is usually in the 10- or 12-point range; subheads are usually around 14 points; and headlines are 20 points and up.

The Other option on the Size cascading menu lets you enter type sizes that are not on the list. You can enter type sizes in increments as small as a tenth of a point.

APPLYING TYPE STYLES

To emphasize key words and phrases in your documents, you can use a variety of type styles. These styles are listed on the Type Style cascading menu. Figure 4.3 shows examples of each style in Times New Roman.

You are probably familiar with the styles and have a good idea of when to use them. However, applying the reverse type style requires some special considerations.

FIGURE 4.3: *The type styles*

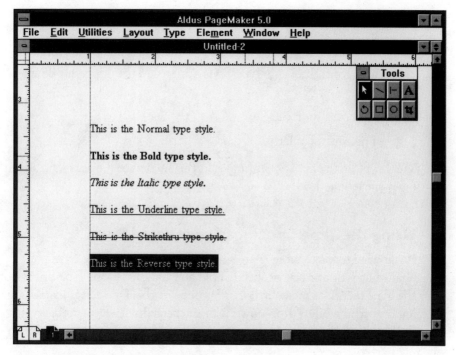

Using Reversed Type

The reverse type style switches the character color from black to white. If these characters are on a white background (such as the paper), the result is white text on white paper—invisible type. Therefore, when you specify a reverse type style, you must also change the background to black or some other color or shade. To shade the background of reversed type, draw a shape around the text with one of the drawing tools, and then fill this shape. Chapter 10 explains this process in detail.

Large, bold, sans serif fonts are the easiest to read in the reverse type style. When reversed, small and serif type-faces tend to be difficult to read.

ASSIGNING TYPE CHARACTERISTICS

PageMaker offers several ways to assign fonts, sizes, and type styles:

- ➤ The Type Specifications dialog box
- ➤ The Font, Size, and Type Style options on the Type pull-down menu
- ➤ Keyboard shortcuts
- ➤ The control palette

We'll explore the above techniques in this section and discuss the advantages of each method.

Using the Type Specifications Dialog Box

If you need to make more than one change to the type (for example, change its font and size or specify bold and italic), choose Type Specs from the Type menu, or press Ctrl+T. This displays the Type Specifications dialog box, which offers drop-down lists for specifying the font and size, as well as check boxes for selecting type styles. This dialog box is shown in Figure 4.4.

FIGURE 4.4: *The Type Specifications dialog box*

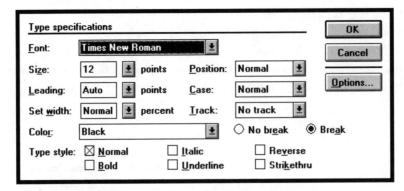

The Type Specifications dialog box provides additional ways to format characters. The Case option's default setting is Normal, which means that the characters will appear in the case in which they were entered. The other options are All Caps and Small Caps.

Using the Case option called Small Caps, you can capitalize all characters, with lowercase letters 70 percent of the size of the uppercase letters. For example, if you formatted 20-point characters as Small Caps, the lowercase letters would be 70 percent of the point size, or 14 points. To change this percentage, click on the Options… button in the Type Specifications dialog box. You can then fill in a different percentage next to Small Caps Size. A higher percentage value brings the size of the small caps closer to the size of the uppercase type.

The other options in the Type Specifications dialog box will be covered in later chapters.

Using the Type Menu Options

When you need to make a single change to the type, you can go directly to the appropriate option on the Type menu (Font, Size, or Type Style). For example, if the current font and style are correct and all you want to do is change the size, use the Size option.

If you have many fonts, they will not all fit on one cascading menu—the font names will display in multiple columns.

The Size cascading menu lists the most commonly used point sizes. To choose a size that's not on the list, or to enter a fractional size, choose the Other option and type in the desired point size.

The type size can be in tenth-point increments, between 4 and 650 points.

Using Keyboard Shortcuts for Styles and Sizes

Another way to specify styles and sizes is with keyboard shortcuts. The shortcuts for changing type styles are listed in Table 4.2. Notice that most of the styles have two keyboard shortcuts. The shortcuts that use Ctrl and Shift are mnemonic (for the most part), but the function keys are faster and easier (if you can remember them). Note that the function keys work on *selected text* only. You cannot use them to turn on a style before you type new text.

The normal style clears all other styles. For example, if the selected text is bold and italic, you can press F5 to choose normal and cancel both styles at once. To cancel only one of the styles, press the appropriate function key or key combination. For instance, to clear only the bold from selected text, use the Bold command (press F6 or Ctrl+Shift+B).

Two of the shortcuts for changing type sizes are Ctrl+Shift+> and Ctrl+Shift+<. Each time you press Ctrl+Shift+>, the type size increases by one point. Ctrl+Shift+< decreases the type size one point at a time. For example, if the current type size were 12 points, the first time you pressed Ctrl+Shift+>, the size would increase to 13 points. The second time, it would increase to 14 points. These shortcuts allow you to play "what-if" games with your type sizes when you aren't sure which size you want. Each time you use the shortcut key, you will immediately see how the selected text looks in the new type size.

TABLE 4.2: *Keyboard Shortcuts for Applying Type Styles*

Style	Key Combination	Function Key
Normal	Ctrl+Shift+Spacebar	F5
Bold	Ctrl+Shift+B	F6
Italic	Ctrl+Shift+I	F7
Underline	Ctrl+Shift+U	F8
Strikethru	Ctrl+Shift+S	
Reverse	Ctrl+Shift+V	

The Ctrl+> and Ctrl+< keyboard shortcuts work like the combinations with Shift, except that they only increase or decrease to type sizes on the size list (6, 8, 9, 10, 11, 12, 14, 18, 24, 30, 36, 48, 60, and 72). For example, if the selected text were currently 12 points and you pressed Ctrl+>, the text would increase to 14 points. Press Ctrl+> again, and the text becomes 18 points. In other words, it skips over the point sizes that are not on the list.

You should be aware that each time you press the key combination, you must wait for the screen to be re-drawn. If you have only a few lines selected, or if you are increasing or decreasing the size by one or two points, you won't mind the wait. If you are making more dramatic changes, you may want to take a trip to the Size cascading menu.

Using the Control Palette

Version
5.0

The *control palette* is a feature new to Version 5.0. The palette, shown in Figure 4.5, lets you apply formatting without going to the menu or a dialog box. The palette is context-sensitive and changes according to the tool you are using and the item that is selected. For instance, if the text tool is active, the palette will display options appropriate for text (font, type styles, size, leading, and so forth). Or, if a graphic object is selected, the palette will display options for manipulating the graphic (size, position, scaling, rotating, and so on). Here, we are going to look at the options that display when the text tool is active; this is called the palette's *character view*.

FIGURE 4.5: *The control palette in character view*

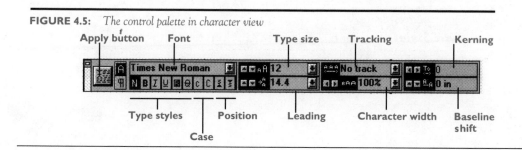

To display the control palette, choose Control Palette on the Window menu or simply press Ctrl+' (apostrophe). The palette appears at the bottom of the window. If it's in the way, you can drag it anywhere in the window; to move the palette, click and drag the vertical bar that's on the left side of the palette. To get rid of the palette, choose the Control Palette command again or click on the dash that's in the upper-left corner of the palette.

Figure 4.5 points out the options available in character view. Some of these options are discussed in Chapters 6 and 9. For now, we are going to concentrate on the font, size, type style, and case options.

Fonts To display your font list, click on the down arrow in the font field. You can then click on the font you want to select. If you have many fonts, use the scroll bar.

Another way to select a font is to click at the beginning of the font field, and start typing the name. The first letter you type will display the first font that starts with that letter. If this is not the font you want, type the second letter of the font name. When the desired font name is displayed, click on the Apply button (see Figure 4.5) or press Enter.

Type Size There are several ways to change the point size:

➤ Double-click in the type-size field, type the new size, and press Enter.

➤ Click on the down arrow in the size field and select the size from the list; use the scroll bar if necessary.

➤ To increase the size by 0.1 point increments, click on the up arrow to the left of the field. To decrease by 0.1 point increments, click on the down arrow. This is called *nudging*.

➤ To adjust by one-point increments, hold down Ctrl as you click on the arrow. This is called *power nudging*.

Type Style The control palette has options for setting the following type styles: Normal, Bold, Italic, Underline, Reverse, and Strikethru. Once you have turned on an attribute, its button is reversed. If the selected text is already set to a particular style, choosing the same style again will turn it off. The Normal style will clear all type styles assigned to the selected text.

Case   Two case options are available in the palette. The small C selects the Small Caps option while the large C turns on All Caps.

TYPING SPECIAL CHARACTERS

PageMaker offers keyboard shortcuts for inserting special characters into your text. The shortcuts are listed in Table 4.3. These special typographical characters are much more professional looking than their typewriter equivalents. Although it requires a little more effort, always use the typographical quotation marks. Also, use an em-dash (—) instead of two hyphens, and an en-dash instead of a single hyphen to specify a range of values (for example, 1–5).

TABLE 4.3:   *Keystrokes for Inserting Special Characters*

Character	Description	Keystrokes
"	Opening quotation mark	Ctrl+Shift+[
"	Closing quotation mark	Ctrl+Shift+]
'	Opening single quotation mark	Ctrl+[
'	Closing single quotation mark	Ctrl+]
—	Em dash	Alt+0151 (numeric keypad)
–	En dash	Alt+0150 (numeric keypad)
©	Copyright mark	Ctrl+Shift+O
®	Registration mark	Ctrl+Shift+G
§	Section mark	Ctrl+Shift+6
¶	Paragraph mark	Ctrl+Shift+7
•	Bullet	Ctrl+Shift+8 or Alt+0183
	Em space	Ctrl+Shift+M
	En space	Ctrl+Shift+N
	Thin space	Ctrl+Shift+T

Note

Although Ctrl+Shift+= is PageMaker's designated keyboard combination for em dashes, it does not work reliably. It actually forms an em dash by placing two dashes close together. In some fonts, this will look like a true em dash; in others it will look like two hyphens. To consistently get an em dash, use Alt+0151.

Version
5.0

In Version 5.0, PageMaker offers an option that, when turned on, will automatically display the typographical quotes when you press the apostrophe/inch-mark key. This option (called Use Typographer's Quotes) is located in the Other Preferences dialog box; choose File ➤ Preferences and then the Other button. Once you turn on this option, PageMaker will display an opening quote when you press " at the beginning of a line or or after a space. It will display a closing quote when you press " before a space, at the end of a line, or after a punctuation mark (such as a period or question mark).

Note

When you import a text file, the Convert Quotes option (which is turned on by default) will convert inch marks and apostrophes to typeset-style double and single quotation marks. It will also convert double dashes to em-dashes.

The only time you should press the Spacebar is between words. Do not insert two spaces between sentences or use the Spacebar to align text. Many novices make the mistake of trying to align text with the Spacebar. They might spend hours inserting spaces, printing out the document, inserting and deleting more spaces, reprinting the document, pulling out their hair, screaming—until finally everything almost lines up.

However, there are occasions when you may want extra spaces between letters or words; for example, between the state and zip code in an address or after a numbered step. To insert additional space, use one of these special characters instead of pressing the Spacebar:

➤ An *em space* (Ctrl+Shift+M) is equivalent to the amount of space a capital M occupies in the current point size.

➤ An *en space* (Ctrl+Shift+N) equals half an em space.

➤ A *thin space* (Ctrl+Shift+T) is a quarter of an em space.

The Spacebar can't be trusted as an accurate measure because PageMaker might vary the width of a space as it fits text on a line. However, Page-Maker keeps its hands off of fixed spaces—they will always be the width described in the above list. There is no way to guarantee the width of a plain old space.

INSERTING SPECIAL CHARACTERS WITH THE CHARACTER MAP ACCESSORY

Windows 3.1 comes with an accessory called *Character Map* that lets you insert special characters. Most of these characters will be from symbol fonts, such as Wingdings, Symbol, and Zapf Dingbats; Figure 4.6 shows the character map for Wingdings.

If you want a bullet other than the standard round shape—such as a square or diamond—you can use Character Map to copy and paste the symbol into PageMaker.

Here is the basic procedure for inserting special characters:

1. Go back to Program Manager, open the Accessories group, and load Character Map.

2. From the Font list, select the desired font (such as Wingdings).

FIGURE 4.6:   *The Character Map accessory with the Wingdings font displayed*

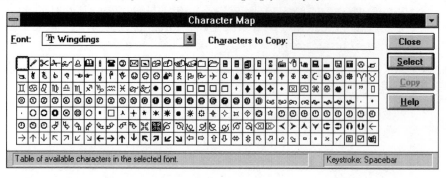

3. Click on the symbol you want.

4. Choose the Select button, and then Copy.

5. Close or minimize Character Map, and return to PageMaker.

6. Paste the symbol in the desired location: With the text tool, click where you want to insert the symbol and choose Paste on the Edit menu.

INSERTING BULLETS WITH THE BULLETS AND NUMBERING ADDITION

Version
5.0

The Bullets and Numbering addition included with Version 5.0 numbers a list or inserts bullets in front of each paragraph in a list; it automatically inserts a tab symbol between the number or bullet and the text. Figure 4.7 shows the Bullets and Numbering dialog box. To display this box, choose Aldus Additions from the Utilities menu and then select Bullets and Numbering.

The first thing to decide is whether you want bullets or numbers. By default, the dialog box displays options for bullets. If you want to number paragraphs, click on the Numbers button. Your dialog box will then look like Figure 4.8. The Bullets button will take you back to the original dialog box.

FIGURE 4.7: *The Bullets and Numbering dialog box*

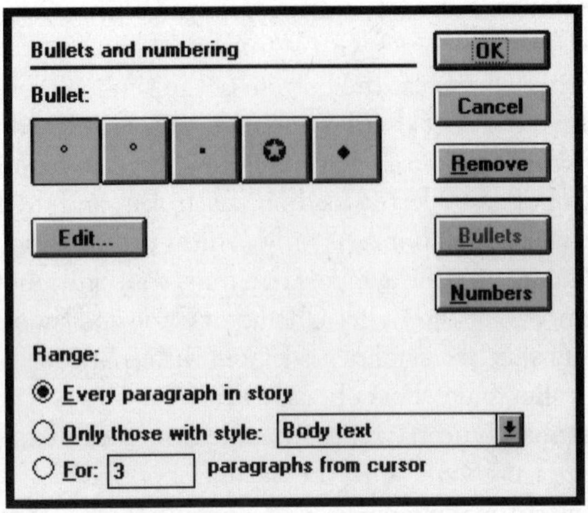

FIGURE 4.8: *When you click on the Numbers button, you will be able to choose a numbering style.*

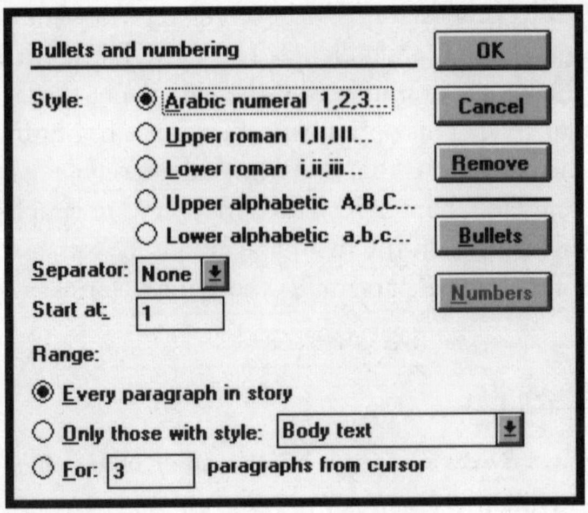

PageMaker offers several bullet styles, including hollow and solid round bullets (see Figure 4.7). Just click on the bullet style you prefer, or click on the Edit button to specify a custom bullet. In the Edit Bullet dialog box, you specify a Bullet Character Code, Font, and Size.

The Bullet Character Code is the ANSI code for a particular symbol. Determining the code is not an easy matter. For some symbols, you can use the Character Map accessory that comes with Windows. When you click on the symbol, the keystroke appears at the bottom of the window. For example, when you click on the checkmark symbol, Alt+0252 is listed as the keystroke. You then know to enter 252 as the Bullet Character Code. However, some of the symbols have letters as their keystrokes, and the Bullet Character Code field will accept numbers only. Unless you can find a chart that lists the ANSI codes for the symbols in a font, your only choice is to type in different numbers for the Bullet Character Code and then click on the Example box to see the symbol associated with that code. After filling in the Edit Bullet dialog box, choose OK.

If you selected the Numbers button, you can choose from several different numbering styles (see Figure 4.8). With the Separator option, you can select a symbol to come after the number (such as a period or parenthesis). Use the Start At field to change the starting number in the list.

It's imperative that you tell PageMaker what text to format; this is done in the dialog box, not by selecting the text. Most often you will want to limit the number of paragraphs that are bulleted. The Only Those with Style option will insert the bullets or numbers in the paragraphs that were formatted with a particular style. This option will start at the beginning of the story and skip over the paragraphs that don't have the designated style. (The Style feature is covered in Chapter 7.) The option For Paragraphs from Cursor assumes your cursor is on the first paragraph to be formatted; just fill in the number of consecutive paragraphs you want to format.

! **WARNING**

> By default, the whole story is numbered or bulleted; this is potentially disastrous if you didn't intend to format the entire story this way. You can't cancel the operation while it's in process nor can you undo it. Fortunately, the Bullets and Numbering dialog box contains a Remove button.

After changing a bullet or numbering style and selecting the appropriate range, choose OK. PageMaker will then insert the bullets or numbers in the range you specified. It will also insert a tab after each bullet or number. You will usually want to change the tab settings because the default tab stops are set at every half inch; this is too much space between the bullet and text. (Tabs are covered in Chapter 6.)

CORRECTING MISTAKES

The three most common typing mistakes are to leave out characters, to type the wrong characters, or to type extra characters.

An important part of the editing process is moving the cursor to the mistakes you want to correct. You have already learned how to scroll the screen using the scroll bar or grabber hand. Once the screen displays what you want to correct, you can click the I-beam or use the keyboard controls to place the cursor in the text.

INSERTING TEXT

PageMaker is always in insert mode. Whatever you type, wherever you type it, the text is added to what is already there. To insert text, click the I-beam where you want to add characters and start typing. Text to the right of the cursor is pushed forward as you type.

DELETING TEXT

Version
5.0
PageMaker offers two ways to delete text while you are using the text tool. To delete a single character, click the I-beam to the right of the incorrect character and press the Backspace key. If the cursor is to the right of the character to be deleted, press Del (or Delete); this capability is new to Version 5.0. To delete larger amounts of text, select the text and then press Del.

REPLACING TEXT

Sometimes you might want to replace one word or phrase with another. Rather than selecting the text, deleting it, and inserting the new text, you can simply select the text you want to replace and then type the new text. The selected text immediately disappears as soon as you begin typing.

To replace multiple occurrences of a word throughout a story, you can use the Story Editor's Change command, as explained in Chapter 5.

UNDOING MISTAKES

PageMaker's Undo feature is a lifesaver if you delete text accidentally. To bring back text you deleted with Del or Backspace, choose Undo from the Edit menu or press Alt+Backspace. You must issue the Undo command immediately, however. If you give another command or even reposition the cursor, you cannot restore the text. When it's too late to undo a command, the Undo option is dimmed on the Edit menu.

The Undo feature is not limited to restoring deleted text. You can also undo other types of editing you've done with the text tool, such as inserting, replacing, and cutting and pasting. However, you cannot undo type specifications.

CUTTING AND PASTING TEXT

To move text such as a sentence or a paragraph, you can use an electronic cut-and-paste method. Select the text to be moved, choose Cut from the Edit menu (or press Shift+Del or Ctrl+X), click the I-beam where you want to move the text, and then choose Paste from the Edit menu (or press Shift+Ins or Ctrl+V).

COPYING TEXT

The procedure for copying text is not too different from moving. Instead of *cutting* the selected text to the Clipboard, you *copy* it; you can either use

Using Windows' Clipboard

When you cut text out of a document, it is sent to Windows' Clipboard. The *Clipboard* is a temporary storage area that holds data that you want to transfer elsewhere—to another location in the same publication, to a different publication file, or even to a different software application. Here are a few examples of ways you can use the Clipboard:

➤ You can cut a paragraph and paste it in another location on the page, or on another page in the same document.

➤ You can cut or copy a block of text or a graphic from one PageMaker publication and paste it into another. Copy the element from one document, open the other publication, position the cursor, and then paste.

➤ You can cut or copy an image from a graphics program and paste it into a PageMaker publication. For example, copy the drawing in CorelDRAW, switch to PageMaker, and paste it into a publication. Because Windows allows you to have several applications running at once, you can perform this transfer quickly.

➤ You can cut or copy text from any program (word processor, spreadsheet, database, and so on) and paste it into a PageMaker publication.

The Clipboard only holds the last thing you cut or copied to it. Once you cut or copy something else, the previous Clipboard contents are thrown out. Therefore, make sure you don't cut or copy a second item before pasting the first item, or you will lose the first thing you sent to the Clipboard. To see the contents of your Clipboard, display the control menu (click on the hyphen in the upper-left corner of the PageMaker application window) and choose Clipboard.

the Copy option on the Edit menu or press Ctrl+C or Ctrl+Ins. (When you copy, the selected text remains in the story.) Then, place the cursor where you want to insert the copy and paste it.

Version
5.0
    If you want to make more than one copy of the selected text, you can use the Multiple Paste option on the Edit menu. This command will ask you for the number of copies you want to make. When you OK the dialog box, the specified number of copies are pasted in the cursor location. Don't use this option if you want to paste the copies in different locations.

WORKING WITH TEXT BLOCKS

In the previous section, you saw how to use the text tool's cut-and-paste technique to move text to another spot on the page. Another way to move text is to use the pointer tool to reposition an entire text block.

A *text block* is a rectangular body of text. In Figure 4.9, there are three text blocks: the line of type at the top of the page, the large block in the middle, and the text at the bottom of the page.

To see the boundaries of a text block, choose the pointer tool and click anywhere in the text. Solid lines appear above and below the text block, and *window shade handles* are attached to these upper and lower boundaries. These handles can be clicked and dragged to lengthen or shorten the text block. The corners of the block contain *text block handles*. You can click and drag these handles to widen, narrow, lengthen, or shorten the text block. Figure 4.9 points out these two types of handles.

FIGURE 4.9: *A selected text block*

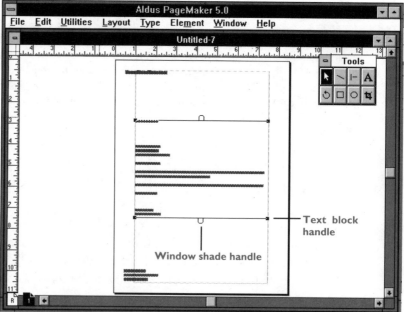

MOVING A TEXT BLOCK

You might remember that you moved a text block (the caption) in Chapter 2. You did this by dragging the block to the new location. Here are the precise steps:

1. Select the text block with the pointer tool.

2. Click inside the block and hold down the mouse button. If you do this correctly, a four-headed arrow appears.

3. Drag the box to the new location.

If you want to move the block to another page spread, you won't be able to drag it there. In this case, you would want to use the cut and paste commands as follows:

1. Select the text block with the pointer tool.

2. Choose Cut on the Edit menu.

3. Go to the page you want to move the text to.

4. Choose Paste on the Edit menu.

5. Drag the block to the desired position.

COPYING A TEXT BLOCK

Version **5.0** To copy a text block to another location in the same publication (whether it's on the same page or not), use the copy-and-paste routine. To copy text to another open publication, you can either copy and paste, or use a technique called *drag-and-drop*. Just open both publications and choose Tile on the Window menu to see the two windows side by side (see Figure 4.10). Then, drag the text block from one window and drop it in the other. The block will remain in its original location and will be copied to the other publication.

Version **5.0** The Multiple Paste option is also available to text blocks. In addition to asking you for the number of copies, it will ask you for a horizontal and vertical offset. These offsets are measured from the top-left corner of the text block.

FIGURE 4.10: *With tiled windows, you can drag text from one publication and drop it in another*

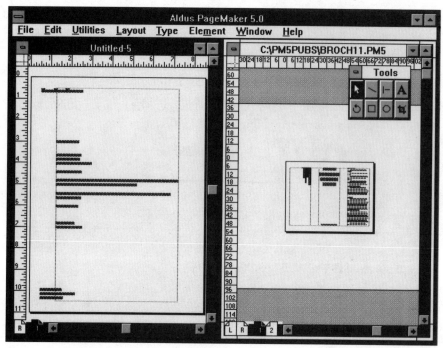

USING A RULER GUIDE TO ALIGN TEXT BLOCKS

When you are positioning text blocks and graphics, you may want to use PageMaker's *ruler guides* to align elements in the same way you would use a T-square or a ruler. These guides can be horizontal or vertical, and you are allowed up to 40 ruler guides per publication. Like your margin guides, the ruler guides do not print.

To insert a vertical ruler guide, click in the vertical ruler and drag the guide to the right. To insert a horizontal ruler guide, click in the horizontal ruler and drag the guide down onto the page. (If your rulers are not displayed on the screen, choose Guides and Rulers on the Layout menu and then select Rulers.)

Positioning text blocks is even easier if the Snap to Guides option is turned on. This option creates a magnetic effect between the object you are moving and the various guides on the page (ruler, margin, and column).

To see if the Snap to Guides option is turned on, choose Guides and Rulers on the Layout menu. If a check mark appears next to Snap to Guides, it is turned on.

When you are finished with a ruler guide, you can either leave it on the page or drag it back into the ruler with the pointer tool.

RESIZING A TEXT BLOCK

To resize a block, just click and drag the text block handles. There are many reasons for needing to do this. One common reason is to flow text across multiple columns, as shown in Figure 4.11. The boxed story is a single column of text, two columns wide. Also, if you change your margins *after* you have placed text on the page, you must resize the text blocks so that they fit within the new margin guides.

FIGURE 4.11: *The text block has been resized to spread text across two columns*

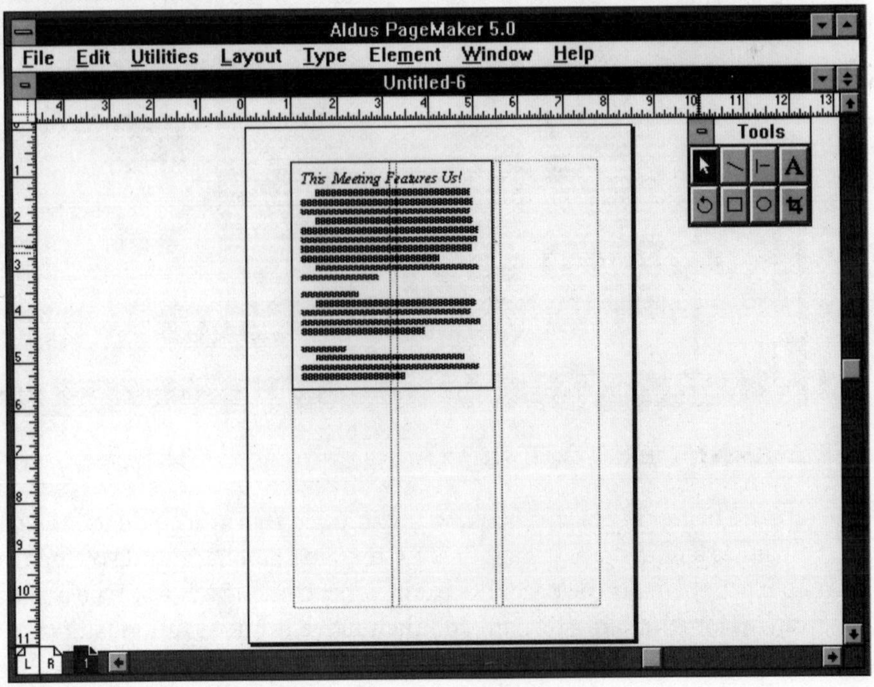

Figure 4.12 shows what happens when the left and right margins have been changed from $1/2$ to 1 inch. The margin guides shift to the new settings, but the text blocks remain in their original locations. To fix this problem, you must resize the text blocks so that the boundaries touch the left and right margin guides. In a long publication, this process could be quite tedious. Therefore, you'll want to give a lot of thought to your margin settings before creating a long publication.

FIGURE 4.12: *The text blocks do not automatically conform to the new margin guides*

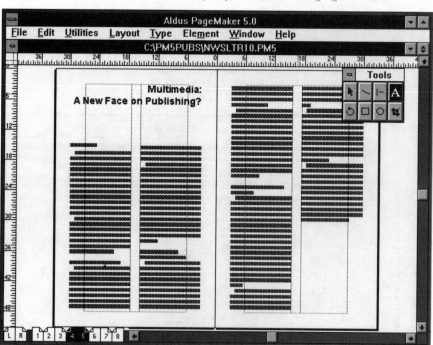

DRAWING A TEXT BOX

At the beginning of this book, we mentioned that you could use the pasteboard as a temporary storage area for text and graphics until you are ready to place them on the page. For example, you might want to type a headline or caption on the pasteboard and then move it into position later.

When you type text to the right of the page, the width of the text block is equivalent to the active page area (the area between the margin guides). The first text block in Figure 4.13 shows you how wide this block is—much wider than it needs to be. Because this extra-wide block would be cumbersome to work with, you would want to drag one of the right text block handles to narrow the block, either before or after you moved the block onto the page.

An alternative is to draw a *text box* the approximate width of the text before you begin typing. The second text block in Figure 4.13 was created with this method. To draw a text box, follow these general steps:

1. Choose the text tool.

2. Click on the page or pasteboard where you wish to type the text, and then draw a box by dragging down and to the right.

FIGURE 4.13: *The first text block is the default width; the second block's width was defined before the text was typed*

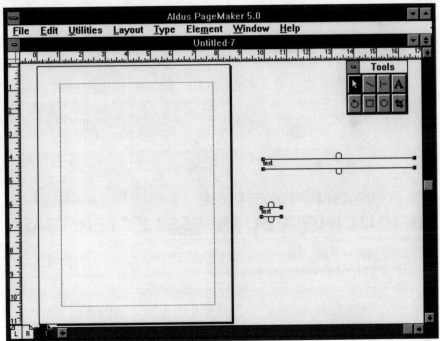

3. When the box is the size of the text block you will be typing, release the mouse button.

Although the text box disappears as soon as you release the mouse button, PageMaker remembers its size when you type. If a line of text is longer than the width of the invisible text box, it will word wrap, just as if you were typing the text between column guides.

DELETING A TEXT BLOCK

You can delete a text block using either the text tool or pointer tool. With the text tool, click and drag across the entire text block, and then press Del. The pointer tool offers a faster way: Simply click on the text block and press Del.

To delete all the text in a story, click anywhere in the story with the text tool, choose Select All on the Edit menu, and then press Del. To delete all the text blocks on a page or page spread, make sure the pointer tool is active, choose Select All on the Edit menu, and press Del.

SUMMARY

In this chapter, you learned how to type and format characters with the text tool. Although you can correct typing mistakes with this tool, the Story Editor is the editing specialist. The next chapter introduces you to this powerful feature.

HANDS-ON PRACTICE: PRODUCING A BUSINESS LETTERHEAD

Now you will use the techniques we've described so far to design a business letterhead and then type a letter. After completing the exercises in this chapter, your final letter will look similar to Figure 4.14. You will also save the letterhead in its own file so that you can use it again with other letters.

FIGURE 4.14: *At least disappointing news can be presented well*

BLUE CHIP REALTY

December 15, 1993

Ms. Betty Johnson
1234 State Street
San Francisco, CA 95123

Dear Ms. Johnson:

Thank you for sending us your resume. Your experience is impressive, and you seem to be very qualified. However, the position has already been filled.

We will keep your resume on file in case another position for which you are qualified becomes available.

Sincerely Yours,

Jody Peterson
Personnel Director

P.O. Box 1234
Menlo Park, CA 55555
(415) 555-CHIP

CREATING A LETTERHEAD

In the following exercise, you will create the letterhead for a company called Blue Chip Realty.

1. Pull down the File menu and choose New.

2. Turn off the Double-Sided option.

3. Specify **1.25** inches for the Left and Right margins.

4. Specify **.5** inch for the Top and Bottom margins.

5. Click on OK.

6. Activate the text tool (the A in the toolbox).

7. Click the I-beam in the upper-left corner of the page (just under the top margin guide and to the right of the left margin guide). The cursor appears at the beginning of the line.

8. Press Ctrl+1 to switch to Actual Size view so that you can read your text.

9. Type **Blue Chip Realty** and press Enter.

10. Type the remaining lines of the letterhead, pressing Enter after each line (press Backspace to erase mistakes as you are typing):

P.O. Box 1234
Menlo Park, CA 55555
(415) 555-CHIP

The completed text for the letterhead is shown in Figure 4.15.

FORMATTING THE LETTERHEAD

Now it's time to format this text. First, you'll format the company name as shown in Figure 4.16.

1. Place the I-beam anywhere in the line *Blue Chip Realty* and triple-click to select the paragraph.

2. Press Ctrl+T to display the Type Specifications dialog box.

FIGURE 4.15: *Letterhead text*

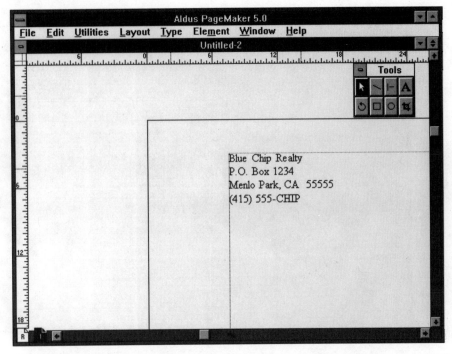

3. Display the Font drop-down list and choose Arial. (You may need to use the scroll bar.)

4. Type **20** in the Size field.

5. Turn on the Bold check box.

6. Display the Case drop-down list and choose Small Caps.

7. Click on OK.

Now let's format the remainder of the letterhead as 12-point Arial with the italic type style.

8. Click right before *P.O. Box*.

9. Hold down Shift and click right after *555-CHIP*. The address and phone number should be selected.

10. Press Ctrl+T, display the Font drop-down list, and choose Arial.

FIGURE 4.16: *Blue Chip Realty is in small caps*

11. If necessary, display the Size drop-down list and choose 12.

12. Turn on the Italic check box.

13. Click on OK.

14. Use the Save option in the File menu to save the file with the name **LETHEAD1**.

Your letterhead is now complete and should look like Figure 4.17.

TYPING THE LETTER

Now that the letterhead is complete, you can type the letter. As with a word processor, the text you create in PageMaker automatically *word wraps* as you type, so you do not need to press Enter at the end of each line in a paragraph. You only need to press the Enter key at the end of short lines

FIGURE 4.17: *The formatted letterhead*

(such as *Dear Ms. Johnson:*), to create blank lines, and at the end of paragraphs.

When typing this letter, press the Spacebar only once between sentences. We know that your high school typing instructor taught you to insert two spaces after the period, but this rule does not apply to typeset documents. Extra spaces can cause large ugly gaps between sentences (especially when text is justified).

For your letterhead, you formatted existing text. Since the entire letter is going to be one font and one size, it will be easier to make the specifications before you start typing.

1. Click an inch or so below the letterhead. Precise positioning is unimportant because you can adjust the text placement later.

2. Specify 12-point Times New Roman (this font and size might already be set).

3. Type the following text (remember, press the Spacebar once, not twice, between sentences):

December 15, 1993

Ms. Betty Johnson
1234 State Street
San Francisco, CA 95123

Dear Ms. Johnson:

Thank you for sending your resume. Your experience is quite impressive, and you seem to be very, very qualified. However, the job has already been filled. (It seems that the president's daughter was also quite qualified.) We will keep your resume in case another position for which you are qualified becomes available.

Very Sincerely Yours,

Jody Peterson
Personnel Director

4. Italicize *Personnel Director* at the bottom of the letter. Figure 4.18 shows the completed letter.

5. Use the Save As option on the File menu to save the file with a new name: **JOHNSON**.

CORRECTING MISTAKES IN THE LETTER

Now we'll insert, delete, and replace words in the business letter. First, insert the underlined words in Figure 4.19 (the text on your screen should *not* be underlined).

1. Place the I-beam just to the left of the word *your*, click, type **us**, and press the Spacebar.

FIGURE 4.18: *Completed body of the letter*

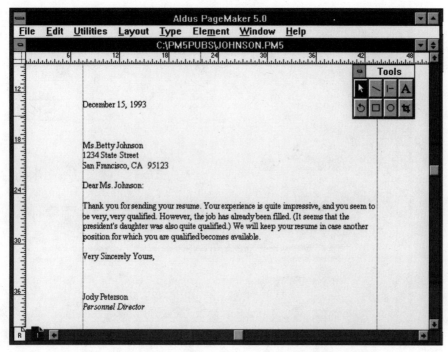

2. Move the cursor just to the right of the word *qualified* in the sentence in parentheses, press the Spacebar, and type **for this position**.

3. Insert the words **on file** after *resume* in the last paragraph.

4. To insert an extra blank line after *Very Sincerely Yours*, click the I-beam at the end of this line (or on one of the blank lines below it) and press Enter.

5. To divide the letter into two paragraphs, click the I-beam on what will be the beginning of the second paragraph, *We will keep*, and press Enter twice.

Now delete the words marked in Figure 4.20.

6. Delete the word *quite* in the first line of the letter by double-clicking on it and pressing Del.

FIGURE 4.19: *The letter, with words to insert (underlined)*

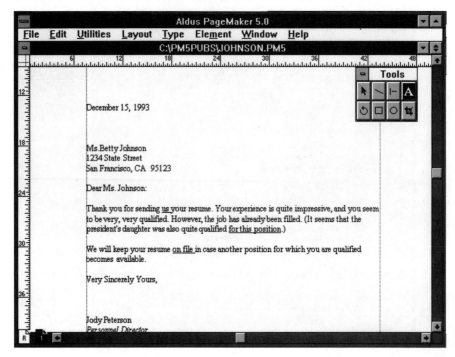

7. Delete *very*, on the second line. Be sure to delete the comma and space.

8. Select the whole sentence in parentheses (including the parentheses) and press Del to remove it.

9. Double-click on the *Very* in the closing and press Del.

Follow these steps to replace a word in the JOHNSON letter:

10. Place the I-beam on the word *job* and double-click to select the word.

11. Type **position** and press the Spacebar.

12. Press Ctrl+S to resave the file.

FIGURE 4.20: *The document, with words to delete marked*

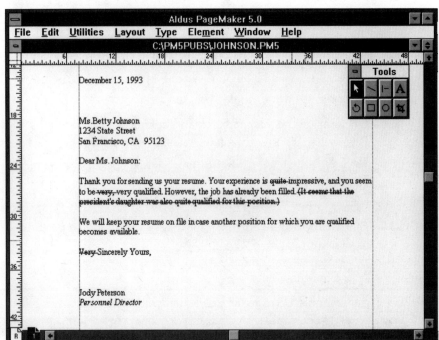

In the following steps, you'll use the Cut and Paste commands to move part of the letterhead to the bottom of the page.

1. Position the screen so that you can see the letterhead at the top of the page. (You should be in 75% or Actual Size view.)

2. Select the address and phone number (but not *Blue Chip Realty*).

3. Pull down the Edit menu and choose Cut (or press Ctrl+X). The text is removed from the page.

4. Scroll down until you can see the bottom-left corner of the page.

5. Click the I-beam about an inch above the bottom margin guide. Don't worry about the exact position; you will place it more precisely in a moment.

6. Pull down the Edit menu and choose Paste (or press Ctrl+V).

The address and phone number are now positioned near the bottom of the page. The easiest way to get the address and phone number aligned at the bottom margin guide is to move the text block. Follow these steps to move this block:

7. Choose the Pointer tool.

8. Click inside the address block and hold down the mouse button. If you do this correctly, a four-headed arrow appears.

9. Drag the box down so that its bottom border touches the margin guide at the bottom of the page. Make sure the box's left border touches the left margin guide.

10. Release the mouse button. This text block should be positioned as shown in Figure 4.21.

FIGURE 4.21: *The address text block positioned at the bottom of the page*

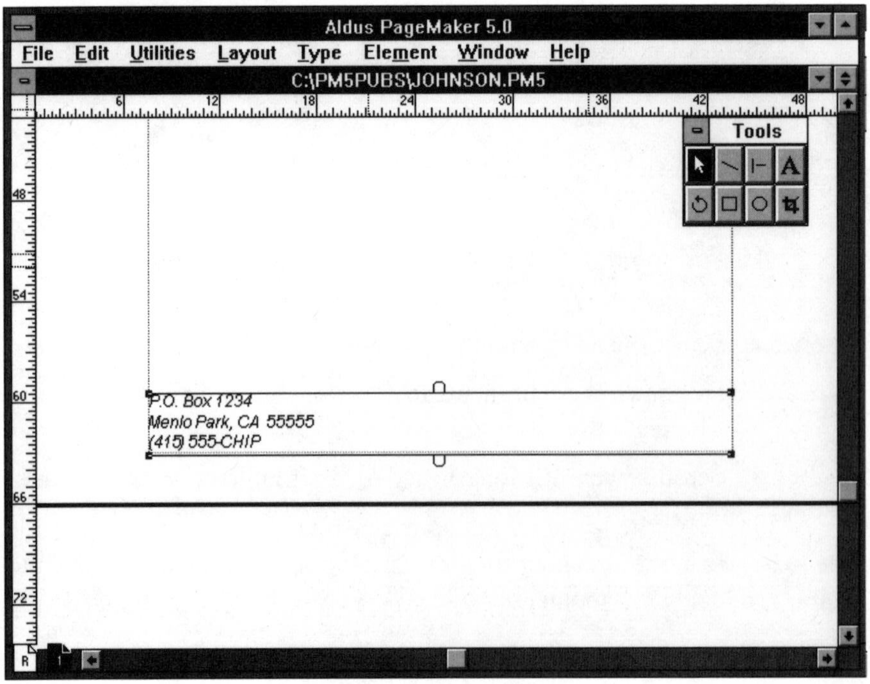

11. You may also want to reposition the middle text block, the one containing the body of the letter. In Fit in Window view, move the text block so that it is centered on the page.

As you can see in Figure 4.22, the two letterhead text blocks have been moved into the left margin. To align the two blocks with each other, you need a vertical ruler guide at the $1/2$-inch mark. Follow these steps to insert this guide and then move the text:

12. Press Ctrl+7 to switch to 75% view, and scroll the screen until you can see the upper-left corner of the page.

13. Click in the vertical ruler and drag to the right. As soon as you move the pointer (a double-headed arrow) onto the pasteboard, you will see the vertical ruler guide.

FIGURE 4.22: *The letterhead moved into the left margin*

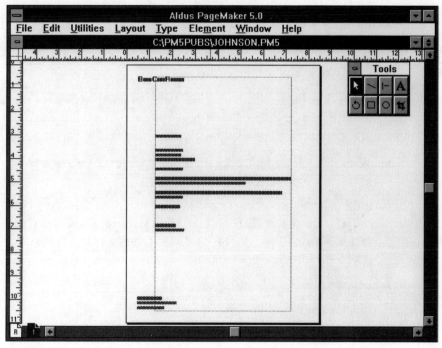

14. Continue dragging until the guide is at the $1/2$-inch mark in the horizontal ruler.

15. Release the mouse button.

If you release the button too soon, you can use the click-and-drag technique to move the ruler to the correct position.

16. Now that you have the ruler guide in place, move the two letterhead blocks (one at a time) so that the left edge touches the ruler guide.

RESIZING THE LETTER TEXT BLOCK

Let's change the left and right margins in the letter from $1\frac{1}{4}$ to 1 inch. After doing this, you'll need to resize the letter text block so that it fits the new margins.

1. Pull down the File menu and choose Page Setup.

2. Enter **1** for the Left and Right margins.

3. Click on OK.

4. Press Ctrl+W to see the entire page.

The margin guides have shifted to the new settings you specified, but the text blocks are still in their original locations. You need to resize the middle text block so that the boundaries touch the left and right margin guides.

5. With the pointer tool, click on the middle text block (the body of the letter) to select it.

6. On the left side of the text block, click on either the top or bottom text block handle (the small black dots) and hold down the mouse button. If you do this correctly, the pointer turns into a double-headed, diagonal arrow.

7. Drag until the left border touches the left margin guide.

8. Release the mouse button.

9. Repeat the procedure to resize the right side of the text block. The text rewraps to fit in the new text block size.

If you accidentally shorten the text block, you may cut off the last line of text. The lower window shade handle will turn red as a warning. Use either window shade handle to lengthen the text block a bit, until the missing line reappears.

10. Press Ctrl+S to save the file.

11. Press Ctrl+P and print the final letter.

CREATING A SECOND LETTERHEAD

In the beginning of this section, you saved your letterhead under the name LETHEAD1. You have since revised the letterhead, placing the company name at the top and the address at the bottom. Now you will save this version of the letterhead in a file with a different name, LETHEAD2. Before you do this, however, you will delete the body of the letter, so the file will become a template to be used with other letters.

Follow these steps to save your second version of the letterhead:

1. With the pointer tool, click on the body of the letter.

2. Press Del. The text block is removed.

3. Use the Save As option on the File menu to save the file with the name **LETHEAD2**.

You now have two styles of letterhead that you could use on different business documents.

*U*sing the Story Editor

*f*ast tracks

To replace one word or phrase with another: 167

Load the story into the Story Editor and move the cursor to the beginning. Choose Utilities ➤ Change. Enter the text you wish to search for in the Find What field, and enter the replacement text in the Change To field. To replace all occurrences, choose the Change All button. Otherwise, click on the Find and Change & Find buttons.

To check the spelling of a story: 172

Load the story into the Story Editor, choose Utilities ➤ Spelling, and click on the Start button. If the unknown word is correctly spelled, choose Ignore or Add. If the word is misspelled, select the word from the list of suggestions or type the correct spelling yourself in the Change To field; then select Replace.

To switch from story to layout view: 175

Choose Story ➤ Close Story.

To place a new story from the Story Editor onto the page: 178

In the Story Editor, choose Story ➤ Close Story. When warned that the story has not been placed, select the Place button. Position the text icon where you wish to place the text and click the mouse button.

THE STORY EDITOR IS YET ANOTHER way to type and edit text in PageMaker. Just click on the text you want to edit, press Ctrl+E, and your story appears in its own word processing window. All the text tool's editing commands (insert, delete, cut, and paste) are available in the Story Editor.

The Story Editor is also equipped with two powerful features that aren't offered when you use the text tool: a spelling checker and a search-and-replace feature. You are probably familiar with these features from your word processing program, and you will see that they work much the same way in PageMaker.

WHAT THE STORY EDITOR CAN (AND CAN'T) DO

You will probably not format text very often in the Story Editor (even though you are allowed to) because it does not display most formatting effects on the screen. When you are in the Story Editor, you are concerned about content, not form. You view only the text, not the page layout, formatting, or graphics.

When you are in the Story Editor, you are in what is referred to as *story view*, as opposed to the view you have been using so far, *layout view*. Figure 5.1 shows the story view of a newsletter article, while Figure 5.2 shows the same article in layout view.

Although the story looks different in the two views, it contains exactly the same text. Any editing changes you make in story view are automatically made in layout view, and vice versa. Each view simply shows the same text in a different form. Story view focuses on the publication text; layout view shows you the big picture.

There are a couple of ways you may want to use the Story Editor. First, you can use it to edit text that is already placed in your publication. You can correct typing mistakes, check the spelling in the story, or use the search-and-replace feature.

FIGURE 5.1: *A newsletter article in story view*

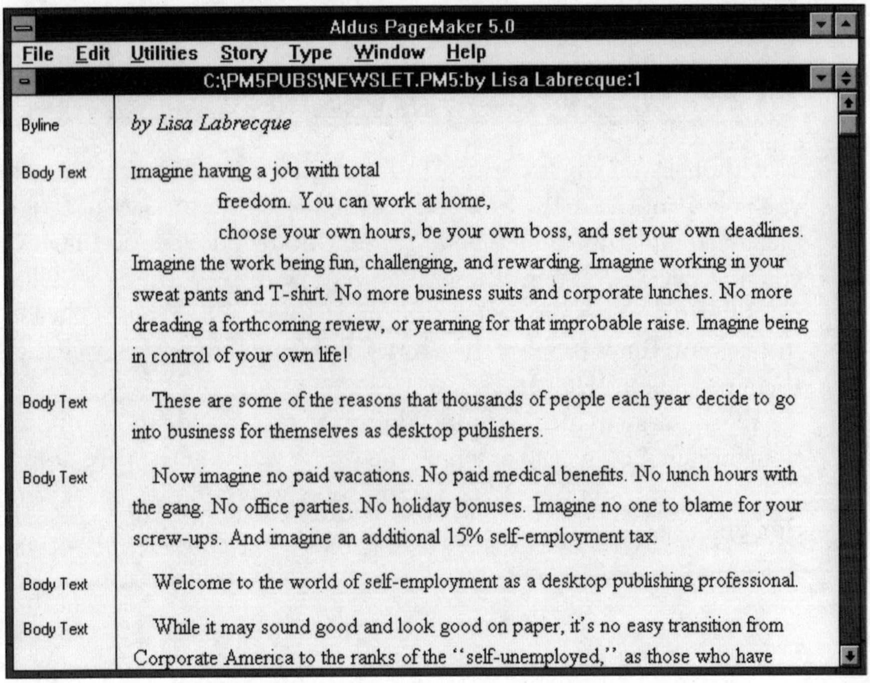

FIGURE 5.2: *The same article in layout view*

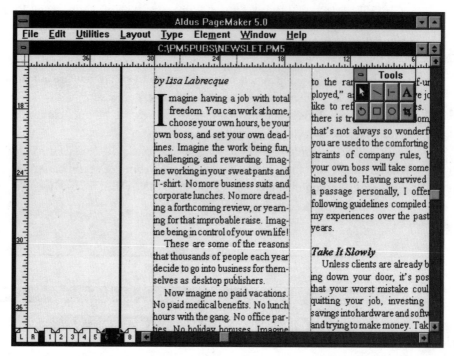

Although you won't want to do your initial formatting in story view, you may want to use the Story Editor to *change* your formatting. For example, if you underlined ten different titles throughout your document, and you now decide you want those titles in italic instead, the Story Editor can substitute the italic style for the underlining. Or if your subheads are in 14-point Times Roman, the Story Editor can automatically change them to 16-point Helvetica.

Another way to use the Story Editor is to create and type an entire story from scratch. So, instead of typing the text directly on the page or in your word processor, you can create a publication and then type its text in the Story Editor.

The Story Editor offers several advantages. You can type and edit much faster in story view than in layout view because the Story Editor does not display fonts and graphics on the screen, nor does it concern itself with line or page breaks. Furthermore, you do not need to load a separate piece of software to create a story—you can type it right in PageMaker.

USING THE STORY EDITOR

To edit an existing story in the Story Editor, click in the text with the text tool, or select the text block with the pointer tool, and press Ctrl+E. You can also load an existing story into the Story Editor by triple-clicking on the text block with the pointer tool.

To create a new story in the Story Editor, press Ctrl+E without any text or text blocks selected. Ctrl+E is the keyboard shortcut for the Edit Story option on the Edit menu. At this point, you can either type in the story or, if it already exists in a word processing file, you can import it into the Story Editor.

THE STORY WINDOW

When you load the Story Editor, you are actually opening a window. Your story window lies on top of your publication window, and it has its own buttons and scroll bars. Most of the time, you will want to click on the maximize button so that your story window fills the PageMaker window.

When you are creating a new story, the title bar says the name of the publication followed by *Untitled*. When you edit an existing story, the first few words of the story are entered into the title bar as the story name. In

Figure 5.1, the name is shown as *by Lisa Labrecque,* the beginning text in the article. The *:1* after the story title indicates that this is the first open story with that name. If you were to open a second story that began with the same exact words, the title bar would show *:2* after the name.

The Story Editor's menu bar is slightly different from the one you see in the publication window because you have different capabilities in each view. A new option, Story, is available. The Element menu is not offered because you do not see graphics in story view. The Layout menu is gone because it is also irrelevant in story view; you work with a continuous stream of text rather than with pages.

The story window is partitioned into two vertical areas separated by a solid line (see Figure 5.1). The right area is where you type your story; the left area displays style names. (Chapter 7 describes the style feature.) Toggle the style names column on and off by choosing Display Style Names on the Story menu.

Version
5.0

Version 5.0 has an Addition that will open a window for each story in a publication. Choose Aldus Additions on the Utilities menu and then select Edit All Stories. PageMaker will then create a cascade of windows for the stories in the current publication, as shown in Figure 5.3. To move to another story window, click on its title bar, or select the publication name from the Window menu and then click on the story name. Bear in mind that headlines, captions, and other short text blocks are considered stories too, and windows will be opened up for them.

TYPING IN THE STORY EDITOR

As when you are using the text tool, you have an insertion point (the cursor) and an I-beam (the mouse pointer) in story view. You should keep the following in mind when you are typing in the Story Editor:

- Press the Spacebar once—and only once—between sentences.

- Let the text word wrap as you type. Press Enter only at the end of paragraphs.

- Do not double-space between paragraphs. To add interparagraph spacing, use a paragraph formatting command (see Chapter 6). You may notice that the Story Editor automatically puts a little

FIGURE 5.3:   *The Edit All Stories Addition will open a window for each story in the publication*

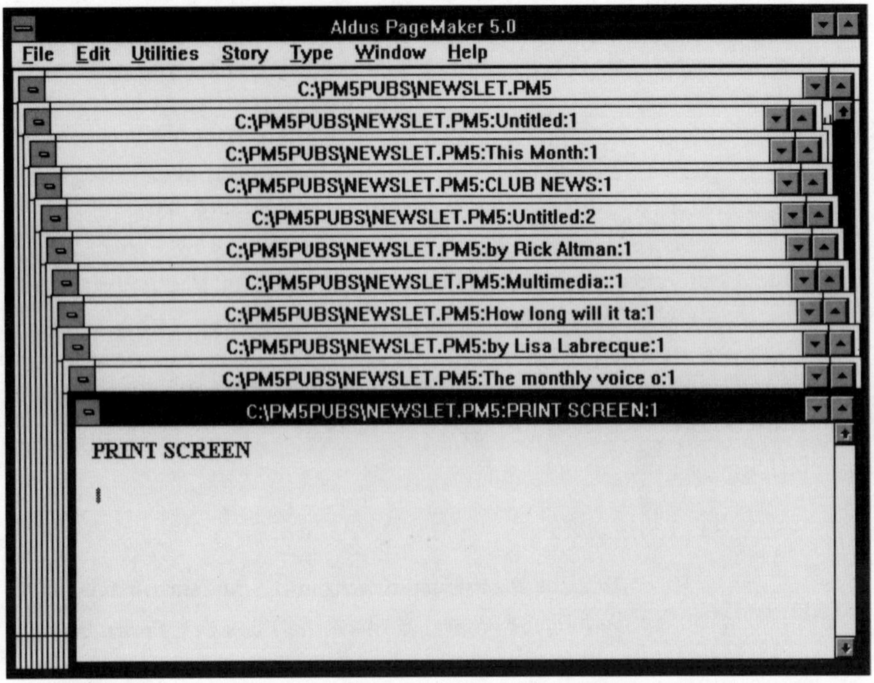

```
┌────────────────────────────────────────────────────────────┐
│ ▣            Aldus PageMaker 5.0                    ▼ ▲      │
│ File  Edit  Utilities  Story  Type  Window  Help            │
│ ┌──────────────────────────────────────────────────────┐   │
│ │ ▫          C:\PM5PUBS\NEWSLET.PM5              ▼ ▲     │   │
│ ┌──────────────────────────────────────────────────────┐   │
│ │ ▫     C:\PM5PUBS\NEWSLET.PM5:Untitled:1       ▼ ▲     │   │
│ ┌──────────────────────────────────────────────────────┐   │
│ │ ▫    C:\PM5PUBS\NEWSLET.PM5:This Month:1      ▼ ▲     │   │
│ ┌──────────────────────────────────────────────────────┐   │
│ │ ▫     C:\PM5PUBS\NEWSLET.PM5:CLUB NEWS:1      ▼ ▲     │   │
│ ┌──────────────────────────────────────────────────────┐   │
│ │ ▫     C:\PM5PUBS\NEWSLET.PM5:Untitled:2       ▼ ▲     │   │
│ ┌──────────────────────────────────────────────────────┐   │
│ │ ▫   C:\PM5PUBS\NEWSLET.PM5:by Rick Altman:1   ▼ ▲     │   │
│ ┌──────────────────────────────────────────────────────┐   │
│ │ ▫    C:\PM5PUBS\NEWSLET.PM5:Multimedia::1     ▼ ▲     │   │
│ ┌──────────────────────────────────────────────────────┐   │
│ │ ▫  C:\PM5PUBS\NEWSLET.PM5:How long will it ta:1 ▼ ▲  │   │
│ ┌──────────────────────────────────────────────────────┐   │
│ │ ▫ C:\PM5PUBS\NEWSLET.PM5:by Lisa Labrecque:1  ▼ ▲    │   │
│ ┌──────────────────────────────────────────────────────┐   │
│ │ ▫ C:\PM5PUBS\NEWSLET.PM5:The monthly voice o:1 ▼ ▲   │   │
│ ┌──────────────────────────────────────────────────────┐   │
│ │ ▫ C:\PM5PUBS\NEWSLET.PM5:PRINT SCREEN:1       ▼ ▲    │   │
│ │                                                       │   │
│ │  PRINT SCREEN                                         │   │
│ │                                                       │   │
│ │   ▌                                                   │   │
│ │                                                       │   │
│ └──────────────────────────────────────────────────────┘   │
└────────────────────────────────────────────────────────────┘
```

extra space between paragraphs so that you can more easily identify your paragraphs. This extra space appears only in story view; it disappears in layout view (and on your printout).

➤ Do not press Tab at the beginning of paragraphs. If you want the first line of each paragraph indented, use a paragraph formatting command (see Chapter 6).

These are actually the same rules that apply to typing text in your word processor.

Type styles are one of the few formatting options that display in story view. As in layout view, you specify the style (bold, italic, and so on) in story view by turning it on and off as you type the text, or by selecting the text after it is typed and then turning on the style. The only paragraph formatting that displays in story view are indents and space before and after.

IMPORTING TEXT INTO THE STORY EDITOR

As previously mentioned, the Story Editor allows you to import a text file into a story window. You might want to do this so that you can edit the file before placing it on a publication page; for example, perhaps you'll want to run it through the spelling checker or do a search-and-replace operation. What types of files can the Story Editor import? It all depends on which import filters you selected when installing PageMaker. There are about a dozen to choose from, including Word for Windows, WordPerfect, and Ami Pro. (Chapter 8 explains file importing in more detail, and Appendix A discusses how to install import filters.)

To import a file, use the Place command on the File menu and select the desired file name. The story will display in a new window (even if an empty story window is already displayed).

To place the imported story in the current window (assuming it's empty), turn on the Replacing Entire Story option in the Place dialog box after you click on the file name.

SEARCHING FOR TEXT

Using the Story Editor's Find command is probably the fastest way to move your cursor in a long story. You can use this feature to go directly to a word or phrase you need to correct or to move the cursor quickly to the heading of a section you want to work on. Use the Find command instead of scrolling through your story, scanning for the passage you need to correct. Your eyes will thank you.

USING THE FIND COMMAND

The Find command searches for the specified characters from the cursor location forward through the story. To begin a search from the top of the story, press Ctrl+PgUp before you initiate the Find command. If you begin the search from somewhere in the middle of the story, the Story Editor will ask you

```
Continue from beginning of story?
```

when it reaches the end, so you can search through the entire story if necessary.

Here are the basic steps for finding a word or phrase:

1. Pull down the Utilities menu and choose Find (or press Ctrl+8). The Find dialog box is shown in Figure 5.4.

2. To the right of Find What, type the word or phrase you are looking for, in either uppercase or lowercase letters.

3. Click on the Find command button.

4. If a story contains multiple occurrences of the word you want to find, continue the search by clicking on the Find Next button.

5. To exit the Find feature, click anywhere outside the dialog box.

If the Story Editor cannot locate a word, perhaps because you mistyped the text in the Find dialog box or in the story, it will display the message

```
Search complete
```

FIGURE 5.4: *The Find dialog box*

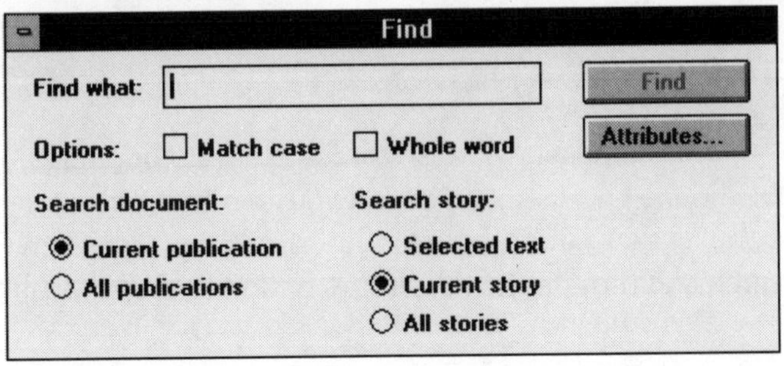

When this happens, check your typing and try again.

If, after exiting the Find feature, you decide you want to continue the search, you don't need to display the Find dialog box again. Just use the Find Next command on the Utilities menu or press Shift+Ctrl+9.

NARROWING THE SEARCH

To save yourself the effort of choosing the Find Next command many times, make the text you enter in the Find What box—the *search string*—as unique as possible.

One way of narrowing the search is to enter a phrase rather than a word. For example, in an article about tennis, don't search for the word *tennis*— there will be too many occurrences. Instead, search for the particular phrase you want, such as *tennis strokes*.

Another way to reduce the number of occurrences that the Story Editor finds during a search is to use the Whole Word and Match Case options in the Find dialog box. The Whole Word option finds your search string only if it appears as a complete word. Without this option, PageMaker locates the word even if it's in the middle of another word. For example, if you search for *other* using this option, you will just find that complete word, not *another*, *smother*, or *others*.

The Match Case option only finds text in the story that matches the exact case you enter. So, if you search for *Tennis*, the Story Editor will not locate *TENNIS* or *tennis*.

You can choose both of these options at the same time to narrow your search even further. The options remain selected for subsequent searches unless you turn them off or exit PageMaker.

SEARCHING ACROSS ALL STORIES AND PUBLICATIONS

Version **5.0**

With Version 5.0 of PageMaker, you can search for a word or phrase in all stories in a publication. This feature is nice if you aren't sure which story or stories contain the text you are looking for. Just open one story when you inititate the search and turn on the All Stories option in the Find dialog box; if the search string is located in other stories, PageMaker will automatically open story windows for them.

Furthermore, you can search all stories in all open publications by turning on the All Publications option. (When you turn on this option, the All Stories option is automatically selected.) Again, PageMaker will open a window for each story in each publication that contains the search string.

CHANGING TEXT

The Story Editor's Change feature takes the Find feature one step further. The Change command searches for a word, phrase, or formatting attribute and replaces it with another. For example, if you find that you have consistently misspelled someone's name throughout a story, you can search for the incorrectly spelled name and replace it with the correctly spelled one.

Another way you can use the Change command is to have it replace shorthand codes typed throughout the story. If a cumbersome word or phrase, such as a company name or a technical term, appears frequently in a story, type an abbreviation in its place. You can then use the Change command to automatically replace all abbreviations with the long word or phrase.

REPLACING TEXT AUTOMATICALLY

Here's the procedure for globally replacing one word or phrase with another:

1. Move the cursor to the beginning of the story.

2. Pull down the Utilities menu and select Change, or press Ctrl+9. The Change dialog box is shown in Figure 5.5.

3. Next to Find What, type the text you wish to find.

4. Next to Change To, type the replacement text.

5. If desired, turn on the Match Case and Whole Word options. (These options work the same way as they do with the Find command.)

6. To replace text in all the stories in the publication, turn on the All Stories option. Or to replace text in all stories in all open publications, turn on the All Publications option.

7. Choose the Change All command button to replace all occurrences.

8. To exit the Change feature, click anywhere outside the dialog box.

FIGURE 5.5: *The Change dialog box*

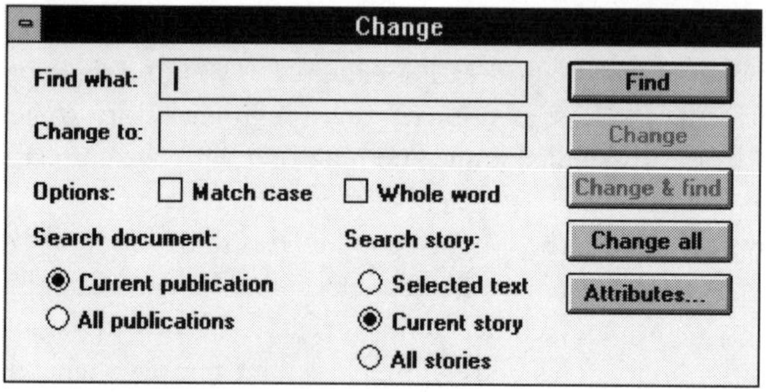

! **WARNING**

Be very careful when you use the Change All command button. If you are not 100 percent certain that you want every occurrence automatically replaced, do *not* use Change All; instead, choose the Find and Change & Find command buttons, as described in the next section.

REPLACING WORDS ONE BY ONE: PLAYING IT SAFE

If you do not want every occurrence of a word replaced, or you aren't sure if you do, play it safe and use the Find and Change & Find command buttons. For example, suppose that you want to replace all occurrences of *her* with *him* in a story. If you forget to turn on the Whole Word option and you choose Change All, the Story Editor replaces the letters *her* in *here*, forming the word *hime*. The word *other* becomes *othim* and *there* becomes *thime*.

You would then have to use the Change command again to search for *him* and replace it with *her*—but this time do not choose *Change All*.

After filling in the Change dialog box, choose the Find button. Page-Maker then stops at the first occurrence of the word. If you want to replace the word, choose the Change & Find button to change the word and find the next occurrence. If you don't want to replace the word, choose Find Next to search for the next occurrence.

REPLACING SPECIAL CHARACTERS

The Change command can also find and replace special characters, such as carriage returns and tabs. This capability is invaluable when you have imported a text file that has two returns between paragraphs, or has a tab at the beginning of each paragraph. As already mentioned, this is not how you format paragraphs in PageMaker.

To rid a text file of extra codes, use the Change command. The carriage return code is ^p, and the tab code is ^t. You should actually type the caret (^); don't press Ctrl. To replace a double carriage return with a single return, search for *^p^p* and replace it with *^p*. To remove tabs, search for *^t* and don't type anything in the Change To text box, because you want to replace the tab space with nothing.

Table 5.1 lists the codes you can enter in the Find What and Change To fields in order to search and replace punctuation and special characters.

REPLACING FORMATTING ATTRIBUTES

An extremely powerful use of the Change command is to search for and replace formatting attributes. You can replace fonts, sizes, type styles, and paragraph styles (this last feature is covered in Chapter 7). This capability makes it easy to revise a story's formatting.

To replace one or more attributes, use the Attributes command button in the Change dialog box. The Change Attributes dialog box is shown in

TABLE 5.1: *Codes for Finding Punctuation and Special Characters*

PUNCTUATION	
Carriage return	^p
New line	^n
Tab	^t
Thin space	^<
En space	^>
Em space	^m
Nonbreaking space	^s
White space or tab	^w
Discretionary hyphen	^-
Nonbreaking hyphen	^~
Computer-inserted hyphen	^c
En dash	^=
Em dash	^_
Nonbreaking slash	^/
SPECIAL CHARACTERS	
Bullet (•)[*]	^8
Copyright (©)	^2
Section mark (§)	^6
Paragraph mark (¶)	^7
Registered trademark (®)	^r
Open double quote (")	^{
Close double quote (")	^}
Open single quote (')	^[
Close single quote (')	^]
Caret (^)	^ ^

[*]*Only bullets created with Ctrl+Shift+8.*

Figure 5.6. In the left half of the box, you indicate the attributes you want to locate. In the right half, you specify the new attributes.

Suppose all the headings in your publication are in 20-point Helvetica, and you decide you'd rather they be in 16-point Garamond. Rather than formatting each heading individually, you can replace the attributes. Here's how it's done:

1. Save the file. It's always a good idea to save your work before you use the Change command, just in case you make a mistake along the way.

2. Move the cursor to the beginning of the story.

3. Pull down the Utilities menu and choose Change.

4. Delete any text next to Find What and Change To.

5. Click on the Attributes command button.

6. In the Find section of the dialog box (the left side), specify the attributes you wish to change (such as Helvetica for the Font and 20 for the Size).

7. In the Change section (the right side), specify the replacement attributes (such as Garamond for the the Font and 16 for the Size).

FIGURE 5.6: *The Change Attributes dialog box*

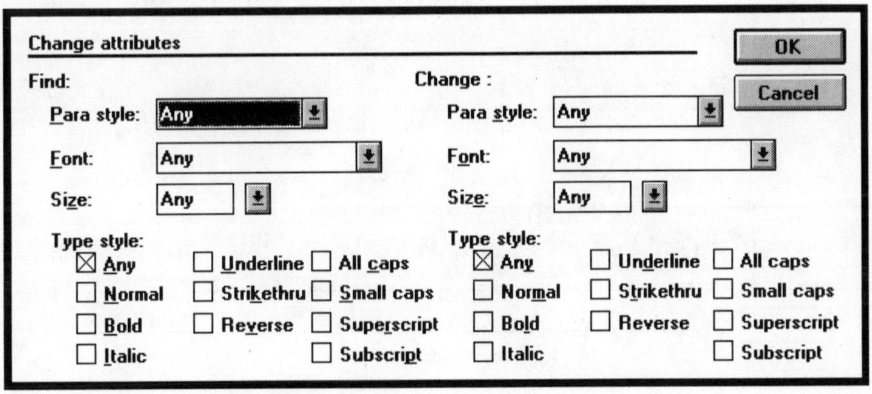

8. Choose OK to close the Change Attributes dialog box.

9. If you know that you want to replace all occurrences of the attributes, choose the Change All command button. Otherwise, use the Find and Change & Find buttons.

10. Close the Change dialog box.

CHECKING YOUR SPELLING

The Story Editor's spelling checker scans your story and stops at words that are potentially misspelled, allowing you to correct them. Even if you won all your school spelling bees, you still may want to use the spelling checker because it also locates typing mistakes (unless you were also the school typing champ). If you have ever used your word processor's spelling checker, you realize the value of this feature.

CORRECTING UNKNOWN WORDS

Pull down the Utilities menu and choose Spelling, or press Ctrl+L, to have the Story Editor check the spelling of each word in your story against Page-Maker's 100,000-word dictionary. If a word is not in the dictionary, the Story Editor stops at the word and presents a dialog box to let you correct it. Figure 5.7 shows the spelling checker dialog box displayed for the unknown word *strongst*. This dialog box contains the following command buttons:

→ Ignore: Leaves the word as it is, and bypasses all future occurrences of the word throughout the story.

→ Replace: Replaces the word with the corrected spelling that appears in the Change To box.

→ Add: Inserts the word in the dictionary so that the Story Editor will recognize it as correctly spelled the next time you check any story in any publication.

FIGURE 5.7: *The Spelling Checker dialog box*

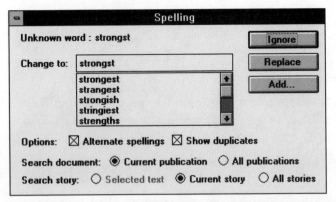

Like your word processor's spelling checker, PageMaker's checker some-times stops at words that are correctly spelled. Proper names, abbreviations, acronyms, and technical terms may not be in the dictionary. Thus, the spelling checker would think the words *Rumpelstiltskin*, *DMV*, and *sulfathia-zole* are misspelled. When the spelling checker finds these types of words, you can choose either the Ignore or Add option. If you are not likely to use a particular word in other stories, choose Ignore. If you will use the word frequently, add it to the dictionary by choosing Add.

When the word is indeed misspelled, you can choose the correct spelling from the list by double-clicking on it. The list displays scroll bars if addi-tional suggestions are available. If the correct spelling is not in the list, you will need to edit the word in the Change To text box. Click the I-beam in the text box to place the cursor there, and then use the regular editing keys to correct the mistake. After you've chosen the correct spelling from the list or edited the word in the Change To box, press Enter or click on the Replace button.

USING THE SPELLING CHECKER

The spelling checker starts correcting at the cursor location and checks all words after that point in the story. If your cursor is not at the beginning when you start the spelling check, the Story Editor checks the words from the cursor to the end of the story and then asks you if you want to continue the check at the beginning of the story.

Follow these steps to spell check a story:

1. Move the cursor to the beginning of the story.

2. Pull down the Utilities menu and choose Spelling, or press Ctrl+L.

Version
5.0

3. To check the spelling of all the stories in the publication, turn on the All Stories option. Or, to check the stories in all open publications, choose the All Publications option.

4. Click on the Start command button. The Story Editor highlights (selects) the first word that is not in the dictionary.

5. As the spelling checker proceeds to find words, choose to Ignore, Replace, or Add them, as explained previously.

When the spelling checker can't find any more misspelled words, it displays the message

```
Spelling check complete.
```

6. Close the spelling checker dialog box by clicking anywhere outside the dialog box.

To speed up the spell-checking process, you can turn off the Alternate Spellings and Show Duplicates check boxes. The Alternate Spellings option lists possible correct spellings for the unrecognized word; the Show Duplicates option shows repeated words (such as *the the*). When PageMaker doesn't have to worry about these two tasks, spell checking is speeded up.

CHECKING A SINGLE WORD'S SPELLING

On occasion, you might want to check a single word to see if you spelled it correctly. Follow these general steps to check a word:

1. Select the word (for example, double-click on it).

2. Press Ctrl+L. The Selected Text option will automatically be turned on in the Spelling dialog box.

3. Select the Start button.

4. If the word is misspelled, select the correct spelling from the list of suggestions. If the word is spelled correctly, the dialog box will display the message "No spelling errors detected."

5. Click anywhere outside the dialog box to close the box.

SWITCHING BACK TO LAYOUT VIEW

Once you are done editing a story in the Story Editor, you'll want to switch back to layout view. PageMaker offers five ways to do this:

➤ Pull down the Edit menu and choose Edit Layout (or press Ctrl+E).

➤ Pull down the Window menu, choose the name of your publication, and select Layout.

➤ Pull down the Story menu and choose Close Story.

➤ Double-click on the control-menu box in the story window.

➤ Minimize the story window.

Some of the commands close the story window, and others leave it open, as summarized in Table 5.2.

TABLE 5.2: *Commands for Switching to Layout View*

Command	Window Status
Story ➤ Close Story	Closed
Double-click on control-menu box	Closed
Edit ➤ Edit Layout (or Ctrl+E)	Open
Window ➤ *publication name* ➤ Layout	Open
Click on minimize button	Open (Minimized)

All these different methods of switching between story and layout view may seem overwhelming. When you are first learning to work with the Story Editor, you might want to stick to one method; for example, use Ctrl+E because it switches you both in and out of the Story Editor.

If you are not sure whether a story window is still open, pull down the Window menu and check to see if there is a right-pointing triangle next to the name of the publication. If there is, click on the publication name, and you will see a list of story names that are currently open.

KEEPING THE STORY WINDOW OPEN

If you leave the story window open, it lies under your publication window, and you may see part of it hiding underneath. If you can see the story window, you can simply click on it to return there. If you can't see the story window, you must use the Window pull-down menu to go back to it.

After you have left story view, you don't see the story window or the story icons unless the publication window is smaller than the PageMaker application window. In other words, your publication window cannot be maximized. Figure 5.8 shows an example of a story window behind a

FIGURE 5.8: *The story window behind the publication window*

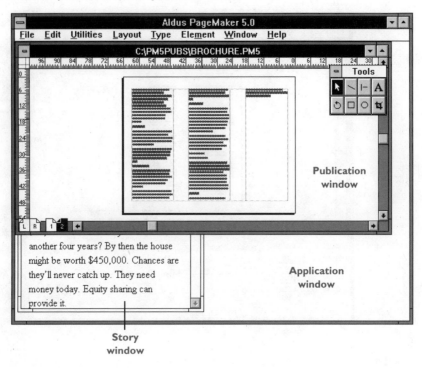

publication window. Figure 5.9 shows a minimized story icon in the application workspace underneath the publication window.

There are a few minor advantages to keeping the story window open rather than closing it. First, you do not need to select the story before you edit it. Just click on the story window, double-click on its minimized icon, or choose the story name from the Window pull-down menu. Also, if your publication has multiple stories, you can keep each story in its own window. Then, to edit a particular story, you don't have to go to that page and select it. You just select the story name from the Window menu.

FIGURE 5.9: *The minimized story icon in the application workspace*

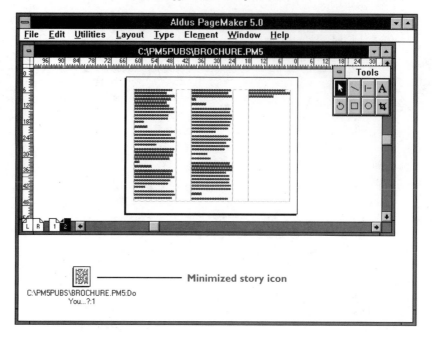

Minimized story icon

PLACING A NEW STORY

There are two ways to create a new story in the Story Editor. You can
either press Ctrl+E in layout view, with no story selected, or choose New
Story from the Story menu when you are in story view.

When you create a new story in the Story Editor, it exists only in the
Story Editor—it is not part of the publication. To incorporate it into your
document, you must close the story window and place it on the page. You
can close the window using any of the techniques described in the previous
section—for example, the Close Story command on the Story menu.

After you close the window, the cursor turns into a loaded text icon. Just
place the icon at the top of the first column in which you want to place the
text, and click. Repeat this procedure for each column.

Before you close the story window, be sure to save your publication. If you don't, and you make a mistake in the placement process, you could lose the story you just created.

SUMMARY

Each of PageMaker's views, story and layout, has its unique capabilities and advantages. In story view, you can type and edit text quickly, without having to wait for the page layout to adjust as you make changes. You also have access to the powerful find and change features, as well as the spelling checker. Although you can't see most formatting in the Story Editor, you can use the Change command to make fast, global formatting changes.

On the other hand, layout view lets you see the actual page layout with its formatting and graphics. The next chapter describes additional ways to format your page.

HANDS-ON PRACTICE: CREATING A BROCHURE

If you want to use the Story Editor to type a story from scratch, you must first open or create a publication. In this chapter, you will begin creating a three-panel brochure that, when folded, fits into a standard business envelope. The final brochure, shown in Figure 5.10, is for the same company for which you designed the letterhead, Blue Chip Realty. You will type most of the text in the Story Editor.

FIGURE 5.10: *The brochure for Blue Chip Realty*

BLUE CHIP REALTY
P.O. Box 1234
Menlo Park, CA 55555
(415) 555-CHIP

Picture Yourself in Your New House!

Do You...?
...want to stop making rent payments?

...want to stop paying so much in taxes?

...want to take advantage of one of the strongest housing markets in the nation?

...feel that you could afford payments if you only owned a house?

If you answered yes to the above questions, keep reading.

Blue Chip Realty is a company whose main goal is to help you buy a house. Our specialty is helping qualified buyers to own their own home. One of these ways is through equity sharing.

Futility
Unlike most areas of the country, buying a home in the Bay Area has become down payment sensitive. There are hundreds of potential homeowners in the Silicon Valley that make great salaries, have good credit, but simply cannot save the lump sum necessary to make a down payment.

Let's assume a couple, who can save $5,000 a year, had $40,000 saved toward a down payment in 1991. They make enough money to cover mortgage payments but need another $10,000 for a 20% down payment on a $250,000 house. So they decide to wait and save.

In the two years it took them to save $10,000, the house appreciated

BLUE CHIP REALTY

$100,000. Now it's 1993 and they need $70,000 for a down payment on the same house, and they only have $50,000. What can they do? Save another four years? By then the house might be worth $450,000. Chances are they'll never catch up. They need money today. Equity sharing can provide it.

Concepts
Equity sharing is an arrangement where an investor puts up money toward a portion of the down payment. In return, he/she will receive a share of the equity from the home buyer.

For example, suppose a buyer, with the help of an investor, purchases a house in 1993 for $300,000. Here's a hypothetical breakdown of the up-front costs:

	Investor	Buyer
Down Payment	$40,000	$20,000
Closing Costs	5,000	5,000
House Payments	None	All
% of Appreciation	40	60

Numerous benefits accrue to you, the buyer, in return for the portion of the appreciation you relinquish in an equity sharing deal. First, you get to fulfill your own American dream: home ownership.

Other benefits include large tax deductions, saying goodbye to rent payments, and getting a leveraged

investment in one of the strongest real estate markets in the world. If these benefits sound good to you, then Blue Chip Realty can help.

Our Focus
Blue Chip Realty specializes in serving home buyers. We do not list property. Instead, we simply act as agents to help people like you find a house here on the Peninsula. So how do we get paid? By receiving a percentage of the commission that the home seller pays to the listing agent. That's all.

We are members of several Multiple Listing Services (MLS) throughout the region. Our geographic area spans Santa Clara and San Mateo counties. Here's an outline of our services:

- **We help determine your price range.** By analyzing your income and savings, Blue Chip Realty uses a computerized worksheet to determine the range of home prices you can reasonably afford.
- **We arrange equity sharing.** If you need cash for a down payment, Blue Chip Realty will match you with an investor.
- **We help you shop for your house.** Blue Chip Realty will work with you to find a house that's just right for you.

- **We handle the transaction.** Blue Chip Realty will write up the offer, negotiate to your advantage, and arrange inspections.
- **We hand you the house keys.**

Matchmaking
Because investors supply the majority of cash, they define most of the terms of the transaction. Blue Chip Realty simply acts as a matchmaker. An investor looks for buyers who have solid cash flow, are credit worthy and debt-free, and are eager to buy a house. Buyers look to match with an investor who fits the buyers' financial needs and desires.

Results
If you are interested in owning your own home and would like Blue Chip Realty to help you achieve this goal, call for an appointment now.

CHANGING YOUR MEASUREMENT SYSTEM

Starting with this chapter, the remaining exercises in the book will use the pica/point measuring system. Because your fonts are measured in this system, you will find it much easier to measure everything in picas and points. If you are not from the typesetting world, the pica/point measuring system may seem like a foreign language. You will probably find it helpful to invest in a pica/point ruler. Remember, there are 6 picas to an inch, 12 points to a pica, and, therefore, 72 points to an inch.

Follow the steps below to change your default measuring system and vertical ruler:

1. If necessary, close any open publications.

2. Pull down the File menu and choose Preferences. The Preferences dialog box appears.

3. Change the Measurement System to Picas.

4. Change the Vertical Ruler to Picas.

> **The Preferences dialog box has several options that pertain to the Story Editor. These options are accessed by clicking on the Other button. At the bottom of this sub-dialog box you can choose a font and size for the Story Editor. These options control the display of text on the screen in story view, not how the text will print.**

5. Close the dialog box.

Until you change them, these settings will apply to all future publications you open or create. If you ever want to go back to working in inches or millimeters, select those measurements in the Preferences dialog box.

SETTING UP THE PAGE

To get the brochure to fold in the white space between columns (called the *gutter*), you need to give careful consideration to your page setup. The rule in publishing is that your gutters should be twice the size of your left and right (or inside and outside) margins, and your left and right (inside and outside) margins must be identical.

Now that your measurement system is in picas, you are ready to create a new publication with the appropriate margin and column settings. Strangely enough, the column settings are not in the Page Setup dialog box; they are in their own dialog box (accessed from the Layout menu), so you'll have to go through two dialog boxes to set up the page.

Follow these steps to set the page specifications for the brochure:

1. Pull down the File menu and choose New. The Page Setup dialog box appears.

Notice the current page size is now in picas. If you are wondering where the 51 × 66 measurement came from, follow this math lesson: multiply 8.5 inches by 6 picas/inch to get 51; 11 inches multiplied by 6 picas/inch equals 66.

2. Specify a Wide orientation.

3. Enter 2 for the number of pages.

4. Enter 3 for both the Inside and Outside margins (3 picas = 0.5 inch).

5. If necessary, enter **4p6** for the Top and Bottom margins (4 picas, 6 points = 0.75 inch). Your Page Setup dialog box should match the one in Figure 5.11.

6. Choose OK. The first page of your brochure appears in landscape orientation. Also, your rulers are in pica increments.

7. Pull down the Layout menu and choose Column Guides.

FIGURE 5.11: *The brochure's page setup*

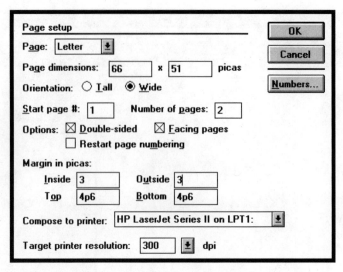

8. Type **3** for the Number of Columns.

9. Type **6** (picas) for the Space Between Columns.

Notice that this setting follows our basic rule: the gutter is twice the size of the inside and outside margins. This setting will ensure that you can fold the brochure in the gutters.

10. Choose OK. Page 1 now displays three columns, each surrounded by column guides, as shown in Figure 5.12.

11. Click on the page 2 icon to move to page 2.

12. Repeat steps 7 through 10 to place the column guides on the second page.

13. Click on the page 1 icon to return to the first page.

14. Save your publication with the name **BROCHURE**, in the C:\PM5PUBS directory.

FIGURE 5.12: *The page layout for the brochure*

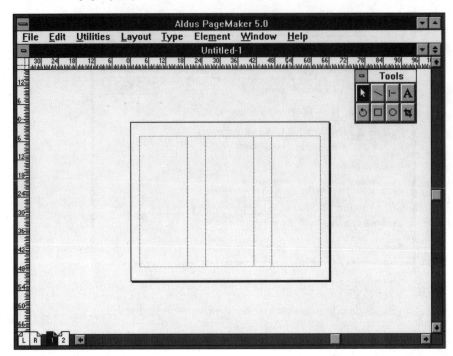

If you have many pages in a publication, placing column
guides individually on each page would be quite tedious.
To automatically place column guides on all pages, you
can use the master pages. See Chapter 14 for details.

ENTERING THE NEW STORY

The story you create in the Story Editor uses your publication's default font
and size (probably 12 points). The text should be 11-point Times New Roman, and you can format it as such while in the Story Editor, even though
you won't see the formatting in story view.

Follow these steps to format and enter the text:

1. To load the Story Editor, press Ctrl+E or pull down the Edit menu and select Edit Story.

2. Click on the maximize button so that your story window fills the screen. Your window should look similar to the one shown in Figure 5.13.

3. Press Ctrl+T and specify the Font as Times New Roman and the Size as 11 points.

4. Choose OK.

5. To remove the style names column, choose Story ➤ Display Style Names.

FIGURE 5.13: *The maximized story window*

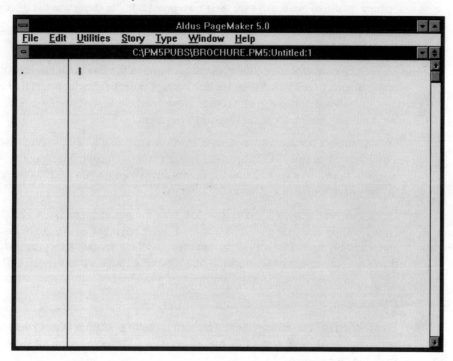

Now you are ready to type the text of the brochure, which is shown in Figure 5.14. (If typing isn't your favorite pastime, you can import the file, BROCHURE.DOC—skip to the section that follows, "Importing BROCHURE.DOC.")

FIGURE 5.14:   *Brochure text*

Do You...?

...want to stop making rent payments?

...want to stop paying so much in taxes?

...want to take advantage of one of the strongest housing markets in the nation?

...feel that you could afford payments if you only owned a house?

If you answered yes to the above questions, keep reading.

BCR is a company whose main goal is to help you buy a house. Our specialty is helping qualified buyers to own their own home. One of these ways is through equity sharing.

Futility

Unlike most areas of the country, buying a home in the Bay Area has become down payment sensitive. There are hundreds of potential homeowners in the Silicon Valley that make great salaries, have good credit, but simply cannot save the lump sum necessary to make a down payment.

Let's assume a couple, who can save $5,000 a year, had $40,000 saved toward a down payment in 1991. They make enough money to cover mortgage payments but need another $10,000 for a 20% down payment on a $250,000 house. So they decide to wait and save.

In the two years it took them to save $10,000, the house appreciated $100,000. Now it's 1993 and they need $70,000 for a down payment on the same house, and they only have $50,000. What can they do? Save another four years? By then the house might be worth $450,000. Chances are they'll never catch up. They need money today. Equity sharing can provide it.

Concepts

Equity sharing is an arrangement where an investor puts up money toward a portion of the down payment. In return, he/she will receive a share of the equity from the home buyer.

FIGURE 5.14: *Brochure text (continued)*

For example, suppose a buyer, with the help of an investor, purchases a house in 1993 for $300,000. Here's a hypothetical breakdown of the up-front costs:

(insert table here)

Numerous benefits accrue to you, the buyer, in return for the portion of the appreciation you relinquish in an equity sharing deal. First, you get to fulfill your own American dream: home ownership.

Other benefits include large tax deductions, saying goodbye to rent payments, and getting a leveraged investment in one of the strongest real estate markets in the world. If these benefits sound good to you, then BCR can help.

Our Focus

BCR specializes in serving home buyers. We do not list property. Instead, we simply act as agents to help people like you find a house here on the Peninsula. So how do we get paid? By receiving a percentage of the commission that the home seller pays to the listing agent. That's all.

We are members of several Multiple Listing Services (MLS) throughout the region. Our geographic area spans Santa Clara and San Mateo counties. Here's an outline of our services:

(insert list here)

Matchmaking

Because investors supply the majority of cash, they define most of the terms of the transaction. BCR simply acts as a matchmaker. An investor looks for buyers who have solid cash flow, are credit worthy and debt-free, and most of all, are eager to buy a house. Buyers look to match with an investor that fits the buyers' financial needs and desires.

Results

If you are interested in owning your own home and would like BCR to help you achieve this goal, call for an appointment now.

As you are typing, remember not to press Enter at the end of lines, just at the end of paragraphs. Don't try to match the line endings shown in the figure.

6. Type the text shown in Figure 5.14. Be sure to make the subheadings bold (you can use the keyboard shortcut Ctrl+Shift+B). You'll see the bold format in story view.

After you type the text, you can go back and make corrections. The techniques for moving the cursor and editing text in the Story Editor are identical to those that you use with the text tool. Refer to Chapter 4 if you need to refresh your memory.

7. Press Ctrl+PgUp to go to the beginning of the story.

8. Proofread your document and correct some of your typing mistakes, but be sure to leave in a few typos so the spelling checker can find mistakes when you use this option later. (If you are a perfect typist, make a few mistakes to give the spelling checker something to do!)

9. Press Ctrl+S to save the file.

IMPORTING BROCHURE.DOC

The text for the brochure is located in the file BROCHURE.DOC in the PM5PUBS directory. If you haven't installed the companion disk yet, see the companion disk instruction page at the back of this book.

Follow these steps to import BROCHURE.DOC, a Word for Windows document:

1. Pull down the File menu and choose Place.

2. Change to the PM5PUBS directory on drive C.

3. Click on BROCHURE.DOC.

4. Click on the Replacing Entire Story option so that the text will import into the current window. (Otherwise, the story will be placed in a new window.)

5. Choose OK. The brochure text is now imported into the story window.

6. Press Ctrl+S to save the file.

The text is imported with the formatting specified in the Word for Windows document. Let's check to see which font and size are used:

7. Click anywhere in a word, and press Ctrl+T to display the Type Specifications dialog box. It just so happens that the text was formatted with the font and size we want—11-point Times New Roman.

8. Choose Cancel to remove the dialog box from the screen.

FINDING A WORD

In the following steps, you will use the Find command to move the cursor to the Matchmaking subhead in the brochure text you just entered. Once there, you can correct some mistakes in this section.

1. Press Ctrl+PgUp to move the cursor to the beginning of the story.

2. Pull down the Utilities menu and choose Find (or press Ctrl+8). You will see the Find dialog box.

3. To the right of Find What, type **matchmaking** (in either uppercase or lowercase letters).

4. Click on the Find command button.

Matchmaking has been found, and it is selected on your screen.

5. To exit the Find feature, click anywhere outside the dialog box.

Now you can edit the text in this portion of the story.

6. Delete the text *most of all,* in the first paragraph of the Matchmaking section. This text is selected in Figure 5.15.

7. In the last sentence of the Matchmaking section, replace the word *that* (underlined in Figure 5.15) with *who*.

FIGURE 5.15: *Delete the selected text*

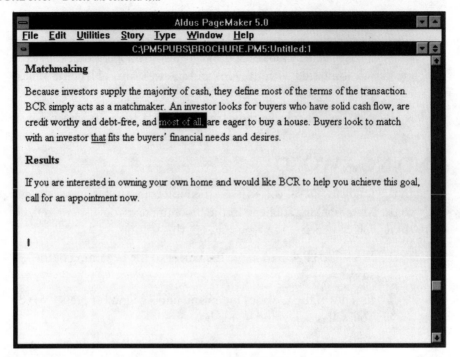

SPELL CHECKING THE BROCHURE TEXT

Now you can use the spelling checker to check your brochure text. Follow these steps:

1. Press Ctrl+PgUp to move the cursor to the beginning of the story.

2. Pull down the Utilities menu and choose Spelling, or press Ctrl+L.

3. Click on the Start command button.

The Story Editor highlights (selects) the first word that is not in the dictionary. Figure 5.16 shows the word *BCR* selected. This word is actually an abbreviation for Blue Chip Realty; it is not misspelled, so it should be ignored.

FIGURE 5.16: *An unknown word*

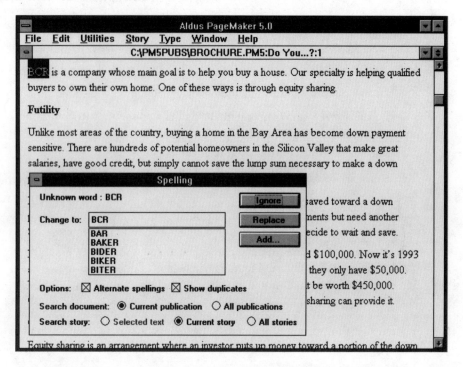

4. Click on the Ignore button.

5. As the spelling checker proceeds to find words, choose to Ignore or Replace them.

When the spelling checker can't find any more misspelled words, it displays the message

```
Spelling check complete.
```

6. Close the spelling checker by clicking outside the dialog box.

PUTTING YOUR TEXT ON THE PAGE

Your brochure text will begin in the third column of page 1 and continue onto page 2. (The first column is actually the back page of the brochure, and the second column is the cover page.)

Follow these steps to place your brochure text onto the page:

1. Save your file with the same name.

2. Pull down the Story menu and choose Close Story. A dialog box displays to let you know the story has not been placed.

3. Choose Place, and a loaded text icon appears.

4. Pull down the Layout menu, and check to see if Autoflow is checked. If it is, press Esc twice to cancel the command. If it's not, choose Autoflow to turn it on.

Now you can shoot the text into the third column on page 1. Because the first two columns are the front and back covers of the brochure, you do not want the story to flow into those columns.

5. Go to page 1.

6. Place the loaded text icon at the top-left corner of column 3 and click. The text flows into this column and then continues flowing into the first two columns of page 2.

Figure 5.17 shows the text placed on page 2. Notice the window shade handles in each selected text block. (Remember, a text block is the text between window shade handles.)

A plus sign (+) in a top handle indicates the story is continued from another text block. A plus sign in the bottom handle indicates the story continues to another text block. An empty bottom handle appears at the end of a story, and an empty top handle appears at the beginning. These handle symbols let you know which part of the story you are viewing.

FIGURE 5.17: *The text flowed onto page 2*

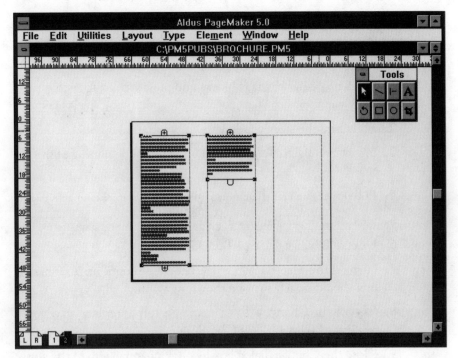

FORMATTING THE STORY IN LAYOUT VIEW

Now that the text is in layout view, you can see formatting effects as you format. Format the brochure's six subheads as follows:

1. Select the text tool.

2. Switch to 75% view.

3. Select each subhead and increase the size to 14 points.

In Chapter 7, you will learn how to speed up the formatting process when sections of text are formatted identically.

4. Repeat steps 2 and 3 for page 1.

5. Save your file with the same name.

REPLACING TEXT IN THE BROCHURE

In the brochure text, *BCR* was typed as a shorthand code for *Blue Chip Realty*. Now you will replace the code with the complete name in one easy procedure.

1. Click on one of the text blocks and press Ctrl+E to switch to story view.

2. Maximize the story window.

3. Press Ctrl+PgUp to move the cursor to the beginning of the story.

4. Pull down the Utilities menu and select Change, or press Ctrl+9.

5. Next to Find What, type **BCR**.

6. Next to Change To, type **Blue Chip Realty**.

7. Turn on the Match Case and Whole Word options. Your dialog box should match the one shown in Figure 5.18.

8. Choose the Change All command button to replace all occurrences of *BCR* with *Blue Chip Realty*.

9. Close the Change dialog box by clicking anywhere in the story.

You can scroll through the story and notice that *Blue Chip Realty* now appears throughout.

FIGURE 5.18:   *Replacing* BCR *with* Blue Chip Realty

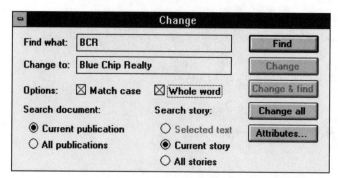

REPLACING FORMATTING

In our brochure, the subheads will be in Arial instead of Times New Roman. Rather than switching to layout view and formatting each subhead individually, you can replace the 14-point Times New Roman with 14-point Arial. Follow these steps to change the attributes:

1. Save the file by pressing Ctrl+S.

2. Press Ctrl+PgUp to move the cursor to the beginning of the story.

3. Pull down the Utilities menu and choose Change.

4. Delete the text next to Find What and Change To.

5. Click on the Attributes command button.

6. In the Find section of the dialog box (the left side), specify Times New Roman for the Font and 14 for the Size.

7. In the Change section (the right side), specify Arial for the Font and 14 for the Size.

8. Choose OK to close the Change Attributes dialog box.

9. Choose the Change All command button to replace the attributes automatically.

10. Close the Change dialog box.

Since story view doesn't display formatting attributes, it's best to switch to layout view to make sure the Change command worked properly.

Follow these steps to switch to layout view and check the format of your subheads:

1. Press Ctrl+E to switch to layout view.

2. Switch to Actual Size view. The subheads should be displayed in Arial (sans serif) instead of Times New Roman (serif).

3. To double-check the format, select a heading and press Ctrl+T to display the Type Specifications dialog box. Arial should appear in the Font box.

4. Press Esc.

5. Save the file.

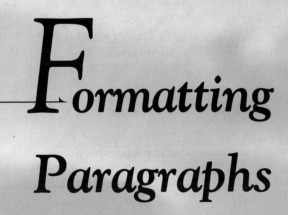

Formatting Paragraphs

*f*ast
tracks

To change the alignment of paragraphs: **204**

Select the paragraphs to be aligned, and choose Type ➤ Alignment. Select the type of alignment (Left, Center, Right, Justify, or Force Justify).

To indent the first line of paragraphs: **204**

Select the paragraphs to be indented, and choose Type ➤ Paragraph. Type the amount of indent in the First field. Choose OK.

To create a hanging indent for bullets: **208**

Select the paragraphs to be indented, and choose Type ➤ Indents/Tabs. In the ruler, drag the left indent (the bottom triangular symbol at the 0 mark) to where you want the text to wrap. Drag the first-line indent (the top triangular symbol) to where you want the bullet to go. Next, you need to set a tab at the same spot as the left indent: Click on the left indent symbol, click on the Position button and choose Add Tab. Choose OK.

To set a tab stop: **211**

Select paragraphs if necessary, and choose Type ➤ Indents/Tabs. Click in the ruler where you wish to set a tab. Select the appropriate tab alignment icon (left, right, center, or decimal).

To change the leading of text: 217

Select the text you wish to change, and choose Type ➤ Leading. Choose the desired leading from the list. If the leading size is not on the list, choose Other and enter the value.

To add spacing between paragraphs: 221

Do not use the Enter key! Instead, select the paragraphs, and choose Type ➤ Paragraph. Enter a value in the Before or After field, and choose OK.

To align a paragraph on the leading grid: 224

Select the paragraph whose odd leading is causing the grid misalignment. Choose Type ➤ Paragraph. Click on the Rules button, and then the Options button. Turn on the Align to Grid option, and then enter a value in the Grid Size field. Press Alt as you click on OK to close all the dialog boxes.

To turn off automatic hyphenation: 226

Select the paragraphs, and choose Type ➤ Hyphenation. Select Manual Only, and choose OK.

To insert a discretionary hyphen: 227

Place the cursor where you want the hyphen to go, and press Ctrl+hyphen.

To avoid widows and orphans: 229

Select the paragraphs, and choose Type ➤ Paragraph. Turn on the Widow Control and Orphan Control options. Choose OK.

I N CHAPTER 5, YOU USED THE TEXT
tool to format individual characters. You changed fonts, sizes, and type
styles. In this chapter, you will learn how to use formatting options that
affect paragraphs. The options that apply to entire paragraphs or groups of
paragraphs include centering, justification, and indenting. You can also
control vertical spacing, hyphenation, and paragraph breaks at the end of
a column or at the end of a page.

Version
5.0

Most of these options are in the Paragraph Specifications dialog box, accessed by choosing Paragraph from the Type menu or by pressing Ctrl+M.
You can also make paragraph formatting changes in Version 5.0's control
palette. To access the control palette's paragraph formatting options, click
on the paragraph symbol (¶) as pointed out in Figure 6.1; this is called the
palette's *paragraph view*. To return to character view, click on the capital A.

SELECTING PARAGRAPHS TO FORMAT

A *paragraph* is defined as a block of text that ends in a carriage return. A
paragraph can be made up of multiple lines that are word-wrapped, a single
line, or even a blank line that you created with the Enter key.

FIGURE 6.1: *The control palette in paragraph view*

Character view button

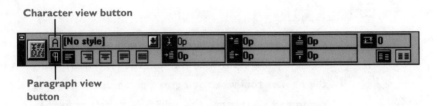

Paragraph view
button

In the Story Editor, you can see your paragraph marks by turning on the Display ¶ option on the Story menu. Figure 6.2 shows a story window with paragraph marks displayed. You cannot display paragraph marks in layout view.

FIGURE 6.2: *Paragraph marks displayed in the Story Editor*

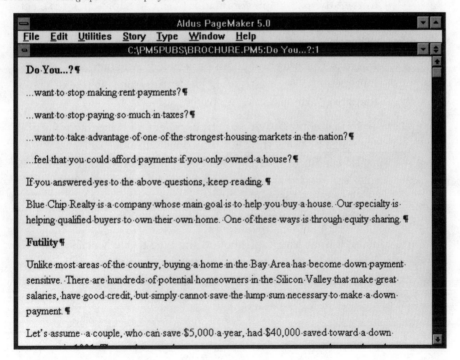

**All the paragraph formatting options require you to se-
lect the paragraphs with the text tool. If you are using
the pointer tool when you give a paragraph formatting
command, you change the publication's default format,
and any new paragraphs you type will have this format.**

Depending on how many paragraphs you want to format, choose the appropriate selection technique below:

➤ To format a single paragraph, you don't need to select all the
text; just place the cursor anywhere in the paragraph before you
initiate the paragraph command. (You can triple-click to select
the entire paragraph, but it's not necessary.)

➤ To format all the paragraphs in a story, place the text cursor anywhere in the story and choose the Select All command on the
Edit menu (or press Ctrl+A). The entire story, even text blocks
that are continued on other pages, is selected.

➤ To format consecutive paragraphs, select all the paragraphs in
the range by using the click-and-drag technique or by clicking
at the beginning and Shift+clicking at the end. You do not need
to select every character in the range; just make sure at least
part of each paragraph is selected. You cannot simultaneously select paragraphs that are not consecutive.

You can also format paragraphs before you type them. Make sure the cursor
is not in any existing text and that no text is selected, and then choose
your formatting options and begin typing. As you type, your paragraph will
be formatted properly.

ALIGNING PARAGRAPHS

PageMaker offers four ways to align text: left, right, centered, or justified. The default paragraph alignment is left; that is, text is lined up at the left edge of the text block. And, unless you have moved the text block, its left edge is at the left column guide.

Left-aligned text is sometimes referred to as *ragged right* because the right side of the paragraph is uneven. To eliminate this ragged look, you can choose justified alignment. With this alignment, small amounts of space are inserted between words so that the right and left ends of the paragraph are even and smooth. The last line of a paragraph is not justified unless you choose the Force Justify alignment option.

Just because it's easy to do, don't feel that you need to justify your body text. The main advantage to justified text is that you can fit more text on the page because more words are hyphenated. If space is a precious commodity in your publication, you might want to justify the text.

Left-aligned text is the easiest to read because fewer words are hyphenated and because the eye doesn't have to skip over extra spaces between words. Furthermore, the uneven line endings create white space, which lightens the page.

If you insist on the more formal look of justified text, make sure the Hyphenation option on the Type menu is turned on (the default setting) so that you don't get large gaps between words. These gaps can create unattractive rivers of white space that run through your paragraphs.

The other types of alignment, centered and right, are usually applied to single-line paragraphs or special text designed to stand out from the rest. Centered alignment is popular for headlines and titles. Designers typically use right alignment to create a special effect. The Force Justify option is also most often used on a single-line paragraph so that the text spans the entire width of the text block (usually the column width).

CHANGING ALIGNMENT

You can change the alignment of a paragraph in several different ways: by using the Alignment cascading menu, filling in the Paragraph Specifications dialog box, pressing key combinations, or with the control palette.

If the only paragraph formatting option you need to change is alignment, use the Alignment option on the Type menu. Or, if you have a good memory, memorize the keyboard shortcuts for paragraph alignment shown in Table 6.1.

TABLE 6.1: *Keyboard Shortcuts for Paragraph Alignment*

Shortcut	Description
Ctrl+Shift+L	Align left
Ctrl+Shift+C	Align center
Ctrl+Shift+R	Align right
Ctrl+Shift+J	Justify
Ctrl+Shift+F	Force justify

Version
5.0

To change alignment with the control palette, click on the appropriate alignment button. These buttons are marked in Figure 6.3.

If you know that you want to change other paragraph formatting options in addition to alignment, display the Paragraph Specifications dialog box by pressing Ctrl+M or by choosing Paragraph from the Type menu. Click on the Alignment field to display the list of alignment choices.

FIGURE 6.3: *The alignment buttons in the control palette*

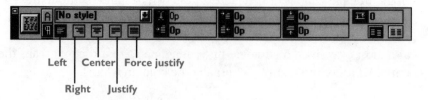

INDENTING PARAGRAPHS

An *indent* is extra space on the left or right side of the paragraph. For example, if you have a quotation or a list, you will want to indent it on the left (and perhaps the right) so that it stands out from the rest of the text.

Figure 6.4 shows examples of the different types of indents available in PageMaker.

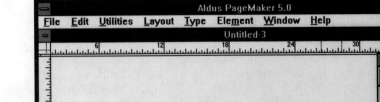

FIGURE 6.4: *Paragraph indents*

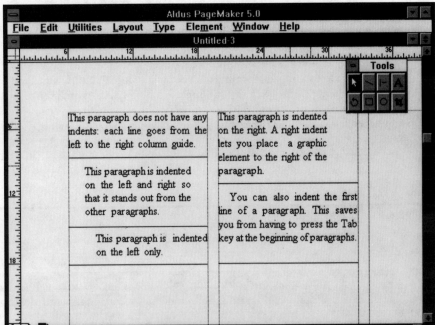

SETTING INDENTS

PageMaker offers two basic ways to set indents: numerically or visually. When you know the numeric value of your indent (for example, 0.25 inch or 1 pica), enter a numeric value in the Paragraph Specifications dialog box or in the control palette. Figure 6.5 points out the three indent fields in the palette.

USING FIRST-LINE INDENTS

Frequently, the first line of each paragraph of body text is indented. On a typewriter, you press the Tab key to indent a paragraph; in PageMaker, you specify a *first-line indent*.

After you set up a first-line indent, you don't need to press Tab at the beginning of each paragraph. And, if you later decide you want more or less space, you don't need to insert tabs or adjust tab stops; you simply change the amount of the indent.

How large should a first-line indent be? If the indent is too small, the purpose of the indent is lost—one paragraph is not easily distinguishable from the next. On the other hand, when a first-line indent is too large, it looks out of place or amateurish. In most cases, a one-pica first-line indent works fine, unless your lines of body text are long, in which case you might want to go up to two picas.

FIGURE 6.5: *The indent fields in the control palette*

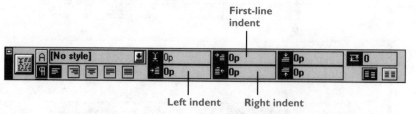

If you find it difficult to distinguish the indent fields in the control palette, study the arrows in the fields. The first-line indent field has an arrow pointing next to the first line; the right indent field has an arrow pointing next to the right side; and the left indent field has an arrow pointing next to the left side.

If you want to "eyeball" your indent settings, the on-screen ruler is the way to go. With the Indents/Tabs option (Ctrl+I), you can set indents and tab stops by clicking and dragging symbols in a ruler.

Figure 6.6 points out the various symbols in the ruler. The default tab stops are set every 3 picas, or $1/2$ inch. You will learn about tab stops shortly.

FIGURE 6.6: *The Indent/Tab ruler*

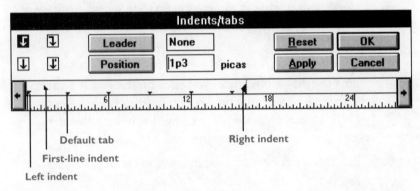

To change an indent, you click and drag the appropriate symbol. The text box in the middle of the dialog box indicates the amount of indent (for example, 2p0 for 2 picas) as you drag the symbol. The best way to understand how the ruler works is to experiment with it. Here is the general procedure:

1. Select the text to be indented.

2. Pull down the Type menu and choose Indents/Tabs (or press Ctrl+I). A ruler and dialog box appear on the screen. The beginning of the ruler (the zero point) is at the beginning of the column. This positioning lets you set the indents with respect to the text. All indents are set relative to the edges of the text blocks.

3. Drag the appropriate indent symbol to the desired position.

oTe

The left indent is linked to the first-line indent symbol: When you move the left indent symbol, the first-line indent also moves, so that it keeps the same relative distance from the left indent. If you want to move the left indent without moving the first-line indent, hold down Shift as you drag the left indent symbol.

Version
5.0

4. In Version 5.0, you can see the effect of your indent before closing the dialog box. After you click on the Apply button, the selected text will be indented as you indicated—but the dialog box will remain on-screen. That way, if you don't like the results, you needn't bring up the dialog box again.

5. When you are done with your indents, click on OK.

CREATING HANGING INDENTS

Another type of indent is called a *hanging indent* because text (such as a bullet or a number) "hangs" to the left of the indented paragraph. Figure 6.7 shows a numbered list with hanging indents.

To create this type of indent, you need to set a left indent, a first-line indent, and a custom tab stop. You can make the indent settings in the Paragraph Specifications dialog box (Ctrl+M), in the control palette, or on the Indent/Tabs ruler (Ctrl+I). However, the only way to set a tab is in the Indent/Tabs dialog box. The first-line indent is where the number or bullet will go. It is always a negative value because it is set as the distance from the left indent, not from the left column guide. The left indent and the tab stop are set at the same place: where you want the text to wrap. In Figure 6.8, the first-line indent is set at −2 picas, the left indent is at 2 picas, and the custom tab stop is at 2 picas.

FIGURE 6.7: *A numbered list with hanging indents*

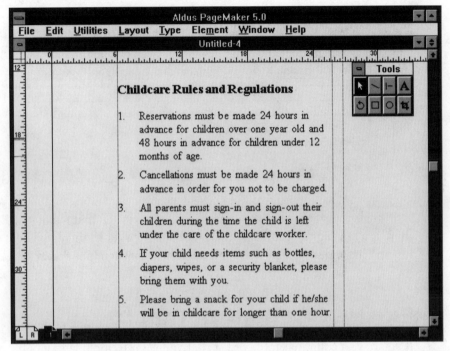

To set a tab at the same spot as the left indent, place the mouse pointer on the left indent symbol and click once. Then click on the Position button and choose Add Tab. You'll learn more about setting tabs in the next section.

Once the indents and custom tab are set, you are ready to type the text in the list. First type the number or bullet. (Ctrl+Shift+8 is PageMaker's code for inserting a bullet; you may also want to insert a special symbol from the Character Map accessory—see Chapter 4 for details.) Then press Tab and type the text for the paragraph. Because of the hanging indent you set, the text will word-wrap to the left indent, not the left edge of the text block. Press Enter to complete the paragraph. The tab and indent settings from the preceding paragraph automatically carry forward to the next paragraph when you press Enter.

FIGURE 6.8: *The Indent/Tabs ruler for a hanging indent*

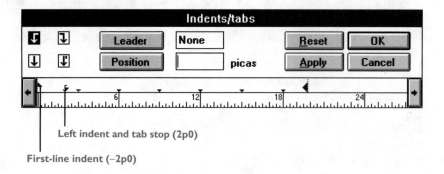

Left indent and tab stop (2p0)

First-line indent (−2p0)

If the list was typed before a hanging indent was set, first make sure there is a tab (not spaces) after each number or bullet in the list. Then, select the list and set the indents and tab in the Indents/Tabs dialog box.

CREATING COLUMNAR TABLES

If you have a columnar table or list that you want to include in a publication, you can either type it directly in the publication, use the Table Editor, or import it from a file. This section describes how to type the table with the text tool. Chapter 13 discusses the Table Editor and Chapter 8 explains how to import text files.

There are two things to remember when typing a table with the text tool. First, set and use tab stops for each column. Do not use the Spacebar to align text because it won't work with proportional fonts. You will also want to specify the appropriate tab alignment.

The second rule for typing tables is to use the *line break* command (Shift+Enter) instead of pressing Enter at the end of each line in the table. The line break command moves the cursor down to the next line without creating a new paragraph. That way, the table is a single paragraph, and you can format it without having to select every line in the table. Because tables often require special formatting and fine tuning, you will find it more efficient to select it by clicking anywhere in the table, rather than clicking and dragging across all its lines.

SETTING, ADJUSTING, AND DELETING TABS

PageMaker provides four kinds of tab alignments:

- A left-aligned tab aligns the column on the left.
- A right-aligned tab lines up the column on the right.
- A centered tab centers the text around the tab stop.
- A decimal tab lines up numbers at the decimal point.

If you select the appropriate tab alignment, your columns will be properly aligned without any fudging with the Spacebar. Figure 6.9 shows an example of each type of tab alignment.

The default tab alignment is left. To specify the other tab types, you need to click on the appropriate icon in the Indents/Tabs dialog box. The icons are labeled in Figure 6.10.

Setting Tab Stops

Follow these steps to set tab stops:

1. Place the cursor where you want the new tab settings to take effect (select existing text if necessary).

2. Press Ctrl+I to display the Indents/Tabs dialog box and ruler. The ruler lines up with your column guides, making it easy to set your tabs with respect to the column.

FIGURE 6.9: *Tab alignment examples*

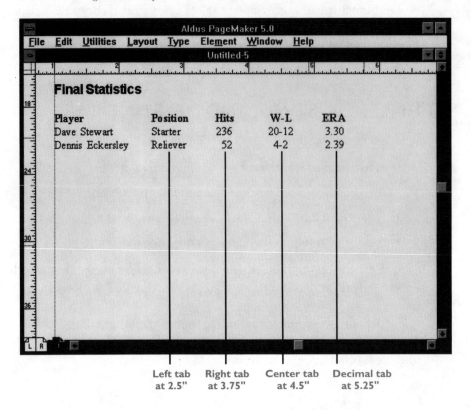

Left tab at 2.5"   Right tab at 3.75"   Center tab at 4.5"   Decimal tab at 5.25"

FIGURE 6.10: *The tab alignment icons in the ruler*

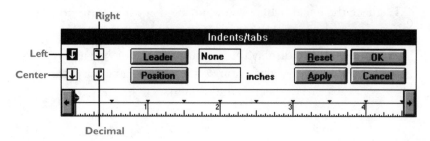

3. Place the pointer where you wish to insert the tab in the ruler and click. A tab symbol will appear, and the precise position will fill in next to the Position button. If you didn't click in the right spot, you can drag the symbol. Notice that when you set a custom tab stop, the default tab stops to the left of your new tab disappear.

4. Click on the appropriate tab-alignment icon (left, right, center, or decimal).

5. Repeat steps 3 and 4 for each tab stop.

6. To see the effect of your tab stops before closing the dialog box, click on the Apply button—the selected text will reflect the tab settings you indicated. If the settings aren't quite right, you can adjust them without having to bring up the dialog box again.

PageMaker offers an alternative method for setting tab stops, when you know the exact numeric value of where you want to set the tabs. For example, if you know you want a tab stop at 4.5 picas or 0.75 inches, you can enter this value in the Indents/Tabs dialog box. Here's how this technique works:

1. Place the cursor where you want the new tab settings to take effect (select existing text if necessary).

2. Press Ctrl+I to display the Indents/Tabs dialog box.

3. In the text box next to the Position button, type the numeric value of the desired tab stop position. This position is measured from the left edge of the current column (not from the left margin or the left edge of the page). If picas are your current measurement system, and you want to enter the value in inches, type an **i** after the number (for example, 0.75i). Or, if your default measurement is in inches and you want to enter the value in picas, type a **p** after the value (for example, 10p).

4. Click on the Position button, and select Add Tab.

5. Click on the appropriate tab-alignment icon (left, right, centered, decimal).

6. Repeat steps 3–5 for each tab stop.

Specifying Leader Characters

By default, PageMaker inserts spaces before a tab, but you may choose to place *leader characters* in this space. Probably the most commonly used leader character is the period, as shown in Figure 6.11. You will frequently see this leader character in tables of contents, and occasionally you'll see it in lists and tables. To create a tab with leader characters, follow these general steps:

1. Press Ctrl+I to display the Indents/Tabs dialog box.

2. Set the desired tab stop, or if the tab has already been set, click the mouse pointer on the tab symbol in the ruler.

3. Click on the Leader button, and choose the desired leader character (dots, dashes, or solid underline). To enter a different leader character, choose Custom and then enter one or two characters in the box next to the Leader button.

FIGURE 6.11: *In this table of contents, leader characters fill the space before the right-aligned tab*

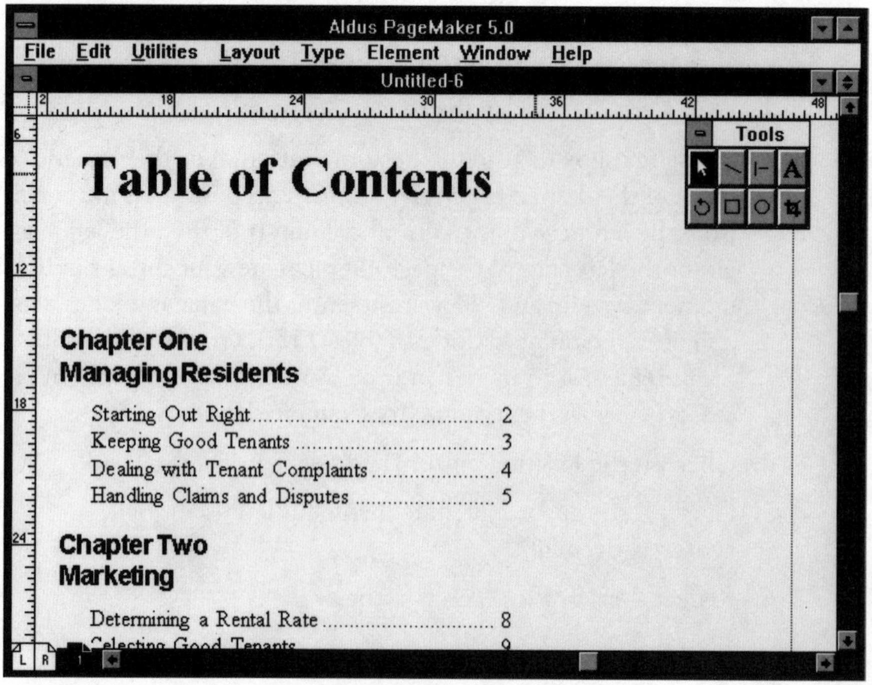

4. Choose OK.

Adjusting Tab Settings

To adjust a tab setting in a table, first make sure the table is selected. If you set up the table as a single paragraph (by pressing Shift+Enter at the end of each line), you can easily select the whole table by clicking anywhere in it with the text tool. If you pressed Enter at the end of each line instead, you have to select all the lines in the table to change the tab stops. After the table is selected, you adjust a tab stop by simply clicking and dragging the tab symbol in the Indents/Tabs ruler.

Clearing Tab Stops

If your ruler contains extra tab stops that you no longer need (or that you set accidentally), you can remove all the custom tabs or delete them one by one. The Reset button in the Indents/Tabs dialog box clears all the custom tabs and displays the default tab stops. To delete a single tab, click on the tab symbol in the ruler, click on the Position button, and then choose Delete Tab. Another way to clear a single tab is to drag the symbol off the ruler.

ADDING VERTICAL SPACING

White space is an important part of a page layout, and a well-designed page uses white space liberally. White space helps break up the "sea-of-gray" syndrome, especially if you are short on art and photos. Furthermore, extra space around subheads helps differentiate them from the body text. Figure 6.12 shows a page with no extra white space; it's not very inviting, is it?

PageMaker offers three ways to control the vertical spacing on your page:

➤ Adjust the leading

➤ Add extra space before or after the paragraph

➤ Use the Align to Grid feature

FIGURE 6.12: *This page desperately needs more white space*

Do You...?

...want to stop making rent payments? ...want to stop paying so much in taxes? ...want to take advantage of one of the strongest housing markets in the nation? ...feel that you could afford payments if you only owned a house?

If you answered yes to the above questions, keep reading.

Blue Chip Realty is a company whose main goal is to help you buy a house. Our specialty is helping qualified buyers to own their own home. One of these ways is through equity sharing.

Futility

Unlike most areas of the country, buying a home in the Bay Area has become down payment sensitive. There are hundreds of potential homeowners in the Silicon Valley that make great salaries, have good credit, but simply cannot save the lump sum necessary to make a down payment.

Let's assume a couple, who can save $5,000 a year, had $40,000 saved toward a down payment in 1991. They make enough money to cover mortgage payments but need another $10,000 for a 20% down payment on a $250,000 house. So they decide to wait and save.

In the two years it took them to save $10,000, the house appreciated $100,000. Now it's 1993 and they need $70,000 for a down payment on the same house, and they only have $50,000. What can they do? Save another four years? By then the house might be worth $450,000. Chances are they'll never catch up. They need money today. Equity sharing can provide it.

Concepts

Equity sharing is an arrangement where an investor puts up money toward a portion of the down payment. In return, he/she will receive a share of the equity from the home buyer.

For example, suppose a buyer, with the help of an investor, purchases a house in 1993 for $300,000. Here's a hypothetical breakdown of the up-front costs:

(insert table here)

Numerous benefits accrue to you, the buyer, in return for the portion of the appreciation you relinquish in an equity sharing deal. First, you get to fulfill your own American dream: home ownership.

Other benefits include large tax deductions, saying goodbye to rent payments, and getting a leveraged investment in one of the strongest real estate markets in the world. If these benefits sound good to you, then Blue Chip Realty can help.

Our Focus

Blue Chip Realty specializes in serving home buyers. We do not list property. Instead, we simply act as agents to help people like you find a house here on the Peninsula. So how do we get paid? By receiving a percentage of the commission that the home seller pays to the listing agent. That's all.

We are members of several Multiple Listing Services (MLS) throughout the region. Our geographic area spans Santa Clara and San Mateo counties. Here's an outline of our services: (insert list here)

Matchmaking

Because investors supply the majority of cash, they define most of the terms of the transaction. Blue Chip Realty simply acts as a matchmaker. An investor looks for buyers who have solid cash flow, are credit worthy and debt-free, and are eager to buy a house. Buyers look to match with an investor who fits the buyers' financial needs and desires.

Results

If you are interested in owning your own home and would like Blue Chip Realty to help you achieve this goal, call for an appointment now.

One golden rule: Do not insert extra space with the Enter key. The problem with hard returns is that they are always there, even when they land at the top of a column. When you use any of the three methods described above, you do not have to worry about deleting space at your column tops.

CHANGING THE LEADING

Leading controls the amount of space between successive lines of type. When you increase the leading value, the amount of space between lines of type is increased. Figure 6.13 displays several examples of text with the same font and size but with different leading. As you increase the leading, some of the extra space goes above the character and some goes below. To be precise, two-thirds of the leading is above the baseline and one-third is below.

Unless you specify otherwise, PageMaker automatically sets your leading as 120 percent of the type size. Thus, 10-point type has 12-point leading; 12-point type has 14.4-point leading. If your line of type contains multiple type sizes, the leading is based on the largest type size. The automatic leading ensures that two lines of type will never be too close together, although it may not always look right or be appropriate for your layout.

FIGURE 6.13: *Examples of different amounts of leading*

This paragraph is typed in
12-point Times Roman with
12-point leading.

This paragraph is typed in
12-point Times Roman with
auto leading (14.4).

This paragraph is typed in
12-point Times Roman with
16-point leading.

This paragraph is typed in

12-point Times Roman with

24-point leading.

≋ *Note*

**Even though leading is almost always applied to entire
paragraphs, PageMaker considers it to be a type specification, not a paragraph spec. The reason for this is one of
convenience: People usually enter the leading value at
the same time as they enter the type size. Therefore,
leading and type size are available in the same dialog box.
(Users would grumble if they had to go to two dialog
boxes to specify the type size and leading.) Also note that
because leading is a character specification, you must select *all* the text in a paragraph when you change the
leading—you cannot just click in the paragraph.**

You can change the leading by choosing the size from the Leading cascading menu, or by entering it in the Type Specifications dialog box. If the
only type specification you want to change is the leading, choose the Leading option from the Type menu. Frequently, however, you enter the leading
as you are specifying the font and type size, so you will want to go through
the Type Specifications dialog box and do everything at once.

Version
5.0

Another way to specify leading is in the control palette. The leading
field is marked in Figure 6.14. Note that this field is available in character
view, not paragraph view. Therefore, you must make sure the character
view button (the large A) is selected in order to have access to this field.

FIGURE 6.14: *The leading field is in the control palette's character view*

Leading

Using a Leading Grid

On a professionally produced page, all textual and graphic elements have depths that are numerically related. They are multiples of a predetermined magic number. If the magic number is 12, all headlines, callouts, graphic boxes, and other page elements have depths of 12, 24, 36, 48, and so on.

This magic number is the size of the leading for your body copy. Don't think of your page's dimensions in terms of inches or points. Instead, think of your page as being divided in increments that match your magic number. Designers refer to this as a *leading grid*.

When all your elements are multiples of your magic number, something magical happens: The baselines in one column exactly line up with the baselines in the adjacent column. Figure 6.15 has a ruler pulled down so that you can see that the baselines match. If your baselines are not aligned, as in Figure 6.16, you might be advertising to discerning eyes that your publishing efforts are less than professional.

FIGURE 6.15: *Perfectly aligned baselines of text*

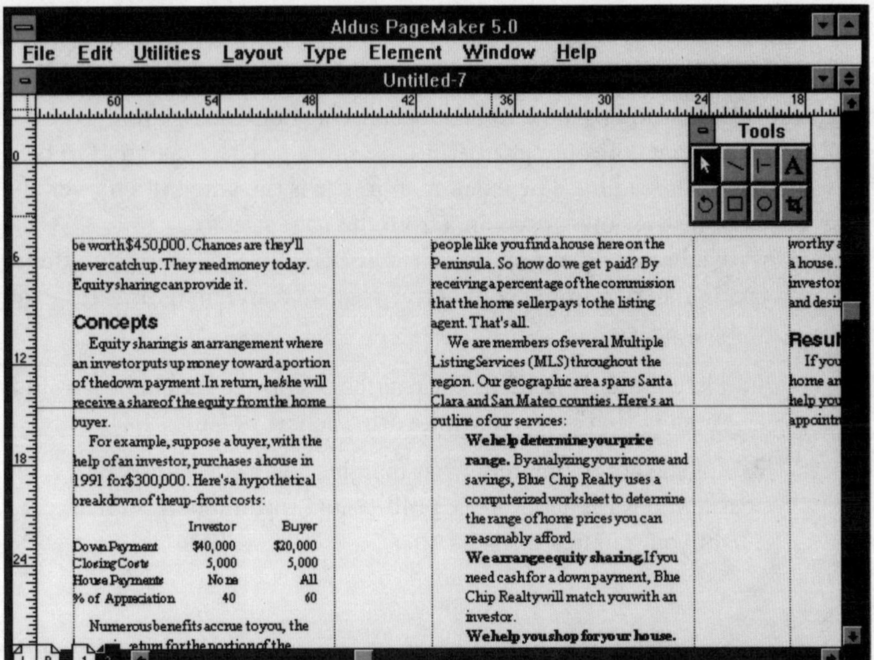

FIGURE 6.16: *Misaligned baselines of text*

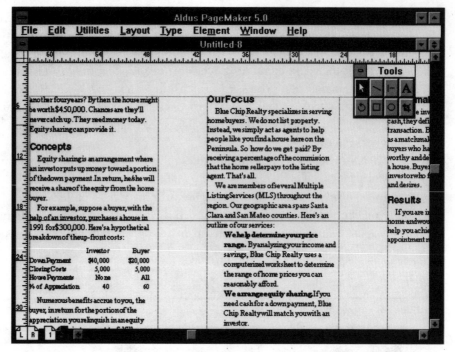

Your top and bottom margins are key players in your leading grid, although they do not have to be multiples of your leading. Your goal is to get the active area of your page (your page size minus the margins) to be a multiple of your leading. The exact margin size is the amount left over after subtracting the active page area from the page size.

With a handheld or pop-up calculator close by, follow this mathematical progression to determine your active page area and margins. This example is for a landscape page.

1. Determine the leading for your body copy. It should be a round number that's easy to work with, such as 14 (not 14.4).

2. Decide approximately what margins you want. For instance, let's say you want about 4-pica (48-point) top and bottom margins for your publication.

3. Subtract both of these margins (96 points) from the page size (612) to get the current active page size (516 points). Note: A landscape letter-size page is 612 points high—8½ inches multiplied by 72 points per inch. (A portrait letter-size page is 792 points high.)

4. Divide the current active page size calculated in step 3 by your leading. If the page size is 516 points and your leading is 14, the result is 36.86 lines. If the number of lines results in an integer, you lucked out and can stop here—your initial margins will work perfectly on the leading grid. If not, continue with steps 5 through 7.

5. Take the integer of the number of lines calculated in step 4 (36) and multiply it by your leading (14) to get an active page size that is a multiple of your magic number. Your active page size in this example is 504 points.

6. Subtract the active page size (504) from the total page size (612) to get the total area available for top and bottom margins (108).

7. Divide the total margins (108) by two to get the value for each of the margins (54 points).

Figure 6.17 illustrates a landscape page set to a 14-point leading grid. The active page size is 504 points (which gives you 36 lines of 11/14 type) and the top and bottom margins are 54 points each. Note: 11/14 means 11-point type on 14-point leading.

Although calculating your leading grid requires quite a bit of math, you will find that the time it saves you as you lay out your page makes it well worth the initial effort.

ADDING PARAGRAPH SPACING

As mentioned earlier, you shouldn't press Enter to insert an extra space between paragraphs. There are several reasons for avoiding blank lines created with a carriage return:

➤ If the blank line lands at the top of a column, this extra space will cause the column to start lower than the other columns.

FIGURE 6.17: *The leading grid for 14-point leading on a landscape page*

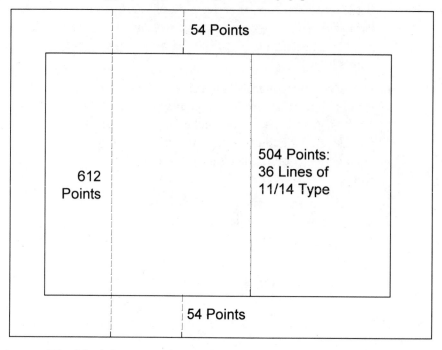

54 Points

504 Points:
36 Lines of
11/14 Type

612
Points

54 Points

➤ The blank lines could possibly throw off the leading grid, so that the baselines of the type do not align.

➤ You cannot precisely control the amount of space—one carriage return might not add enough space and two might add too much.

Version
5.0

None of these problems arise when you use PageMaker's paragraph spacing options. In the Paragraph Specifications dialog box, you can set the amount of space before and after your paragraphs. In Version 5.0, another way to specify the paragraph spacing is in the control palette; these fields are marked in Figure 6.19.

In determining how much space to add before and after a subhead, you should keep in mind that a subhead introduces a new topic and should therefore be separated from the text above it and tied to the text below it. You can show this relationship by placing more space above the subhead than below it.

LEADING METHODS

PageMaker has three ways in which it can measure leading: Proportional, Baseline, and Top of Caps. (The Baseline method is new to Version 5.0.) Proportional is Page-Maker's default; with this method, two-thirds of the leading goes above the baseline and one-third goes below. Thus, if you specify 24 points of leading, 16 points will go above the baseline and 8 points will go below. Although Proportional is the default, it is not the method used in traditional typography; Baseline is. With the Baseline method, the leading is measured from baseline to baseline. If you specify 24 points of leadings, the entire 24 points goes above the baseline. In the Top of Caps method, the leading is measured from the top of the tallest letter in a line. This method can sometimes give you undesirable results (for example, when the first letter in the paragraph is enlarged—see Figure 6.18).

Which method is best? Well, if you are an experienced PageMaker user and are accustomed to working with the Proportional method, you might want to stick with it. Otherwise, we recommend that you switch to the more intuitive Baseline method. To change the leading method, press Ctrl+M to display the Paragraph Specifications dialog box and choose the Spacing button. In this sub-dialog box, you will find the three options for leading method.

Exactly how much space? The leading of your subhead plus the space above and below it should be a multiple of your magic number (the leading of the body text). Once you determine the appropriate paragraph spacing for your subheads, use this spacing for all subheads in the publication. This consistency and uniformity not only looks more professional, but it helps your readers visually identify each level of subheading. PageMaker's style feature offers an easy way to apply consistent formatting to your subheadings (see Chapter 7).

For example, suppose the leading of your publication's body text is 12 (i.e., your magic number is 12), and your subheads have 14-point leading. To keep on the leading grid, you should add 10 points of space above the subheads (14-point leading plus 10-points of space equals 24—a multiple of the magic number).

FIGURE 6.18: *With the Top of Caps leading method, the interline spacing isn't always what you expect.*

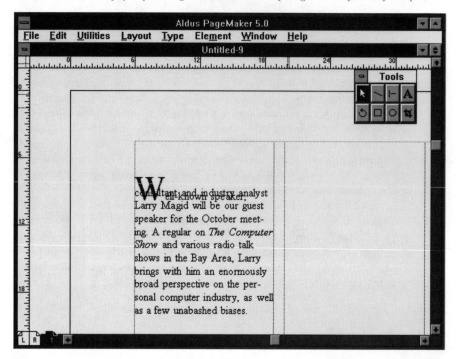

FIGURE 6.19: *The space before and after fields in the control palette*

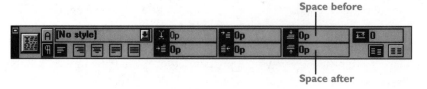

USING THE ALIGN TO GRID OPTION

Sometimes you'll have a particular item, such as a table, that uses a different leading from the body text, causing the baselines of type to fail to line up on the leading grid. You could get out your calculator and determine how much space is required above and below the table to keep the body text on the leading grid, but that would be a grueling job. It would also be frustrating, because you would have to constantly adjust the spacing each time you altered the number of lines in the table. Instead, you can use Page-Maker's Align to Grid option. This option, when applied to a paragraph (such as a table), will position the following paragraph on the leading grid. (Notice that we said the *following*, not the *current*, paragraph.

You access the Align to Grid option through the Paragraph Specifications dialog box, but it is hidden several dialog boxes deep in the Paragraph Rule Options box (although it has absolutely nothing to do with paragraph rules). Here's how to align a paragraph to the leading grid:

1. Place the cursor in the paragraph which is causing text to be off the leading grid. (PageMaker will add extra space after this paragraph so that the next paragraph wil be properly aligned to the grid.)

2. Press Ctrl+M to display the Paragraph Specifications dialog box.

3. Click on the Rules button.

4. Click on the Options button.

5. Click on the Align to Grid option.

6. Next to Grid Size, type the value of your body text leading (your magic number).

7. Hold down Alt and click on OK to close all three dialog boxes.

Version
5.0

Alternatively, if your control palette is displayed, you can enter your grid size in the field marked in Figure 6.20. Then turn on the Align to Grid option by clicking the right-hand button (also marked in Figure 6.20). The left-hand button turns the option off.

FIGURE 6.20: *The align-to-grid fields*

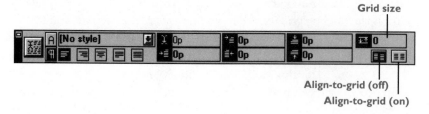

Grid size

Align-to-grid (off)

Align-to-grid (on)

Use the Align to Grid option with discretion. Don't use it for repeating elements, such as subheads, because you may get different amounts of spacing around them. You cannot be assured of consistent spacing from one element to the next when you use Align to Grid. Save this feature for special cases or exceptions.

GIVE YOURSELF A BREAK

PageMaker offers a number of ways to control how your lines, paragraphs, columns, and pages break. For example, you can tell PageMaker not to split a paragraph between two columns, or to always place certain paragraphs at the top of a column or page.

HYPHENATION

By default, the hyphenation feature is turned on for all paragraphs. To turn off hyphenation, choose Hyphenation on the Type menu or press Ctrl+H; you can then click on the Off button in the Hyphenation dialog box. You can turn off hyphenation for single paragraphs or for an entire story. If you turn off hyphenation before you type the story, none of the text will be hyphenated. If you type a story and then decide you don't want hyphenation, you must select all the paragraphs (Ctrl+A) before you turn off hyphenation. For a single paragraph, simply click in the paragraph and then turn off hyphenation.

Types of Hyphenation

When you select Hyphenation from the Type menu or press Ctrl+H, you will see the dialog box shown in Figure 6.21. This dialog box offers three different types of hyphenation: Manual Only, Manual Plus Dictionary, and Manual Plus Algorithm. Each option progressively puts more hyphens in your text.

When you initially select the Manual Only option, it is as if you turned off hyphenation; no hyphens are used. However, you can add your own hyphens when and where you want by inserting *discretionary hyphens* (Ctrl+hyphen). Use this option if you want very light hyphenation or if you want total control over the hyphenation.

If you see a big gap at the end of a line, you can hyphenate the word at the beginning of the next line. Just place the cursor where you want the hyphen to go and press Ctrl+hyphen to insert a discretionary hyphen. The first part of the word will be hyphenated and move up to the previous line, assuming there's enough room for it. If you change the text and a hyphen is no longer needed because the word does not appear at the end of a line any more, the discretionary hyphen disappears. However, the hyphen is simply hidden, and if it is ever needed again, it will reappear.

FIGURE 6.21: *The Hyphenation dialog box*

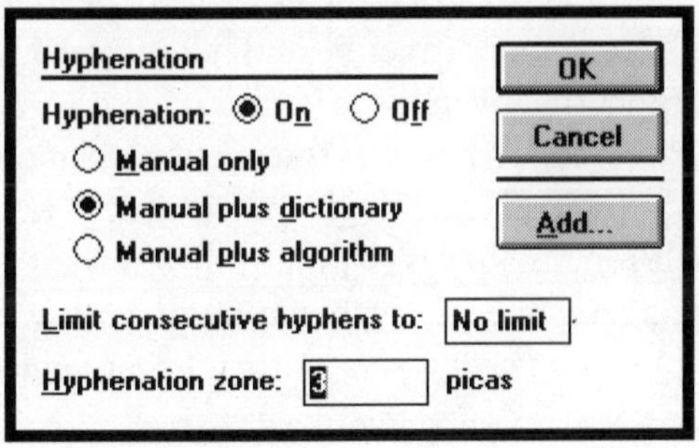

Wait until the final stage of your publication production before you insert discretionary hyphens. If you insert them too early in the process, the line endings will inevitably change, and you will find that different hyphenation is required.

The Manual Plus Dictionary option (the default) also lets you enter discretionary hyphens, but it automatically hyphenates other words when necessary, using its 100,000-word hyphenation dictionary. This is actually the same dictionary that the Story Editor's spelling checker uses. If a word is not in the dictionary, it will not be hyphenated.

Of the three types of hyphenation, the Manual Plus Algorithm option inserts the most hyphens. Along with your discretionary hyphens and the dictionary hyphens, it also inserts hyphens (as necessary) in words not found in the dictionary by following a set of guidelines (an algorithm) for their placement.

Other Hyphenation Controls

Another way to control the amount of hyphenation in a paragraph is with the two options at the bottom of the Hyphenation dialog box.

We highly recommend you limit the number of consecutive hyphens. By default, the setting for the Limit Consecutive Hyphens To option is No Limit, which means you can have an *unlimited* number of hyphens in a row. Because a stack of hyphenated words is unattractive and hard to read, you should limit the number of consecutive hyphens to 2.

The Hyphenation Zone option tells PageMaker the maximum amount of white space you will accept at the end of a line. It therefore does not apply to justified text. The default zone is 3 picas ($\frac{1}{2}$ inch). If you want a less ragged right margin, enter a smaller value for Hyphenation Zone; it will hyphenate more words. To hyphenate fewer words, enter a larger value for Hyphenation Zone.

Figure 6.22 shows three paragraphs, each with a different hyphenation zone. The first paragraph has a 2-pica hyphenation zone, the second has the default zone of 3 picas, and the third has a 4-pica zone.

FIGURE 6.22: *Comparing hyphenation zones*

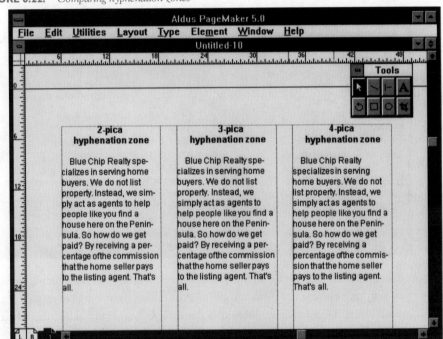

AVOIDING WIDOWS AND ORPHANS

In PageMaker, widows and orphans are straggling words that appear at the top or bottom of a column. A *widow* is the beginning of a paragraph that sits at the bottom of a column. An *orphan* is the end of a paragraph at the top of a column. Figure 6.23 shows a lonely orphan at the top of the column on the right.

By default, PageMaker's widow and orphan controls are turned off. However, you can define exactly how many lines constitute a widow or orphan (1, 2, or 3). For example, if you specify 2 for both the widow and orphan

FIGURE 6.23: *An orphan*

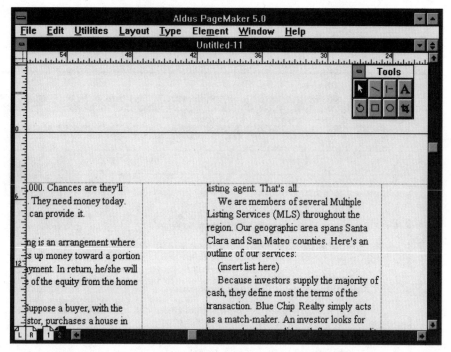

control options in the Paragraph Specifications dialog box, PageMaker will not permit two lines of a paragraph to end up at the top or bottom of a column. Thus, if the first two lines of a paragraph begin at the bottom of a column, the lines will be placed at the top of the next column. Or, if the last two lines of a paragraph land at the top of a column, a line from the previous column will be brought up, so that three lines are at the top.

To add widow or orphan control to existing text, first select the text. Generally, you should select the entire story with Ctrl+A. Otherwise, fixing a widow or orphan in one location may cause one to appear elsewhere.

When widow or orphan control is activated, your columns may end up with ragged bottoms, but most designers prefer ragged bottoms to widows and orphans. In fact, the white space created from ragged bottoms might contribute to a friendlier, more open feeling to your page.

Note that single-line paragraphs, such as subheads, are *not* considered widows. So, even if you have widow/orphan control turned on, your subheads might fall at the bottom of the column. However, PageMaker offers a different way to avoid this kind of problem, as described in the next section.

PARAGRAPH AND LINE BREAKS

The Paragraph Specifications dialog box offers a variety of options for controlling your paragraph and line breaks.

The Keep with Next__Lines option in the Paragraph Specifications dialog box will prevent your subheads from being stranded at the bottom of a column. It essentially glues two paragraphs together so they won't be separated. When you check this option, the number 1 automatically appears as the number of lines. This setting works fine as long as the paragraph of body text is indeed on the next line. If an extra carriage return somehow found its way between the subhead and body text, the Keep with Next value would have to be 2 lines.

The Keep Lines Together option prevents a paragraph from being split between columns. This option is ideal for tables whose lines shouldn't be separated. If you don't want any paragraphs to be split between columns, you could select the entire story and specify this formatting option. (Keep in mind that your columns will be very uneven and your text will probably flow onto more pages.)

To start a particular section of your story on a new page or column, use the Page Break Before or the Column Break Before option. Click in the single paragraph that should appear at the top of the page or column before turning on the option. These types of breaks are sometimes referred to as *hard*, or *forced*, breaks. Your other column and page breaks are *soft*, and their positions will vary according to the amount and format of text in the column.

The position of a hard break is always the same. It appears before the paragraph formatted with Page Break Before or Column Break Before.

CONTROLLING LINE BREAKS

Version 5.0 has an option for controlling line breaks; the Break and No Break options are located in the Type Specifications dialog box (Ctrl+T). If you don't want a line break at a certain location in your text, you can select the text and turn on No Break. When you do this, the text you selected is essentially glued together and will not split onto multiple lines.

The No Break option is commonly used to keep dates from separating onto two lines; for example, with the date *May 5, 1993*, you wouldn't want *May* at the end of one line and *5, 1993* at the beginning of the next. By selecting the date and turning on No Break, you can ensure that the date will not be split. Figure 6.24 shows an example of this. Other cases when you might want to use the No Break option are with phone numbers (to prevent the area code from splitting from the rest of the number), times (to keep the a.m. or p.m. with the time), numbers containing dashes(such as a part number or social security number), as well as words with hard hyphens (such as *hit-and-run* or *brush-off*).

FIGURE 6.24: *In the first paragraph, the date is split onto two lines; in the second paragraph, the No Break option was used to keep the date on one line.*

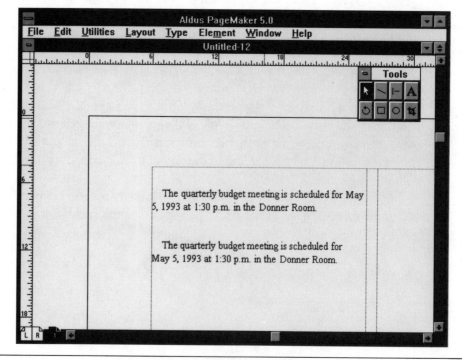

SUMMARY

When we refer to paragraph formatting, we are talking about commands that affect entire paragraphs, not single lines or characters. Alignment, indents, tabs, hyphenation, and extra space above and below are some of the ways you can format your paragraphs.

One of the topics discussed in this chapter is not actually a paragraph format: leading. Because leading is closely associated with the type size, this specification is officially a character format, and it is an option in the Type Specifications dialog box. However, except in rare cases, a paragraph has the same leading throughout.

In the next chapter, you will learn how to apply both character and paragraph formats quickly and uniformly throughout a publication.

HANDS-ON PRACTICE: FORMATTING PARAGRAPHS IN THE BROCHURE

This exercise continues with the brochure that was started in Chapter 5. In this portion of the chapter, you will do the following:

- ➤ Type centered text on the cover page
- ➤ Indent the first line of each paragraph of body text
- ➤ Type a bulleted list with hanging indents
- ➤ Type and set tabs for a three-column table
- ➤ Adjust the leading of body text, subheads, and the table
- ➤ Add space above the table and subheads

CENTERING TEXT ON THE BROCHURE COVER PAGE

In the following steps, you will type and center the paragraphs on the cover page of the brochure.

1. Open the BROCHURE publication you created in Chapter 5 and display page 1. Or, you can open the file BROCH6.PM5 in the C:\PM5PUBS directory.

2. Activate the text tool and click at the top of the second column.

3. Specify the font as Arial, the size as 36 points, and the type style as Bold.

4. Pull down the Type menu and choose Alignment.

5. From the cascading menu, choose Align Center. The cursor centers itself between the column guides.

6. Type **Picture Yourself in Your New House!** Let the text wrap, and PageMaker will automatically center it as you type. Compare your title to the one shown in Figure 6.25.

FIGURE 6.25: *The centered title on the brochure's cover page*

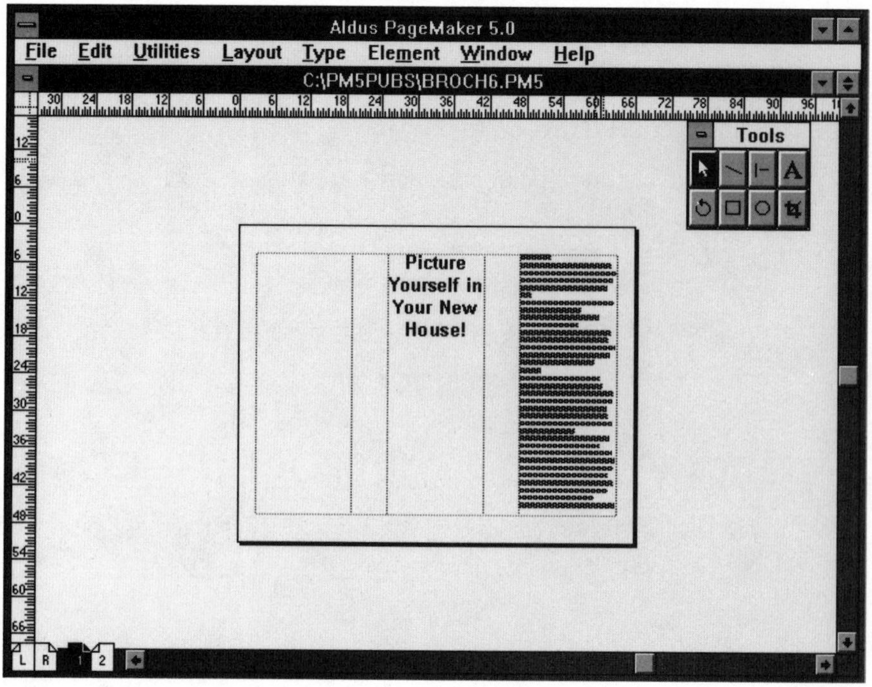

Now you will center the company name at the bottom of the cover page. This time, you'll enter the text and then format it.

7. Click right above the bottom column guide in the second column, and switch to Actual Size view.

8. Type **Blue Chip Realty**.

To establish consistency between the brochure and the letterhead you created in Chapter 4, the company name should be formatted the same way in both publications.

9. Select the text and specify the font as Arial, the size as 20 points, and the type style as Bold. Also turn on the Small Caps case option.

10. Press Ctrl+Shift+C to center the company name.

11. Switch to the pointer tool and move the text block so that the baseline of the text is aligned with the bottom margin guide, as shown in Figure 6.26.

JUSTIFYING THE BROCHURE TEXT

To see how the brochure body text looks when it is justified, follow these steps:

1. Switch to the text tool and click anywhere in the text in the third column.

2. Pull down the Edit menu and choose Select All (or press Ctrl+A).

3. To see that all the text in the story is selected, go to page 2.

4. Press Ctrl+Shift+J to justify the selected text.

Notice that the story is a little shorter when it is justified. However, the brochure has enough space for its contents, and Blue Chip Realty wants to project a warmer and friendlier image, so you should switch back to left-aligned paragraphs.

5. Make sure the story is still selected, and press Ctrl+Shift+L to return to the default left alignment.

FIGURE 6.26: *The company name aligned at the bottom margin guide*

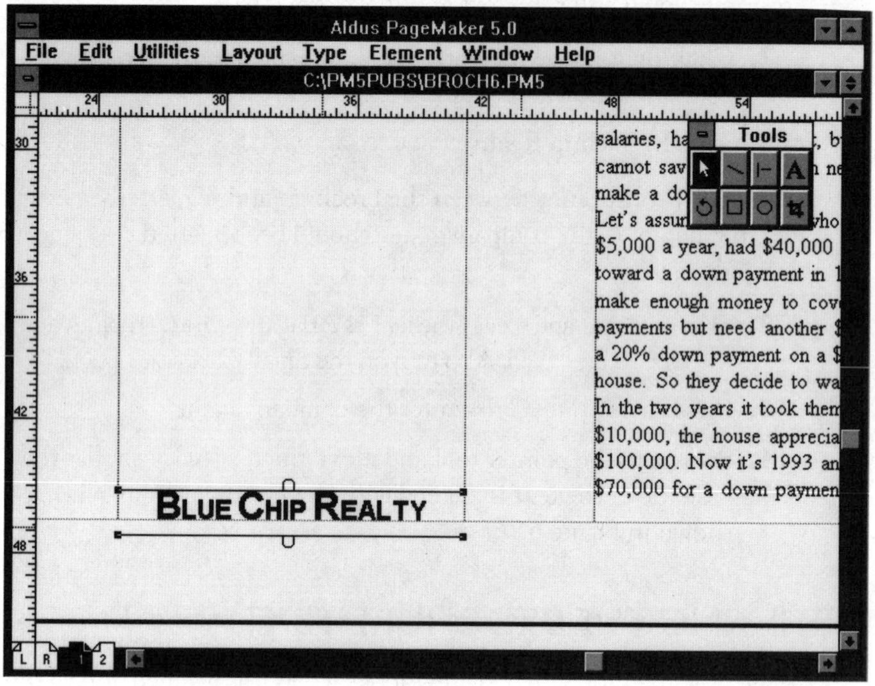

INDENTING THE BROCHURE PARAGRAPHS

In the following steps, you'll set a 1-pica first-line indent for the brochure body text. Since you know the numeric value of the indent, you can either set the indent in the Paragraph Specifications dialog box or in the control palette.

NOTE

If your default measurement system is not picas, you will need to go to Preferences dialog box to change it.

Follow these steps to set the indent:

1. Make sure the main story is still selected.

2. Pull down the Type menu and choose Paragraph (or press Ctrl+M).

3. In the Indents section in the dialog box, next to First, type **1**.

4. Choose OK.

5. If necessary, switch to 75% view to see the indents.

Figure 6.27 shows some of the indented paragraphs on page 2. Notice that every paragraph is indented, even the subheads that aren't supposed to be. You could remove the subhead's indent now by selecting each heading and changing the first-line indent to zero. However, we will be adding other formatting to the subheads later, so let's wait and do all the subhead formatting at once.

FIGURE 6.27: *Paragraphs with a 1-pica first-line indent*

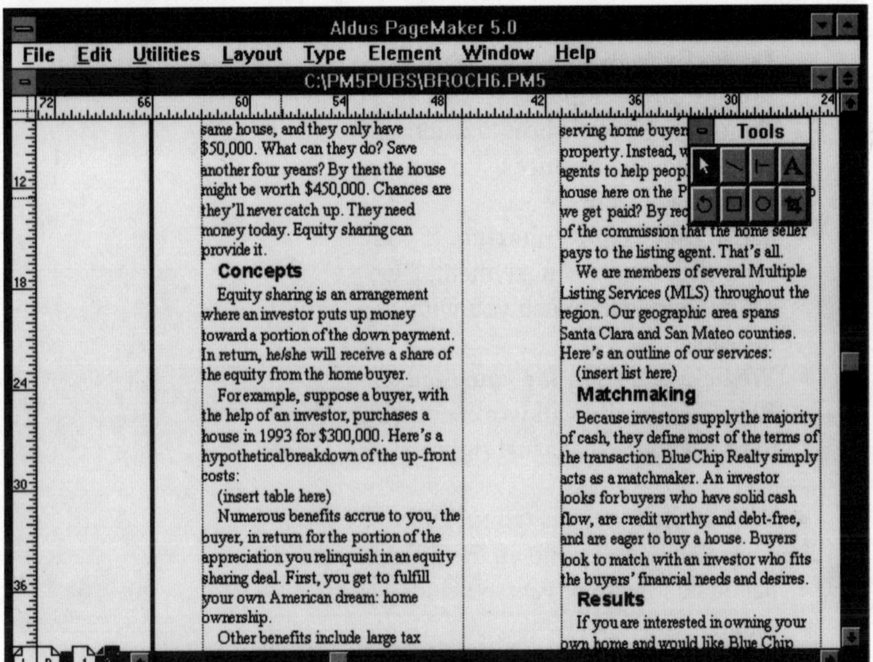

TYPING A BULLETED LIST

Figure 6.28 shows a bulleted list with hanging indents that needs to be inserted into the brochure. Follow these steps to type the bulleted list:

1. Select the text (*insert list here*), which is in the second column of page 2, and delete it. You should still have a blank line, and the cursor should be on this line.

2. Press Ctrl+I to display the Indents/Tabs dialog box and ruler.

3. Hold down Shift and drag the left indent to 2p0.

4. Click on the first-line indent symbol. If necessary, drag it until the Position field reads −1p0.

FIGURE 6.28: *A bulleted list with hanging indents*

- **We help determine your price range.** By analyzing your income and savings, Blue Chip Realty uses a computerized worksheet to determine the range of home prices you can reasonably afford.
- **We arrange equity sharing.** If you need cash for a down payment, Blue Chip Realty will match you with an investor.
- **We help you shop for your house.** Blue Chip Realty will work with you to find a house that's just right for you.
- **We handle the transaction.** Blue Chip Realty will write up the offer, negotiate to your advantage, and arrange inspections.
- **We hand you the house keys.**

5. To set a tab at the same spot as the left indent, place the mouse pointer on the left indent symbol and click once. The text box should read 2p0. Then click on the Position button and choose Add Tab.

A tab symbol appears. Note that custom tabs have different symbols from the default tabs. Your ruler should match the one shown in Figure 6.29.

FIGURE 6.29: *A ruler set for hanging indents*

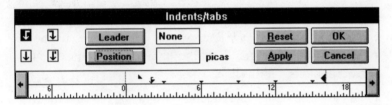

6. Click on OK.

The cursor is already at the first-line indent. You are now ready to type the bulleted list.

7. Press Ctrl+Shift+8. This key combination is PageMaker's code for inserting a bullet.

8. Press Tab.

9. Press Ctrl+Shift+B to turn on the bold type style and type **We help determine your price range.** Press Ctrl+Shift+B to turn off the bold style.

10. Type the rest of the paragraph: **By analyzing your income and savings, Blue Chip Realty uses a computerized worksheet to determine the range of home prices you can reasonably afford.**

11. Press Enter to complete the paragraph. The tab and indent settings from the preceding paragraph automatically carry forward to the next paragraph when you press Enter.

12. Repeat steps 7 through 11 to enter the remaining bulleted items shown in Figure 6.28. Do not press Enter after the last item; if you did, delete the blank line.

13. Save the file.

SETTING UP AND TYPING THE TABLE

Now you will set up and enter a three-column table, which requires two right-aligned tabs. Follow these steps to add the table to your brochure:

1. On page 2, switch to the text tool and Actual Size view.

2. Select the text (*insert table here*), which is in the first column of page 2, and delete it. You should still have a blank line, and the cursor should be on this line.

3. Press Ctrl+I to display the Indents/Tabs dialog box and ruler.

4. Drag the first-line indent to 0p0 to remove the indent.

5. Move the pointer to the 10-pica mark on the ruler and click. A left-aligned tab symbol appears. If you didn't click in the right spot, you can drag the symbol to 10p0.

6. To change the tab stop alignment, click on the right-align tab icon. (This icon is shown in the margin.)

7. Set a right-aligned tab stop at 14p0.

8. Click on OK.

Before you begin typing the table, you should consider your type specifications. For this table, a 10-point font will work fine.

9. Specify the font as Times New Roman, the size as 10 points, and the type style as Bold.

10. Press Tab to go to the first tab stop, and then type **Investor**. As you type, the text moves to the left. Because the tab is right-aligned, the text is lined up on the right.

11. Press Tab to go to the second tab stop and type **Buyer**. Press Ctrl+Shift+B to turn off the Bold style. These bold entries are the headings for the table's columns.

Do not press Enter! If you already did, press Backspace to remove it.

12. Press Shift+Enter to go to a new line without creating a new paragraph.

13. Press Shift+Enter again to create a blank line.

14. Beginning at the left column guide, enter the following table. The most important thing to remember is to press Shift+Enter at the end of each line instead of Enter. But do not press Shift+Enter or Enter at the end of the last line.

Down Payment	$40,000	$20,000
Closing Costs	5,000	5,000
House Payments	None	All
% of Appreciation	40	60

ADJUSTING A TAB STOP IN THE TABLE

While the column spacing is sufficient, the extra space at the end of each line indicates there's enough room to spread the columns out a little more. You can do this by manipulating the existing tab stops.

1. Click anywhere in the table and press Ctrl+I to display the Indents/Tabs dialog box and ruler.

2. Drag the second tab symbol to 15p0.

3. Click on OK. Now the columns are spaced evenly, as shown in Figure 6.30.

4. Save your file.

If only part of your table contains the new tab settings, you have hard returns in your table instead of line breaks. To replace a return with a line

FIGURE 6.30: *The table, with adjusted tab settings*

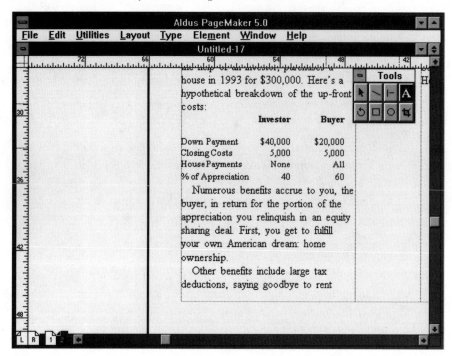

break, place the cursor at the beginning of the line following the hard return, press Backspace, and then press Shift+Enter.

ADJUSTING VERTICAL SPACING IN THE BROCHURE

So far, we have been ignoring the vertical spacing in the brochure. None of the elements on the page (body text, subheads, or the columnar table) has any extra space around it.

In our brochure, we are going to use 14 for the body text leading. Fourteen-point leading is just slightly larger than the automatic leading for 11-point type (13.2). Each subhead will also have 14 point leading and 14 points of extra space around it in order to keep the elements on the leading grid. Thus, 14 is our "magic number."

Specifying Fixed Leading

Follow these steps to change the leading of the body text and the table:

1. Switch to Fit in Window view on page 2. This is only so that you can see how the length of the text automatically adjusts with the leading change.

2. Click anywhere in the story with the text tool.

3. Press Ctrl+A to select all the text.

4. Pull down the Type menu and choose Leading.

5. From the cascading menu, choose 14. The text adjusts to 14-point leading.

6. Switch to 75% view and select the table (you can triple-click on it since it is one paragraph). Notice that there is currently too much space between lines in the table when 10-point type has 14-point leading.

7. Specify 12-point leading.

There is still too much space between the column headings and the rest of the table. You should now adjust the leading of this single line.

8. Double-click on the blank line to select it.

9. From the Leading cascading menu, choose Other.

10. Type 2.

11. Press Enter.

12. Click elsewhere in the text to unselect the blank line.

Your table should now be spaced as shown in Figure 6.31. You'll add space above and below the table in the next section.

Now, let's reflow the extra text from column 2 into column 3:

13. With the pointer tool, click on the text block in column two.

14. Drag the bottom window shade up so that it is even with the bottom margin guide.

FIGURE 6.31: *The table with the new leading values*

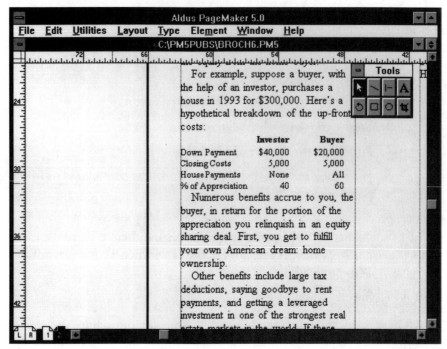

15. To flow the extra text into the next column, click on the triangle in column 2's bottom window shade, use the scroll bar to display the top of column 3, and then click at the top of the column. The text now flows into this column. (Text flow is discussed in more detail in Chapter 8.)

Adding Space above the Subheads

The best way to control spacing around subheads is with PageMaker's space before/after attributes. Let's add 14 points of space above the subheads:

1. Click on one of the subheads with the text tool.

2. Press Ctrl+M to display the Paragraph Specifications dialog box.

3. To eliminate the paragraph indent, type 0 next to First.

4. Next to Before, type **0p14** (14 points).

5. Press Enter. Your subhead should be spaced as shown in Figure 6.32.

6. Repeat steps 1 through 5 for the remaining five subheads.

FIGURE 6.32: *The properly spaced subheads*

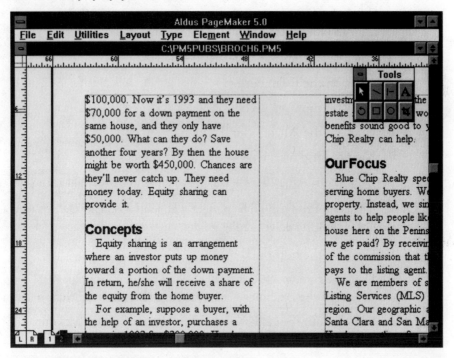

Aligning the Table to the Grid

The table needs extra space around it. Since you typed it as a single paragraph, you can specify the paragraph spacing as you would for any other paragraph. Also, because the table uses a different leading from the rest of the publication, you will need to use the Align to Grid feature to keep the page elements on the leading grid.

Follow these steps to add spacing and then align the paragraph after the table to the leading grid:

1. With the text tool, click anywhere in the table and press Ctrl+M.

2. Specify **0p6** before and **0p6** after, and then choose OK.

Now that the paragraph spacing is set, you can return to the Paragraph Specifications dialog box and find the Align to Grid option.

3. Click in the table and press Ctrl+M.

4. Click on the Rules button.

5. Click on the Options button.

6. Click on the Align to Grid option.

7. Next to Grid Size, type **14**.

8. Hold down Alt and click on OK to close all three dialog boxes.

Now all the baselines should be perfectly aligned. You can see this in your document by pulling down a ruler guide.

9. Click on the horizontal ruler.

10. Drag the ruler guide down to a line of type underneath the table. All the baselines across the page should sit on this guide.

11. Switch to the pointer tool and drag the ruler guide back into the ruler.

CONTROLLING PARAGRAPH AND COLUMN BREAKS

You can look through your brochure for single-line widows and orphans in 75% view. Regardless of whether you find any, let's turn on the widow/orphan control. That way, if you change the page layout in the future, you won't have to worry about straggling lines.

1. Select the entire story with the text tool.

2. Press Ctrl+M and turn on Widow Control and Orphan Control.

3. Click on OK.

Now you will use the paragraph break options to control the breaks in the brochure.

4. Select a subhead and press Ctrl+M.

5. Turn on the Keep with Next option and click on OK. This will keep the subhead with the body text.

6. Repeat steps 4 and 5 for each subhead.

7. Select the table, press Ctrl+M, turn on the Keep Lines Together option, and click on OK. Now the list will never be divided between columns.

8. Turn on the Keep Lines Together option for the paragraphs in the bulleted list.

9. Press Ctrl+S to save the file.

10. Press Ctrl+P to print the brochure.

Going in Style

*f*ast
tracks

To display the style palette: 253

Choose Window ➤ Style Palette.

To create a style: 254

Format a paragraph with the desired character and paragraph attributes.
Choose Type ➤ Define Styles and click on the New button. Enter a
name and choose OK.

To create a style with the control palette: 255

Format a paragraph with the desired character and paragraph attributes.
Select the paragraph-style field (for example, click and drag across the
current entry in the field) and type the new name. Press Enter and
choose OK to add the style.

To apply a style: 257

Select the paragraphs to be formatted and click on the style name in the
style palette.

To apply styles with the control palette: 258

Select the paragraphs to be formatted. Click and hold on the arrow in
the paragraph-style field and drag to the desired style name.

To edit an existing style: 260

Choose Type ➤ Define Styles. Select the style name from the list and click on the Edit button. Choose the appropriate button—Type, Para, Tabs, or Hyph—depending on the type of formatting you wish to revise. Make the change and close the dialog boxes.

To display style names in the Story Editor: 264

In the Story Editor, choose Story ➤ Display Style Names. The names appear in a sidebar to the left of the text.

To search and replace style names: 265

Display the story in the Story Editor, and choose Utilities ➤ Change. Click on the Attributes button. On the left side of the dialog box (labeled Find) display the Para Style drop-down list and select the style you wish to find. In the right side of the dialog box (labeled Change) display the other Para Style drop-down list, and select the replacement style.

To copy styles from another publication: 266

Display the publication into which you wish to copy the styles. Pull down the Type menu and choose Define Styles. Click on the Copy button, and select the name of the publication that contains the styles you want to copy.

N THE PREVIOUS CHAPTERS, you've learned how PageMaker formats blocks of text and individual paragraphs. Now you will take a giant leap forward and learn how to use a very powerful method of formatting: paragraph styles. By creating and applying styles, you not only make formatting more efficient, but you also give yourself the flexibility to reformat your publication quickly and easily.

THE BENEFITS OF USING STYLES

Paragraph styles allow you to automate the formatting, and the inevitable reformatting, of your publication. If you worked through the Hands-On Practice exercise in Chapter 6, you had to individually format each subhead in the brochure with its specifications: 14-point Arial bold with 14 points of leading, 14 points of space above, and kept with the next paragraph. With styles, you only have to format one paragraph. You can then apply this exact formatting to any other paragraph with just two mouse clicks.

Imagine that you decide that your publication's body text would look better in a 12-point type size instead of a 10-point type. Making this formatting change without styles would be a tedious process, requiring you to increase the point size of each group of consecutive paragraphs of body text (making sure you don't change the type size of subheads or other non-body text paragraphs). However, if you had assigned a style to all the paragraphs of body text, you could simply edit the style to automatically change the type size of every paragraph of body text.

Another benefit to using styles is that they ensure consistent formatting. When you are formatting paragraphs one at a time, you risk forgetting to turn on a particular option. Although you might not notice this inconsistent formatting right away, you probably will see it clearly in the final print-out. With styles, on the other hand, every paragraph associated with a certain style name will be formatted identically.

The set of styles in a publication is called a *style sheet*. This might sound like the styles are stored in a separate file, but they are not; styles are stored within the publication.

USING THE STYLE PALETTE

While you are formatting your publication and creating styles, you will want to turn on the *style palette*. This is a box that lists the styles contained in your publication. The name of the style of the currently selected paragraph is highlighted. You can use the style palette to create, assign, and edit styles. Figure 7.1 shows an example of a style palette. To display this palette, pull down the Window menu and choose Style Palette, or press Ctrl+Y. Like the toolbox, the style palette can be dragged anywhere on the screen to keep it out of the way of your document. It also can be lengthened if your publication has many style names.

FIGURE 7.1: *A style palette*

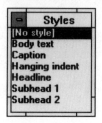

In every publication, there are several default style names: Body text, Caption, Hanging indent, Headline, Subhead 1, and Subhead 2. You can use these styles as they are, edit their formatting specifications, or delete them. The first item in the palette, [No style], applies to paragraphs to which no style is assigned.

CREATING A STYLE SHEET

Creating a style is easy. You simply use the Define Styles dialog box to assign a style name to a formatted paragraph, and the formatting contained in that paragraph is then associated with the name. The style contains instructions on character formatting (such as font, size, leading, and type style), as well as paragraph formatting (such as indents, tabs, space above and below, hyphenation, widow/orphan control, and column breaks). Note that only one font can be associated with a style.

You can create styles at any point in the design and layout process, but the earlier the better. If the publication already has text, you can create the style as you come across the various elements. For example, the first time you encounter a subhead, format it as fully as you can, and then create a style for it. You can always refine the style later.

1. With the text tool, click anywhere in the formatted paragraph for which you wish to create a style.

2. Pull down the Type menu and choose Define Styles (or press Ctrl+3).

When the dialog box appears, [Selection] is highlighted. This indicates the style is based on the formatting in the selected paragraph. The paragraph's formats are listed at the bottom of the dialog box. We'll explain how to decipher and change these formats in the "Editing a Style" section.

3. Click on the New button. The Edit Style dialog box, shown in Figure 7.2, appears.

4. Next to Name, type a name for the style (up to 31 characters).

5. Hold down Alt and click on OK to close both dialog boxes.

FIGURE 7.2: *The Edit Style dialog box*

```
Edit style                          [    OK    ]

Name:     [                    ]    [  Cancel  ]

Based on:  No style          [±]

Next style: Same style        [±]    [  Type... ]

next: Same style + face: Arial + bold + italic +    [  Para... ]
size: 14 + leading: auto + flush left +
hyphenation                                          [  Tabs... ]

                                     [  Hyph... ]
```

The new style is now listed in your style palette. However, this style is not yet applied to any paragraph, not even the current one, because creating a style does not apply that style. See the section "Assigning Styles" for information on applying styles to paragraphs.

PageMaker offers a couple other ways to create a style. These techniques bypass the menu and are even faster than the Ctrl+3 keyboard shortcut. The first shortcut uses the keyboard: Hold down Ctrl and click on [No style] in the style palette. This takes you directly to the Edit Style dialog box.

Version
5.0   The second shortcut uses Version 5.0's control palette. The style field is available in the palette's paragraph view, so you may have to click on the ¶ button to see this field. The paragraph style field is marked in Figure 7.3. To create a new style in the control palette, select the paragraph style field (for example, click and drag across the current entry in the field) and type

FIGURE 7.3: *The paragraph style field*

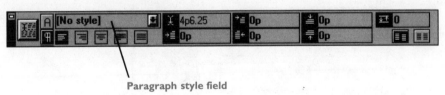

Paragraph style field

the new name. When you press Enter, PageMaker will display the following message:

```
Style name does not exist.
Press OK to add this style.
```

After you click on OK, the style name will be added *and* the style is automatically applied to the currently selected paragraph(s). This is the only technique that creates and assigns style names in one step.

BASING A STYLE ON ANOTHER STYLE

The Based On option in the Edit Style dialog box creates a link between the current style and an existing style. When you change the format of the Based On style, you automatically change the format of all styles that are linked to it.

Suppose your publication has a special style for the first paragraph after a subheading—it has the same font, size, and leading as your body text but the paragraph does not have a first-line indent. By linking the First Para style to the Body Text style, you will save time when you make formatting changes. If you change the type size associated with the Body Text style, this change will be automatically reflected in the First Para style.

Figure 7.4 shows the Edit Style dialog box for a style named First Para that is based on the Body Text style. In the format list at the bottom of the

FIGURE 7.4: *The First Para style is based on the Body Text style*

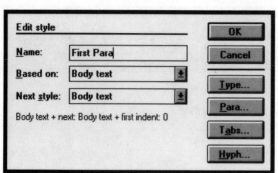

dialog box, all formatting characteristics that match those in the Body Text style are replaced with the style name. The formatting specification that is not a part of Body Text—the first-line indent—is still listed.

SPECIFYING THE NEXT STYLE

The Next Style option in the Edit Style dialog box specifies the style of the paragraph that follows the current style. The default setting for the Next Style option is Same Style. This setting is appropriate for body text because one paragraph of body text usually follows another. Sometimes, however, a certain style will always proceed another. For example, after a subhead, you will usually have a paragraph of body text.

 oTe

The Next Style setting has no effect when you apply styles to existing text. The only time it takes effect is when you are creating *new* paragraphs, in either layout or story view. For example, if you formatted text with the Subhead style and pressed Enter to go to the next paragraph, that next paragraph would be formatted with the Body Text style. But if the paragraphs were already typed, assigning the Subhead Style would *not* format the next paragraph with the Body Text style.

ASSIGNING STYLES

Once you have created a style for every element in your publication, you can begin assigning styles. This is sometimes called *paragraph tagging* (*tag* is another word for style). The fastest way to assign styles is to click on the paragraph with the text tool, and then click on the name in the style palette. You can also use the Style option on the Type pull-down menu, but the style palette is quicker and more convenient.

Version
5.0

If your control palette is displayed, you can choose the name from the paragraph style list. The field displays [No style] unless a particular style has been assigned. To display the list, click on the down arrow in the paragraph style field and hold the mouse button down. You can then drag to the de-sired style name and release the mouse button when the name is highlighted.

Since most of the paragraphs in a story will be some sort of body text style, we recommend that you assign this style first, to all the text. (Ctrl+A will select all text in a story.) You can then go through the story and assign the other styles (heads, subheads, and so forth) on a paragraph by para-graph basis. In most cases, we have found this method to be the fastest way to tag a story. However, do *not* apply a style to all the text until you have created styles for the other items! If you do, you will lose all formatting you may have done to the other paragraphs.

An alternative technique for assigning styles is to start at the beginning of the story, and tag the paragraphs as you come to them. When consecu-tive paragraphs use the same style, you can select the text by clicking and dragging across the paragraphs; when you click on a style in the palette, the same style will be applied to all selected paragraphs.

ASSIGNING TAGS IN YOUR WORD PROCESSOR

If you are aware of the structure of your publication as you are typing a story in your word processor, you can embed the style names right in the document. Or, if your word processor has its own style feature, you can as-sign the tags while you are creating the document. Then, when you import the file into PageMaker, the paragraphs will already be tagged. All you have to do is define the formatting associated with each style.

Chapter 8's section on importing styles describes exactly how this works.

WATCHING FOR LOCAL FORMATTING

Local formatting refers to formatting specifications within a paragraph that are not part of the style. For instance, an italicized word is considered local formatting. You apply a local format by selecting and formatting the text. Your changes have no effect on other paragraphs with the same style.

As you are creating your styles, pay close attention to where the cursor is positioned in the paragraph. If the cursor is on a character that is locally formatted (in bold or italic, for example), this formatting will be part of the style. Then, when you apply the style, the entire paragraph will have this unintentional formatting.

When you see a plus sign next to the style name in the style palette, the current paragraph contains some kind of local formatting. You will only see the plus sign when the cursor is positioned on the locally formatted text. In Figure 7.5, the cursor is on a boldfaced word, and the style palette indicates the local formatting by a + after the style name (Bullet List).

FIGURE 7.5:   *Bullet List+ indicates that the cursor is located in text that contains local formatting*

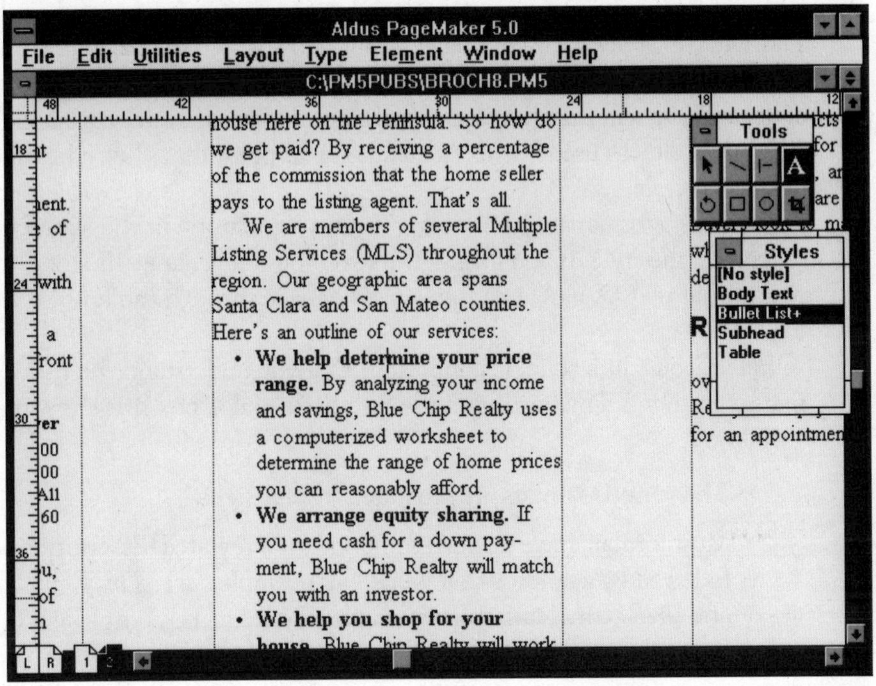

EDITING A STYLE

When you change one of the formatting characteristics associated with a style, the change affects all the paragraphs that have been assigned that style. This global and automatic reformatting lets you quickly and easily play what-if games with your page layout. How would the page look if the subheads were in Avant Garde instead of Helvetica? Edit the Subhead style, and you will instantly see this change. How would the page look if a 12-point font was used for text instead of a 10-point font? Just edit the Body Text style.

To make a formatting change to a style, you do not edit the actual text; you revise the style. If you format the text, you only change the local format of that text. A global change must be made through the Edit Style dialog box.

Before you edit a style, it's important that you understand the list of formats it contains. The bottom of the Edit Style dialog box lists the formats as follows:

→ The various formats are separated by plus signs.

→ Most formats have a short, sometimes abbreviated, description followed by a colon and a value. For example, *face: Tms Rmn* and *size: 11* indicate the paragraph is typed in 11-point Times Roman.

➤ Formats that don't require a value are simply listed with a brief description. For example, *flush left* indicates the text is left-aligned.

To revise the formatting associated with a style, click on the appropriate button—Type, Para, Tabs, or Hyph—and make your changes.

One way to get to the Edit Style dialog box is by choosing Define Styles on the Type menu. You then select the style name from a list and click on the Edit button. A faster way is to hold down the Ctrl key as you click on the style name in the style palette.

REMOVING STYLES

If you don't plan on using the default styles in your publication, you should delete them so they won't be confused with the ones you will create. Or, if you created a style that you no longer need, you can remove it.

To remove style names, follow these basic steps:

1. Pull down the Type menu and choose Define Styles (or press Ctrl+3). You will see the Define Styles dialog box.

2. Click on the style name to be removed.

3. Click on the Remove command button.

4. Repeat steps 2 and 3 to remove any other style names.

5. Click on OK. The styles you removed are no longer listed in the style palette. If the deleted style had been assigned to a paragraph, that paragraph has no style associated with it now.

If you remove a style name accidentally, and you discover the error before you choose OK in the Define Styles dialog box, click on the Cancel button. Any styles you removed will be restored.

To eliminate the default styles from all new publications you create, remove the style names when no publication is open. Your new publications will then have empty style palettes.

LISTING STYLE NAMES

Version 5.0

Version 5.0 includes two Aldus Additions that produce lists of style names used in a publication. The first one, called List Styles Used, displays the styles used in a particular story; Figure 7.6 shows an example of this. Note that the list indicates the number of paragraphs that are tagged with each name. This list will clue you in as to whether some of the paragraphs are tagged incorrectly. For example, you may see a style name on the list that doesn't belong in the story. Or, if every paragraph is supposed to be tagged and the list comes up with two paragraphs that don't have a style name, you will immediately know that you need to tag these paragraphs. However, the list does not tell you which paragraphs are tagged with which names. For this detective work, you'll need to use the Story Editor, as described in the section "Using Styles in the Story Editor."

To use the List Styles Used Addition, use the pointer tool to select one of the text blocks in the story you want to check. It doesn't matter which block you select but you'll get an error message if you don't select any blocks or if you select more than one. Then choose Utilities ➤ Aldus Additions ➤ List Styles Used. PageMaker will display the list of style names in its own text block. You can zoom in and read this list, move it around, and when you're finished, delete it.

FIGURE 7.6: *A list of style names used in a story*

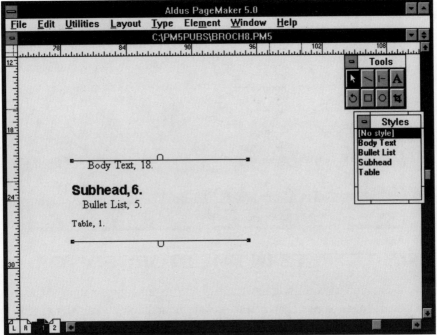

Another Aldus Addition, Display Pub Info, will list all the style names in the entire publication. As Figure 7.7 shows, this dialog box lists each style name, what it's based on, and its next style. This addition will also give you two other pieces of information about the publication—the fonts used and the files to which the document is linked. If you're interested in only the style names, turn off the Fonts and Links check boxes at the bottom of the dialog box.

Unlike the List Styles Used addition, Display Pub Info does not create a text block of the style name data. However, there is a way to view and print the information outside of the dialog box: with the Save command button. When you click on this button, you will be prompted for a file name; the file will be stored with an .INF extension. To view this text file, you can bring it into your word processor or place it in a PageMaker publication.

FIGURE 7.7: *A list of style names used in a publication*

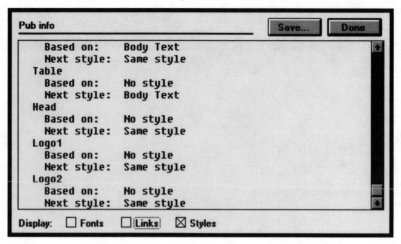

USING STYLES IN THE STORY EDITOR

When you use the style palette in the Story Editor, you can see the style names next to each paragraph—a feature unavailable in the standard layout view. Another advantage of styles in the Story Editor is that you can find and change style names.

DISPLAYING STYLE NAMES

In story view, style names appear in a sidebar to the left of the text. This bar only appears when the Display Style Names option on the Story menu is turned on. Figure 7.8 shows a story with the style names displayed. When a paragraph has no style associated with it, a small dot appears in the style area.

You can select a paragraph by clicking on the style name in the sidebar.

FIGURE 7.8: *The style names are in a sidebar to the left of the paragraphs*

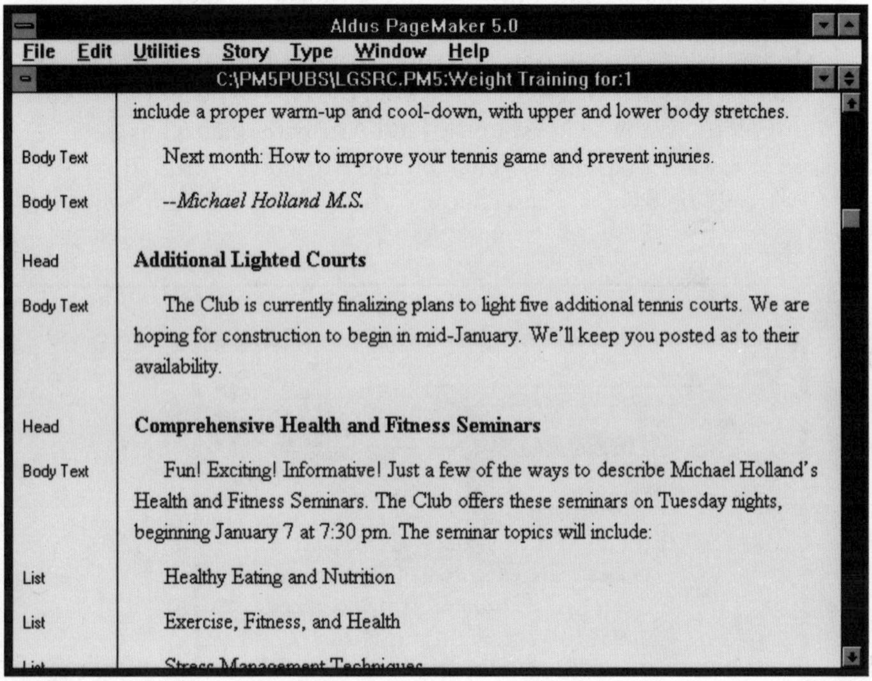

As in layout view, you can assign styles by clicking on the style name in the style palette. Keep in mind that you won't actually see the formatting until you return to layout view. Use the style sidebar to keep track of the styles.

FINDING AND CHANGING STYLE NAMES

The Story Editor's Find and Change commands can search for and replace paragraph styles. Here are a few examples of how you can use these commands:

➤ Use the Find command to quickly discover whether a certain style is used in the story. (It's a good idea to do this before removing a style.)

➤ Search for a subhead style to jump from one section to the next.

➤ If many paragraphs were tagged incorrectly, just replace one style name with another using the Change command.

To locate a style name, click on the Attributes button in the Find (Ctrl+8) dialog box. Then choose the style from the Para Style drop-down list. Figure 7.9 shows the style list in the Find Attributes dialog box.

To replace a style name, click on the Attributes button in the Change (Ctrl+9) dialog box. Then choose the styles from the Para Style lists.

FIGURE 7.9: *The Para Style list in the Find Attributes dialog box*

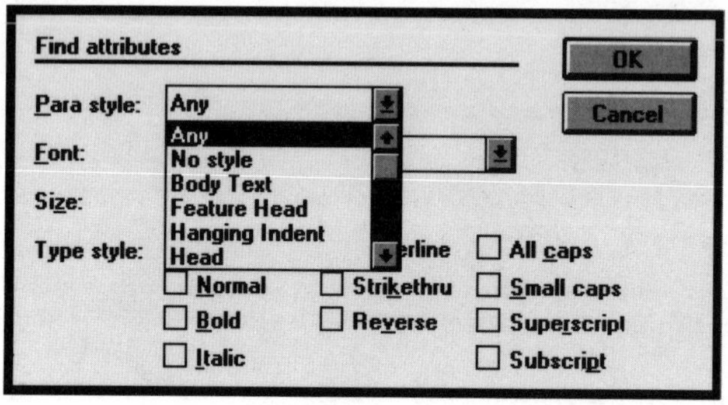

COPYING STYLES
FROM ANOTHER PUBLICATION

Suppose that you have created a flier for one of your clients, and you liked its formatting so much that you want to use the styles in another flier. Rather than recreating these styles, you can simply copy them from the existing publication to the new one. You cannot pick and choose which styles to include; all the styles will be copied.

Follow these general steps to copy styles between publications:

1. Open the publication into which you want to copy the styles.

2. Pull down the Type menu and choose Define Styles.

3. Click on the Copy button.

4. Choose the name of the publication that contains the styles you want to copy.

5. Click on OK.

These styles are added to the current publication's style sheet. You can then edit the styles in the new publication or immediately format the text with these styles. In the case of duplicate style names, you are asked if you want to copy over the existing styles. If you choose OK, the imported styles will replace the existing styles with the same name. If you choose Cancel, none of the styles will be imported.

SUMMARY

In this chapter, you learned that the most efficient way to format a publication is with paragraph styles. Global formatting changes are a couple of clicks away when you have assigned styles to your paragraphs; formatting revisions can be an absolute nightmare without styles.

Not only are styles a big time saver, but they also promote formatting consistency. When you use styles, each subhead is formatted exactly like every other subhead. Styles also make it easier to work with imported text files, as you will see in the next chapter.

HANDS-ON PRACTICE: CREATING STYLES FOR THE BROCHURE

In this practice exercise, you will create and assign the following styles for the Blue Chip Realty brochure:

- ➤ Body Text
- ➤ Subhead
- ➤ Bullet List
- ➤ Table

To begin, follow these steps to open the brochure file and turn on the style palette:

1. Open the BROCHURE.PM5 publication you have worked on in previous chapters. Or, open the file BROCH7 in the C:\PM5PUBS directory.

2. Pull down the Window menu and choose Style Palette, or press Ctrl+Y.

REMOVING THE DEFAULT STYLES

Because we will not be using the default styles in the brochure, you can delete them.

1. Pull down the Type menu and choose Define Styles (or press Ctrl+3). You will see the Define Styles dialog box, as shown in Figure 7.10.

2. Click on the first style name, Body text.

3. Click on the Remove command button.

4. Repeat step 3 to remove the remaining style names.

FIGURE 7.10:   *The Define Styles dialog box*

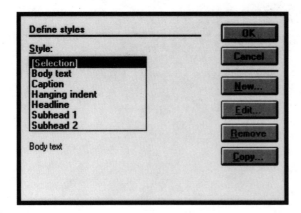

5. Click on OK. The style palette is now empty except for the [No style] item.

CREATING THE BROCHURE STYLES

First, you'll create a style for your body text, appropriately named Body Text.

1. Switch to the text tool and, in 75% view, click anywhere in a paragraph of body text.

2. Pull down the Type menu and choose Define Styles (or press Ctrl+3).

When the dialog box appears, [Selection] is highlighted. This indicates the style is based on the formatting in the selected paragraph.

3. Click on the New button. The Edit Style dialog box, shown in Figure 7.11, appears.

4. Next to Name, type **Body Text**.

5. To finish creating the Body Text style, hold down Alt and click on OK to close both dialog boxes.

FIGURE 7.11: *The Edit Style dialog box for Body Text*

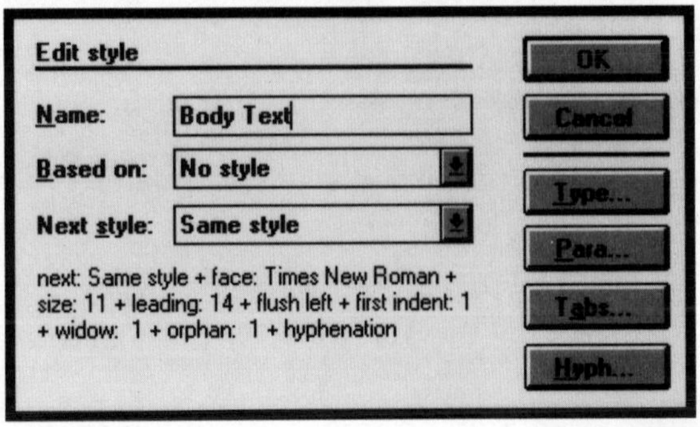

Body Text is now listed in your style palette. However, this style is not yet applied to any paragraphs. (We'll do this later.)

Follow these steps to create the Subhead style:

6. Click on any of the subheads.

7. Press Ctrl+3 to display the Define Styles dialog box.

8. Click on the New button.

9. Type the name **Subhead**.

10. Pull down the drop-down list to the right of Next Style.

11. Select Body Text. Your dialog box should match the one shown in Figure 7.12.

12. To finish creating the Subhead style, close the dialog boxes.

FIGURE 7.12: *The Edit Style dialog box for the Subhead style*

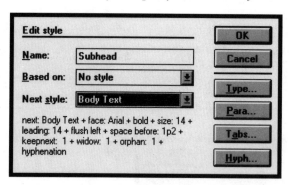

Subhead is now listed along with Body Text in your style palette. Follow these steps to create the Bullet List style:

13. Click anywhere in one of the bulleted paragraphs on page 2, *except* in the first sentence (or the style will have the bold type style associated with it).

14. Press Ctrl+3 and click on the New button in the Define Styles dialog box.

15. Type the name **Bullet List**.

16. Pull down the drop-down list to the right of Based On.

17. Select Body Text. Your Edit Style dialog box should match Figure 7.13.

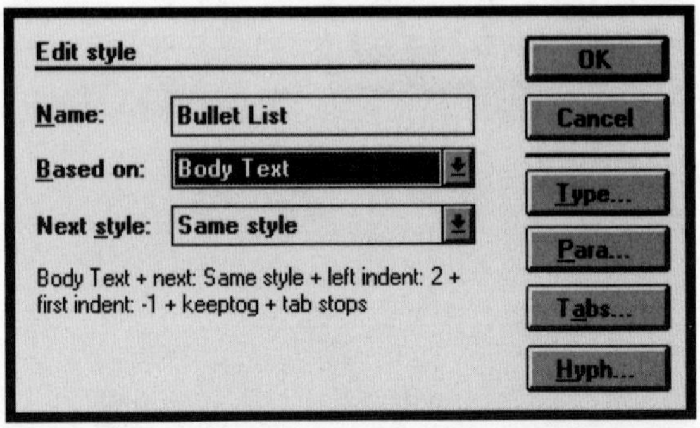

FIGURE 7.13: *The Edit Style dialog box for the Bullet List style*

The format list at the bottom of the dialog box changes to reflect this new setting. All formatting characteristics that match those in the Body Text style are replaced with the style name. The formatting specifications that are not a part of Body Text, such as the hanging indent settings and the tab stop, are still listed.

18. Close the dialog boxes.

Now create the Table style:

19. Click anywhere in the table in the first column of page 2, except in the line with the bold type style.

20. Hold down Ctrl and click on [No style] in the style palette. This takes you directly to the Edit Style dialog box.

21. Type **Table** for the style name.

22. Select Body Text as the Next Style. The dialog box should match the one shown in Figure 7.14.

FIGURE 7.14: *The Edit Style dialog box for the Table style*

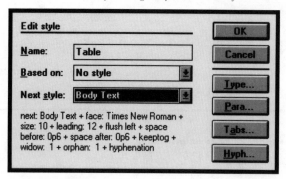

23. Click on OK.

24. Save your file.

APPLYING THE BROCHURE STYLES

Since most of the type is body text, you will assign this style first.

1. Click anywhere in the story with the text tool.

2. Press Ctrl+A to select the entire story.

3. Click on Body Text in the style palette.

All your text is now formatted with the Body Text style, including the subheads, table, and bulleted list. This is not the disaster that it appears to be. You have created styles for these other elements and will soon apply them to restore the formatting.

To format the rest of the brochure, follow these steps:

4. In 75% view, click on one of the subheads.

5. Click on Subhead in the style palette. The paragraph is instantly reformatted.

6. Repeat steps 1 and 2 to reformat the remaining subheads.

If you have trouble formatting a subhead, select it, press F5, and then apply the Subhead style again. This clears any local formatting.

7. The bulleted paragraphs are consecutive, so select all of them together, and then click on Bullet List in the style palette. All the selected paragraphs are formatted at once.

8. Click anywhere in the table, which is a single paragraph, and choose Table from the style palette.

9. The blank line underneath the column headings needs to be formatted to 2-point leading. Select the link and specify this leading.

10. Press Ctrl+S to save the file.

Your publication is now completely tagged and formatted. It should look exactly like it did before you began creating styles. You might be wondering what you have gained from all this work—the end result is exactly the same. The real value of a style sheet becomes apparent when you make formatting changes.

MAKING GLOBAL FORMATTING CHANGES

Let's see how the brochure looks with 12-point body text. By editing the Body Text style, we can change all the paragraphs at once.

1. Hold down Ctrl and click on Body Text in the style palette. You will go directly to the Edit Style dialog box for the Body Text style.

2. Click on the Type button.

3. Change the type size to 12.

4. Close the dialog boxes.

All the body text is now reformatted in 12-point type. The paragraphs in the bulleted list are also in 12-point type because you based the Bullet List style on the Body Text style. If you had not applied styles, you would have had to select each portion of body text and make the formatting change.

You might suspect that the story consumes more space in 12-point type. If you switch to Fit in Window view on page 2, you will see that the story is indeed longer, but it still fits on the page with a little room to spare. (Later in the book, we will use this extra space for a graphic.)

Next, let's change the first-line indent of Body Text to 1.5 picas.

5. Hold down Ctrl and click on Body Text in the style palette.

6. Click on the Para button.

7. Change the first-line indent from 1 to 1.5 picas.

8. Close the dialog boxes.

9. Save the file.

Figure 7.15 shows a paragraph with the new specifications for the Body Text style. The additional indent adds a bit more definition to the body text paragraphs.

You can continue to explore the possibilities. Try changing the font of the Subhead style to Times New Roman. Which do you prefer: Arial or Times? Print the page and see what you think.

FIGURE 7.15: *A paragraph formatted with the new Body Text style*

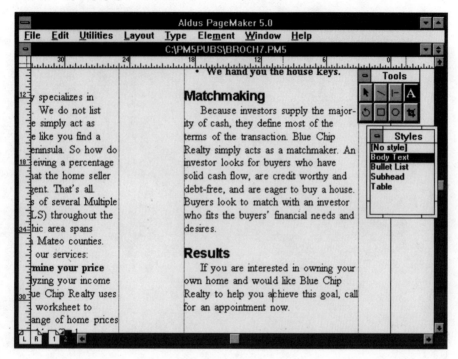

Importing and Flowing Text

fast tracks

To flow text across multiple or partial columns: 295

Place the loaded text gun in the upper-left corner of where you want to place the text. Click and drag a box the size of the desired text block.

To embed style tags in your word processing documents: 298

Type the style name at the beginning of the paragraph, enclosed in angle brackets. You don't need to tag a paragraph if it uses the same style as the preceding paragraph. When importing a tagged file, turn on the Read Tags option in the Place File dialog box.

To import a story from another publication: 304

Open the publication into which you wish to copy the story. Choose File ➤ Place and select the name of the publication. The Place Page-Maker Stories dialog box will then display the first few words of each story—double-click on the story to be imported.

To update a story after the text file has changed: 309

Choose File ➤ Links. Click on the name of the changed file and choose the Update button.

To thread one text block into another: 312

Select the text block with the pointer tools and choose Edit ➤ Cut. Switch to the text, and place the cursor in the text block to which you wish to thread the block. Choose Edit ➤ Paste.

To unthread a text block: 317

With the pointer or text tool, select tht text you want to unthread. Choose Edit ➤ Cut. With no text selected, choose Edit ➤ Paste.

SO FAR, YOU HAVE SEEN TWO WAYS to place text on a page: with the text tool and with the Story Editor. Both involve you actually composing text directly in PageMaker. Another, perhaps more common, way is to import text from your word processor. PageMaker can import files from a wide variety of word processors, such as Word, Ami Pro, WordPerfect, and others. You can even import stories from other PageMaker documents. A publication can contain any number of imported text files; each file becomes a separate story within the publication.

After we explore techniques for importing text, we'll cover some ways to handle text blocks. By manipulating the text blocks, you can control the flow of text in the publication.

HOW TO IMPORT FILES

It has often been said that one of the keys to PageMaker's success is its simplicity and approachability. Indeed, a new user need only know about the *Place* command to get started with the program. And while the term is a bit outdated (most programs today refer to the command as Import, not Place), it strikes at the core of what PageMaker does best: placing objects on a page and formatting them. This concept should already be familiar to you, as Chapter 5 discussed placing text typed in the Story Editor.

And speaking of the Story Editor, you can import text into story view as well as layout view, as the Place option is available in the Story Editor's File menu. If you know that the file needs editing (for example, you need to find and remove extra carriage returns), it makes sense to import the file into the Story Editor before placing the story on the page. After your editing is finished and you exit from the Story Editor, you are automatically prompted to place the text on the page.

IMPORTING WORD PROCESSOR FILES

Before you bring in a word processor file, you should make sure that you have set up PageMaker to import that type of file. You should also be sure that the file has been properly prepared to minimize the work you'll have to do after the text is in PageMaker. When you import the file, you can control its placement and format it as necessary.

CHECKING WHICH FILES CAN BE IMPORTED

When you used the Aldus Setup program to install PageMaker on your hard disk, you were asked to specify which file filters you would want to use, so that PageMaker can import files from other programs. (See Appendix A for information about installing filters.) For example, if WordPerfect is your word processor of choice, you should choose this filter in the Aldus Setup program. You can run the Setup utility, located in your Aldus group, any time you need to install more filters.

Table 8.1 lists the word processors for which PageMaker offers filters.

In addition, PageMaker provides filters for dBASE files, Lotus 1-2-3 and Excel spreadsheets, and even for chapter files from its rival Ventura Publisher.

TABLE 8.1: *Text Import Filters*

Format	File Extension
Ami Pro	SAM
Microsoft Word	DOC
Multimate Advantage II	DOC
PC Write	PCW
Rich Text Format	RTF
Text Only (ASCII)	TXT
Windows Write	WRI
Word for Windows	DOC
WordPerfect	WP5
WordPerfect for Windows	WP5
WordStar	WS, WST
XYWrite III	XY3

PREPARING THE TEXT IN YOUR WORD PROCESSOR

There are two general approaches to take when preparing text in your word processor bound for a PageMaker publication:

➤ Preformat your text in your word processor

➤ Format it in PageMaker

The safe approach is to concentrate on your writing while in your word processor (arguably the most important phase of any project), and save the formatting for later.

If you take this approach, you can live by a very simple edict: *Keep It Simple, Stupid!* All you need do is type. Don't format headlines or subheads, don't worry about the flow of your body copy, disregard hyphenation or justification settings, don't indent paragraphs, don't double-space after paragraphs, *don't do nothin'*! Just type. All layout decisions will be made later when you begin formatting your publication—this is the time for brilliant prose.

Okay, that is one school of thought. The other goes something like this: If, while preparing your text, you know how you would like to handle certain textual elements, why not designate them right then and there? Your headlines are to be 14-point bold? Fine, format it and tell PageMaker to retain the format. In fact, that is exactly what the option in the Place dialog box is called: Retain Format.

Figure 8.1 shows a Word for Windows document with a bit of formatting. The headlines, bullets, and subheads are all formatted with Word's style function. The presumption here is that the author of this text knows ahead of time what the final publication is to look like.

FIGURE 8.1: *If you format your document ahead of time, you can tell PageMaker to use this formatting when you place the file.*

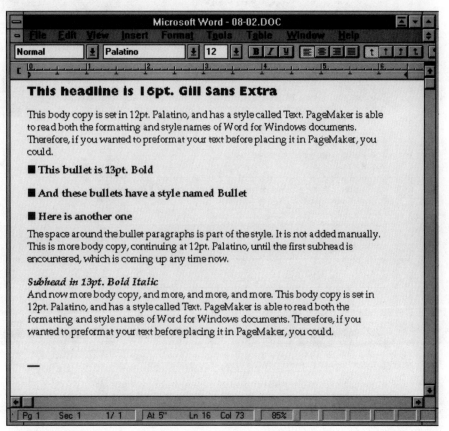

Figure 8.2 shows what happens if you tell PageMaker to place the text without formatting. All of the text comes into PageMaker formatted according to the default settings—12-point Times New Roman unless you say otherwise. Notice the style palette, however. It lists four style names with asterisks. Those names came from Word, not PageMaker. Those are the names of the four styles defined in Word; even though you told PageMaker to disregard the formatting, it still recognizes the style name. We explored styles in detail in Chapter 7. Notice what happened to the bullets, which are actually character number 0110 (lower case n) set in the Zapf Dingbat typeface.

FIGURE 8.2: *Placing text with no formatting produces plain text.*

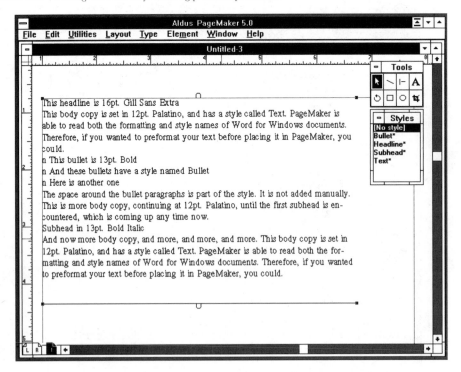

On the other hand, Figure 8.3 shows the result of the Retain Format command in the Place dialog box. Most every style element in the original Word document was read, interpreted, and applied by PageMaker. This is obviously a tremendous time savings if you are working with text that is already formatted.

 !**W**ARNiNG

Keep this in mind: When you tell PageMaker to retain the formatting of an original file, it retains everything, warts and all. So make sure that your text file doesn't have unwanted formatting, unless you enjoy unformatting a document (yuck).

FIGURE 8.3: *Placing text with formatting intact gives you a running start.*

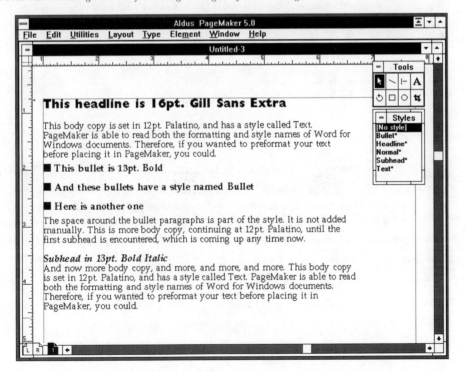

Whether you decide to format before or after, there are certain practices that are always taboo in the word processor. Figure 8.4 shows the gory details. Inexperienced text inputters think they are doing you a favor by spacing a headline over to show that it is to be centered, by adding asterisks for bullets, by underlining with the dash character, or by tabbing to show indents. As you can see, these characters all make the trip over to PageMaker, with or without the Retain Format option, where they then must be removed.

The less formatting you do in your word processor, the less clean-up work you will have to do in PageMaker. PageMaker will try its best to place text files just the way you created them, including spurious spaces, needless tabs, and useless indents. We have found that properly-prepared text files can ease the production process tremendously.

Here are a few things to *avoid* when typing a document that will be imported into PageMaker:

- Two spaces between sentences
- Regular spaces (inserted with the spacebar) to line up columns
- Tabs at the beginning of paragraphs
- Hyphenation
- Justification
- Double-spacing

If you type the text single-spaced without tabs (as the above list implies), you will need some way to see where one paragraph ends and the next begins. While tabs are taboo, you could instruct your word processor to add an indent to the first line of each paragraph. If you place the text in PageMaker without retaining formats, the indents will be ignored.

Most of us, though, are used to including an extra return between paragraphs, and we would be hard-pressed to break ourselves of that habit. Perhaps your best bet is to continue double-spacing between paragraphs, and

FIGURE 8.4: *Amateur hour comes to PageMaker—you are doing nobody a favor by formatting your text file in this manner.*

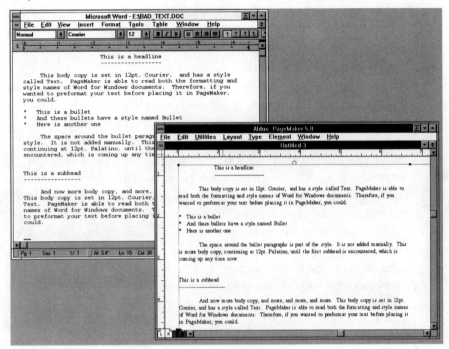

then use your word processor's search and replace command to remove the extra returns before placing the text in PageMaker. Curiously, PageMaker's ASCII text import filter can remove extra returns, but that capability is not extended to the various word processing filters.

You can also search and replace the double returns after placing the text, by bringing the text into the Story Editor and using the Change command. Chapter 5 explains how to find and remove carriage returns in story view.

Don't waste time specifying document layout settings, such as margins, page size, headers, and footers, because these settings will be ignored when the file is imported, regardless of the status of the Retain Format option.

Retaining Formatting

While you are creating text in your word processor, you may choose to do some light formatting, such as boldfacing or italicizing words. This formatting can be imported if you turn on the Retain Format option in the Place File dialog box. The option is turned on by default. You cannot select which formatting to import; it's all or nothing. The type of formatting that is imported depends on your word processor, but PageMaker will retain the basic formatting (such as centering, justification, indents, bold and italic, typefaces, sizes, and line spacing) in most word processors' files.

While importing text and formatting can be a major boon to your efforts to automate your publishing, you should be aware of its drawback: You give up the ability to preformat the text in PageMaker. Before importing text, PageMaker offers you a chance to make basic decisions about the format of your text. For example, you can specify 11-point Times New Roman with a 1-pica first-line paragraph indent before you choose the Place command. Then, when you import the text, it will automatically be formatted according to your specification. This preformatting is ignored if the Retain Format option is turned on.

Figure 8.5 shows a WordPerfect file that was placed in PageMaker twice. The text in the column on the left was imported without formatting. That is, the Retain Format option and the Convert Quotes option were turned off. Convert Quotes transforms inch marks (") and apostrophes (') into the more professional-looking typographical opening and closing curly quotation marks (" " and ' '). For the text in the right column, both of these default

FIGURE 8.5: *The text in the second column was imported with formatting retained and quotes converted.*

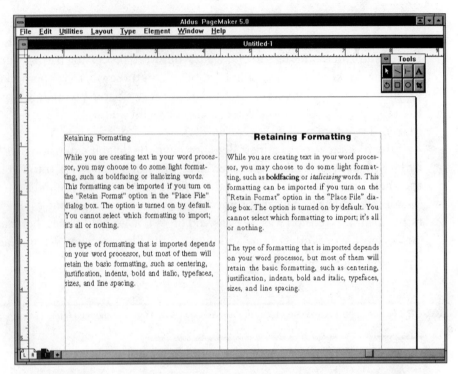

options were left on. Compare the text in the two columns. In particular, note the following items:

- ➤ In the original text file, the headline is centered and set in a heavy typeface, several words are bolded and italicized, and the text is justified.

- ➤ PageMaker assigned the default font of 12-point Times New Roman to the unformatted block, but brought in the original formatting of 13-point Adobe Garamond on the formatted block.

- ➤ The quote marks on the right are true quotes, not inch marks.

PLACING IMPORTED TEXT

When you are ready to insert your word processor file into a PageMaker publication, choose the Place option from the File menu and navigate the Drives and Directories lists to change to your word processing path. By default, PageMaker lists only the importable files—those with the appropriate extensions whose filters were installed in the Aldus Setup program. Using the List Files of Type option, you can choose to list all files, only Page-Maker files, or only older PageMaker files.

If the file you want to import does not have the default extension used by PageMaker (see Table 8.1), PageMaker will stop you halfway through the import process and ask you for the format. In Figure 8.6, a standard WordPerfect file was chosen for import into PageMaker, with one exception: The file extension was .WP instead of .WP5. We find this rather curious, as most WordPerfect users we know use the file extension WP instead of a version-specific one like WP5.

FIGURE 8.6: *If PageMaker doesn't recognize an extension, it asks you to choose a filter.*

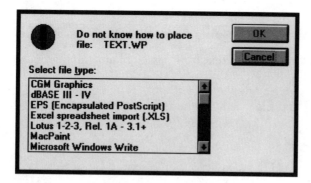

If you don't normally use the extension that PageMaker uses as a default, you might grow tired of having to manually edit the file name extension each time you place a file, or answer PageMaker's query about the file's format. Sadly, Version 5.0 does not provide the user any means for changing the default, short of using a binary file editor and making changes to one of the program files. Version 4.0 kept these references in a user-editable INI file—that's the price of progress, we suppose.

SPECIAL TEXT IMPORT OPTIONS

Version **5.0**

Several of the text import filters have additional options available that allow you to be a little more specific on what you import. For example, in Word for Windows, you can choose whether or not to import table of contents and index entries, page breaks, or tables. By holding down the Shift key when you click on OK in the Place Document dialog box, you will see the options specific to the filter. Figure 8.7 shows the options dialog box for Word for Windows.

WordPerfect 5.0/5.1 and Word for DOS also display an import filter dialog box when you hold down Shift as you click on OK. These two filters offer options pertaining to styles.

FIGURE 8.7: *The Word for Windows Import Filter dialog box*

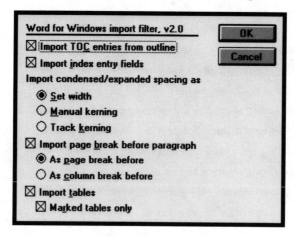

Word for Windows import filter, v2.0
☒ Import TOC entries from outline
☒ Import index entry fields
Import condensed/expanded spacing as
   ◉ Set width
   ○ Manual kerning
   ○ Track kerning
☒ Import page break before paragraph
   ◉ As page break before
   ○ As column break before
☒ Import tables
   ☒ Marked tables only

OK
Cancel

FLOWING IMPORTED TEXT

PageMaker offers three ways to flow text into columns:

→ Automatically

→ Manually

→ Semiautomatically

Each technique has its own advantages.

Manual Text Flow

With manual text flow, you shoot the text into each column, on each page. Before each shot, you reload the text gun by clicking on the bottom window shade handle. The advantage to this method is that you can select exactly where the text is placed. If you don't want the text flowed into one of the columns, you simply skip over it and shoot the text into the next column. Manual text flow is the default. When manual text flow is in effect, the Autoflow option on the Layout menu is not checked.

To place imported text using manual text flow, follow these steps:

1. Pull down the Layout menu and check to see if Autoflow is turned on. If it's checked, turn off the option. Otherwise, press Esc twice (or click outside the menu) to cancel the command.

2. Use the Place command (Ctrl+D) to select the file you wish to import. After you close the dialog box, you will see the manual text flow icon, which looks like a box of greeked text.

3. Go to the first column where you want the text, place the text gun, and click the left mouse button.

The text flows into this one column and is enclosed in window shades, as shown in Figure 8.8. The triangle inside the bottom handle indicates there is more text to flow; you no longer have a text gun.

4. To reload the text gun, click on the bottom window shade handle. The text gun reappears.

5. Shoot the text at the top of the next column.

6. Repeat steps 4 and 5 until all the text is placed. When the bottom window shade handle is empty, there is no more text to flow.

Semiautomatic Text Flow

Semiautomatic text flow gives you the best of both worlds. You can select which columns to flow the text into, but you don't have to reload the text gun for each column. Unfortunately, there is no menu option for turning on semiautomatic text flow. You must hold down the Shift key as you shoot the text into each column. You can use semiautomatic text flow regardless of whether Autoflow is turned on or off.

1. Use the Place command (Ctrl+D) to select the file you wish to import. After you close the dialog box, you will see a text gun.

2. Hold down Shift, and the text gun appears as a semiautomatic text icon—a squiggly, dotted-line arrow. Keep the Shift key down as you click the text icon where you want to place the

FIGURE 8.8: *The triangle in the bottom handle indicates that there is more text to be placed.*

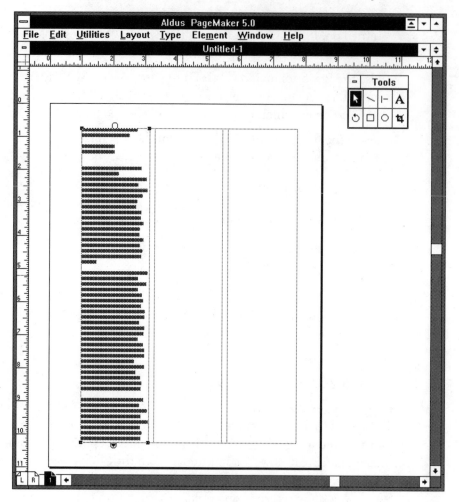

text. The text flows into this one column, and the text gun is still loaded.

3. Hold down Shift as you shoot the text in each column.

When all the text is flowed, the text gun disappears, and the bottom window shade of the text block is empty.

Automatic Text Flow

With automatic text flow, you shoot the text only once, in the first column into which you want the text to flow. Text automatically ripples into subsequent columns on subsequent pages. If the text is longer than the number of pages in the publication, PageMaker creates the necessary number of pages. This type of text flow is ideal for long documents. You turn on automatic text flow by choosing Autoflow on the Layout menu.

1. Pull down the Layout menu and check to see if Autoflow is turned on. If it's not checked, turn on the option. Otherwise, press Esc twice to cancel the command.

2. Use the Place command (Ctrl+D) to select the file you wish to import. After you close the dialog box, you will see the automatic text flow icon, which looks like a squiggly arrow (not dashed like the semiautomatic icon).

3. Go to the first column where you want the text, place the text gun, and click the left mouse button. The text automatically flows onto subsequent columns.

Note

If the page already has text placed on it, PageMaker will flow the text above the existing text block, but not below it. Text flow will then continue on the next page. If Page-Maker encounters a graphic during autoflow, the text will overlay the graphic. However, you can use the Text Wrap option on the Element menu to wrap the text around the graphic. See Chapter 11 for more details on text wrap.

Drag-Placing Text

When you click the text gun at the top of a column, the text flows into the entire column. But what if you want the text to flow across the width of two columns, or into part of one column? The point-and-shoot technique of flowing text will not work in these circumstances. Instead, use the *drag-place* method.

With the drag-place technique, you define the shape of the block by clicking and dragging. The shape can be any rectangular size and can span multiple or partial columns. Figure 8.9 shows a text block that is placed across three columns. Here is the general procedure for drag-placing text.

FIGURE 8.9: *A text block drag-placed across multiple columns*

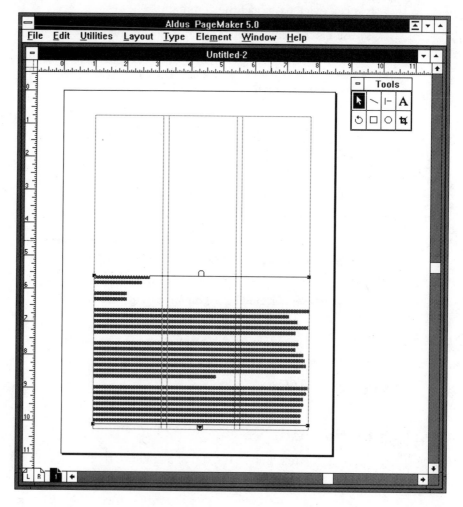

1. Place the loaded text gun in the upper-left corner of where you want the text placed.

2. Use the click-and-drag method to draw a box the size of the desired text block.

3. Release the mouse button.

This technique works regardless of the type of text flow in effect.

IMPORTING STYLES

Because PageMaker can import styles, the assignment of paragraph styles can begin right in your word processor. When you embed style names in your word processing document, the text is imported with style names already assigned to each paragraph. If you get in the habit of tagging paragraphs in the word processing stage, all you have to do in PageMaker is define the formatting associated with each style.

Bear in mind that assigning style names in your word processor is not the same as formatting the text; you will usually wait to do most of the formatting in Page-Maker. In your word processor, just assign names to the major elements in the story, such as body text and headings.

PageMaker offers two ways to import styles from a word processing document into a PageMaker publication, depending on whether your word processor has a style feature.

USING YOUR WORD PROCESSOR'S STYLE FEATURE

Word for Windows, Word for DOS, Ami Pro, and WordPerfect are a few of the word processors that allow you to define and assign styles. Figure 8.10 shows an example of a style list in Word for Windows. If you aren't familiar with how to create styles in your word processor, refer to the program documentation or a book about the software.

FIGURE 8.10: *A Word for Windows style list*

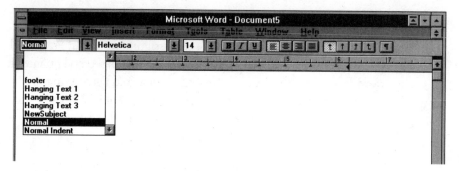

After you place the file in a PageMaker publication, the style palette will list the imported style names. An asterisk appears next to each style that wasn't previously defined in the current publication. The asterisk will disappear once you define the style's formatting in the Edit Style dialog box.

Remember, we are talking about the style name, not its formatting. Whether or not the imported text retains its formatting depends upon the status of the Retain Format option in the Place Document dialog box.

EMBEDDING STYLE TAGS

If your word processor doesn't have its own style feature, you can type style names directly into your word processing document. Figure 8.11 shows a Windows Write document that contains PageMaker style names.

FIGURE 8.11:   *A Write document with embedded style names*

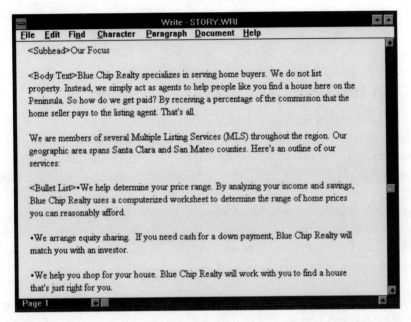

Follow these rules for embedding style names in your word processing documents:

➤ Enclose the name in angle brackets.

➤ Type the tag at the beginning of the paragraph.

➤ Do not tag a paragraph if it uses the same style as the preceding paragraph. In other words, you need only to enter tags when the style changes.

Notice that the third paragraph of text in Figure 8.11 does not have a tag. This paragraph will automatically be assigned the same tag as the previous paragraph (Body Text).

To import a tagged file, turn on the Read Tags option in the Place File dialog box. When a tag name matches an existing style name, the style is automatically assigned to the paragraph, and it is formatted accordingly.

When the tag name doesn't already appear on the publication's list of styles, the style name will still be imported, and the paragraph will be tagged. However, since PageMaker doesn't know how to format this new style, its name appears in the style palette with an asterisk next to it. After you edit the style to format the text, the asterisk disappears.

IMPORTING ASCII FILES

If PageMaker does not provide a filter for your word processor (if it's *not* listed in Table 8.1), don't despair. PageMaker can import files that are in standard ASCII text format. An ASCII file contains only text; any special formatting, such as fonts, bold, centering, and indents, is stripped out when you save the file in ASCII format. Almost every program has a way of creating an ASCII file; check your software's documentation for details.

Two other types of file formats are DCA (Document Content Architecture) and RTF (Rich Text Format). Unlike ASCII, these file formats retain some of the file's formatting. Not all programs can create these file types, however.

To import a file in one of these formats, you must install the appropriate filters in Aldus Setup (see Appendix A).

USING THE TEXT-ONLY IMPORT FILTER

After you specify the name of the ASCII file you want to place (in the Place Document dialog box), you are presented with the Text-Only Import Filter dialog box shown in Figure 8.12. This dialog box allows you to reduce the amount of clean-up work needed on the imported ASCII file. ASCII files typically contain unwanted carriage returns and spaces. This dialog box lets you filter them out as you bring the text into PageMaker.

By default, extra returns and spaces are not filtered out. When your file has carriage returns at the end of each line and two carriage returns between paragraphs, turn on the At End of Every Line option. Also be sure to turn on the But Keep Tables, Lists, and Indents As Is option, if necessary. You can imagine what a mess a table would be if its line endings were removed.

FIGURE 8.12: *The Text-Only Import Filter dialog box*

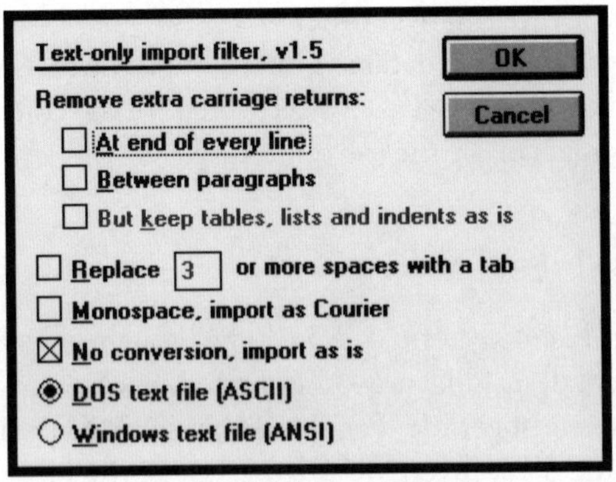

```
Text-only import filter, v1.5          [   OK   ]

Remove extra carriage returns:         [ Cancel ]
   ☐ At end of every line
   ☐ Between paragraphs
   ☐ But keep tables, lists and indents as is

☐ Replace [ 3 ]  or more spaces with a tab
☐ Monospace, import as Courier
☒ No conversion, import as is
◉ DOS text file (ASCII)
○ Windows text file (ANSI)
```

! **WARNING**

> Be careful—if your file does not contain double-spacing
> between paragraphs when you turn on the **At End of
> Every Line** option, the file comes in as one gigantic
> paragraph!

When the ASCII file has two carriage returns between paragraphs (but does not have returns at the end of each line), turn on the Between Paragraphs option.

Two of the dialog box options deal with extra spaces. Let's say you create an ASCII file in your database program. Instead of a tab between each of the columns, the ASCII file might have a series of spaces. If you set this text in a proportional font, the columns will not line up. In this case, you could either format the text with a fixed-space font (the Monospace option), or have PageMaker replace the spaces with tabs.

IMPORTING SPREADSHEET INFORMATION

PageMaker's import capabilities are smart in other ways also—most notably in the ability to import spreadsheet and database information. Import of columnar data is often tricky business, but PageMaker's filters for the common spreadsheet and database formats make the job quite easy.

IMPORTING SPREADSHEETS

Spreadsheets from Microsoft Excel or Lotus 1-2-3 can be brought into Page-Maker with the Place command, just like any other text. When you invoke Place and choose an Excel spreadsheet file, PageMaker presents you with the dialog box shown in Figure 8.13. If you know the name of the range you want, you can choose it from the list of named ranges. If you want a specific range that is not named, you will need to enter it manually—for example, A1:D36.

You can control the handling of tab alignment, styles, and cell boundaries, and you can even import the spreadsheet as a graphic instead of text. You would not be able to edit the contents of the spreadsheet if it were imported as a graphic, but you could easily size and scale the entire image, as you would any other image file.

The Lotus 1-2-3 filter behaves in a similar fashion, but doesn't offer the choice of importing a worksheet as a graphic, or cutting off information at cell boundaries.

WARNING

If the imported range is too wide for the column you place it into, each line will wrap onto multiple lines, creating a garbled mess. To fit each row onto a single line, you can reduce the type size, adjust tab stops, and/or widen the text block.

FIGURE 8.13: *The dialog box for placing an Excel spreadsheet*

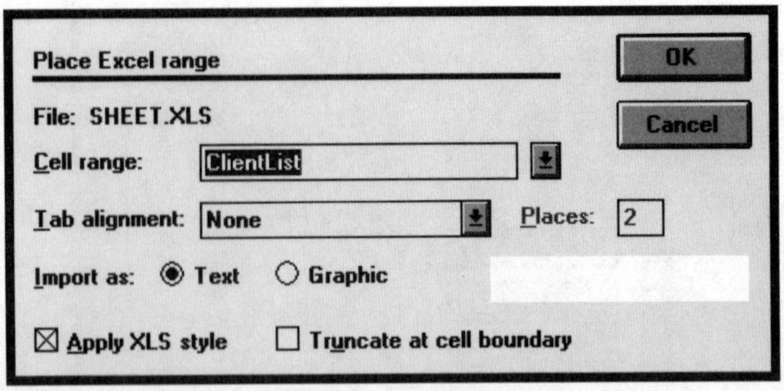

IMPORTING DBASE FILES

Bringing in database information is even easier—the only requirement is that the data be in dBASE format. To import dBASE data, use Place, find the DBF file, and answer the questions asked of you in Figure 8.14. Choosing the Directory format presents the data horizontally, with Field names as column headings. Choosing Catalog formats the data vertically, with each field on its own line.

You can use the Add or Add All button to choose the fields you want to include, and once that is done, you can use the Style button to dictate how the fields are to be formatted. For instance, in Directory format, you can designate that the NAME and COMPANY fields are to be left-aligned, while the AMOUNT OWED is to be decimal-aligned. In Catalog format, you can designate that two fields, such as FIRSTNAME and LASTNAME, are to be on the same line.

You must click on the field name in the Fields Selected list before you can choose the Style button.

FIGURE 8.14: *The Place dBASE File dialog box*

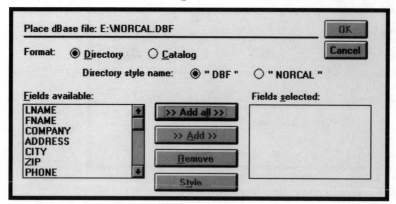

IMPORTING FROM PAGEMAKER TO PAGEMAKER

Version
5.0

As of Version 5.0, there are three ways to extract a story from one publication and place it in another: You can use the Place command and the Page-Maker import filter, you can open a second publication (5.0 lets you do that) and transfer the story across the Clipboard, or you can show two publications on screen at once, and simply drag from one to the other. To use the Place command, follow these general steps:

1. Open the publication into which you want to copy a story.

2. Choose Place from the File menu (or press Ctrl+D) to display the Place File dialog box.

3. Choose the .PM5 file from which you want to import. You will see the Place PageMaker Stories dialog box, as shown in Figure 8.15.

This dialog box lists the first few words of each story in the publication. If you need to see more of a story, select the story name and click the View button. The text will display in its own window, labeled View Story:1. To see more of the story, you can maximize the window and scroll through the document. When you're finished viewing the story, double-click on the control-menu box to close the window.

FIGURE 8.15:   *The Place PageMaker Stories dialog box*

You can control which stories are listed by specifying the minimum length of the stories. To do so, change the default of 20 characters at the bottom of the dialog box, and then choose the Relist button.

4. Click on the story name and choose OK.

Your text is now loaded into a text gun. To place the text, position the text gun where you want the story, and click the left mouse button. For more information on placing text, see the section "Flowing Imported Text."

Because Version 5.0 supports multiple open documents, you could also do the following:

1. Open the publication into which you want to copy a story.

2. Open another publication, the one that holds the text you seek.

3. Select the text, either with the text tool or pointer tool.

4. Choose Edit ➤ Copy to copy the text.

5. Switch to the publication that will hold the text.

6. Choose Edit ➤ Paste.

The Windows Clipboard is a well-traveled route used by anyone intending to share data between applications. If the donor of the data were not Page-Maker, but, say, Word for Windows, Excel, or any other text-generating program, the steps would be the same.

If the text file that you want to place spans more than one page (or two facing pages), then you should use the import method, as you cannot select and copy text across more than one page spread. However, if you need to place several elements from one publication to another—including graphic elements—the second method would likely be more handy for you.

Finally, now that more than one publication can be opened, drag-and-drop comes to PageMaker, in the form of quick and easy story transfer. To move a story from one publication to the other, your best bet might be to choose Window ➤ Tile (to display them side-by-side), and then drag the text block across the window boundary. The story will disappear for a moment, quickly to reappear in the other window. Release the mouse, and you're done.

RELATING STORIES TO TEXT FILES

Normally, importing a text file is a one-way street. Once you import it, there is no further connection between the original text file and the publication. If you edit the text in the publication, that does not alter the text file. Likewise, if you edit the text file after it's imported, the publication does not change. PageMaker offers several ways to change this, making text-editing a two-way street.

CREATING A TEXT FILE FROM A STORY

The Export option on the File menu creates a text file out of a PageMaker story. This text file can be exported using any of the export filters that were installed with the Aldus Setup program. If you export the file to Word format, you can then edit the file in Microsoft Word. If you export to Text Only format, you can open the file in any word processor or text editor (refer to your software's documentation for instructions on retrieving an ASCII file). After you export a file, you can return it to the PageMaker publication by placing it again.

When you export a file, some of the formatting might be stripped from the file; it depends on the type of formatting in the story and what type of exporting procedure you use. If you export the story, then add more text to it in your word processor, and finally place it in the same PageMaker publication, the new story will not necessarily be formatted like the original.

The key to retaining the story's formatting through the exporting process is to use paragraph styles instead of local formatting wherever possible. Then, when you export the file, turn on the Export Tags option to create a file with embedded tag names.

Figure 8.16 shows part of a story that has been exported to a file and then opened in Windows Write. Each style name appears inside angle brackets. To export a story, follow these basic steps:

1. Place the text cursor in the story you want to export. You must be using the text tool; the Export option is unavailable with the pointer tool.

2. Pull down the File menu and choose Export.

3. Type a file name.

4. To include the paragraph styles with the document, turn on the Export Tags option.

5. Select a file format from the list. Keep in mind that local formatting will be stripped from a Text Only file; to preserve local formatting you'll want to choose one of the word processing formats or RTF format.

6. Choose OK.

FIGURE 8.16: *An exported text file with style tag names*

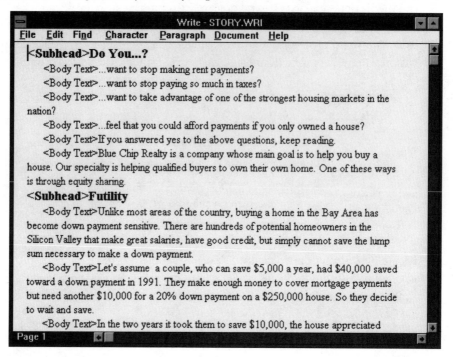

When the export operation is complete, you have a file that can be viewed and edited in a word processor. The file is assigned an extension appropriate to the file type to which you exported (for example, .TXT for Text Only or .DOC for Word).

After editing the story in your word processor, you might want to place it in your PageMaker publication again. Several options in the Place File dialog box are important for replacing a file. First, if you exported the tags, you want to be sure to turn on the Read Tags option. Second, to bring in local formatting, you need to turn on Retain Format. Finally, the Replacing Entire Story option enables you to place the same story in the same location in a publication, without having to delete the old text before importing the new story, and without having to indicate into which columns to flow the text. Note that the Replacing Entire Story option is available only if the text cursor is in the story before you display the Place File dialog box.

One frequent reason to use the Export command is a change to the layout of your publication. If you change the margins or columns after you have placed the text, the text blocks will not automatically adjust to fit the new column guides. Rather than adjusting the size of each text block (which could take an hour or so in a lengthy publication), you would be better off to export the file with its tags, delete the story, and then place the file again. (Because the text block is a different size, you can't use the Replacing Entire Story option here.) Although this sounds like a lot of work, it is much faster than moving and sizing the multitude of text blocks that would exist across a lengthy publication.

ESTABLISHING LINKS TO YOUR TEXT FILES

Another way to connect your PageMaker story with its external text file is with PageMaker's Links option. When a link is established, changes in the text file are reflected in the story inside the publication. This feature is especially useful when other people are supplying you with stories for your publication. If someone makes a change to a text file after you have placed it, file linking can save you from having to import the file again. It also ensures that the publication story matches the contents of the external file.

To display the Links dialog box, choose Links from the File menu, or press Shift+Ctrl+D. The Links dialog box is shown in Figure 8.17.

Whenever you import a file with the Place command, a link is automatically established between the PageMaker publication and the imported file. While the process of file linking is automatic, the process of updating the story to match the linked file is not—you must explicitly issue that command. Select a document in the Links dialog box by clicking on it. When your text file matches your story, the Status message reads

```
This item is up to date.
```

When you make a change to the external file, the Status message reads

```
The linked file has been modified since the last time it
was placed.
```

FIGURE 8.17: *The Links dialog box*

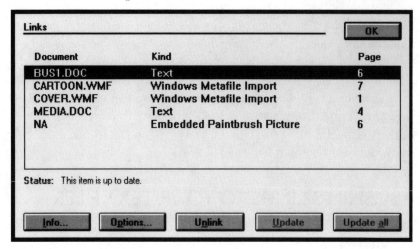

The Update All button reimports all linked files that have been modified *and* that are set up for automatic updating. Notice the NA next to the Embedded PaintBrush Picture. This is a graphic that was brought into Page-Maker across the Clipboard, and therefore has no file name associated with it.

You can also tell PageMaker to replace automatically the internal version of the story with the changed external file. Click on the Options command button in the Links dialog box to display the Links Options dialog box, and then turn on the Update Automatically option. Whenever you open the publication, the story will automatically reflect any changes made in the text file. You may also want to turn on the Alert Before Updating option, so that as you open a file, PageMaker notifies you when a story needs updating. You can then cancel the updating if you want to leave the story as it is.

You might *not* want the story updated with the new external file if you have made any changes to it in PageMaker. If both the internal story and the external text file have been changed, you have a problem: Which version do you go with? If you replace the story with the linked file, you lose any changes you made to the text and any formatting you have done in PageMaker. With the Update Automatically option turned on, PageMaker always warns you when the internal and external versions of the text have both been modified.

To get information about the text file, click on the Info command button in the Links dialog box. The Link Info dialog box, shown in Figure 8.18, lets you know when the file was originally placed, when it was last modified, and when (if applicable) the contents of the internal copy were last modified. You can also use this dialog box to link and import a different text file in the place of the current one; just select a different file in the Drives and Directories lists.

The Retain Cropping Data option retains data to imported graphic files only. Cropping is discussed in Chapter 11.

Another way to get to the Link Info and Link Options dialog boxes is through the Element menu. You must select part of the story (with either the pointer or text tool) before choosing these commands. If you don't, the Link Info option will not be available, and the changes you make to the Link Options dialog box will change the defaults for any new stories you place, but they won't affect existing stories.

FIGURE 8.18: *The Link Info dialog box*

Link info: BUS1.DOC

File name:

broch11.pm5
broch6.pm5
broch7.pm5
broch8.pm5
broch9.pm5
brochtxt.doc
brochtxt.sty
brochure.doc
brochure.pm5
brochure.pt5
chap1.doc
chap1.pm5
chap2.doc
chap2.pm5
chap3.doc
chap3.pm5

Directories:
c:\pm5pubs

c:\
pm5pubs

Location:
c:\pm4\pm5docs\bus1.doc
Kind: Text
Size: 12K
Placed: 10/22/92, 4:34 PM
Document modified: 3/4/93, 11:17 AM
Internal copy Modified: 10/10/93, 11:19 AM

Drives:
c: dos

Link
Cancel

☐ Retain cropping data

Finally, Figure 8.19 shows the Aldus Addition called Display Pub Info. This handy window shows font information, status of linked files, and styles used. Here it is providing a quick look at all linked files. By clicking on the Save button, you can save all of this information to a file for future reference or comparison.

FIGURE 8.19: *The Display Pub Info dialog box shows linked files.*

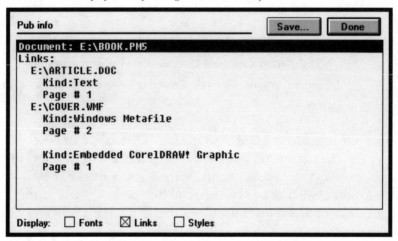

PLAYING WITH TEXT BLOCKS

As you flow text into different columns, the story is divided into multiple text blocks, one text block per column. These text blocks are connected to one another, as indicated by the plus sign (+) in the window shade handles. When you see a + in the handle, the text block is *threaded* (connected) to another text block in the same story. Threaded text blocks are part of the same story.

An empty handle at the top of a window shade indicates that the block is the beginning of a story while an empty handle at the bottom of a window shade indicates the end of a story.

The advantage to threaded text blocks is that the copy flows freely from one block to another. When you format the text or change the size of a

Version
5.0

UNLINKING DOCUMENTS

When you place a file or paste from the Clipboard, the file or object is automatically linked to the PageMaker publication. Thus, PageMaker will always remember the origin of every item that comes from an outside source. Linking is a nice feature when the source file changes and you want your publication to reflect these changes. However, there are occasions when you may not want to retain this link:

➤ If you have edited the text in the publication and always want to use this version of the file, not the file you originally placed

➤ If you no longer have the original text file

➤ If you pasted something from the Clipboard

➤ If you are giving someone else your publication and you don't want or need to give that person the source files

File linking takes extra time when you are opening a file so you want to unlink those items you won't ever need to update. To unlink a document, click on its name in the Links dialog box and then choose the Unlink button.

---

text block, the text automatically reflows between text blocks. If, for example, you shorten a text block, the overflow is automatically sent to the next block, which then pushes text into the third block. This rippling effect continues to the end of the story. If the last text block is not large enough to accommodate the additional text, a triangle appears in the bottom window shade handle, notifying you that additional text needs to be placed.

SEPARATING A TEXT BLOCK

There are several situations in which you might need to divide a text block into two separate blocks. Adding a graphic or pull-quote to a column is probably the most common reason to separate a text block. Figure 8.20 shows two separate text blocks in the first column, with a callout in between.

FIGURE 8.20: *A text block that has been divided in two*

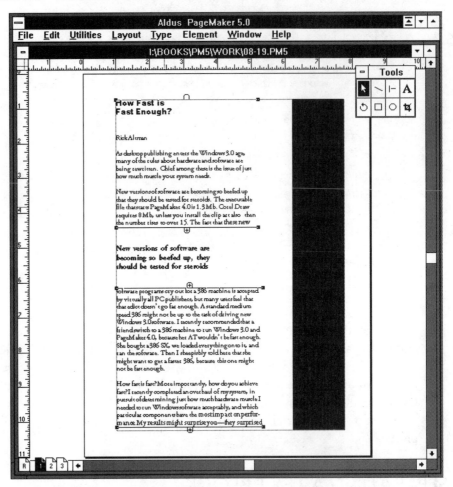

To divide a text block into two threaded blocks, follow these steps:

1. Shorten the text block by dragging the bottom window shade handle up.

2. Click on the bottom window shade handle to load the text gun.

3. Shoot the gun where you want the second block to go. You can also drag-place the text if you don't want the text to fill the rest of the column.

COMBINING TEXT BLOCKS

Sometimes, after you have separated a text block into multiple blocks, you will want to recombine them into a single text block. Your first instinct might be to move the text blocks so that they are close together, but this technique still leaves two separate text blocks. Your second instinct might be to delete the lower text block and resize the upper one, but this deletes the text in the lower block. The process of combining text blocks is not at all intuitive, so you will just have to memorize the steps or refer back to this section when you need to.

Follow these steps to combine two threaded text blocks:

1. With the pointer tool, select the second text block.

2. Drag the bottom window shade up until it meets the top window shade.

If you do this correctly, the text in the block disappears (although it is still there). Make sure your text block looks like Figure 8.21 before you proceed. If you still see a line or two of text, shorten the block until it is entirely collapsed upon itself.

3. Select the first text block.

4. Drag the bottom window shade handle so that it covers where the collapsed text block is.

When you release the mouse button, the text is now contained in a single block. To summarize—in order to combine two text blocks, you must *collapse* the lower block into "nothingness" and then run over it with the upper block. (Note that once you select the upper block, you will no longer see the collapsed lower block—you will need to remember where it was when you pull down the window shade handle of the upper block.)

FIGURE 8.21: *A text block that has been shortened so that no text is displayed between window shade handles*

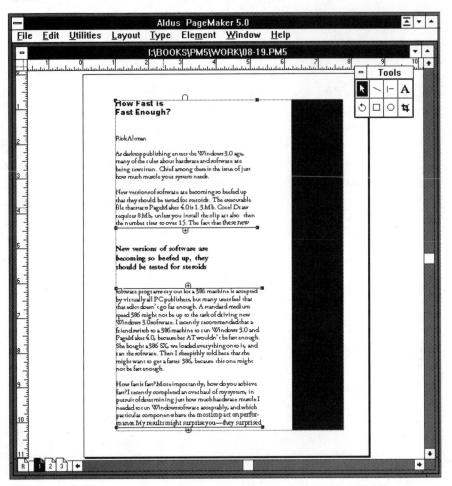

THREADING A TEXT BLOCK

Occasionally, you will inadvertently create a separate text block that was supposed to be connected to the main story. If, say, you click the I-beam outside of a text block to which you intended to add the text, that text becomes its own story in its own block, *not* threaded to the main story. To make this unthreaded text part of another story, you need to cut the unthreaded block with the pointer tool and then paste it with the text tool. If the text you want to rethread is in more than one text block, select all text blocks (by pressing Shift as you click on each block) before cutting to the Clipboard.

UNTHREADING A TEXT BLOCK

At times you may want purposely to disconnect text from a story. If you typed the headline as part of the main story, you may want to pull it out of the text block so that you can spread it across multiple columns. Or, you may have imported a text file that is made up of two articles. When you place this file, it is a single, threaded story. Because you want to place each article separately, you need to unthread one of the articles so that it is in its own story.

To unthread text, follow these general steps:

1. With the text or pointer tool, select the text you want to unthread.

2. Cut the text to the Clipboard.

3. Display the page on which you want the unthreaded text to appear.

4. With the pointer tool active, paste from the Clipboard. You can also paste with the text tool active—just make sure the cursor is not in an existing text block (otherwise, the text will be threaded to *that* text block). The text tool offers the advantage of letting you specify the target location for the new story.

After you perform the above steps, the group of pasted text blocks becomes its own story, completely unrelated to the original story.

USING THE TEXT FLOW ADDITIONS

Version
5.0

While the meat and potatoes of text flow reside with the tools and functions just described, there are several handy tools found in the new Aldus Additions that can assist with your text flow issues.

Find Overset Text

This Addition will take you to the end of a text thread that includes text that has not been placed on a page. In other words, the Find Overset Text addition shows you text that does not fit in your publication. Text can be overset because you forgot to finish flowing it when you initially placed the file or because you inserted text into a story.

To use this Addition, and most of the Additions that involve text flow, you must first select a text block, either with the pointer or the text tool. Find Overset Text will traverse any number of pages to find the last visible occurrence of text in a thread. It is then up to you to place the text: First click on the triangle in the window shade handle and then click where you want to flow the text. If all of the text is placed—if there is no text yet to be threaded—then PageMaker will indicate that there is no overset text.

Balance Columns

The Balance Columns Addition does just what its name implies: It evens out columns so that they are the same length. Figure 8.22 shows the same story before and after column balancing. Notice that the columns on the right-hand page have roughly the same length. To accomplish this task without the Addition would be tedious and time-consuming.

The Balance Columns dialog box, shown in Figure 8.23, offers a couple of options. First, you can choose to align the columns at the top or the bottom. (These icons are marked in Figure 8.23.) If you choose to align them at the top, PageMaker adjusts the bottom window shades until the selected text blocks are balanced. All the columns start at the topmost text block (usually the top margin guide). If you choose to align the columns at the bottom, the top window shades are adjusted. All the columns end at the bottommost text block (usually the bottom margin guide).

The second option in the dialog box lets you indicate what to do with leftover lines in case there is a remainder when the total number of lines in the selected blocks is divided by the number of selected columns. Take a close look at page 3 in Figure 8.21—notice that the first two columns on page 3 each have one more line than the last column. In this case, the first

FIGURE 8.22: *Both pages contain the same story; the columns on the right-hand page were evened out with the Column Balancing Addition.*

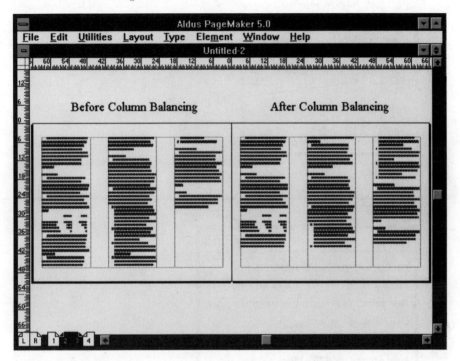

icon for Add Leftover Lines was chosen so that the remaining lines were added from left to right. With the second icon, the remaining lines are added from right to left. Note that the leftover lines are not lumped into a single column—they are spread out.

Story Info

The Story Info Addition simply tells you about the selected text, as Figure 8.24 shows, but in a very efficient manner. Of particular interest is the measure of column inches consumed by the story (great for publication editors copy-fitting stories on deadline), the number of pages spanned by the story, and whether there is any overset text (text that is not placed).

FIGURE 8.23: *The Balance Columns dialog box*

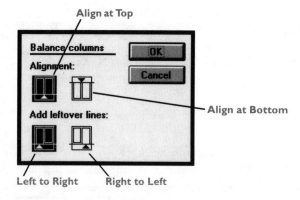

FIGURE 8.24: *The Story Info dialog box*

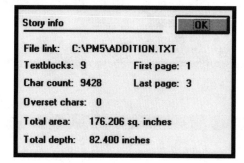

Textblock Info

This Addition is similar to Story Info, except that it returns information about a particular text block, rather than the entire story. As Figure 8.25 indicates, Textblock Info tells how this text block fits into the whole of the story, how much space it consumes, and how many characters it contains.

Traverse Textblocks

Figure 8.26 shows the simplicity of the Traverse Textblocks Addition, allowing you to quickly move through a story that spans multiple, possibly even discontiguous, pages. When a story has been broken up into many text blocks, this Addition can help you locate and follow the thread across the pages in your publication.

FIGURE 8.25: *The Textblock Info dialog box*

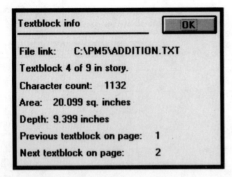

FIGURE 8.26: *The Traverse Textblocks dialog box*

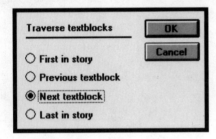

Continuation

Figure 8.27 shows the simple beauty of this feature. We did not add the jump line at the top of this text block; PageMaker did it for us. If this story continued onto the next page, we could automatically add a continuation line at the bottom. To create a "Continued From" notice, select the Bottom of Textblock option in the Continuation dialog box, or to create a "Continued To" line, select the Top of Textblock option. The Continuation Addition creates the thread of text, assigns the correct page number, and creates a unique style for the continuation line, to ensure that you can format them globally. The style for the continuation notice at the top of a column is called Cont. From; the one at the bottom of a column is called Cont. To. A very cool featurette.

FIGURE 8.27: *The Continuation Addition in action*

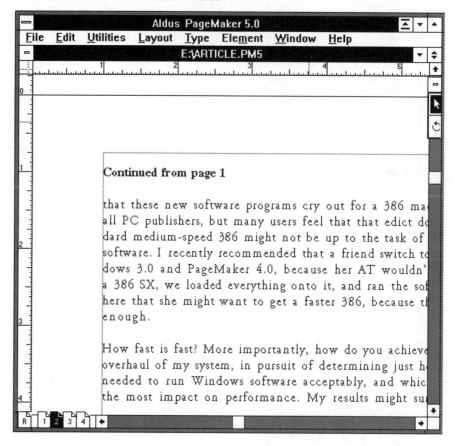

SUMMARY

In previous chapters of this book, you have used PageMaker in somewhat of a vacuum—meaning that all text and graphics came from *inside* Page-Maker. In this chapter, you started bringing the outside world into PageMaker. In most publications, especially the longer ones, the main text will be imported from external text files, so the techniques and concepts discussed in this chapter are important.

HANDS-ON PRACTICE: IMPORTING AND EXPORTING TEXT

In this hands-on exercise, you will have the opportunity to practice techniques for importing, flowing, and exporting text (you will not actually be building a publication).

FLOWING TEXT

In the following sections, you'll use each of the text-flowing methods: manual, semiautomatic, and automatic. For the exercises, you need a short (one- or two-page) single-spaced text file. You can use the FLOW.DOC file in your C:\PM5PUBS directory, or choose one of your own files.

Set up your PageMaker publication as follows:

1. Create a new publication with the following specifications: tall orientation and 3-pica margins all the way around.

2. Create four column guides.

3. Change the type size to 10 points. Making this change before you import the text file will cause the text automatically to be formatted in this type size.

4. Save the publication as **FLOWTEST** in the C:\PM5PUBS directory.

Flowing Text Manually

First, let's place the imported text using manual text flow.

1. Pull down the Layout menu and check to see if Autoflow is turned on. If it's checked, turn off the option. Otherwise, press Esc twice (or click outside the menu) to cancel the command.

2. Pull down the File menu and choose Place (or press Ctrl+D).

3. If necessary, navigate the Drives and Directories lists to change the path to C:\PM5PUBS.

4. Click on the FLOW.DOC file. (Don't double-click or you won't have a chance to select the Place Document options).

5. Turn off the Retain Format option. If you don't do this, the text will not be formatted to your earlier specification of 10 points.

6. Click on OK.

After a few seconds, you will see the manual text flow icon, which looks like a box of greeked text.

7. Shoot the text at the top of column 1.

The text flows into this one column and is enclosed in window shades. The triangle inside the bottom handle indicates that there is more text to flow. Notice that you no longer have a text gun.

8. To reload the text gun, click on the bottom window shade handle. The text gun reappears.

9. Shoot the text at the top of the next column.

10. Repeat steps 8 and 9 until all the text is placed. When the bottom window shade handle is empty, there is no more text to flow.

Flowing Text Semiautomatically

Manual text flow is a bit tedious, so let's flow in the same file using the semiautomatic technique. First, get rid of the text you imported.

1. Choose the Revert option from the File menu. (You could also select all the text with the text or pointer tool and press Del.)

2. Press Ctrl+D to display the Place Document dialog box.

3. Click on the FLOW.DOC file. Notice that the Retain Format option is still turned off.

4. Click on OK.

5. When you see the text icon, hold down Shift, and the text gun changes to a semiautomatic text icon—a squiggly, dotted-line arrow. Keep the Shift key down as you click the text icon at the top of column 1. The text flows into this one column, and the text gun is still loaded.

6. Hold down Shift as you shoot the text at the top of each column.

When all the text is flowed, the text gun disappears, and the bottom window shade of the text block is empty.

Flowing Text Automatically

Revert back to your last saved version and try the third way of flowing text:

1. Select Revert from the File menu.

2. Pull down the Layout menu and choose Autoflow.

3. Press Ctrl+D to display the Place Document dialog box.

4. Click on the FLOW.DOC file. Make sure the Retain Format option is still turned off.

5. Click on OK. The autoflow text gun appears.

6. Click the autoflow text gun at the top of the first column. The text automatically flows onto subsequent columns.

7. Close the file (you don't have to save it).

IMPORTING THE LETTERHEAD INTO THE BROCHURE

In the brochure you've been working on in previous chapters, the company name and address will appear on the back page. This will be the same text that is in the letterhead created in Chapter 4. Because this text requires special formatting, importing it from the LETHEAD1 publication will be quicker than retyping the address. (Note: If you didn't create LETHEAD1, use the file LETHEAD8 in your PM5PUBS directory.)

Follow these steps to import the PageMaker story:

1. Open the BROCH8 publication and display page 1 in Fit in Window view (press Ctrl+W).

2. Choose Place from the File menu (or press Ctrl+D) to display the Place Document dialog box.

3. Click on LETHEAD1.PM5 or LETHEAD8.PM5.

4. Turn on the Retain Format option, sice we want to bring in formatted text.

5. Coose OK. You will see the Place PageMaker Stories dialog box, shown in Figure 8.28. This particular publication has only one story (the letterhead).

6. To see the contents of the story, click on the story name (Blue Chip Realty...) and choose the View button. A small window containing the letterhead text pops up onto the screen; note that this window does not show the text's formatting.

7. Double-click on the View Story window's control-menu box to close this window.

8. Click on OK. After a moment, you will see a text gun.

9. Place the loaded text gun at the top of column 1 and shoot the text.

10. Switch to 75% view. Your screen should resemble Figure 8.29.

11. Save the file.

FIGURE 8.28: *The publication has only one story.*

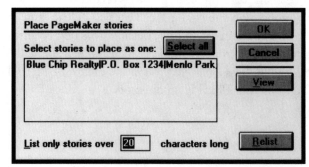

FIGURE 8.29:   *The return address on the back page of the brochure*

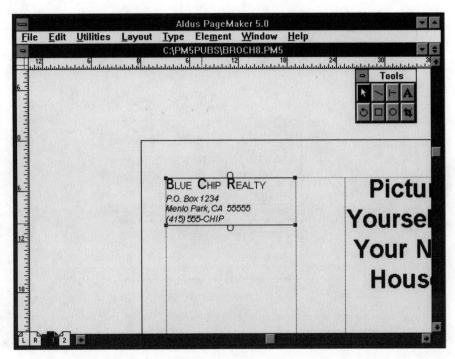

In the next chapter, you will position the address more precisely.

EXPORTING THE BROCHURE STORY

As mentioned earlier in the chapter, one common reason to export a story is because you changed margins or columns after you have placed the text. Instead of adjusting manually the size of each text block, you can export the file with its tags, delete the story, and then place the file again. Let's try this on the brochure.

1. In the Page Setup dialog box, change the top and bottom margins to 0p40. As Figure 8.30 shows, the text blocks do not span the new top and bottom margins.

FIGURE 8.30: *After changing margins, text blocks are too small.*

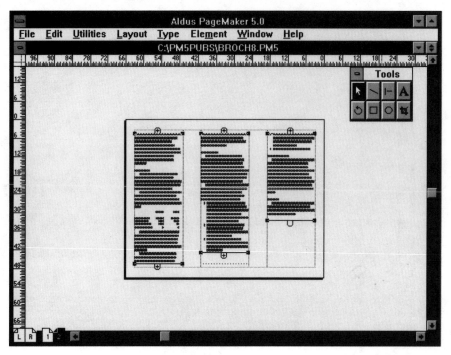

2. Switch to the text tool and click anywhere in the main story.

3. Pull down the File menu and choose Export.

4. Type **BROCHTXT** for the file name.

5. Turn on the Export Tags option.

6. Display the file format list, and choose a format such as Word-Perfect 5.0.

7. Choose OK.

Once the text is exported with its tag names, you can delete the story and import it again.

8. Press Ctrl+A to select all the text.

9. Press Del to delete the selected text.

10. Pull down the File menu and choose Place.

11. Select the BROCHTXT file from the list.

12. Turn on the Read Tags option and make sure Retain Format is turned on.

13. Choose OK.

14. Using the automatic flow feature, place the text in column 3 of page 1; text will automatically flow into columns 1–3 of page 2.

When you are finished, the text blocks conform to the new margins.

SHORTENING AND LENGTHENING A TEXT BLOCK

Now let's shorten a text block in your brochure so that you can see the automatic reflow of threaded text. Follow these steps:

1. Display page 2 in Fit in Window view.

2. Select the first column on page 2.

3. Drag the bottom window shade up until the text block is about half of its original length. When you release the mouse button, you can see that the text reflowed into the other columns.

4. Drag the bottom handle back down to the end of the column. The text automatically reflows.

THREADING TEXT INTO ANOTHER STORY

In the following exercise, you will make a common mistake in PageMaker: accidentally creating a separate text block that should have been part of the main story. After making this mistake, you will learn how to correct it. In the following steps, you will add Blue Chip Realty's phone number underneath the last paragraph in the story.

1. With the text tool in Actual Size view, click underneath the last paragraph in the third column, allowing a couple lines of white space above the cursor.

2. Press Ctrl+Shift+B to turn on the bold style.

3. Type **(415) 555-CHIP**.

4. Press Ctrl+Shift+C to center the line.

5. Switch to the pointer tool and click on the phone number.

The empty window shade handles indicate that this text block is its own story. Because it is not threaded to the preceding paragraph, it will not flow with the main story. This could create future problems when you change the size of other text blocks or reformat the text. As Figure 8.31 shows, text from the main story could actually flow over this unthreaded text block. To make the unthreaded text block part of the main story, you need to cut the block with the pointer tool and then paste it with the text tool. The phone number should already be selected with the pointer tool.

6. Pull down the Edit menu and choose Cut. The text block is sent to the Clipboard.

7. Switch to the text tool.

FIGURE 8.31: *One story flowing over another*

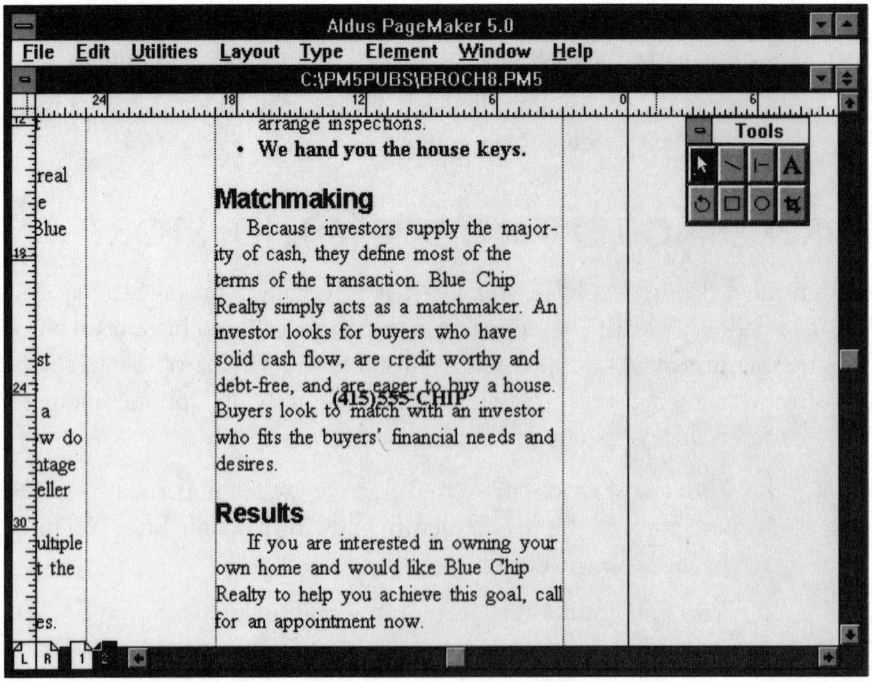

8. Click at the end of the last paragraph in the main story and press Enter twice.

This is actually what you should have done before typing the phone number in the first place. If you had, you would not have created the separate text block.

9. Pull down the Edit menu and choose Paste. The phone number is pasted from the Clipboard.

10. Switch to the pointer tool and click on the phone number.

As you can see from the text block handles, the phone number is now part of the main story.

11. We are finished working on the brochure for now, so close the file without saving the changes you made in this chapter.

Advanced Text Formatting Techniques

To rotate text with the control palette: 338

Select the text block with the pointer tool. Type a degree value in the rotation field and press Enter. A negative value will rotate the block clockwise; a positive value will rotate it counterclockwise. You can also click on a nudge button to increase or decrease the rotation by 0.1 degree. To rotate in increments of 1 degree, hold down the Ctrl key as you click on the nudge button.

To rotate text with the rotation tool: 339

Select the text block with the pointer tool and then choose the rotation tool. Place the starburst cursor at the location around which you want to rotate the selected text block (usually the center). Then drag the cursor in the direction you want to rotate the text. The text will rotate on your screen as you drag the cursor.

To skew text: 340

Select the text block with the pointer tool. Type a degree value in the skewing field and press Enter. A positive value slants the text to the right and a negative value slants the text to the left. You can also use the nudge buttons to increase the value in 0.1 degree increments (or 1 degree increments if you hold down Ctrl as you nudge).

To create a drop cap: 341

With the text tool, click anywhere in the paragraph. Choose Utilities ➤ Aldus Additions ➤ Drop Cap. Enter the number of lines and choose OK.

To kern two characters: 346

Place the cursor between the characters to be kerned. Press Ctrl+minus on the number pad to bring the characters closer together. Press Ctrl+plus to "unkern."

To tighten the spacing of a selected range of text (to *Track*): 350

Select the text, pull down the Type menu and choose Track. Choose either Normal, Tight, or Very Tight.

To adjust character width: 352

Pull down the Type menu and choose Set Width. To create narrower characters, enter a value less than 100; to create wider characters, enter a value over 100.

OU HAVE ALREADY LEARNED many typographical formatting controls, such as the ones discussed in Chapter 4 for adjusting fonts, sizes, and type styles; and those in Chapter 6 for leading controls. But PageMaker provides even more ways to fine tune the appearance of your type.

This chapter describes how to adjust the spacing between letters and words in PageMaker. However, before we get into these more complicated aspects of typography, you will learn how to create several special effects with your type.

CREATING SPECIAL EFFECTS

PageMaker does not have the sophisticated controls for manipulating type that CorelDRAW and other drawing and illustration programs offer. For example, you wouldn't be able to turn text inside out, fit it to a curved path, or give it a three-dimensional look. However, there are several special effects you can produce right in PageMaker. You can rotate text to any angle, you can skew (slant) type, and you can create drop caps.

ROTATING TEXT

Use the text rotation option when you want part of the page oriented differently. Figure 9.1 shows rotated text used for a headline. Text rotation was available in Version 4.0 of PageMaker, but you could flip a text block in only 90-degree increments. Now, in Version 5.0, you can rotate text in any increment, and in one of two ways: with the control palette or the rotation tool. Regardless of which method you use, you must first select the text block with the pointer tool.

You cannot rotate *part* of a text block (in other words, text selected with the text tool). You can, however, rotate a threaded text block.

FIGURE 9.1: *A rotated headline*

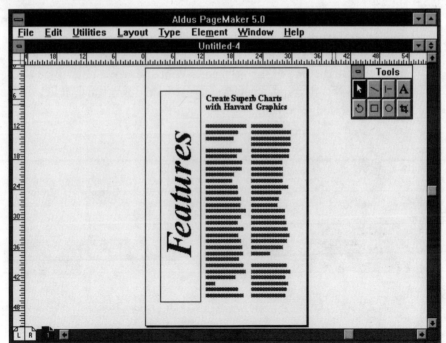

Once text is rotated, Version 5.0 also allows you to edit and format it directly—you don't have to go into the Story Editor as you did in Version 4.0.

Rotating with the Control Palette

The control palette's rotation option is pointed out in Figure 9.2. One way to specify the degree of rotation is to type a degree value into the rotation field and press Enter. A negative value will rotate the block clockwise; a positive value will rotate it counterclockwise. For example, the text in Figure 9.1 was rotated 90 degrees counterclockwise. If you wanted this text to face in the opposite direction, you would enter –90 for the rotation value. To return the text to its original position, enter a value of 0. The value can be any number between –360 and 360, in increments of 0.01 degrees.

The number you enter is always measured from the starting position of 0 degrees. Let's look at an example. Suppose you first rotated the text 90 degrees counterclockwise and now you decide you want to rotate it so that it's upside-down. You do not enter 90 to rotate the text another 90 degrees; instead, you pretend that the block is in its original location and you enter a value of 180.

A second way to specify the rotation angle is to use the nudge buttons (marked in Figure 9.2). Each time you click on a nudge button, the rotation is increased or decreased by 0.1 degree. The button that points up increases while the one that points down decreases the rotation. To rotate in increments of 1 degree—a *power nudge*— hold down the Ctrl key as you click on the nudge button.

FIGURE 9.2: *The control palette's rotation and skewing options*

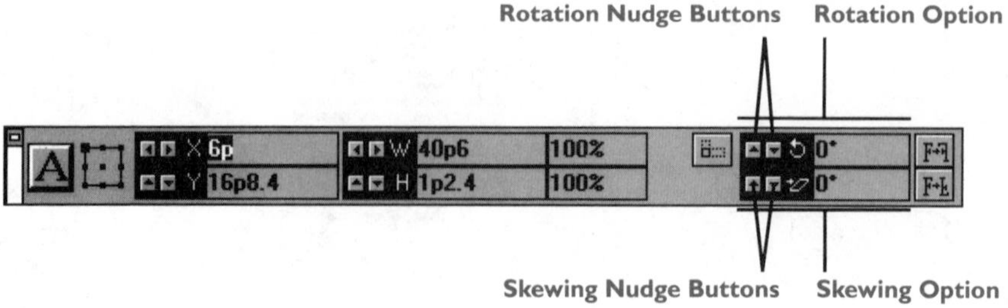

Rotating with the Rotation Tool

Version
5.0

The second way to rotate text—the rotation tool—allows you to forget about rotation degrees and lets you physically move the block to the position you want. If geometry is not your forte and you have a difficult time with degrees, you'll probably prefer to use Version 5.0's new rotation tool, which is marked in Figure 9.3.

First, select the text block with the pointer tool. Then select the rotation tool in the toolbox. You will see a new kind of cursor, called a *starburst.* Move this cursor to the location around which you want to rotate the selected text block (usually the center). You then drag the starburst cursor in the direction you want to rotate the text. The text will rotate on your screen as you drag the cursor. For example, if you drag to the left, the block rotates 180 degrees (upside-down text). Or, if you drag straight up, the block rotates 90 degrees counterclockwise.

As you drag, you'll see a *rotation lever,* which controls the amount of rotation. Dragging the starburst away from the starting point will give you more control over the rotation. With a longer lever, in other words, you'll be able to rotate the text in smaller increments. With a short lever, you may be able to rotate the block in only 2- or 3-degree increments, but with a longer lever, you'll be able to rotate in increments of tenths of degrees.

To rotate the text block in 45-degree increments, hold down Shift as you drag the starburst cursor. This makes it easy to turn text sideways or upside-down.

FIGURE 9.3: *The rotation tool*

Rotation Tool

SKEWING TEXT

Version
5.0

With the control palette's skewing option, you can provide your display type with a sense of movement by slanting it to the right or left. Slanting type to the right makes it similar to the italic type style, except that in this case you have control over how much the text is slanted. Figure 9.4 illustrates an example of a special effect created with skewed text; in this example, a gray-shaded, slanted copy of the text is placed behind the original text to create an illusion of shadowed type.

The skewing option is pointed out in Figure 9.2. As with the rotation option, you must choose a text block with the pointer tool before you can skew it, and you can either enter a degree value in the field or use the nudge buttons to increase the value in 0.1-degree increments (or 1-degree increments if you hold down Ctrl as you nudge). A positive value slants the text to the right while a negative value slants to the left. In Figure 9.4,

FIGURE 9.4: *Skewed text*

the text is skewed −20 degrees. The skew value can range from -85 to 85 degrees, in 0.01-degree increments.

CREATING DROP CAPS

A dropped capital letter, called a *drop cap,* is the first character of a paragraph that has been enlarged and hangs down into the body of a paragraph. Drop caps are frequently used at the beginning of a story, or to introduce new sections of a story, as shown in Figure 9.5. When set correctly, drop caps can add a professional touch to your publication.

Version **5.0** The easiest way to create a drop cap is with the Drop Cap Addition. All you have to do is place the text cursor in the paragraph and choose Drop Cap from the Aldus Additions menu. You'll be asked to enter the size of the drop cap; three lines is the default. The number of lines will determine how large the drop cap is. Needless to say, you won't want the size to be

FIGURE 9.5: *A drop cap*

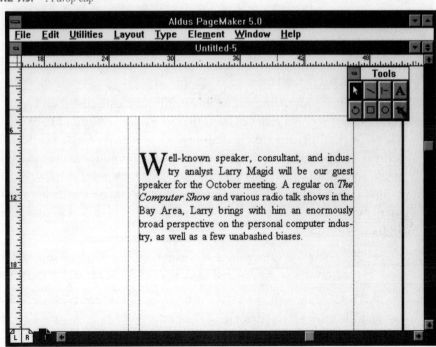

greater than the number of lines in the paragraph. In fact, drop caps would look out of place on short paragraphs—save this effect for long, introductory paragraphs.

Before clicking on OK to create the drop cap, you may want to click on the Apply button to preview this special effect. (You may need to move the dialog box out of the way to see the paragraph—just drag the box's title bar until you can see the drop cap.) Then, if you don't like the size, you can enter a different number of lines without leaving the dialog box. Note that you must eliminate the current drop cap with the Remove button before you can apply a new size.

The Prev and Next buttons allow you to move the cursor to other paragraphs without having to leave the Drop Cap dialog box.

Paragraphs that begin with a drop cap should not have a first-line indent. Be sure to remove any indents *before* running the Drop Cap Addition—you will have trouble removing them after the fact.

Behind the Scenes

You may be curious to know how this Addition creates the drop cap. Actually, it runs through a series of steps that in earlier versions of PageMaker had to be performed manually. This procedure uses type specifications to control the size and position of the enlarged letter and uses tabs and line breaks to control the wrapping of the body text around the drop cap.

Take a look at Figure 9.6. This figure shows the type specifications and type options for the drop cap shown in Figure 9.5. Here is a summary of the drop cap settings:

➜ The point size is increased; the exact size is given by a formula based on the point size and leading of the body text.

➜ The leading is the same as the body text's leading. (Auto leading will throw off the spacing of the paragraph.)

FIGURE 9.6: *The typographical controls for a drop cap*

Type specifications			
Font:	Times New Roman		**OK**
Size:	33.6 points	**Position:** Subscript	**Cancel**
Leading:	14 points	**Case:** Normal	**Options...**
Set width:	Normal percent	Track: No track	
Color:	Black		
Type style:	☒ Normal ☐ Bold		

Type options		
Small caps size:	70	% of point size
Super/subscript size:	100	% of point size
Superscript position:	33.3	% of point size
Subscript position:	41.6	% of point size
Baseline shift:	0 points	◉ Up ○ Down

OK   Cancel

→ The position is set to Subscript.

→ The Super/Subscript Size is 100%. This setting makes the subscripted character 100 percent of the point size; in other words, the actual point size specified.

→ The Subscript Position has been adjusted to a percentage that lines up the top of the drop cap near the ascenders in the body text, and the bottom with the text baseline.

If you want to manually adjust the vertical alignment of a drop cap, this is where to do it. Select the letter with the text tool, then enter a larger Subscript Position number to move the drop cap down.

Figure 9.7 shows the paragraph in story view with the Display ¶ option turned on. You may notice that the drop cap doesn't display in story view; the letter actually displays in a different size to let you know that it's formatted differently. Find the line break symbol at the end of the first line—this break was created with Shift+Enter. Also note the tab symbol at the beginning of the second line. The Drop Cap Addition set a tab stop to the right of the drop cap and then tabbed in the second line so that it wraps around the enlarged letter.

If you edit text in the first several lines of the paragraph, the tabs and line breaks may move and end up in the wrong places. If this happens, you'll have to delete the original tabs and line breaks and insert new ones in the appropriate places. The easiest place to do this is in the story editor, where you can see the tab and line-break codes.

FIGURE 9.7: *The Drop Cap Addition inserts line breaks and tabs in the appropriate places so that the body text wraps around the drop cap*

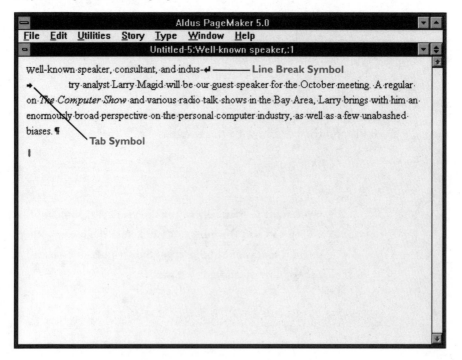

Removing a Drop Cap

If you change your mind and decide you don't want a paragraph to have a drop cap any more, just place the text cursor in the paragraph and display the Drop Cap dialog box. Click on the Remove button and the Addition will go through and reverse the drop cap formatting.

CREATING STANDING CAPS

A similar effect is called a *standing cap* or *raised cap*. As shown in Figure 9.8, a standing cap simply has a larger point size than the body text. Just select the letter and enlarge it—that's all there is to it. Note that the capital letter should have the same leading as the body text.

FIGURE 9.8: *A standing cap*

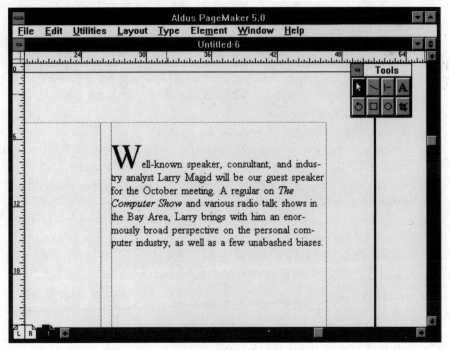

ADJUSTING HORIZONTAL SPACING

PageMaker provides several ways to control the horizontal spacing—the space between words and letters—of your text. Two factors that affect horizontal spacing are alignment and hyphenation. You learned about these controls in Chapter 6. In the following sections, you will learn about kerning, tracking, condensing and expanding character widths, and changing the default word and letter spacing.

KERNING TEXT

In Figure 9.8, notice the large gap between the enlarged capital *W* and the letter *e*. PageMaker tries to correctly control the space between letters, and under normal circumstances, such as straight body copy and moderately sized subheads, its efforts are quite satisfactory.

Not only does PageMaker know how wide each character is, but it also knows that certain pairs of characters need a bit more or less space. The classic example is the combination of capital letters A and V. When these characters are together, their angles require that they be moved closer together, as illustrated in Figure 9.9. By default, PageMaker does this *pair kerning* automatically. You can see the Pair Kerning setting in the Spacing Attributes dialog box (press Ctrl+M and choose Spacing from the Paragraph Specifications dialog box).

Unfortunately, PageMaker doesn't recognize every single combination of characters in every conceivable font that requires adjustment. To fine tune your text, you may have to do some of the adjusting yourself. Increasing the size of a single character, such as the one in Figure 9.8, is a likely situation in which manual letter spacing, or *kerning*, is needed.

To kern two characters, place the cursor between the characters and press Ctrl+minus on the number pad to bring the characters closer together. Press Ctrl+minus until you achieve the desired letter spacing. If you bring them too close together, you can press Ctrl+plus to "unkern" the characters. Each time you press Ctrl+minus, PageMaker kerns characters together 0.04 *em*; Ctrl+plus kerns characters apart 0.04 *em*. (One em equals the width of the letter "m" in the current type size.) To kern by 0.01 em, use Ctrl+Shift+minus and Ctrl+Shift+plus.

FIGURE 9.9: *The effect of kerning*

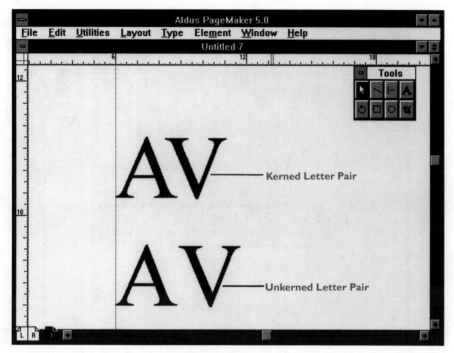

Figure 9.10 shows the result of kerning the large *W* with the small *e*. Ctrl+minus was pressed three times.

To clear manual kerning, press Ctrl+Shift+0 (zero on the top row of the keyboard).

Kerning usually requires accurate screen fonts and some trial and error. You won't really know for sure how accurately you kerned the characters until you print the page. The more accurate your screen display, the fewer rounds of test prints you are likely to need.

347

FIGURE 9.10: *The standing capital letter after kerning*

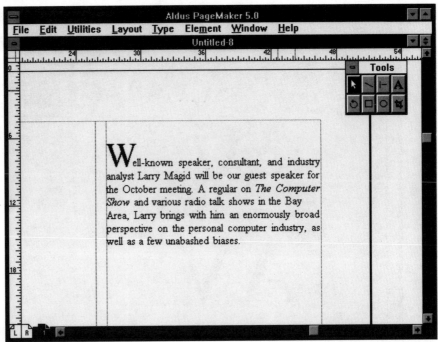

Version 5.0 Version 5.0's control palette also offers a kerning option; this option is pointed out in Figure 9.11. By clicking on the right nudge button, you move the letters apart 0.01 em; clicking on the left nudge button will move the letters together 0.01 em. If you hold down Ctrl as you click on the nudge buttons, you will kern in increments of 0.1 em.

FIGURE 9.11: *The kerning option in the control palette*

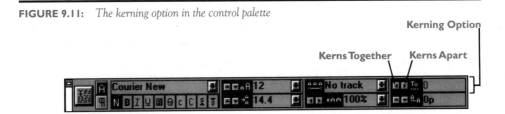

EXPERT KERNING ADDITION

PageMaker's keyboard controls for kerning, such as Ctrl+minus and Ctrl+Shift+minus, allow you to manually adjust the spacing between characters—*you* decide how much kerning you want. Another way to kern is with the Expert Kerning Addition. This Addition not only automates the kerning process, but it also provides more precise kerning control. It first removes any manual kerning you may have already done to the selected text, and then it evaluates each pair of characters and inserts appropriate kerning between them. You will use this Addition to fine-tune the kerning of large text (headlines, posters, and so forth). While it will work on small text, the Addition (and kerning in general) is usually only necessary on large type. Note that Expert Kerning works on PostScript Type 1 fonts only (such as ATM fonts and fonts built into PostScript printers); you will get an error message if you try to use it with TrueType fonts.

Here's how it works: With the text tool, you select the characters you want to kern and then display the Expert Kerning dialog box. You can enter a new value for the Kern Strength, or leave the default value of 1.0. The kern strength governs the tightness of the character spacing. A value of 0.0 offers the loosest kerning while 2.0 offers the tightest. For a starting point, you'll probably want to stick with the default. If you're not satisfied with the results, you can adjust the strength in tenths of a point—adjust up to bring the characters closer together or down to spread them further apart. Figure 9.12 shows several examples of text that has been kerned.

The Design Class field lets you specify the original master design of the font: Text, Display, or Poster. Some fonts were intentionally designed to be used for display type while others were designed to be used for body text. For example, Helvetica Black and Futura Extra Bold are display fonts while Times Roman and Bookman are text fonts. (Many fonts designed for display purposes are so heavy as to be virtually illegible in small text sizes.) If you aren't sure of the design class, leave this field at its default (Text).

After the Addition is finished kerning your text, the end result is as if you had kerned each character pair manually, with a different amount of kerning for each pair. You can adjust the kerning further using your manual keyboard controls, or you can run the Kerning Addition again. To remove all the kerning, press Ctrl+Shift+0 (zero). Because of the amount of time the automatic kerning takes, the PageMaker documentation recommends that you use the Expert Kerning Addition judiciously and only on small blocks of text.

FIGURE 9.12: *Examples of different kern strengths*

AVERY BROWN

No Kerning

AVERY BROWN

1.0 Kern Strength

AVERY BROWN

2.0 Kern Strength

AVERY BROWN

0.5 Kern Strength

TRACKING LETTER SPACING

Another way to adjust letter spacing is with *tracking*. PageMaker's tracking feature lets you adjust the spacing of a selected range of text, such as complete lines or entire paragraphs. If your story is too long to fit in a required amount of space, you can tighten the letter spacing in the story. Large type sizes typically have too much space between the characters; use tracking to tighten up the spacing. Looser spacing is sometimes used for special effects.

Five different levels of tracking are available, as illustrated in Figure 9.13. In the figure, notice that the paragraph's length varies from eight to ten lines, depending on the tracking. By default, PageMaker doesn't use any tracking. Normal tracking is a little tighter than no tracking at all.

Version
5.0

For even more precision in your letter spacing, you can edit the tracking settings for a particular font, using the Edit Tracks Addition. The average desktop publisher will probably have neither the need nor the skill to delve into this complex procedure. This Addition was designed for scrupulous typographers who place the utmost importance on precise letter spacing.

FIGURE 9.13: *A comparison of tracking levels*

No Tracking:

Well-known speaker, consultant and industry analyst Larry Magid will be the speaker for October. A regular on The Computer Show and various radio talk shows in the Bay Area, Larry brings with him an enormously broad perspective on the personal computer industry, as well as a few unabashed biases.

Very Loose Tracking:

Well-known speaker, consultant and industry analyst Larry Magid will be the speaker for October. A regular on The Computer Show and various radio talk shows in the Bay Area, Larry brings with him an enormously broad perspective on the personal computer industry, as well as a few unabashed biases.

Very Tight Tracking:

Well-known speaker, consultant and industry analyst Larry Magid will be the speaker for October. A regular on The Computer Show and various radio talk shows in the Bay Area, Larry brings with him an enormously broad perspective on the personal computer industry, as well as a few unabashed biases.

Normal Tracking:

Well-known speaker, consultant and industry analyst Larry Magid will be the speaker for October. A regular on The Computer Show and various radio talk shows in the Bay Area, Larry brings with him an enormously broad perspective on the personal computer industry, as well as a few unabashed biases.

Loose Tracking:

Well-known speaker, consultant and industry analyst Larry Magid will be the speaker for October. A regular on The Computer Show and various radio talk shows in the Bay Area, Larry brings with him an enormously broad perspective on the personal computer industry, as well as a few unabashed biases.

Tight Tracking:

Well-known speaker, consultant and industry analyst Larry Magid will be the speaker for October. A regular on The Computer Show and various radio talk shows in the Bay Area, Larry brings with him an enormously broad perspective on the personal computer industry, as well as a few unabashed biases.

You can specify tracking either through the Track option on the Type menu or in the Type Specifications (Ctrl+T) dialog box. First select the quantity of text whose letter spacing you want to change, and then specify the tracking level.

Version **5.0** You can also choose the tracking level in the control palette. This option is marked in Figure 9.14. To display the list of levels, click on the down arrow in the field; then choose the desired setting. The level (No Track, Loose, Very Loose, Normal, Tight, or Very Tight) will then display in the control palette's tracking field.

FIGURE 9.14: *The tracking option in the control palette*

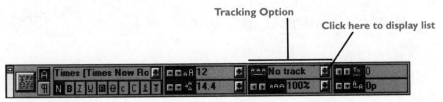

Tracking Option

Click here to display list

CHANGING THE CHARACTER WIDTH

The Set Width option, which appears on the Type pull-down menu and in the Type Specifications dialog box, changes the width of the letters as well as the spacing between them. The height of the characters—the type size—remains constant. All character and space widths are changed proportionally so that the font will not be distorted.

Figure 9.15 shows how different the same type size looks with varying character widths. By changing the character width, you can give the illusion of choosing a different type size.

You set the width as a percentage of the normal width. To create narrower characters, enter a value less than 100 for Set Width; to create wider characters, enter a value over 100. The standard settings are 70, 80, 90, 110, 120, and 130; however, you can enter any value in $\frac{1}{10}$% increments, from 5% to 250%.

FIGURE 9.15: *Proportional character-width changes*

Picture Yourself in Your New House!	**70%**
Picture Yourself in Your New House!	**80%**
Picture Yourself in Your New House!	**90%**
Picture Yourself in Your New House!	Normal
Picture Yourself in Your New House!	110%
Picture Yourself in Your New House!	120%
Picture Yourself in Your New House!	130%

Version
5.0

The Set Width option in the control palette is pointed out in Figure 9.16. You can either enter a percentage in this field or use the nudge buttons to increase/decrease the width in 1% increments. A power nudge (hold down Ctrl as you click) will increase/decrease the width in 10% increments.

FIGURE 9.16: *The Set Width option in the control palette*

Set-Width Option

ADJUSTING WORD AND LETTER SPACING

Another way to control horizontal spacing is through the Spacing Attributes dialog box. (Spacing is a command button in the Paragraph Specifications dialog box.) The Spacing Attributes dialog box, shown in Figure 9.17, lets you define the range of acceptable intra-word and intra-letter spacing. Before you dive into this section, be aware that word and letter spacing are not easy concepts to grasp, and only the most diligent (and brave) typographers will find it necessary or wise to venture into the Spacing Attributes box.

FIGURE 9.17: *The Spacing Attributes dialog box*

Spacing attributes

Word space:	**Letter space:**	OK
Minimum 75 %	Minimum -5 %	Cancel
Desired 100 %	Desired 0 %	
Maximum 150 %	Maximum 25 %	Reset

Pair kerning: ☒ Auto above 4 points

Leading method: ◉ Proportional ○ Top of caps ○ Baseline

Autoleading: 120 % of point size

The word spacing values are based on the font's *space band*, which is the amount of space created when you press the spacebar. In word spacing, the default Desired value is 100%. This means that PageMaker tries to keep the space between words equivalent to the size of the font's space band. If you want more or less space between words, you can adjust the Desired value.

When text is justified, PageMaker frequently needs to manipulate the word spacing to something other than the Desired value. It might need to shave off a little space between words or add some. The Minimum and Maximum values tell PageMaker exactly how much space it can add or subtract.

A Minimum value of 50% word space indicates that you will allow the intra-word space to be as small as half of the font's space band. A Maximum value of 200% indicates that you will accept a space that is twice the width of the font's space band. By decreasing the Minimum value, you are saying that you are willing to accept a smaller amount of space between words. When you increase the Maximum value, you are likely to see larger gaps between words.

Figure 9.18 compares different word spacing percentages, using extreme values so that you can easily discern the differences. The Desired, Minimum, and Maximum word space settings for each paragraph are shown above it. Notice how the paragraph is longer with 200% word spacing, which places two space bands between words.

The letter spacing values are entered as percentages of the font's space band. Ideally, each character uses the exact space built into the character; this built-in space is called its *pen advance*. Pen advance is measured from the left edge of one character to the left edge of the next character. The Desired value of 0% indicates that no extra space should be added between letters. 0% is the ideal, but PageMaker needs to cheat sometimes to accommodate all the different character widths in a line. It's up to you to tell PageMaker just how much it can cheat.

The Minimum value for letter spacing (entered as a negative number) defines the amount of space you will allow PageMaker to remove from the

FIGURE 9.18: *Comparison of word spacing percentages*

Default Spacing: Desired 100%, Min 75%, Max 150%

Because investors supply the majority of cash, they define most of the terms of the transaction. Blue Chip Realty simply acts as a matchmaker. An investor looks for buyers who have solid cash flow, are credit worthy and debt-free, and are eager to buy a house. Buyers look to match with an investor who fits the buyers' financial needs and desires.

Desired 100%, Min 100%, Max 100%

Because investors supply the majority of cash, they define most of the terms of the transaction. Blue Chip Realty simply acts as a matchmaker. An investor looks for buyers who have solid cash flow, are credit worthy and debt-free, and are eager to buy a house. Buyers look to match with an investor who fits the buyers' financial needs and desires.

Desired 25%, Min 25%, Max 25%

Becauseinvestorssupplythemajorityofcash,theydefinemostofthe termsofthetransaction.BlueChipRealtysimplyactsasamatchmaker.Aninvestorlooksforbuyerswhohavesolid cashflow,arecreditworthyanddebt-free,andareeagertobuyahouse.Buyerslooktomatchwithaninvestorwho fitsthebuyers'financialneedsandde-sires.

Desired 200%, Min 200%, Max 200%

Because investors supply the majority of cash, they define most of the terms of the transaction. Blue Chip Realty simply acts as a matchmaker. An investor looks for buyers who have solid cash flow, are credit worthy and debt-free, and are eager to buy a house. Buyers look to match with an investor who fits the buyers' financial needs and desires.

normal pen advance when necessary. These numbers are not percentages of the pen advance; they are percentages of the space band. Thus, the default value of −5% indicates that character spacing can be narrowed by as much as 5% of the space band. The Maximum value defines the greatest amount of space that can be added to the normal pen advance. The default Maximum value of 25% means that you will allow PageMaker to insert a quarter of a space band between characters.

Occasionally, PageMaker cannot stay within the ranges you specify for acceptable word and letter spacing. For example, you will sometimes see lines that are too loose (with lots of white space in the line) when hyphenation is turned off, or when a word cannot be hyphenated.

To help you locate the lines in which PageMaker had to override your spacing attributes, choose Preferences from the File menu and turn on the Show Loose/Tight Lines option in the Preferences dialog box. The lines that are looser or tighter than the range in the Spacing Attributes dialog box are then shaded in the publication, as shown in Figure 9.19. You might choose to kern or track these particular lines or to change the hyphenation.

FIGURE 9.19: *Lines that are too loose or too tight are shaded*

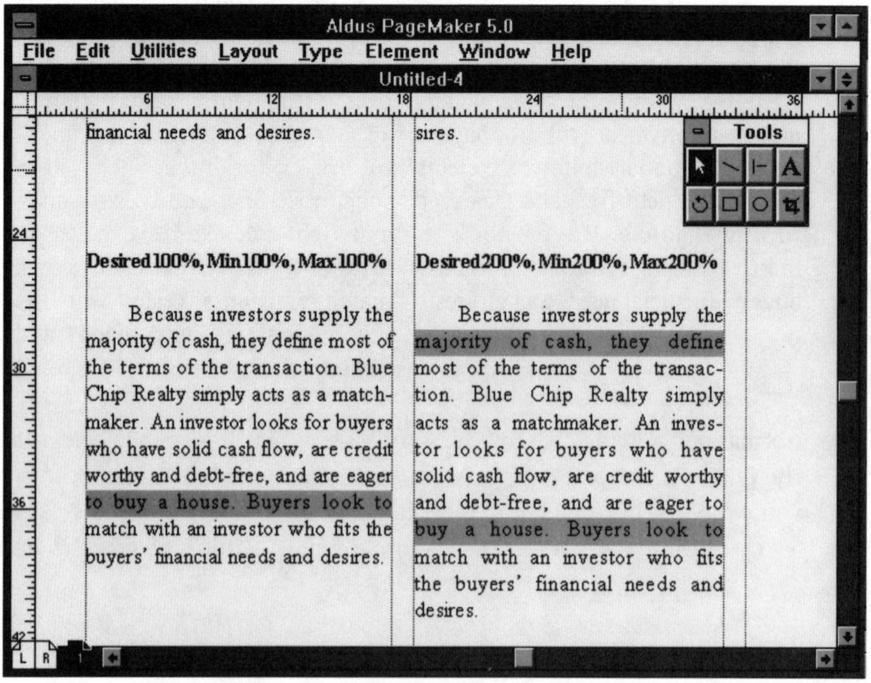

SUMMARY

Depending upon your experience with typography, the letter and word spacing could make all the difference in the world, or none at all. Rest assured, however, that virtually all documents will have readers who notice and appreciate good kerning.

HANDS-ON PRACTICE

In Chapter 8's hands-on practice exercise, you placed the company name and address in column 1 of the brochure. If you rotate this text, it becomes a return address, and you can use the brochure as a self-mailer. Follow these steps to rotate the text 90 degrees clockwise:

1. Open the BROCH9.PM5 publication in the C:\PM5PUBS directory.

2. With the pointer tool, select the address block.

3. Choose the rotation tool and place the starburst cursor inside the center of the text block.

4. Hold down Shift and drag straight down. (The Shift key constrains the rotation to 45-degree increments).

5. Release the mouse button when the text block has rotated 90 degrees clockwise.

6. Switch to 75% view so that you can see the rotated text.

7. Switch to the pointer tool and drag the text block so that it is aligned in the upper-right corner of the column (inside the margin and column guides). Refer to Figure 9.20 for the location.

8. Save the file.

9. Print page 1 to see how the rotated text looks.

FIGURE 9.20: *The rotated address block*

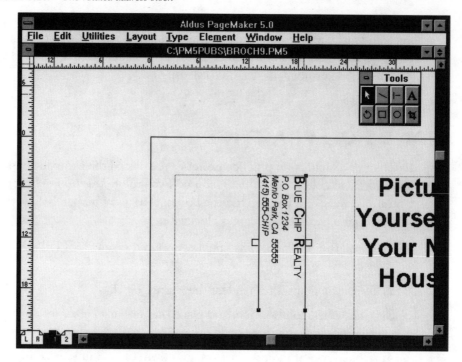

NoTe

Another way to rotate the text block would be to display
the control palette and enter -90 in the rotation field.

part

T h R e e

In this part, you will learn how to enhance your publication with graphic elements—ranging from a vertical rule between columns to detailed drawings. In the first two chapters, you will learn how to create graphics with PageMaker's built-in drawing tools and to import images created with graphics programs. Chapter 12 is devoted entirely to the topic of using color in your publications. Chapter 13 explains how to use the Table Editor that comes with PageMaker. It is grouped with the graphics topics because a columnar table becomes a graphic element once you enhance it with lines and shades; and like a graphic image, a Table Editor table must be imported into PageMaker.

WORKING WITH GRAPHICS

Using the Graphics Tools

⨍ast tracks

To create a box with rounded corners: **365**

Use the rectangle tool to draw the box. With the box selected, choose Element ➤ Rounded Corners. Select the desired rounding and choose OK.

To change the stacking order of objects: **366**

Use the Bring to Front or Send to Back options on the Element menu.

To create reverse type: **376**

Type the text and draw an empty box around it. Select the text with the text tool and choose Type ➤ Type Style ➤ Reverse. Then select the box with the pointer tool, and choose Element ➤ Fill ➤ Solid.

To draw a shadow box: **377**

Draw a box with a paper fill. Copy the box (Ctrl+C) and paste it (Ctrl+V). Fill the second box with a solid shade, and reposition the box if necessary. Send the solid box behind the first box by using the Send to Back option on the Element menu.

To move a graphic: **382**

Select the object with the pointer tool. Click and drag the graphic to the desired location. If the graphic has a fill, you can click anywhere (inside or on the outline). Otherwise, you must click on the object's outline.

To make multiple copies of a graphic object: 383

Copy the selected object to the Clipboard (Ctrl+C). Choose Edit ➤ Multiple Paste. Enter the number of copies to paste, and specify how much to offset the copies.

To create a custom vertical ruler: 387

Pull down the File menu, and choose Preferences. Display the drop-down list next to Vertical Ruler and choose Custom. Enter your body text leading next to Points. Choose OK. Turn on Snap to Rulers on the Guides and Rulers menu—this will create a magnetic effect between your graphic elements and the ruler increments.

To create rules above or below paragraphs: 387

Select the paragraph with the text tool and press Ctrl+M to display the Paragraph Specifications dialog box. Click on the Rules button, and turn on Rule Above Paragraph or Rule Below Paragraph. Select the desired line style, line width, and indents. Use the Options button to adjust the vertical position of the rules.

To anchor a graphic object to text: 393

Cut the object to the Clipboard (Ctrl+X). Choose the text tool and place the cursor where you want to insert the graphic. Paste the object (Ctrl+V). If you want the graphic to overlay the text, specify 0-point leading for the graphic.

HIS CHAPTER CONCENTRATES ON
the interesting ways in which graphic elements can liven up your publications. After a brief review of the PageMaker toolbox drawing tools, you'll
learn how to set different line widths and styles and how to create graphic
effects with fills. We'll also describe how to create two kinds of graphics
that will flow with your text: paragraph rules and inline graphics.

DRAWING GRAPHICS

In Chapter 2 you had an opportunity to practice creating graphics with
PageMaker's tools, and you've seen that they are easy to use. The following
sections provide more details on some of the drawing techniques you've
used in earlier chapters.

TOOL REVIEW

Figure 10.1 identifies the drawing tools in the toolbox. Here's a review of
each tool's function:

- ➤ The line tool draws a line in any direction.

FIGURE 10.1: *The drawing tools*

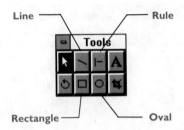

➤ The rule tool restricts the line angle to increments of 45 degrees. Use it to create horizontal and vertical rules.

➤ The rectangle tool draws a box with square corners. To create a perfect square, hold down the Shift key as you draw. Note: Unlike previous versions of PageMaker, version 5.0 doesn't offer a rounded-corner tool. To create a box with rounded corners, see the next section "Tips on Drawing Boxes."

➤ The oval tool creates circular shapes. By holding down the Shift key as you draw, you can produce a perfect circle.

After you choose one of the drawing tools, the pointer becomes a cross-bar shape when you move it onto the page or pasteboard. You draw by clicking and dragging; release the mouse button when the graphic is the desired size.

TIPS ON DRAWING BOXES

After drawing a box, you can use the Rounded Corners option on the Element menu to change the angle of the corners. With this option, you can round the corners of a square-corner box, square the corners of a rounded-corner box, or make the corners less or more round.

A common use of the rectangle tool is to draw a box around text. The box around the *Winter Hours* text in Figure 10.2 was created with the rectangle tool.

FIGURE 10.2: *The boxed text was created with the rectangle tool.*

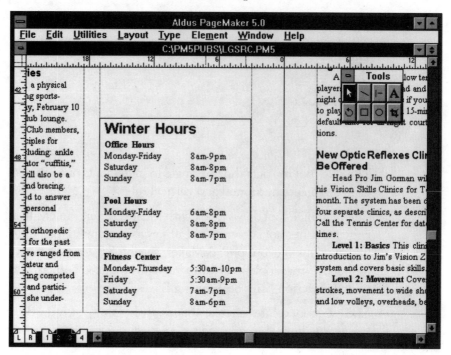

When you draw a box around text, remember to allow space between the outline and the text. If you draw the box on top of the column guides, you need to indent the text on the right and left. One way to indent the text is to adjust the size of the text block with the pointer tool. A more precise way is to select all the text with the text tool and set right and left paragraph indents. In Figure 10.2, 0.5-pica indents were used.

Another way to box text is with the inline graphics feature, described later in the chapter. A third way to box text is using the KeyLiner Addition (see the sidebar below).

CHANGING THE STACKING ORDER OF OBJECTS

Whenever you draw an object—line, rule, rectangle, or oval—that overlaps another object, the last one drawn is placed on top. You can change

Using the Create Keyline Addition

The Create Keyline Addition draws a box around any selected object (for example, a text block or a graphic). With the object's handles as the reference points, the box can be exactly the size of the object or be larger or smaller by a specified number of points (in .01-point increments) on each side. A positive value will make the box larger than the selected object; a negative value will make it smaller. The box can be placed either in front of or behind the object.

For convenience, you can set the box's fill and line attributes directly from the Create Keyline dialog box—just click on the Attributes button. The Overprint, Reverse Line, and Transparent options are discussed later in the chapter.

The box that is created with Create Keyline is exactly like one created with the rectangle tool. Therefore, you can also set the fill and line attributes using the Element menu. In fact, once you've created the box with Create Keyline, any changes must be made via the Element menu. Returning to Create Keyline would create an additional box.

There are many uses for this handy and easy-to-use Addition, including using it for trapping graphics and framing graphics or text.

the stacking order of an object by selecting it and pressing Ctrl+F or Ctrl+B to move the object forward or backward in the order. Or, if you prefer, you can choose Bring to Front or Send to Back from the Element menu.

See Figure 10.3 for an example of five stacked objects. The skewed rectangle and the small circle are on the bottom layer; the horizontal rectangle is on the middle layer; the rounded rectangle and the large circle are on the top layer.

Some thought may be required to obtain the proper stacking order for multiple overlapping objects. For example, if you have more than two objects that you want to arrange in a particular order, you will not be able to move an object one layer at a time. You will have to bring the top object to the front and then send each successive layer to the back until you have the objects in the order you want.

FIGURE 10.3:   *Five objects stacked using the Bring to Front and Send to Back commands*

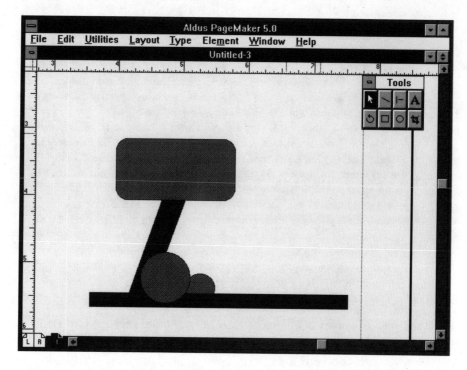

When objects are stacked on top of one another, it is often difficult to select the object you want. If you hold down Ctrl as you click on the stack, PageMaker will select another object. Keep Ctrl+clicking until the desired object is selected.

SETTING LINE WIDTHS AND STYLES

By default, PageMaker lines—those drawn with the line tool or outlining a shape drawn with another tool—are 1-point solid lines. The Line option on the Element menu allows you to change the width, or *weight*, and style of lines.

MAKING LINE SPECIFICATIONS

You can make your line specifications before or after you draw the graphic. If you specify the line characteristics before you draw the graphic, the graphic will be drawn with that line style. To change the style after you draw a graphic, first select it by clicking on it with the pointer tool. (Actually, if you just drew the object, it's already selected.) A selected line has selection boxes, called *graphic handles*, at the beginning and end of the line. A selected shape is surrounded by eight graphic handles.

Pay close attention to which graphic element, if any, is selected when you choose line specifications. If nothing is selected, you will change the default style—this style will apply to any new lines or shapes you draw. If a line, box, or circle is selected, you will change the line specifications of that particular graphic.

A common mistake that you might make when you want to draw two lines of different weights is to draw the first line, and then specify the weight of the second line. But because the first line is automatically selected after you draw it, you end up changing the weight of the first line, not the second one. To avoid this mistake, unselect the first line before you specify the weight of the second line. Unselect by clicking elsewhere on the page or pasteboard. This process is called *clicking off*.

CHOOSING THE POINT SIZE

As you can see from the Line menu, shown in Figure 10.4, lines come in a variety of point sizes, ranging from hairline (the thinnest) to 12 points. The memo form illustrated in Figure 10.5 uses three line weights: The line under the company name is 2 points, the series of thin lines are hairlines, and the heavy line at the bottom is 6 points.

Vertical *rules* (lines) are useful for separating columns, especially when the text is not justified. A 1-point line is probably the maximum weight you would use for this type of line. If you want to repeat between-column vertical rules on every page of a publication, draw them on the master pages, as explained in Chapter 14.

FIGURE 10.4: *The Line menu*

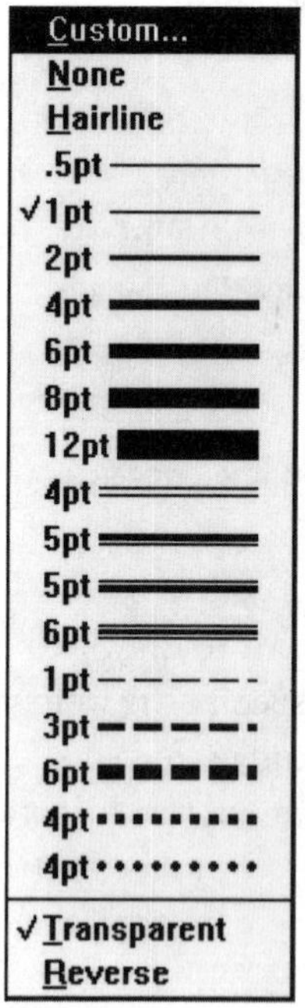

FIGURE 10.5: *The memo form with three line weights*

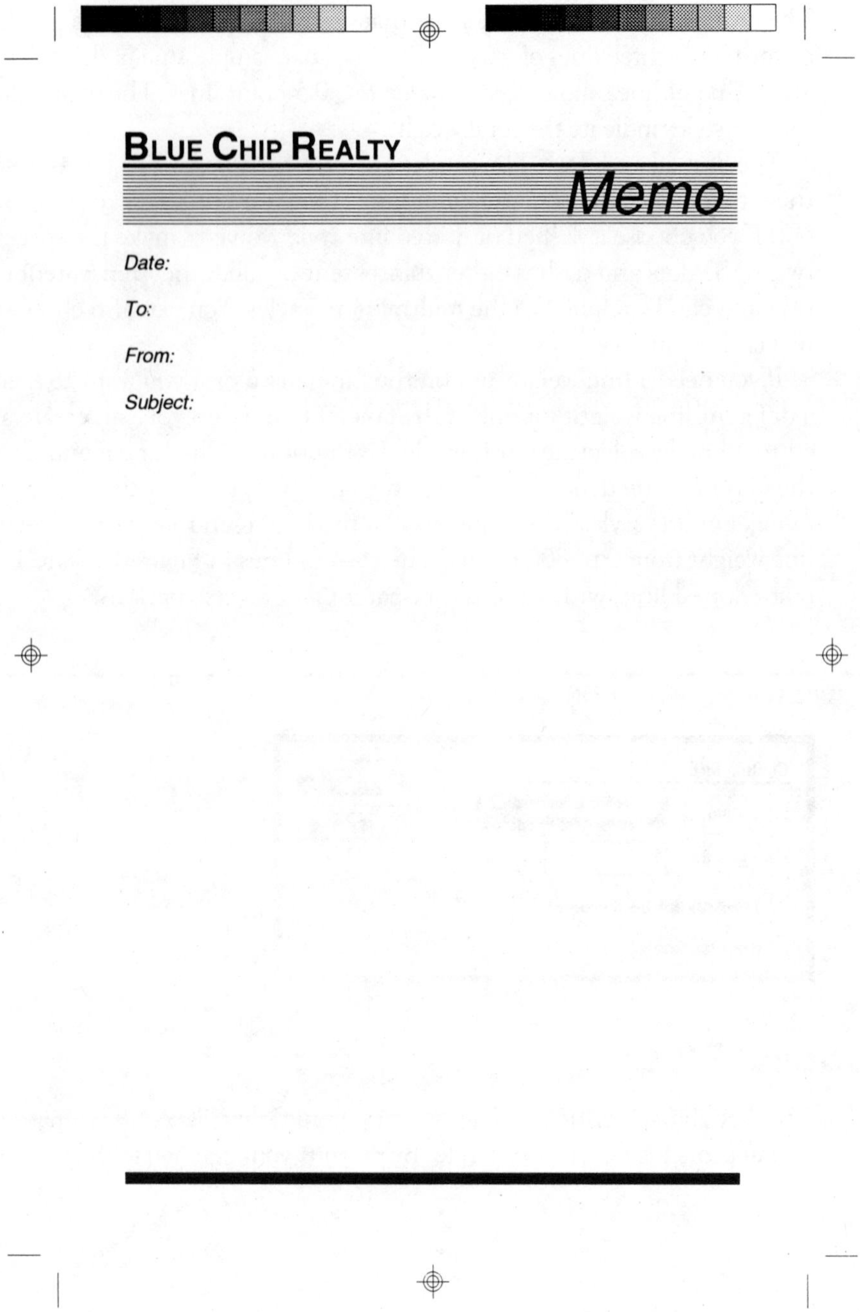

BLUE CHIP REALTY

Memo

Date:

To:

From:

Subject:

SELECTING A LINE STYLE

The Line menu shows the line styles that are available. Some of the line styles create two or three lines of varying weights. For example, one of the styles creates a 2-point line sandwiched between two 0.5-point lines. The sizes next to the line styles indicate the total weight.

The dashed and dotted line styles are frequently used with boxes. Use them to enclose coupons and order forms that you want your readers to cut out. If you choose a dashed or dotted line style, you can make the spaces between the dots and dashes either transparent or solid; the Transparent option also can be applied to the multiple-line styles. You can also choose to reverse any line style.

Version
5.0

If you need a line weight not on the Line menu or if you want to specify a different line weight for one of the fancier line styles, you can create a custom line by selecting Custom, the first option on the Line menu. From the Custom Line dialog box shown in Figure 10.6, you can choose from a number of line styles (the same ones on the Line menu) and then specify a line weight from 0 to 800 points. The custom lines in Figure 10.7 are 10-point dotted lines with various transparent and reverse options.

FIGURE 10.6: *The Custom Line dialog box*

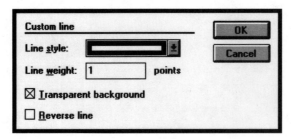

USING FILLS

Another characteristic of a PageMaker graphic is its *fill*. A fill is a pattern that appears inside a box or circle. By default, your geometric shapes are

FIGURE 10.7: *Custom lines with examples of transparent and reverse options*

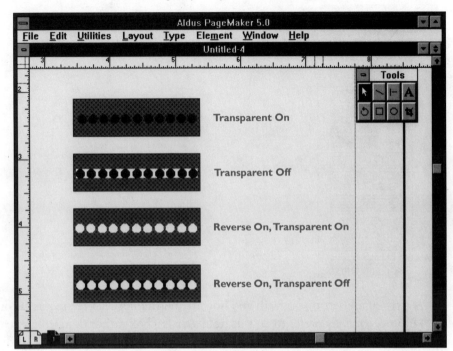

empty. You can fill them with different shades or patterns by using the Fill menu, shown in Figure 10.8.

As with line specifications, you can make your fill specifications before or after you draw the object. Before you specify the fill, make sure the correct object is selected. Otherwise, you could fill the wrong element or change the default fill (if no object is selected).

Eight different line patterns are listed at the bottom of the Fill menu. You can create vertical, horizontal, diagonal, or criss-cross hairlines in two different increments. The number of lines that are created depends on the size of the box you draw. The hairlines in Figure 10.5 were created by drawing a box with the rectangle tool, using a horizontal-line fill pattern, and setting the box's line weight to None. The following sections describe some other ways to use fills.

FIGURE 10.8: *The Fill menu*

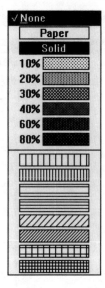

Version
5.0

If you are setting both fill and line attributes for a selected rectangle or ellipse, you may prefer to do this from a dialog box rather than from two separate menus. *Fill and Line* is a new option on the Element menu; its dialog box is shown in Figure 10.9. To save you a trip back to the Line menu, the Fill and Line dialog box contains options for choosing reverse and transparent lines.

This dialog box also contains a setting called Overprint. See Chapter 12 for an explanation of overprinting and knocking out.

USING SCREENS TO SHADE TEXT

The percentages in the Fill menu refer to shades, or *screens*. The higher the percentage, the darker the shade. Unless you are using color, the screens are in shades of gray.

You can create an interesting effect by placing a screen behind text, as shown in the sports page heading in Figure 10.10. This box was drawn with the rectangle tool; a 20% shade was selected from the Fill menu. The outline around the shade was removed by choosing None from the Line menu.

FIGURE 10.9: *The Fill and Line dialog box*

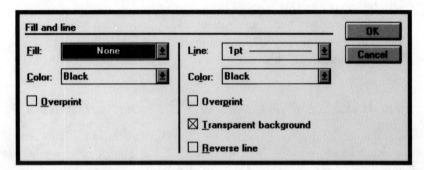

FIGURE 10.10: *A heading with a 20% gray shade*

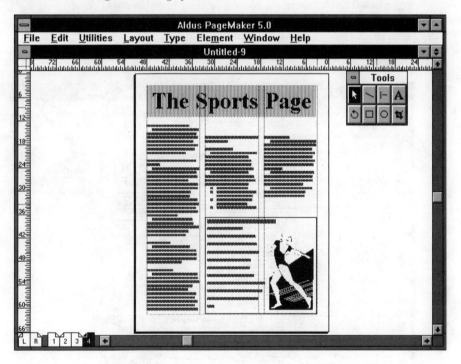

Because screens are actually made up of many small dots, these dots might be too noticeable on a 300-dpi laser printer. If your page contains a screen and you want the best quality, consider printing it on a higher-resolution device, such as a Linotronic 1270-dpi or 2540-dpi typesetting machine. Appendix C describes how to use a typesetting service bureau.

PROVIDING A BACKGROUND FOR REVERSE TYPE

As explained in Chapter 4, the reverse type style switches the character color from black to white (or to the current paper color), so this white text needs to be placed against a shaded background. A solid fill, as opposed to a percentage shade, provides the greatest contrast and legibility. Unless you are using color, the solid shade is black (adding color is discussed in Chapter 12). The sports page heading in Figure 10.11 is an example of reversed type.

FIGURE 10.11:   *A reversed heading*

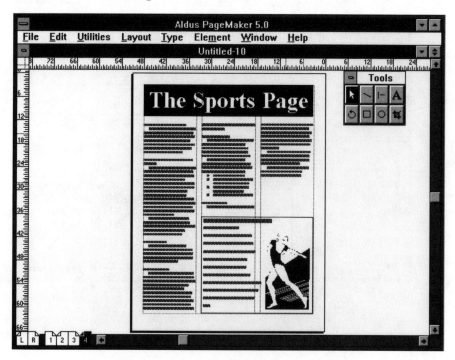

The most legible reverse type is large, sans serif, and bold. Do not reverse small body text because it may be unreadable.

Creating reverse type can be difficult because at one stage you either have white text on a white background or black text on a black background. If you reverse the type first, you can't see the text, so you don't know where to draw the box. If you draw the solid-fill box around black type, you can't see the text to reverse it. The best way to handle this problem is to follow these steps, in the order outlined below:

1. Type and format the text, but do not reverse it yet.

2. Draw an empty box around the text, but do not add the solid fill yet.

3. Select the text with the text tool and then choose Reverse from the Type Style menu.

4. Select the box with the pointer tool and then fill it with the solid shade.

WARNING

Sometimes when you draw a box with a shaded or solid fill over text, you will not be able to see the text because the box is overlaying it. To solve this problem, you need to place the box behind the text. Select the box and choose the Send to Back option from the Element menu (or press Ctrl+B).

DRAWING SHADOW BOXES

A shadow box, such as the one shown in Figure 10.12, is actually made up of two boxes: The one in the front contains text and a graphic, and the box in the back has a solid fill.

FIGURE 10.12:   *The text and graphic are enclosed in a shadow box.*

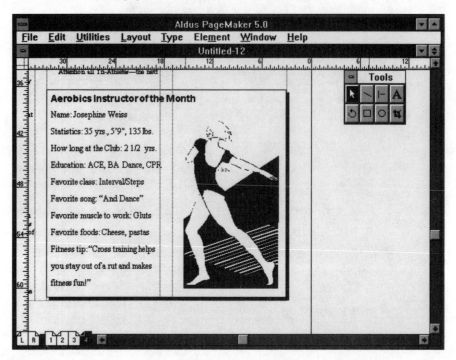

You can either manually draw each of the boxes, or you can draw one box and copy it with the Clipboard. Here are the basic steps for creating a shadow box:

1. Draw a box with a paper fill. *Paper* is an opaque fill that is the color of the paper (usually white).

2. Copy this box to the Clipboard (Ctrl+C) and then paste it (Ctrl+V). It is now on top of the first box, slightly offset to the right and down.

3. Fill the second box with a solid shade.

4. If necessary, reposition the solid box.

5. Send the solid box behind the first box by using the Send to Back option on the Element menu.

CREATING BLEEDS

A *bleed* is a graphic element that extends clear to the edge of the page; margins are disregarded. Just glance through a magazine, and you will notice how frequently bleeds are used. You will often see reversed text inside a band of color that bleeds off the top of the page, and photographs and artwork are sometimes bled off the page as well. Occasionally, an entire page is shaded with a color or screen.

To create a bleed, draw an unlined, filled box that extends beyond the edge of the page, as shown in the example in Figure 10.13. This slight oversizing makes sure that the bleed will indeed extend to the very edge of the page after the paper is cut to the page size. In other words, it allows for error in the paper-cutting process.

Creating bleeds on an $8\frac{1}{2}$-by-11-inch page presents a problem because laser printers cannot print to the edge of the page. These printers have

FIGURE 10.13: *A solid shade that bleeds off the page*

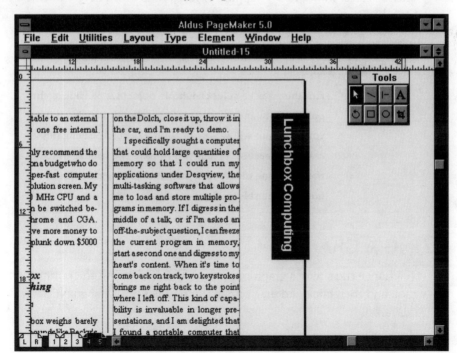

built-in $\frac{1}{4}$- to $\frac{1}{2}$-inch margins on all four sides of the page. One solution is to print the publication on a Linotronic typesetting machine that doesn't have this limitation (see Appendix C). Another solution is to set up a slightly smaller page size—for example, 8 by 10 inches. If a final page size of $8\frac{1}{2}$ by 11 inches is necessary, you can tell the print shop to enlarge the page. But keep in mind that enlarging will lower the resolution.

MANIPULATING GRAPHICS

Adjusting the size and placement of a graphic is similar to changing the size and position of a text block. The main difference is that selected text blocks have window shades and selected graphics have *graphic boundaries*.

To select a graphic, use the pointer tool. If the graphic has a fill, you can select it by clicking anywhere on the graphic—inside it or on the outline. To select a graphic that doesn't have a fill, you must click on the graphic outline. To select multiple objects, hold down Shift as you click on each one. To select multiple overlapping objects, hold down both the Ctrl and Shift keys.

Another way to select multiple objects is to choose the pointer tool and click and drag around the objects. As you drag, you will see a box with a dotted outline; this is called a *marquee*. When you release the mouse button, the marquee disappears but all objects inside the marquee will be selected.

SIZING A GRAPHIC

To change the size of a graphic, you simply select it with the pointer tool, and then click and drag one of the handles until the graphic is the desired size.

The selection handles in the middle of the graphic boundary change either the width or the height. The corner handles adjust both the width and the height as you drag. These handles are pointed out in Figure 10.14.

When you change the length of a line, hold down the Shift key as you drag the selection handle. Without the Shift key, the line will be jagged.

FIGURE 10.14: *Use the handles to change the size of a graphic.*

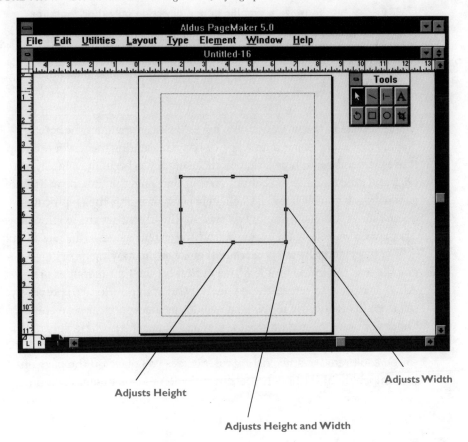

Adjusts Height

Adjusts Height and Width

Adjusts Width

MOVING A GRAPHIC

To move a graphic, just click and drag it to the desired location using the pointer tool. You don't even have to select it first. However, if the graphic is selected, do not click and drag a handle. If you do, you will end up sizing the graphic instead of moving it. Where you click on the graphic depends on whether the graphic is filled or empty. You can click anywhere on a filled graphic (inside or on the outline), but you must click on the outline of an empty graphic.

> To move a graphic in one direction only (horizontal or vertical), hold the Shift key while clicking and dragging. Then, whichever way you drag first is the only way the object will move. This can help maintain alignment between objects.

While you are in the process of moving a graphic, sometimes the actual graphic moves and sometimes a line or box representing the size of the graphic moves, depending on how long you click before you begin dragging. If you click and hold for a second before you start dragging, the actual graphic moves as you drag. If you click and immediately begin dragging, the graphic itself doesn't move; instead a line or box representing the size of the graphic moves. Then, when you release the mouse button, the graphic moves to the new location.

If you accidentally move a column guide while moving or sizing a graphic, use the Undo Guide Move option on the Edit menu, or press Alt+Backspace, to return the guide to its original position. To prevent yourself from inadvertently moving the guides in the future, turn on the Lock Guides option (located on the Guides and Rulers menu). However, you should be aware that this option locks ruler guides as well as column guides, so you can't remove any existing ruler guides you place on the page until you unlock them (although you can still add new ruler guides when the guides are locked).

COPYING A GRAPHIC AND USING MULTIPLE PASTE

To copy a graphic, select it with the pointer tool and choose Copy from the Edit menu or press Ctrl+C. You can then paste the graphic into your publication by choosing Paste from the Edit menu or pressing Ctrl+V. The copied object will be pasted slightly offset (down and to the right) from the original. To place the copied object on a different page, move to that page before pasting. The duplicate will be placed in the same relative location on the new page unless this page has a different view; in this case, the copy will be pasted in the center of the window.

Version
5.0

To paste more than one copy of the graphic, you can use the Multiple Paste option on the Edit menu. (Note that you must first copy the selected object to the Clipboard.) You can choose how many copies to paste and specify how much to offset the copies—horizontally, vertically, or both. The offset is measured from the upper-left corner of the original object. Positive offsets place the copies below and to the right of the original object; negative offsets place them above and to the left.

Figure 10.15 shows an example of a box pasted three times. The copies were offset .75 inches vertically and 0 inches horizontally. The beauty of Multiple Paste is its ability to evenly space several objects. It saves you from having to measure carefully and use ruler guides.

PRECISE POSITIONING

While you are drawing a graphic, don't be overly concerned about its exact size and position. Create the graphic in Fit in Window view so that you can position it with respect to the entire page; then zoom in on the area for precise positioning. We recommend that you do all your graphic positioning in Actual Size or even 200% view. Frequently, elements that look properly aligned in Fit in Window view do not appear aligned in a more magnified view.

One way to make sure graphic elements are aligned is to use your column and ruler guides as guidelines (they aren't called guides for nothing). The Snap to Guides option (choose Layout ➤ Guides and Rulers to locate this option) ensures that graphic and text elements that are drawn near a guide are actually aligned on the guide. This option creates a magnetic effect between the guides and your graphics (as well as text blocks) so that

FIGURE 10.15: *The boxes were copied and evenly spaced with the Multiple Paste command.*

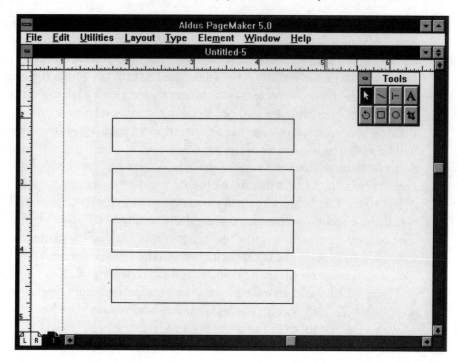

whenever the element gets near a guide, it is pulled to the guide. With the Snap to Guides feature turned on, you can draw a side of a box near a column guide, and the box will be exactly on top of the column guide. You cannot be assured of this precision when Snap to Guides is turned off.

! WARNING

> **While it is to your benefit to keep Snap to Guides turned on most of the time, you will need to turn it off to position elements near, but not on, a margin, column, or ruler guide.**

Don't forget to use the rulers themselves to help you with graphic alignment. A dotted line in the ruler indicates where the cross-bar is on the page.

Ruler guides—the ones you pull out of the horizontal and vertical rulers—are invaluable tools for lining up graphics with each other or with text blocks. For example, you can use ruler guides to make sure several horizontal lines begin and end at the same point. Ruler guides in Actual Size view provide you with much more accurate positioning than the eyeball method. You can have up to 40 ruler guides per publication, so use them freely.

Depending on the line weight and the page view you are in, you may not see a line you draw on top of a column, margin, or ruler guide. For example, you will not see a hairline drawn on a ruler or column guide in any page view. To make sure that these lines are indeed there, you can turn off all the guides (choose Layout ➤ Guides and Rulers ➤ Guides, or just press Ctrl+J). Or if the line is drawn on a ruler guide, you can move the guide out of the way.

POSITIONING AND SIZING
A GRAPHIC USING THE CONTROL PALETTE

Version
5.0

The control palette allows precise positioning and sizing of graphics. Figure 10.16 points out the sizing and positioning fields in the control palette.

The X and Y position options allow you to position a graphic by specifying horizontal (X) and vertical (Y) coordinates, measured from the ruler's zero point. The zero point is at the upper-left corner of a right-hand page or the upper-right corner of a left-hand page, unless you have changed it. The *proxy* (see Figure 10.16) is an important part of positioning an object with the control palette. The proxy is a representation of the selected object, and has nine reference points. The enlarged point is the active reference point from which objects are measured. For example, if you click on the point inside the proxy, the X and Y values reflect the distance from the ruler zero point to the center of the selected object. Or, if you click on the upper-left corner of the proxy, the X and Y values reflect the distance from the zero point to the upper-left corner of the selected object.

FIGURE 10.16: *You can size and position a graphic by using options in the control palette.*

Apply Button   **Position Fields**

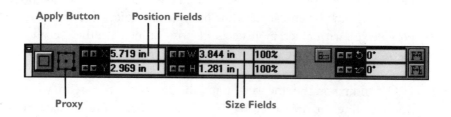

Proxy   **Size Fields**

The W and H options tell you the width and height of the selected graphic.

Any changes made to the control palette affect the graphic. To reposition the graphic, you can change the X and Y or W and H settings a small amount by clicking on the nudge buttons. Each time you click on the button, the value is nudged .01 inch. If you hold down Ctrl as you nudge (a *power nudge*), the value is increased or decreased by about .1 inch. As you nudge, the object immediately moves on the screen. If you know the exact values, you can directly enter them in the size or position fields, and then either press Enter or click on the Apply button.

The size and position fields will accept arithmetic expressions. You can use +, –, *, or / to add, subtract, multiply, or divide numbers.

CREATING A CUSTOM VERTICAL RULER

When you are using a leading grid, you want all elements on the page—your graphics as well as the text—to line up on the grid. This alignment becomes almost automatic if you create a custom vertical ruler that matches your body text leading and then turn on the Snap to Rulers option. After you set these two options, the custom ruler is in increments of your magic number, and there is a magnetic effect between your graphic elements and the ruler increments.

To create a custom vertical ruler, follow these steps:

1. On the File menu, choose Preferences.

2. For the Vertical Ruler, choose Custom and enter your body text leading (your magic number) next to Points.

3. On the Layout menu, choose Guides and Rulers, and then turn on Snap to Rulers (or press Shift+Ctrl+Y).

The tick marks on the custom ruler correspond to your units of leading. If your text is properly aligned on the leading grid, all your text baselines will rest on the tick marks.

As you draw, size, and position your graphics, they will automatically jump to the tick marks on the ruler. The ruler guides you pull out will also automatically line up with these tick marks.

PLACING LINES WITH PARAGRAPHS

The drawing tools aren't the only way to create horizontal lines in Page-Maker. The Paragraph Rules dialog box, accessed through the Paragraph Specifications dialog box, has options that place lines above or below paragraphs, without you having to actually draw the lines.

The main advantages to paragraph rules are that they flow with the text and that they can be part of a style—and therefore, applied automatically.

The disadvantage to drawing a line above a paragraph using a graphic tool is that the line is anchored to the page; if the text reflows, the line doesn't move with the paragraph. A paragraph rule, on the other hand, always remains with the text in its paragraph. Another advantage is that you can automate the position and length of paragraph rules, while with the drawing tools, you must manually position and size each line.

Some uses of paragraph rules are to set off pull-quotes, to create dividing lines between articles, and to emphasize headings or other important paragraphs. Figure 10.17 shows a rule above a subhead.

To add a rule above and/or below a paragraph, place the text cursor in the paragraph and press Ctrl+M to bring up the Paragraph Specifications dialog box. Then choose the Rules command button, and the Paragraph Rules dialog box will display as shown in Figure 10.18. Note that there are identical options for the rules above and below the paragraph. You can turn on either or both rules for a paragraph, and set different options for each rule.

The Line Style list offers options for various weights of single lines (1, 2, 4, 6, 8, and 12 points), double lines, a triple line, dots, and dashes.

FIGURE 10.17: *The rule above the subhead was created with PageMaker's paragraph rule feature.*

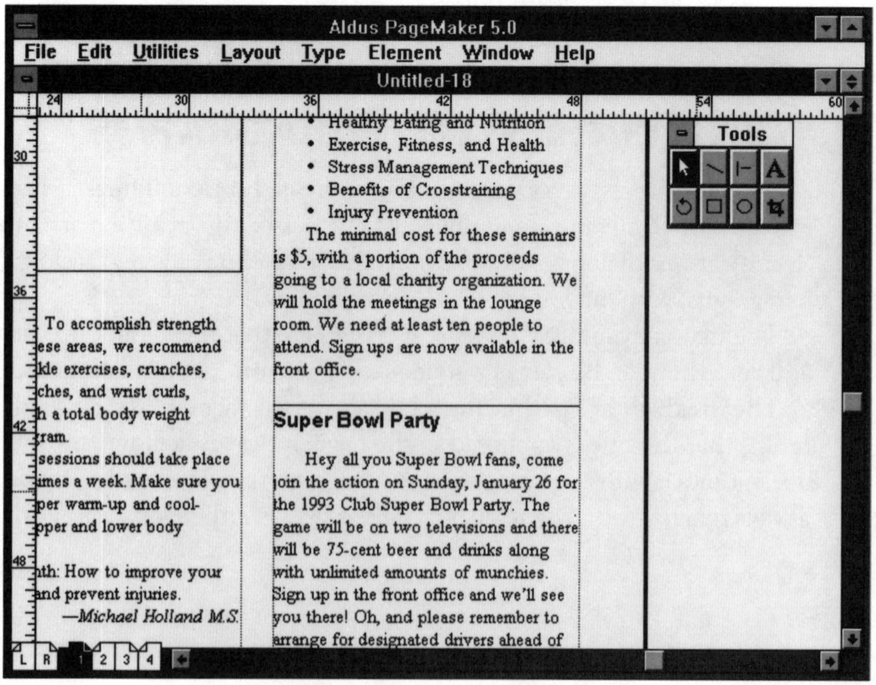

FIGURE 10.18: *The Paragraph Rules dialog box*

Paragraph rules

☐ Rule above paragraph

Line style: 1pt ————— ▼

Line color: Black ▼

Line width: ○ Width of text ◉ Width of column

Indent: Left 0 picas Right 0 picas

☐ Rule below paragraph

Line style: 1pt ————— ▼

Line color: Black ▼

Line width: ○ Width of text ◉ Width of column

Indent: Left 0 picas Right 0 picas

OK

Cancel

Options...

The length of the rule is controlled by three options: Width of Text, Width of Column, and Indent. With the default line width, Width of Column, the line spans the entire column width. With the Width of Text option, the rule's length corresponds to the length of the first line in the paragraph (or the last line, for rules below the paragraph). To create rules that are shorter or longer than the line width, use the Indent option. Enter a positive number next to Left or Right to make the rule shorter; enter a negative number to create a longer rule.

Actually, a more accurate name for the **Width of Column** option is **Width of Text Block.** If the text block goes across two columns, the rule will also span two columns (see Figure 10.19).

FIGURE 10.19: *A paragraph rule that spans two columns*

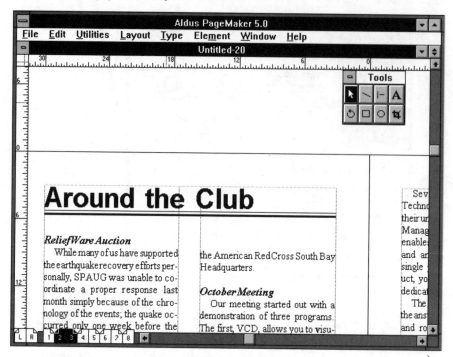

ADJUSTING PARAGRAPH RULES

The distance between the rules and the text is a function of the paragraph's leading. If you find that the rules are too close to the text (which they frequently are), you can add extra space by using the selections in the Paragraph Rule Options dialog box, shown in Figure 10.20. To display this box, press Ctrl+M, click on the Rules button, and then the Options button.

For both the top and bottom rules, the space is measured from the baselines. This measuring system is no problem for the bottom rule because the value you enter is the amount of space added below the baseline. But because the rule above is measured from the baseline and not from the top of the capital letters, you need to add the text's cap height to whatever space you want between the text and the rule. The *cap height* is the height of the capital letters in a given font and size, usually two-thirds of the point size.

FIGURE 10.20: *The Paragraph Rule Options dialog box*

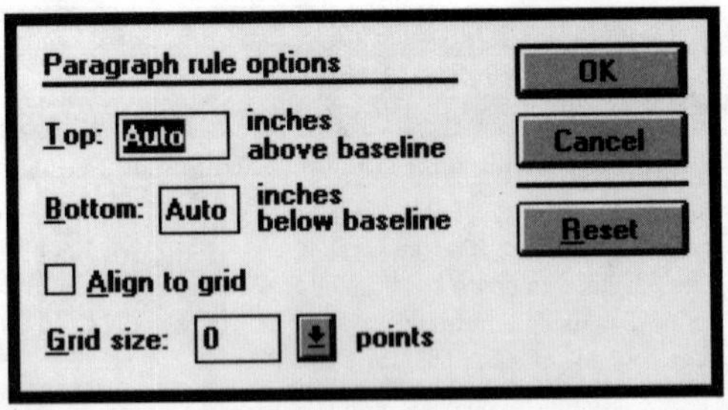

```
┌─────────────────────────────────────────────────┐
│  Paragraph rule options          ┌──────────┐    │
│  ──────────────────────          │    OK    │    │
│              ┌──────┐  inches     └──────────┘    │
│  Top: │ Auto │  above baseline                    │
│              └──────┘            ┌──────────┐     │
│              ┌──────┐  inches    │  Cancel  │     │
│  Bottom: │ Auto │  below baseline └──────────┘    │
│              └──────┘            ┌──────────┐     │
│  ☐ Align to grid                 │  Reset   │     │
│              ┌──────┐ ┌──┐       └──────────┘     │
│  Grid size: │  0   │ │ ± │  points                │
│              └──────┘ └──┘                         │
└─────────────────────────────────────────────────┘
```

For example, if you want 24 points of space and your text is 12 points with a cap height of 8 points, specify 32 points of space above the baseline.

CREATING PULL-QUOTES

Pull-quotes are catchy sentences that are pulled out of an article and placed inside rules, a box, or a circle. They have three purposes: to grab the reader's attention, to add a graphic element to a page that looks too gray, and to lengthen an article that is too short for the allotted space. Figure 10.21 shows how a pull-quote can enhance a page.

The text for the pull-quote should be in a separate, unthreaded text block. Decide where you want the pull-quote to go and adjust other text blocks to create space for it. For example, shorten the text block in the column you want the pull-quote to go into. If the quote is to go in the middle of a column, you'll need to divide the text block into two separate blocks, as described in the "Separating a Text Block" section in Chapter 8. To create the pull-quote text block, you can either type the text in the empty space you created, create a text box on the pasteboard, or copy the sentence from the article. If you go the copy route, you'll want to copy with the text tool and paste with the pointer tool; this procedure will create an unthreaded text block.

Once the text is in its own text block, you can add paragraph rules above or below it, or enclose it in a box or circle. It's important that the pull-quote is distinctive from the body text, but at the same time doesn't conflict with it. For example, you shouldn't set the pull-quote in the same exact typeface, size, and style as your body text. Nor should you set the

FIGURE 10.21: *This pull-quote has paragraph rules above and below it to separate it from the body*

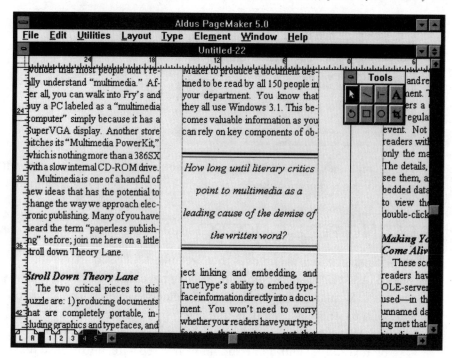

body text in Bookman and the pull-quote in Times Roman (two different serif fonts). Here are a few basic rules to follow when formatting your pull-quote text:

- → Use the same typeface as your body text but with a different style (italic or bold) and a larger size.

- → Add extra leading to make the quote easier to read and to further distinguish it from the body text.

- → Make sure there is adequate space between the pull-quote and the surrounding body text. You may want to set left and right indents.

WRAPPING TEXT AROUND A PULL-QUOTE

Figure 10.22 shows a pull-quote that spans part of two columns. How this effect was created may not be immediately obvious. When you initially place the text block between the columns, the pull-quote overlays the columnar text. PageMaker does have a text wrap feature but it applies only to wrapping text around graphic objects, not text blocks. Therefore, what you have to do is draw a box around the text block and then make the box invisible by specifying None for the line style and the fill. (Unless you want to see the box.) Here are the precise steps for creating the pull-quote shown in Figure 10.22:

1. Create and format the pull-quote. If you like, you can copy text from a story and then paste it on the pasteboard. The dots above and below the paragraph in Figure 10.22 are a rule line style.

2. Use the rectangle tool to draw a box between the two columns. Position and size the box as necessary.

3. With the box selected, pull down the Element menu and choose Text Wrap. Click on the second wrap option, and enter 0 for the Top and Bottom stand-off. (The stand-off is the amount of space between the graphic and the text that wraps around it.) Close the dialog box. The columnar text now wraps around the box.

4. Move the pull-quote text block inside the box.

5. Select the box and specify None for the line style and fill.

Instead of drawing the box yourself, you can place the text block between the columns, and while it is still selected, use the Create Keyline Addition. You will still need to change the Text Wrap and the stand-off values. The line and fill settings can be set with Create Keyline options.

The text wrap feature works for all pull-quotes, not just for ones that span parts of two columns. Instead of shortening or separating text blocks, you can place the quote inside an invisible box and turn on text wrap. For more information about text wrap, see Chapter 11.

CREATING INLINE GRAPHICS

Except for paragraph rules, the graphics you have seen thus far are anchored to the page. They don't move unless you drag them, so consequently they do not flow with the text. Stationary graphics are the way to go when you want your graphic elements in a fixed location on the page.

FIGURE 10.22: *To wrap columnar text around this pull-quote, you need to use the text wrap feature.*

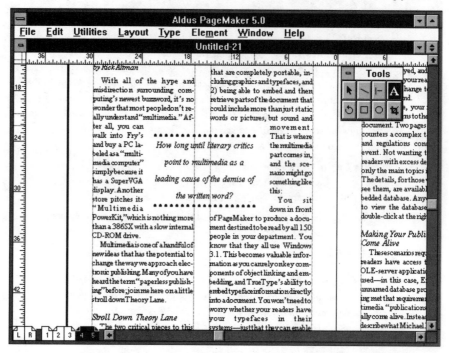

But sometimes you might want a graphic to be anchored with the text it is associated with and to flow with that text. That's where *inline graphics* come into the picture.

An inline graphic is a graphic that is placed or pasted into a text block so that it becomes part of the text block. You might think of it as a cross between a paragraph of text and a graphic—it shares properties of both. Like any graphic, an inline graphic can be filled with different shades and can be stretched or shrunk with its graphic handles. As with a paragraph, you can define its alignment, indents, leading, and space above and below.

Chapter 11 explains how to import an image and place it in a text block as an inline graphic. Here, we will show you how to shade a paragraph with an inline graphic so that the text remains shaded no matter where it flows.

To create an inline graphic, you paste the graphic into the text while you are using the text tool. The graphic is inserted at the cursor position.

As an example, we'll create a shade behind a paragraph, as shown in Figure 10.23.

1. With the rectangle tool, draw a box around the text to be shaded.

2. Fill the box with the desired shade percentage. To remove the outline, choose None from the Line menu.

3. Cut the box to the Clipboard.

4. With the text tool, insert a blank line above the paragraph. Remove any paragraph attributes (indents, space before) from this line, and turn on the Keep With Next option (so that the shade will not be separated from the text).

FIGURE 10.23:   *The shade behind the text is an inline graphic.*

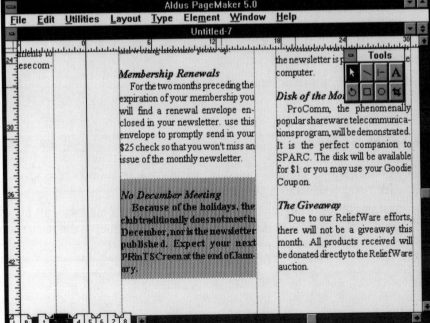

5. With the cursor on the blank line, paste the box.

At this point, the box is inserted as an inline graphic and will flow with the text. However, it is not shading the text below it yet. The trick to getting a box to overlay text is to specify a small amount of leading for the inline graphic; we have found that 0- or 1-point leading works well.

6. Triple-click on the box to select the entire paragraph.

7. Specify 0 leading and press Ctrl+1 to redraw the screen in Actual Size view. The box overlaps the paragraphs but is not positioned properly.

8. With the pointer tool, drag the box so that it covers the text you want shaded. If necessary, lengthen the box by dragging down one of the bottom handles.

For some reason, inline graphics require a lot of screen redrawing. Every time you make a change that affects the inline graphic, you must redraw the screen by issuing one of the page view commands (such as Ctrl+1).

You can use this same technique to shade a drop cap.

SUMMARY

This chapter covered the objects you can draw and effects you can achieve with PageMaker's tools. While lines, shapes, and shades add visual interest to your publications, use them sparingly. When graphic elements are over-used, they lose their impact and confuse your audience—the readers don't know what to look at first.

HANDS-ON PRACTICE: ADDING GRAPHIC ELEMENTS TO A NEWSLETTER

In the exercises in this chapter, you will create graphic elements in a short newsletter. Pages 2 through 5 of the newsletter are shown in Figures 10.24 through 10.27. The NWSLTR10.PM5 file is the starting point for this hands-on practice.

DRAWING VERTICAL RULES BETWEEN COLUMNS

Between the columns on pages 2, 4, and 5 are 1-point vertical rules. Follow these steps to draw these lines:

1. Open the NWSLTR10.PM5 publication in the C:\PM5PUBS directory.

2. In Fit in Window view, use the rule tool to draw a line in the gutter between the columns of text on page 2 (see Figure 10.25).

3. Pull down the Element menu, choose Line, and select 1 pt. (It may already be selected.)

4. Switch to Actual Size view, choose the pointer tool, and move the line so that it is exactly in the middle of the gutter. Adjust the length of the line if necessary.

5. Repeat steps 2–4 for the vertical rules on pages 4 and 5 (see Figures 10.27 and 10.28).

BOXING A COLUMN

Follow the steps below to draw a box around the text in column 2 of page 3 (see Figure 10.25):

1. Go to page 3 in Fit in Window view.

2. Using the rectangle tool, draw a box around column 2.

3. Pull down the Element menu and choose Fill and Line. For Fill select None, and for Line select 1pt.

FIGURE 10.24: *Page 2 of the newsletter*

CLUB NEWS

ReliefWare Auction

While many of us have supported the earthquake recovery efforts personally, SPAUG was unable to coordinate a proper response last month simply because of the chronology of the events; the quake occurred only one week before the October meeting.

But it is never too late to stretch out a hand, and this month SPAUG calls upon all of its members to participate in ReliefWare: An Auction for Action.

Its success depends upon you, the people who will donate computer-related items and buy them. The proceeds will be sent directly to the American Red Cross South Bay Headquarters.

October Meeting

Our meeting started out with a demonstration of three programs. The first, VCD, allows you to visually change directories by moving the cursor around a graphic tree structure. ZDIR displays a directory listing that indicates how much space the files take (unlike DIR which only tells you how much space is remaining). DIRNOTES gives you a way to append comments to filenames, and then view these comments.

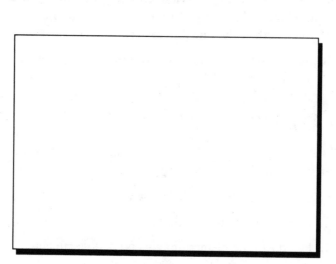

FIGURE 10.25: *Page 3 of the newsletter*

Several representatives from Technology Concepts demonstrated their unique product called Fax Line Manager. This hardware device enables you to use a fax, a modem, and an answering machine on a single phone line. With this product, you do not have to pay for a dedicated phone line.

The Fax Line Manager automates the answering and detecting process and routes the call accordingly. After the first ring, the device picks up and listens for a tone. If it hears the fax tone, the call will be routed to the fax machine. If it hears a touch tone, it will be routed to the modem. If no tones are detected, the answering machine picks up.

Membership Renewals

For the two months preceding the expiration of your membership you will find a renewal envelope enclosed in your newsletter. Use this envelope to promptly send in your $25 check so that you won't miss an issue of the monthly newsletter.

No December Meeting

Because of the holidays, the club traditionally does not meet in December, nor is the newsletter published. Expect your next PRinT SCreen at the end of January.

This Month

This Meeting Features Us!

In somewhat of a break from tradition, this month's guest will be the inanimate objects that make up the heart and soul of our group: our bulletin board and newsletter.

Now that SPARC has received a facelift, it is time to show it off, and in conjunction with our Disk of the Month, you will be treated to a tour of the bulletin board and all of its nooks and crannies. Those of you who are a bit shy of SPARC, come out and see how easy it can be.

Members will also get to see how the newsletter is put together on the computer.

Disk of the Month

ProComm, the phenomenally popular shareware telecommunications program, will be demonstrated. It is the perfect companion to SPARC. The disk will be available for $1 or you may use your Goodie Coupon.

The Giveaway

Due to our ReliefWare efforts, there will not be a giveaway this month. All products received will be donated directly to the ReliefWare auction.

Multimedia:
A New Face on Publishing?

by Rick Altman

With all of the hype and misdirection surrounding computing's newest buzzword, it's no wonder that most people don't really understand "multimedia." After all, you can walk into Fry's and buy a PC labeled as a "multimedia computer" simply because it has a SuperVGA display. Another store pitches its "Multimedia PowerKit," which is nothing more than a 386SX with a slow internal CD-ROM drive.

Multimedia is one of a handful of new ideas that has the potential to change the way we approach electronic publishing. Many of you have heard the term "paperless publishing" before; join me here on a little stroll down Theory Lane.

Stroll Down Theory Lane

The two critical pieces to this puzzle are: 1) producing documents that are completely portable, including graphics and typefaces, and 2) being able to embed and then retrieve parts of the document that could include more than just static words or pictures, but sound and movement. That is where the multimedia part comes in, and the scenario might go something like this:

You sit down in front of PageMaker to produce a document destined to be read by all 150 people in your department. You know that they all use Windows 3.1. This becomes valuable information as you can rely on key components of object linking and embedding, and TrueType's ability to embed typeface information directly into a document. You won't need to worry whether your readers have your typefaces in their systems—just that they can enable TrueType under Windows.

How long will it take until literary critics point to multimedia as a leading cause of the demise of the written word?

FIGURE 10.27: *Page 5 of the newsletter*

Double-Click Here
For More Information

On page 2 of your document, you have important statistics concerning an upcoming event—too involved, you determine, for a simple chart. Instead, you create an icon that simply reads "Double-click here for more information." Said double-click promptly launches Excel and an embedded sound file. As the chart is displayed, audible instructions prompt your reader as to the variables to change to assess the situation at hand.

When done, your reader exits Excel and returns to the PageMaker document. Two pages later, he encounters a complex table of rules and regulations concerning the event. Not wanting to bore your readers with excess detail, you list only the main topics in this table. The details, for those who want to see them, are available as an embedded database. Anyone wishing to view the database need only double-click at the right spot.

Making Your Publications
Come Alive

These scenarios require that your readers have access to the same OLE-server applications that you used—in this case, Excel and an unnamed database program. Having met that requirement, your multimedia "publications" can virtually come alive. Instead of trying to describe what Michael Jordan looks like during one of his flying dunks, you could embed a recorded visual image of it, tongue flapping and all. (I wonder how long it will take until literary critics point to multimedia as a leading cause of the demise of the written word. They might be right...)

Conventional publishing is unable to approach the presentation potential that multimedia and OLE offer. With each new Windows application that gets into the act, the opportunity increases for sharing data—whether written, spoken, or seen.

Companies like Corel and Micrografx, two leaders in graphics software, already have plans to offer an all-in-one graphics station for users making presentations or preparing business communiqués. Imagine how effective your messages could be if you could count on common software being used by your recipients.

You could prepare the message in a presentation module, link to charts produced in another module, use sound and motion as supplied by Windows multimedia resources, and full-color drawings produced by a drawing module. All your readers would have to do is click here and there. Sounds like a commercial being made—bring on the yuppies in their cool business suits.

The text is too close to the box outline—set left and right indents to provide more space between the text and the box.

4. Select the entire story with the text tool. (Note that *This Month* is not part of the story.)

5. Press Ctrl+M to display the Paragraph Specifications dialog box and set Left and Right indents of 0.5 picas. Close the dialog box.

SHADING THE CLUB NEWS HEADING

In the following steps, you will shade the heading shown in Figure 10.28:

1. Display page 2 in the newsletter.

2. Using the rectangle tool, draw a box around the heading, across both columns.

FIGURE 10.28: *The Club News heading has a 30% gray shade.*

3. With the pointer tool in Actual Size view, select the text block and position it so that its location matches Figure 10.28. Your goals are to center the text vertically inside the box and to allow a little extra space to the left of the text.

4. Select the box and choose a 30% shade from the Fill menu.

5. To remove the outline from the box, choose None from the Line menu.

CREATING A REVERSED HEADING

The *This Month* heading on page 3 of the newsletter is reversed type, as shown in Figure 10.29. Follow these steps to create this effect:

1. Zoom in on the top of page 3, column 2.

FIGURE 10.29: *This Month is a reversed heading.*

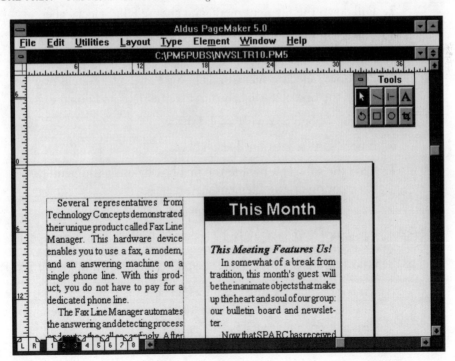

2. Draw a box around the text *This Month*. Do not add the solid fill yet.

3. If necessary, move the text block so that it is vertically centered within the box you just drew.

4. Select the text with the text tool and then choose Reverse from the Type Style menu.

5. Select the box with the pointer tool and then fill it with the solid shade.

CREATING A SHADOW BOX FOR THE CALENDAR

The shadow box in Figure 10.30 will ultimately hold a calendar of events. Follow the steps below to create the shadow box:

1. In the bottom half of page 2, use the rectangle tool to draw a box.

2. Pull down the Element menu and choose Fill. Select Paper.

3. Pull down the Edit menu and choose Copy to copy this box to the Clipboard.

4. Pull down the Edit menu and choose Paste. The copy is now on top of the first box, slightly offset to the right and down.

5. Fill the second box with a solid shade.

6. If necessary, reposition the solid box.

7. Send the solid box behind the first box by using the Send to Back option on the Element menu.

CREATING A PULL-QUOTE

In the following steps, you'll create the pull-quote shown in Figure 10.31:

1. On page 4, shorten the text block in column 2 by dragging the bottom window shade up above the head *Double Click Here*. This will open up space for the pull-quote.

FIGURE 10.30: *The shadow box is actually two boxes: a box with a solid shade behind a box with a paper fill.*

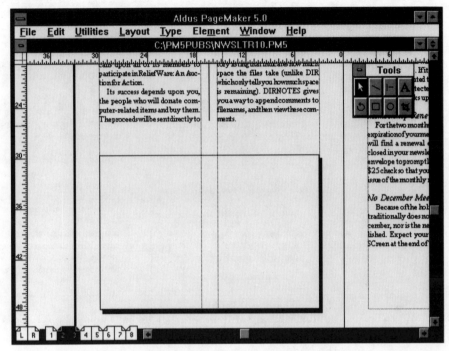

2. On page 5, find the text to be made into a pull-quote. It is near the top of column 2:

```
I wonder how long it will take until literary critics
point to multimedia as a leading cause of the demise
of the written word.
```

3. Select the text with the text tool, and choose Copy on the Edit menu.

4. Switch to the pointer tool, and choose Paste on the Edit menu. The pull-quote is now its own unthreaded text block—however, it needs to be moved into position and sized appropriately.

5. Drag the pull-quote to the empty space you created on page 4, and adjust the text block so that it fits into column 2.

FIGURE 10.31: *A pull-quote*

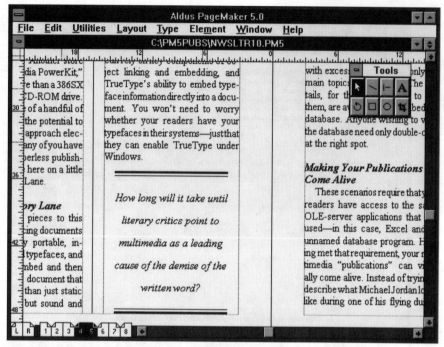

6. Select the text with the text tool, and specify the type as 12-point Times New Roman italic, with 24-point leading.

7. Set the paragraph specifications with a 1-pica left indent, 1-pica right indent, no first-line indent, and centered alignment.

8. Notice that the last line of the quote only has one word on it. One way to fix this problem is to edit the text. Edit the quote so that it reads:

```
How long will it take until literary critics point to
multimedia as a leading cause of the demise of the
written word?
```

9. With the text tool, click inside the pull-quote.

10. Press Ctrl+M to display the Paragraph Specifications dialog box.

11. Choose the Rules command button to display the Paragraph Rules dialog box.

12. Turn on Rule Above Paragraph.

13. Pull down the Line Style list.

14. Choose the 5pt double-line style that has a heavy line above a thin line.

15. Set 1-pica left and right indents.

16. Turn on Rule Below Paragraph.

17. Select the 5pt double-line style that has a thin line above a heavy line (the opposite of the rule above the paragraph).

18. Set 1-pica left and right indents.

19. Close the dialog boxes.

Your pull-quote could use some extra space between the text and the rules; 24-points would work well, since this is the leading of the text. Follow these steps to adjust the spacing:

20. Display the Paragraph Rules dialog box.

21. Choose the Options button.

22. Next to Top, type **0p32.** This was calculated by adding 24 points of space plus two-thirds of the point size (12).

23. Next to Bottom, type **0p24** or 2 picas.

24. Close all the dialog boxes.

25. If necessary, adjust the vertical position of the paragraph, so that the bottom rule is on the margin.

26. Save the publication.

There is now an equal amount of space between the rules and the text, both above and below the paragraph.

*I*mporting

*G*raphics

fast tracks

To import a graphic: **415**

Pull down the File menu and choose Place. Click on the name of the graphic file and choose OK. Click on the page where you want to place the graphic, or drag a box the desired graphic size.

To keep a graphic in its original proportions while adjusting its size: **417**

Select the object and hold down the Shift key as you drag a selection handle.

To scale a graphic: **420**

Select the graphic, and enter the percentages in the H (Height) and W (Width) scaling fields in the control palette.

To wrap text around a graphic: **421**

Select the graphic, and choose Text Wrap from the Element menu. Click on the second wrap option. Select the desired text flow icon.

To customize text wrap: **424**

Select the graphic, and choose Text Wrap from the Element menu. Click on the second wrap option, and specify a 0 standoff all the way around. Choose OK. Look for empty space between the text and the graphic, and create new handles in these locations by clicking on the boundary. Drag the handles to bring the graphic boundary closer to the graphic.

To place an inline graphic: 426

Place the text cursor where you want the graphic to go. Press Ctrl+D to display the Place dialog box and choose the file to be inserted. Make sure the option As Inline Graphic is turned on and choose OK.

To crop an image: 431

Choose the cropping tool in the toolbox or control palette. Click on the graphic. Drag a selection handle—use the corner handles to crop diagonally, the left and right handles to crop horizontally, or the top and bottom handles to crop vertically.

To rotate a graphic: 433

Select the graphic and enter the degree value in the rotation field of the control palette; a negative value rotates clockwise and a postive value rotates counterclockwise. You can also rotate with the rotation tool in the toolbox.

To update an imported image after the graphic file has changed: 441

Choose File ➤ Links. Click on the name of the changed file and choose the Update button.

To import a graphic from the Clipboard: 447

Select the object in your Windows-based graphics program, and copy it to the Clipboard. Switch back into PageMaker and paste the graphic into the publication. The Edit ➤ Paste command inserts an embedded object; the Edit ➤ Paste Special command inserts a linked file.

HILE PAGEMAKER'S DRAWING
tools can add attractive touches to your publications, they produce only
the simplest of graphics. For more sophisticated images and artwork, you
need to look to graphic software packages. With a dedicated graphics program, you can either create images yourself or enhance pictures that come
with the program. These graphics can then be imported into your Page-
Maker publications.

BITMAPS VERSUS VECTOR GRAPHICS

Graphic software can be divided into two broad categories:

➤ Those that create images by a collection of dots, referred to as *paint*
programs because you can use your mouse cursor as a brush and
mark up the screen however you wish. They create images bit by
bit, dot by dot, and so these images are called *bitmap graphics*.

➤ Those that create images by using geometric shapes, such as
ovals, rectangles, lines, and curves. These are known as *drawing*
programs, and they produce *vector graphic* images.

Drawing programs produce images that are usually of a decidedly higher quality than paint programs because they are mathematical shapes, not simply a collection of dots. For instance, when you create a circle with a drawing program, it knows that it is supposed to be a circle, with a certain circumference and radius from the center. If you enlarge or reshape the graphic, it still knows that it is a circle. But a circle from a paint program doesn't know that it is supposed to be a circle; it just happens to look like one at the moment. Resizing usually distorts the image.

Furthermore, paint programs create graphics at a finite resolution, usually between 72 and 300 dpi, depending on the power of the program and the amount of memory your computer has available. The distance between the dots cannot be changed. A low-resolution bitmap image will look equally bad on an Epson dot-matrix printer, a LaserJet printer, or an ultra-high resolution Linotronic imagesetter.

On the other hand, drawing programs produce graphics that are designed to print at the maximum resolution of your printer: 72 dpi on a dot-matrix printer, 300 on a laser printer, and 1200 or more on high-end typesetting machines. Drawing programs essentially tell the printer: "Make a circle with these dimensions and place the dots as close as you know how."

As a result, drawing programs are excellent for high-precision work, such as CAD drawings and other detailed graphics. The best drawing programs for the IBM PC are, in alphabetical order, Adobe Illustrator, Aldus Freehand, CorelDRAW, and Micrografx Designer. All four programs can produce sharp, complex drawings and store them in a form that is acceptable to PageMaker.

However, you would not use one of these drawing programs to create a scanned image for a PageMaker publication, or to edit a screen shot. In those cases, you want direct control over each and every dot that makes up the image, and so you would turn to one of several paint programs on the market, such as Picture Publisher, PhotoStyler, PhotoShop, Photo Finish, or the Paintbrush program that comes with Windows.

Compare the two sunbathers in Figure 11.1. These are two clip-art images from CorelDRAW. Can you tell which one is bitmap and which is a vector graphic?

All the screen images in this book are bitmap images. Each dot represents a tiny portion of the computer screen; drawing programs cannot produce the same effect.

FIGURE 11.1: *The sunbather at the top is a vector graphic; the one at the bottom is a bitmap image.*

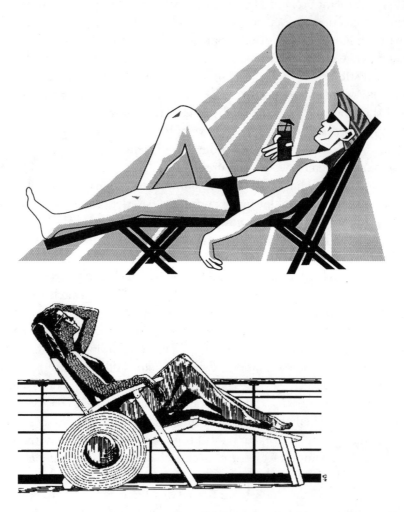

In many cases, you can take a low-resolution image and convert it into a high-resolution drawing. For example, suppose that you are producing an inventory parts list and you have a dozen low-quality photos of exotic nuts and bolts. Halftoning or photostatting won't work because the coffee stains will show. So you purchase a cheap scanner and turn each photo into a digitized bitmap image. Your hand-held scanner produces images that are just as bad as the originals—worse, even—but now you can bring those images into a drawing program and trace around them with high-quality bezier curves and vector graphic tools.

Presto, you now have high-quality line art that can be precisely sized, scaled, and electronically pasted into your parts list. Your coworkers throw you a party, and your boss gives you a raise.

PREPARING A GRAPHIC FOR PAGEMAKER

In order to bring an external graphic into PageMaker, it must be in a format that PageMaker can understand. PageMaker cannot import Corel-DRAW's .CDR files or Arts & Letters' .GED files. However, all graphics programs offer ways to export their files to standard graphic formats. The most popular formats are Encapsulated PostScript (.EPS), Windows Metafile Format (.WMF), and Computer Graphic Metafile (.CGM). For bitmap graphics, picture images (.PCX), and Tagged Image File (.TIF) formats are the standards.

Graphic import filters for some of these formats are built into Page-Maker; others need to be installed through the Aldus Setup program. Table 11.1 lists the graphic formats that PageMaker can import, their type, and whether or not filters for them are built-in.

If you have a PostScript printer, the best format to use for your graphic file is Encapsulated PostScript (EPS) because it provides the highest quality art. An image in EPS format is not a good candidate for a non-PostScript printer, although it can be printed under certain circumstances. If you see a shaded box when you import the graphic, you will not be able to print the graphic on a non-PostScript printer because there is no screen rendition of the PostScript code. If you see an image when you import an EPS file, you can print the graphic, but it will be low quality. Except for the purposes of printing proofs, you shouldn't import EPS graphic files to be printed on a non-PostScript printer (but you have plenty of other formats from which to choose).

Most graphic packages include ready-made drawings and symbols, called *clip art*. CorelDRAW, for example, comes with 12,000 clip-art images, including pictures of people, animals, food, maps, home furnishings, buildings, and arrows, to name a few. You can also purchase clip art packages,

TABLE 11.1: *PageMaker Graphic Import Filters*

Format	Extension	Type	Built In
AutoCAD	PLT, ADI, DXF	Vector	No
Computer Graphic Metafile	CGM	Vector	No
Encapsulated PostScript	EPS	Vector	No
Excel Chart	XLC	Vector	No
GEM	GEM	Vector	No
HPGL	PLT	Vector	No
Kodak PhotoCD	PCD	Bitmap	No
Lotus 1-2-3 graphic	PIC	Vector	No
Table Editor	TBL	Vector	No
Tagged Image File	TIF	Bitmap	Yes
Tektronix PLOT-10	PLT	Vector	No
VideoShow (NAPLPS)	PIC	Vector	No
Windows Draw	PIC	Vector	No
Windows Metafile	WMF	Vector	No
Windows PaintBrush	BMP, PCX	Bitmap	Yes
WordPerfect Graphics	WPG	Vector	No
ZSoft	PCX	Bitmap	No

such as the ones offered by 3G Graphics, Image Art, Art Right, and New Vision Technologies. Like graphic images in general, clip art can either be bitmap or vector graphic.

Some clip art is already in a standard graphic file format, and you can import it directly into PageMaker. However, you may want to import a clip-art image into your drawing program first, so that you can edit it and add colors, shading, or other enhancements. Do this editing and formatting *before* you import the file into PageMaker; once the image arrives in PageMaker, manipulations are limited.

To summarize, your objective in the graphic preparation stage is to produce a file that is in one of the standard graphic file formats listed in Table 11.1. Depending on which file format you choose, you might need to run the Aldus Setup program to install additional import filters.

PLACING A GRAPHIC

Placing a graphic is quite similar to placing text, and you even use the same command: Place on the File menu or Ctrl+D. Instead of a text gun, you get a graphic gun, which differs depending on the type of graphic you are placing. The gun has a pencil inside it for vector graphics, a paintbrush for bitmap graphics, an X for TIFF files, and the letters PS for EPS files.

As with text, you have two methods for placing the file: point-and-shoot or drag-place. When you click the graphic gun at the target location (point-and-shoot), the artwork appears in its original size. When you click-and-drag the graphic gun (drag-place), the graphic fits inside whatever size box you draw. The drag-place technique not only changes the size of the graphic, it changes its proportions as well, creating a distorted image. Unless you intend to distort a picture, always place your graphic with the point-and-shoot method. Then you can resize the graphic proportionally, as will be explained shortly.

Unlike a publication page, which is usually filled with text and other graphic elements, the pasteboard is an uncluttered area that is an ideal target location for an external graphic. You can place the graphic on the pasteboard, resize it or rotate it, and then move it into position on the page.

SIZING A GRAPHIC

How you resize a graphic depends on its format (vector versus bitmap) and whether you want it to keep its original proportions. In Figure 11.2, the graphic on the left shows the distortion that occurs when an image is not proportionally sized. This happens when you click on a graphic handle and start dragging (the way you have been sizing text and graphic elements so far). The graphic on the right in Figure 11.2 was sized proportionally. To keep a graphic in its original proportions as you adjust its size, hold down the Shift key when you drag a handle. As you drag, the graphic jumps to the next proportional size.

Sometimes you might not want proportional scaling. For example, suppose you are sizing an arrow. If you prefer a taller, thinner arrow, you could create this shape by sizing it without the Shift key.

FIGURE 11.2: *The graphic on the left is distorted; the graphic on the right is proportionally sized.*

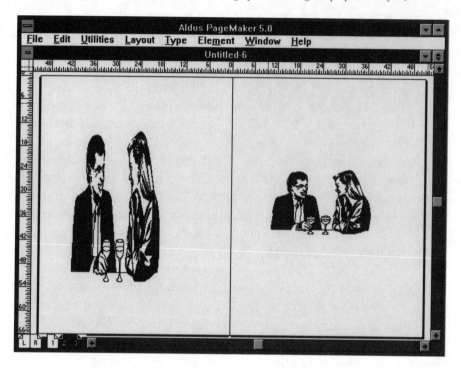

If you forget to hold down **Shift** as you size a graphic, you
don't have to delete the graphic and start over. Just hold
down **Shift** and start dragging a selection handle. The
graphic immediately returns to its original size and proportions; you can then finish resizing it, but proportionally this time.

When sizing a bitmap graphic, use the *magic-stretch* technique. When you hold down Shift and Ctrl as you drag a handle, three things happen at once:

→ You change the size of the graphic.

→ The graphic keeps its original proportions.

→ The magic part: PageMaker will allow only those sizes that are multiples of your printer's resolution.

The magic-stretch technique provides the best output for graphics produced by paint programs. Figure 11.3 compares a graphic that was stretched with a normal click-and-drag technique with a graphic that was magic-stretched.

FIGURE 11.3: *The graphic on the right was magic-stretched; the distorted graphic on the left was not.*

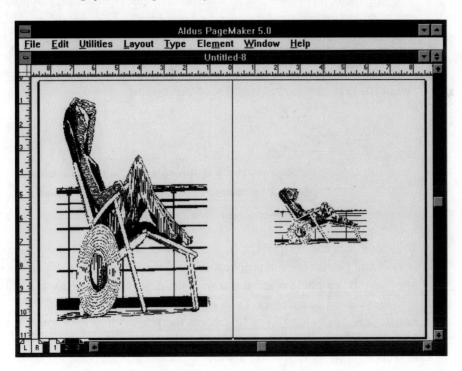

Sizing and Scaling with the Control Palette

Version
5.0
Another way to size an imported graphic is by entering values in the W (Width) and H (Height) fields in the control palette. These fields are pointed out in Figure 11.4. Thus, if you know you want the graphic to be 3 by 5 inches, enter 3 in the width field and 5 in the height field. Click on the Apply button or press Enter after entering the new values.

FIGURE 11.4: *The sizing and scaling fields in the control palette*

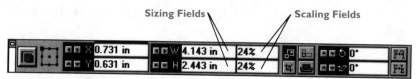

Using the control palette, the width and height of imported graphics can be scaled up or down by a specified percentage. The percentage-scaling fields are adjacent to the fields for specifying the W and H values in inches (see Figure 11.4). Suppose you want the graphic to be half its original size; just enter 50 in both of the percentage-scaling fields. The scaling always refers to the graphic's *original* size, not its *current* size.

The control palette is the only way to do percentage scaling in PageMaker; there is no equivalent command in the menu.

By default, you can control the height and width independently. However, the control palette offers a proportional-scaling option that enables you to maintain the graphic's original proportions. After the proportional scaling option is turned on, whenever you enter a value in the width field, the height field fills in with a size that keeps the graphic in proportion. Or, if you enter 50% in the percentage-scaling field for width, the height scale also changes to 50%.

When proportional-scaling is turned off (as it is by default), the option looks like this:

To turn on proportional-scaling, click on this option. The option will then look like this:

Note that the status of the proportional-scaling option in the control palette has no effect on sizing a graphic with the click-and-drag method (you still must hold down Shift).

The control palette also has an option for scaling bitmap graphics that is the equivalent of the magic-stretch technique; it's called printer resolution scaling. When it is turned on, the option looks like this:

When it is turned off, the option looks like this:

The printer resolution scaling option is available in the control palette only when a bitmap graphic is selected.

WRAPPING TEXT AROUND A GRAPHIC

When you are placing a graphic within columns of body text, you need to decide how you want the text to wrap around the graphic. Do you want the text to flow on top of the graphic, above and below the graphic, above but not below, or on all sides of the graphic? These decisions are made in the Text Wrap dialog box. You might remember that the text wrap feature was introduced in Chapter 10 for wrapping columnar text around a pull-quote.

The Text Wrap dialog box, shown in Figure 11.5, contains icons representing the options. First, there are three Wrap options:

➤ The first icon represents no text wrap; the text flows on top of the graphic. This is appropriate for a background image that has a very light shade; if it's too dark, you won't be able to read the text.

➤ The second icon turns on the text-wrap feature so that the text wraps around the graphic.

➤ The third wrap icon refers to custom wrap, which you can use to adjust the text wrap around graphics with an irregular shape.

Once you turn on text wrap, you can choose from three different Text Flow options:

➤ The first icon inserts a column break after the graphic; text does not flow underneath the graphic.

➤ The second icon flows the text above and below the graphic.

➤ The third icon flows the text on all four sides of the graphic (assuming there is room for text beside the graphic).

Figure 11.6 shows an example of text wrap in which text flows around a graphic. This effect was achieved by choosing the second text-wrap icon and the third text-flow icon in the Text Wrap dialog box.

FIGURE 11.5: *The Text Wrap dialog box*

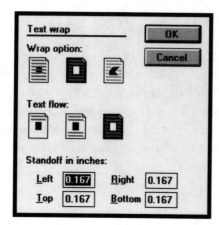

FIGURE 11.6: *To get text to wrap around a graphic, choose the third text-flow icon.*

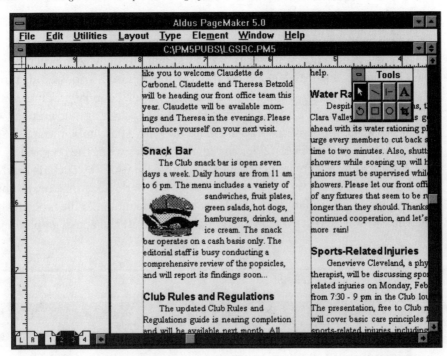

At the bottom of the Text Wrap dialog box there are controls for the amount of white space around the graphic. The *standoff* is the amount of space that separates the text from the graphic. The left, right, top, and bottom sides of the graphic are controlled separately. One way of bringing text closer to a graphic is to decrease the standoff.

When text wrap is turned on, a graphic has two boundaries. The inner boundary is the *bounding box* you have been using to size the graphic. It is comprised of eight square handles. The outer boundary, called the *graphic boundary*, has diamond-shaped handles in each corner. The distance between the two boundaries is the standoff. You adjust the size of a graphic with the square handles. The diamond-shaped handles change the shape of the text that wraps around the text; they are used to create a custom text wrap.

CUSTOMIZING TEXT WRAP

When a graphic is oddly shaped, a rectangular text wrap leaves a lot of white space, gaps between letters, or bad breaks around hyphenated words—even when you specify a zero standoff all the way around the graphic (see Figure 11.7). To get the text to wrap in the nooks and crannies of a graphic, you can create a custom graphic boundary. Compare Figures 11.7 and 11.8. The graphic in Figure 11.7 uses a standard text wrap, while the same graphic in Figure 11.8 has a customized wrap.

For your custom wrap, look for empty space between the text and the graphic, and create new handles in these locations by clicking on the boundary. Then drag the new handles (or any of the existing ones) to bring the graphic boundary closer to the graphic. The more handles you create, the easier it is to get the boundary right up against the actual graphic.

FIGURE 11.7: *Standard text wrap*

FIGURE 11.8: *Customized text wrap*

Each time you drag a graphic-boundary handle, the text reflows around the new boundary. This delay can be annoying when you are making a lot of adjustments to the boundary, but you can turn it off by holding down the Spacebar as you create and drag handles. When you release the Spacebar, the screen is redrawn with the custom text wrap.

In the Text Wrap dialog box, the custom text wrap icon is automatically selected when you start adjusting the graphic boundary (you cannot select this icon). If you don't like the results of your custom wrapping, you can return to the original text wrap by choosing the rectangular text-wrap icon and reentering standoff values.

Customizing a graphic boundary is a skill that requires patience and practice. Try importing a variety of odd-shaped graphics and customizing the wrap. You can also practice wrapping text around a circle or ellipse you have created with PageMaker's drawing tools.

PLACING INLINE GRAPHICS

When you want a graphic to flow with the text, place it as an *inline graphic* as opposed to an *independent graphic*. Indepedent graphics are anchored to the page, wherever you place them. Inline graphics, on the other hand, are anchored to the text—when the text flows to a different spot on the page, the graphic will move with it. (This topic was introduced in Chapter 10; a shaded box was pasted as an inline graphic behind a couple of paragraphs so that the text remained shaded even when the text changed position.)

To insert a graphic so that it is part of a text block, paste or place the graphic with the text cursor positioned where you want the graphic to go. For example, if you want a graphic to go between two paragraphs, insert a carriage return, and with the cursor on this blank line, place the graphic.

When a text cursor is in a text block, you have a new option in the Place Document dialog box: As Inline Graphic, which appears after you select a graphic file from the list. This option is automatically selected. Choose OK. If you don't see the graphic, press Ctrl+1 to refresh the screen. The image is immediately inserted at the cursor location; you do not see a graphic gun when you place an inline graphic.

Figure 11.9 shows a swimmer that was inserted as an inline graphic. If the swimmer were an independent graphic, it would always remain in its current position on the page, even if the text around it flowed to a different position. As an inline graphic, the swimmer floats with the text, and it retains its position between the two paragraphs.

FIGURE 11.9: *The swimmer is an inline graphic.*

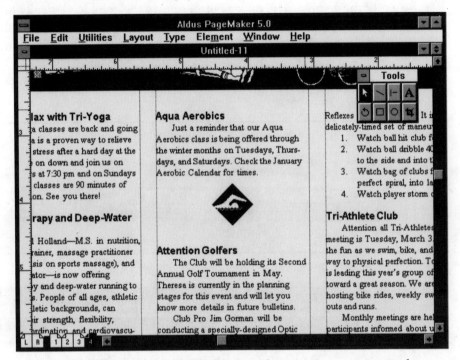

Another advantage of inline graphics is that you can use paragraph controls to align them in the text block. To center an independent graphic, you have to move it manually and either eyeball the center or use several ruler guides to help you position it exactly. To center an inline graphic, press Ctrl+Shift+C or enter the alignment in the Paragraph Specifications dialog box. (The swimmer graphic in Figure 11.9 was centered this way.) You can also use other paragraph controls such as indents and spaces above and below.

When an inline graphic is selected, the control palette offers a special option just for this type of graphic. The baseline offset, pointed out in Figure 11.10, controls the position of the inline graphic in relation to the baseline of the surrounding text. With a baseline offset of zero, the baseline of the graphic rests on the baseline of the text, as shown in Figure 11.11. If you want the baseline of the graphic to be lower than the text baseline, you can specify an offset greater than zero, with the maximum value being the height of the graphic. The nudge buttons move the graphic vertically in increments of 0.01 inch. Use the down-pointing button to lower the graphic; use the up-pointing button to raise the graphic after you have lowered it. Note that you cannot use the baseline offset option to raise the graphic baseline above the text baseline.

FIGURE 11.10: *The baseline offset option in the control palette is for positioning inline graphics.*

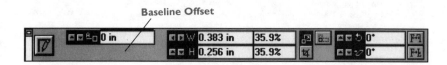

FIGURE 11.11: *The feet graphic is aligned with the text baseline (an offset of zero).*

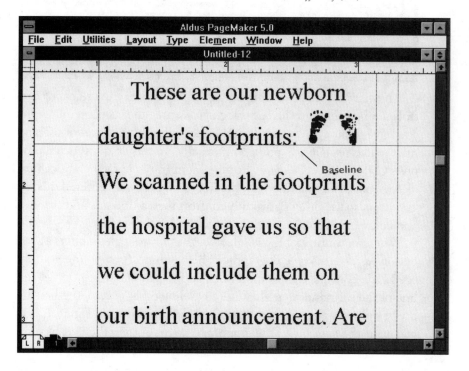

You can raise the graphic above the text baseline by using a type specification. With the text tool, select the inline graphic and a surrounding space. Press Ctrl+T, choose the Options button, and enter a value for Baseline Shift (make sure the Up option is selected).

One limitation to inline graphics is that text wrap options do not apply. To achieve the text wrap shown in Figure 11.12, you have to tab in each line and place line breaks at the end of lines, and change the leading of the graphic to match that of the text. Another drawback to inline graphics is

FIGURE 11.12: *The hamburger is an inline graphic; to get the text to wrap around it, tabs and line breaks were inserted.*

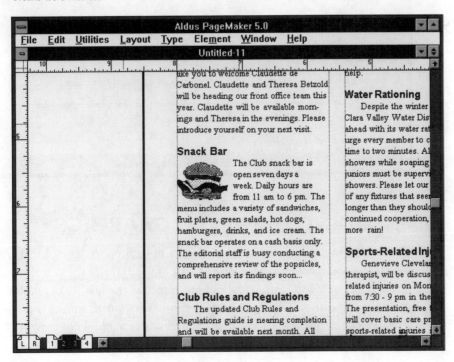

that you must redraw your screen constantly to get an accurate representation of the graphic. The quickest way to refresh your screen is to choose the current page view.

In story view, inline graphics appear as icons, as shown in Figure 11.13. Independent graphics are not indicated in story windows.

FIGURE 11.13: *An inline graphic in story view*

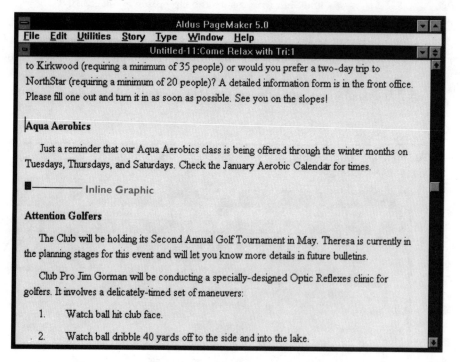

FINE TUNING IMPORTED GRAPHICS

There are a limited number of ways to modify an imported graphic in Page-Maker. As you have already seen, you can move and size these graphics. In this section, you will learn a few ways to improve the quality of graphics you have imported from an external graphics program. Some of these features are not applicable to graphics created with PageMaker's drawing tools.

CROPPING IMAGES

When you *crop* an image, you are trimming it to remove an unwanted portion. Here are a few examples of when cropping is appropriate:

➤ To cut out a distracting person lurking on the side of a photograph

➤ To focus on a person from the waist up instead of including the full body

➤ To trim blank space (such as the sky) from the edge of a picture

In other words, cropping lets you zero in on the important or key part of an image. You can crop your artwork in your graphics program or in PageMaker.

 When you use PageMaker's cropping tool (shown in the margin), the entire graphic is still stored inside the publication; you are simply indicating which part of the graphic you want to see. This fact has its pluses and minuses. On the positive side, you can crop without worrying about deleting part of the image, and if you don't like your cropping job, it's easy enough to uncrop or recrop. On the negative side, a cropped image consumes as much memory and disk space as the original image. If computer memory is at a premium for you, crop the artwork in your graphics program before importing it into PageMaker.

Figure 11.14 shows five different versions of the same image. The graphic at the top of the page is uncropped, and the other images show different ways the picture can be cropped.

Here are the general steps for cropping in PageMaker:

1. With the pointer tool, select the graphic to be cropped.

2. Choose the cropping tool in the toolbox. When the mouse pointer is on the page or pasteboard, you will see the cropping tool.

3. Click and drag one of the selection handles. Use the left and right handles to crop horizontally, the top and bottom handles to crop vertically, and the corner handles to crop both dimensions at once.

FIGURE 11.14: *Different ways of cropping a graphic (the image at the top is uncropped)*

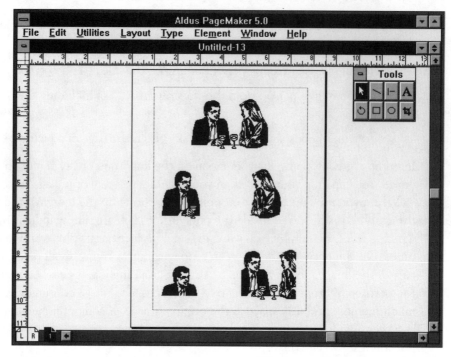

After you crop a graphic to a certain size, you can move the image around inside the bounding box, displaying different parts of the graphic. For example, suppose you have a graphic of a man and woman, and you crop out the woman. By dragging the cropping tool inside the graphic boundary, you can redisplay the woman and crop out the man. When you drag the cropping tool inside the bounding box, you see a grabber hand that allows you to reposition what is displayed.

Version
5.0
The control palette also offers a way to access the cropping tool (pointed out in Figure 11.15). It makes no difference whether you initiate cropping with the toolbox or the control palette; the cropping process is identical. To turn off the cropping option, activate the scaling option (see Figure 11.15). The scaling and cropping options are alternatives—when one is turned on, the other is automatically turned off. Turning on the scaling option simply selects the pointer tool.

FIGURE 11.15:   *The cropping and scaling options in the control palette*

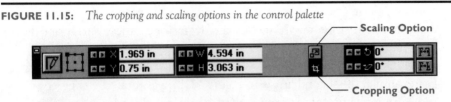

Scaling Option

Cropping Option

Version
5.0

Suppose you carefully cropped a graphic and now you want a different graphic file in place of the cropped one. Do you have to recrop the new graphic? The answer is no, assuming you want the new graphic to be the same size and to be cropped the same way. To do this, select the existing graphic, display the Place dialog box, choose the name of the new graphics file, and then turn on two options: Replacing Entire Graphic and Retain Cropping Data. When you choose OK, the new graphic will be in the same place, the same size, and have the same cropping information as the original graphic.

TRANSFORMING A GRAPHIC

In PageMaker 5.0, you can make your imported graphics do somersaults, backflips, and other gymnastic routines. The control palette has options for rotating, skewing, and reflecting (flipping) graphics. These options are pointed out in Figure 11.16.

To quickly eliminate any of the adjustments you make to a graphic, you can use the Remove Transformation option on the Element menu. The graphic will then display in its original form.

Rotating a Graphic

Version
5.0

Chapter 9 discussed how to rotate a text block, and rotating a graphic works in a similar fashion: You can use either the rotation option in the

FIGURE 11.16:   *The rotating, skewing, and reflecting options in the control palette*

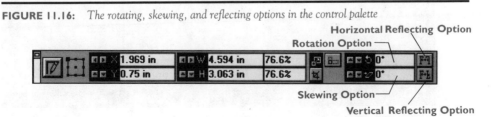

Horizontal Reflecting Option

Rotation Option

Skewing Option

Vertical Reflecting Option

control palette or the rotation tool. For your convenience, we'll repeat the discussion here. One way to specify the degree of rotation is to type a degree value in the rotation field and press Enter. A negative value will rotate the graphic clockwise while a positive value will rotate it counterclockwise. For example, the second arrow in Figure 11.17 was rotated 90 degrees. (The original, unrotated arrow is above this arrow.) If you wanted this graphic to face in the opposite direction, you would enter −90 for the rotation value. To return the graphic to its original position, enter a value of 0. The value can be any number between −360 and 360, in increments of 0.01 degrees.

The number you enter is always measured from the starting position of 0 degrees. Let's look at an example. Suppose you first rotate the graphic 90 degrees counterclockwise and now you decide you want to rotate it so that it's upside-down. You do not enter 90 to rotate the text another 90 degrees; instead, you pretend that the graphic is in its original location and you enter a value of 180.

FIGURE 11.17:   *The original graphic is at the top; a copy of the graphic was rotated 90 degrees.*

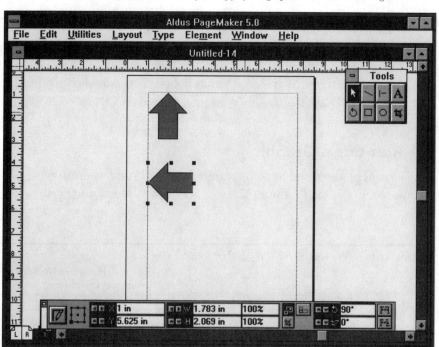

A second way to specify the rotation angle is to use the nudge buttons. Each time you click on a nudge button, the degree is increased or decreased by 0.1. The button that points up increases, while the one that points down decreases the degree. To rotate in increments of 1 degree—a *power nudge*— hold down the Ctrl key as you click on the nudge button.

The second way to rotate—the rotation tool, shown in the margin—allows you to forget about rotation degrees and lets you physically move the graphic to the position you want. When you select this tool, you will see a new kind of cursor, called a *starburst*. You place this cursor at the location around which you want to rotate the selected graphic (usually the center). You then drag the starburst cursor in the direction you want to rotate the graphic. The image will rotate on your screen as you drag the cursor.

While you're dragging, you'll see a *rotation lever*. This lever controls the amount of rotation. By dragging the starburst away from the starting point, you'll have more control over the rotation. In other words, with a longer lever, you'll be able to rotate the text in smaller increments. For example, with a short lever, you may be able to rotate the block in 2- or 3-degree increments, but with a longer lever, you'll be able to rotate in increments of hundredths of degrees.

TIP

To rotate the graphic in 45-degree increments, hold down Shift as you drag the starburst cursor.

Skewing a Graphic

Version
5.0

The skewing option was pointed out in Figure 11.16. As with the rotation option, you can either enter a degree value in the field or use the nudge buttons to increase the value in 0.1-degree increments (or 1-degree increments if you hold down Ctrl as you nudge). A positive value slants the graphic to the right while a negative value slants to the left.The skew value can range from −85 to 85 degrees, in 0.01 increments.

Flipping an Object

PageMaker refers to the flipping options as *reflecting* buttons (see Figure 11.16) because the result is similar to a mirror image. Figures 11.18 and 11.19 show examples of horizontal and vertical flips. The horizontal flip is useful when a person is facing in the wrong direction (people should always face into the page—this draws your readers into the page). If your image has someone facing to the left, and you want to place the graphic on the left side of the page, you can use the horizontal reflecting button to flip the image. The vertical flip can be used to create a reflection. In Figure 11.19, a copy of the graphic was vertically flipped to create the special mirror-like effect.

FIGURE 11.18: *Compare the original graphic (at the left) with a horizontally-flipped copy (at the right).*

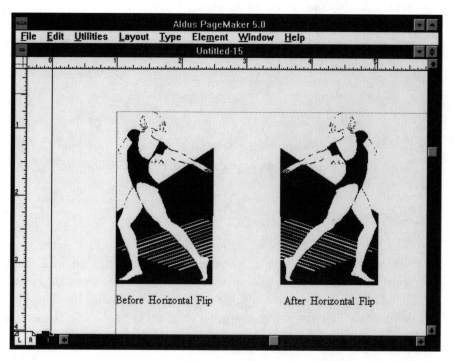

FIGURE 11.19: *This mirror effect was created by vertically flipping a copy of the graphic.*

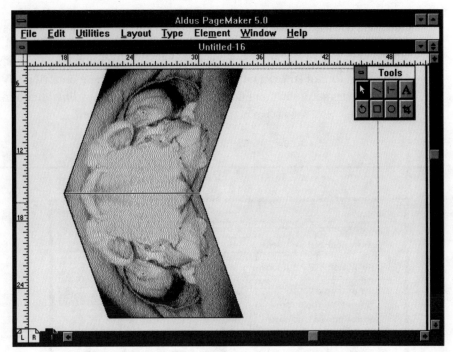

ARNiNG

Be careful when flipping photographs horizontally. If there is a sign in the background, any text would be backwards. Or, if a well-known right-handed tennis player were swinging the racket in his left hand, the discerning eye might discover what you had done.

ADJUSTING THE SCREEN RESOLUTION

There is a trade-off between the screen resolution of your imported graphics and the speed at which the screen is redrawn. The Preferences dialog box, shown in Figure 11.20, offers three ways to display images on your screen: Gray Out, Normal (the default), or High Resolution. These options apply to all imported graphics in a publication; you cannot choose a different option for each image. Also, they have no effect on your printed graphics.

FIGURE 11.20: *Use the Graphics option to control screen resolution.*

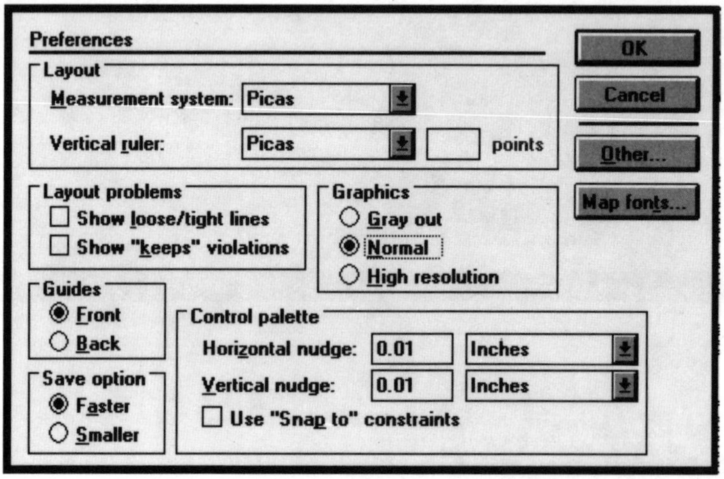

Gray Out, shown in Figure 11.21, offers the fastest screen redrawing because it doesn't actually show your images. It displays gray boxes inside the bounding box.

High Resolution provides the best screen resolution for TIFF images. However, screen redrawing is significantly slower. Figure 11.22 shows a TIFF image in normal resolution. Figure 11.23 shows the same file in high resolution. As you can see, the difference in screen resolution is significant, as is the time it takes to redraw the screen. Turn on High Resolution when you need to size or crop an image; switch to Normal or Gray Out when you want to concentrate on formatting the text.

FIGURE 11.21: *The Gray Out screen resolution*

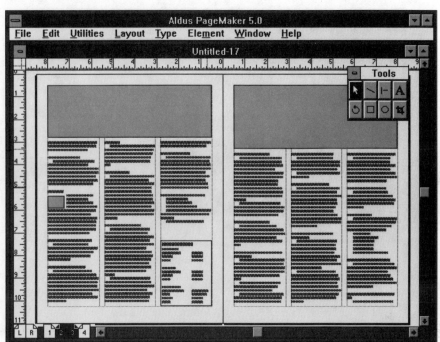

WORKING WITH BITMAP IMAGES

Bitmap graphics have the lowest print quality, but PageMaker offers a way to improve their output.

The Image Control option on the Element menu is specific to black-and-white bitmap images (including TIFF files). The Image Control dialog box, shown in Figure 11.24, allows you to control the lightness and contrast of your images (as on your television set).

Select the bitmap image before displaying the Image Control dialog box. To lighten the image, enter a positive percentage next to Lightness; enter a negative value to darken it. You can also change the lightness percentage with the scroll bar by clicking on the right arrow to lighten, the left arrow to darken.

FIGURE 11.22: *A TIFF image in normal resolution*

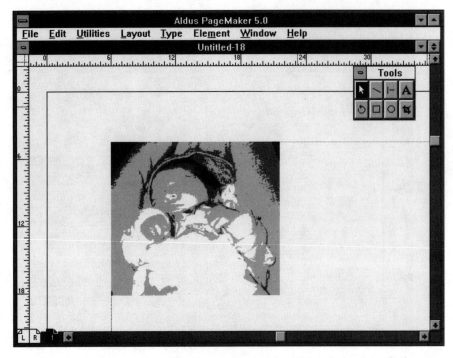

With the Contrast control, you can make the image lighter or darker in relation to the area behind the image. A 50% setting retains the graphic's original black-and-white contrast. Higher percentages increase the contrast between the image and its background. A 0% contrast reverses the black and white.

After adjusting the Lightness or Contrast controls, choose the Apply button. This lets you see how the adjustment affects the image without leaving the Image Control dialog box. If the graphic is hidden under the dialog box, move the box out of the way (drag the title bar). The Default button reverts the controls to their original settings (Lightness 0%, Contrast 50%). When you are satisfied with your results, choose OK.

FIGURE 11.23: *A TIFF image in high resolution*

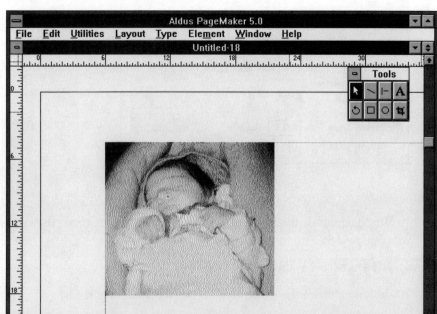

LINKING FILES

Much of what you learned about text file linking in Chapter 8 applies to the linking of graphic files. File linking helps you maintain a relationship between your publication and the original graphic file you imported. When an imported graphic is linked to its external file, you can avoid having to import and size a graphic each time it is modified in the graphics package.

As with text files, the process of file linking is automatic, but the process of updating the screen image to match the external file is not. You must explicitly issue that command. The Update command button is in the Links dialog box.

FIGURE 11.24: *The Image Control dialog box*

Image control
Lightness: [0] % ← ▮ →   [OK]
Contrast: [50] % ← ▮ →   [Cancel]
Printing parameters
Screen patterns: ▮ ▮   [Default]
Screen angle: [DFLT] degrees   [Apply]
Screen frequency: [DFLT] lines per inch

When a graphic file matches the image in the publication, the status message reads:

`This item is up to date.`

If you later change the external file, the status message reads:

`The linked file has been modified since the last time it was placed.`

You can then click on the Update button to reimport the file.

For a summary of all external files the publication is linked to, you can use the Display Pub Info Addition. This Addition lists the name and path of each linked file, the type of file (such as Windows metafile or TIFF), and the page number on which the graphic or text file was placed. Figure 11.25 shows a sample Pub Info dialog box with just the Links checkbox turned on.

FIGURE 11.25: *The Display Pub Info Addition summarizes information about linked files.*

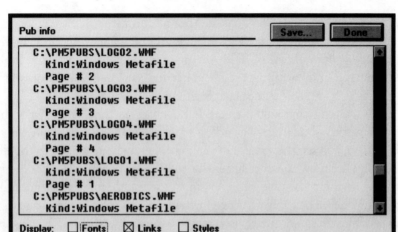

AUTOMATIC UPDATING

If you want PageMaker to automatically replace the internal version of the image with the changed external file, turn on the Update Automatically option in the Link Options dialog box shown in Figure 11.26. Link Options is a button in the Links dialog box, as well as an option on the Element menu. With the Update Automatically option, whenever you open the publication, the image instantly reflects any changes made in the graphic file; you don't need to choose the Update button.

You may also want to turn on the Alert Before Updating option so that as you open a file, PageMaker notifies you when a graphic needs updating. You can then cancel the updating if you want to leave the graphic as it is.

FIGURE 11.26: *The Link Options dialog box*

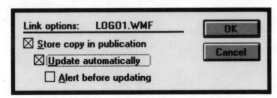

TO STORE OR NOT TO STORE

The Link Options dialog box has another important item: Store Copy in Publication. By default, PageMaker keeps copies of your imported graphic files inside your publication. The graphic is therefore in two places: in the .PM5 file and in its own graphic file. This duplication is a waste of valuable disk space and can sometimes lead to enormous publications.

A less wasteful approach is to tell PageMaker *not* to store a copy of the graphic in the publication. Regardless of whether the files are stored in the publication, you see the graphics because the images are linked to their external files. This approach requires that you keep your graphic files intact—don't delete them! If you delete, rename, or move them, they will not appear in the publication. However, whenever you modify the image in your graphics program, the revised image is automatically used because of the file linking.

By turning off the Store Copy in Publication option, you do two things at once: You minimize the size of your publication and you create an automatic link to the external graphic file. It's up to you to decide which graphics you want to apply the option to. You may want to keep it on for some graphics (such as small clip-art pictures) and turn it off for your larger images.

If you turn off the Store Copy in Publication option, the Update Automatically and Alert Before Updating options are unavailable because, when the graphic is not stored in the publication, PageMaker has no choice but to update. The updating happens automatically, and you are alerted only if it can't find the file.

When you place a large graphic, PageMaker will ask you if you want to include a complete copy in the publication (see Figure 11.27). If you choose No, the Store Copy in Publication option is turned off.

It's important to remember not to delete, move, or rename the graphic files; otherwise, you will see the error dialog box shown in Figure 11.28. If you deleted the file, you have no alternative but to choose the Ignore

---

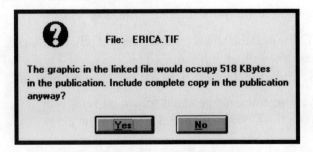

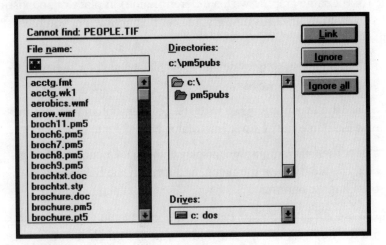

option. If you moved or renamed the file, you can use the File Name and Directories lists to select the new path and name.

REVISING AND REPLACING LINKED FILES

Suppose that you use your graphics package to modify an image you previously imported into a publication, and you save the revised image with the same name. How does this revised image get into PageMaker?

→ If the Store Copy in Publication option is turned off or the Update Automatically link option is turned on, the revised image is automatically imported the next time you open the publication.

→ If the Update Automatically option is turned off (as it is by default), choose the Update command button in the Links dialog box.

Regardless of which method you use, the graphic's original size, proportions, and cropping are maintained.

Now let's look at a slightly different situation: You want a different graphic (or the same graphic with a different name) in place of an existing graphic. In order to link this new graphic to the publication, you have several alternatives:

→ Delete the existing graphic and then place and size the new graphic. Crop if necessary.

→ Select the existing graphic with the pointer tool and choose the new file name in the Link Info dialog box.

→ Select the existing graphic, display the Place Document dialog box, choose the new file name, and turn on the Replacing Entire Graphic option.

Version
5.0

When you use either of the last two techniques, the old graphic is eliminated and the new graphic appears in the same size and location as the original graphic. If you want the new graphic to be cropped the same way as the original, turn on the Retain Cropping Data option. (It is an option in the Place Document and Link Info dialog boxes.)

IMPORTING GRAPHICS FROM THE CLIPBOARD

Another way to bring art into your publication is through the Windows Clipboard. This method eliminates the need for disk files. In your Windows-based graphics program, you create your graphic and then cut or copy it to the Clipboard. You then switch back into PageMaker and paste the graphic from the Clipboard into the publication. If a text cursor is positioned in a text block when you paste, the graphic is inserted as an inline graphic. Otherwise, the graphic is independent and can be positioned anywhere on the page.

With the Clipboard technique, you avoid the export-import routine. The graphic doesn't ever need to exist as a separate file, although it's a good idea to save the image in your drawing program in case you need to modify the graphic in the future.

If you want to paste more than one copy of the graphic on the same page, you can use the Multiple Paste option on the Edit menu. For more information about Multiple Paste, see the section titled, "Copying a Graphic and Using Multiple Paste" in Chapter 10.

Because you are not importing from a disk file, graphics that you import through the Clipboard are not linked to the publication. An item imported with the Paste command is considered an *embedded object*. For more information on this topic, see the discussion on embedded objects in the next section.

If you later decide to link an embedded object to an external file, follow these steps:

1. In the Links dialog box, click on the description of the embedded object.

2. Choose the Info button.

3. Select the file name in the Link Info dialog box.

USING OBJECT LINKING & EMBEDDING

Great news for PageMaker 5.0 users: You now get to use one of the most powerful, efficient, and fun tools that Windows 3.1 has to offer—*Object Linking & Embedding*, known mostly by its spirited nickname, *OLE*. Thanks to Version 5.0, PageMaker users now get access to this nifty way to place and manage external graphics; thanks to Windows 3.1, OLE has proven to be an exceptionally sturdy vehicle for graphics sharing.

If you have ever used the Edit ➤ Paste command to transfer graphics to PageMaker via the Clipboard, then you already know the mechanics of using OLE. But OLE goes one big step further: It empowers PageMaker to recall the original source program that created the graphic for quick and efficient editing. There are two ways in which OLE is implemented—the details of which are to be described soon—but the important thing to know is that when you use OLE to paste a graphic into PageMaker, that graphic becomes instantly editable with nothing more than a double-click.

HOW OLE WORKS

Here's the scenario: You are producing the sports page for your community news weekly during the time when the local race track hosts its annual AnyTown 500 Race. That cool race car you found in the CorelDRAW clip art collection will be perfect for this job. You launch Corel, open the race car, select it, and choose Edit ➤ Copy. Next, you launch PageMaker, open the publication for your magazine, and pull down the Edit menu and choose Paste Special.

Special? What's so special about a paste? Paste Special is the gateway to OLE, and with a bit of use, you might agree with its name. Any program that includes Paste Special on its Edit menu is capable of receiving hot-linked data. The Paste Special dialog box is shown in Figure 11.29. This dialog box lists the different types of formats in which you can paste. To create an OLE hot-link, you'll want to choose the name of the source program (in this case CorelDRAW). Then, when you click on the Paste Link button, the graphic appears on your page. Figure 11.30 shows the race car once it is paste-linked into the magazine.

This race car will neither look different nor print different than if it were pasted through the Clipboard as a static graphic or placed as a Windows

FIGURE 11.29: *The Paste Special dialog box is the gateway to OLE.*

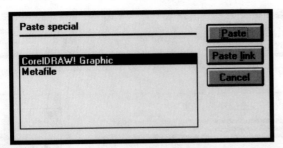

metafile. The formats are all identical. The big difference can be appreciated when your editor instructs you to remove the front guard on the race car. In the pre-OLE days, you would have to trace the steps yourself: You would have to launch CorelDRAW, open the file with the car, make the change, save the file, repeat the copy or export command, return to PageMaker and repeat the Paste or Place command.

But with OLE, everything is different. All you do is double-click on the car and the Windows OLE engine revs into action. It looks at the graphic, determines the source, switches to or launches that program, and then loads the original graphic file. You just sit back and watch. When Corel presents you with the original race car, you make the change, and save. That's it—the graphic in PageMaker has already changed, or is ready to change pending your say-so via the Links dialog box. Figure 11.31 was taken right after the Save command was issued in CorelDRAW—the image in PageMaker was immediately updated.

WHY OLE WORKS

It used to be that when a program like CorelDRAW copied an image to the Clipboard, it supplied only the graphic information necessary for another program to display and print the image. But today, OLE-compliant programs send much more information to the Clipboard:

> ➤ All graphic data in metafile format
>
> ➤ The name of the program that created the graphic
>
> ➤ The name of the original file and its location

FIGURE 11.30: *Thanks to OLE, this race car will be able to trace its tracks back to CorelDRAW.*

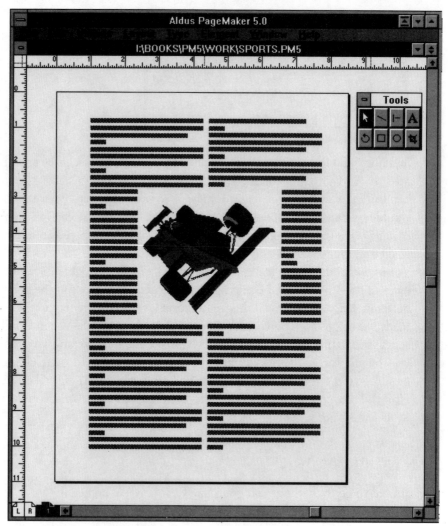

➤ The source data required to recreate the graphic

This last item will become especially significant later in this discussion.

FIGURE 11.31: *A double-click brings up Corel, and a Save command automatically updates the graphic in PageMaker.*

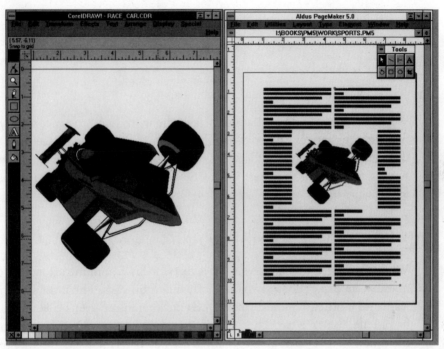

Defining Terms

The two players in this particular game, CorelDRAW and PageMaker, each are given names to identify their roles. As the source of the graphic, Corel is called the *OLE server*. It serves data to other programs. As the recipient of the graphic, PageMaker is called the *OLE client*. It is being served by Corel. When you hear these terms in conjunction with other software, you will be able to tell whether they can play the OLE game and which side of the give-and-take they are on. Some programs can go both ways. Corel-DRAW and most Microsoft programs can act as servers or clients, even at the same time.

In our seminars, we usually get a few oohs and aahs when we set up a three-way communication between OLE-compliant programs. We show an Excel worksheet providing data to an Excel chart. That chart is hot-linked to CorelDRAW, where supporting text and headlines are added. In turn, that embellished chart is hot-linked to PageMaker, where the chart is part of an annual report. In this routine:

- Excel plays the part of server.

- Corel plays the part of client.

- Corel also plays the part of server.

- PageMaker plays the part of client.

When we change one of the numbers in the worksheet, the accompanying Excel chart changes immediately. That promptly sends a message out through Windows for the CorelDRAW chart to change, and that in turn sends a message for the chart in PageMaker to change. It all seems to occur at the same time.

LINKING VERSUS EMBEDDING

While the essential feature of OLE is its two-way communication, this communication can occur in two distinctly different ways. The most straightforward and most easily understood OLE connection is the *linked file*. As a linked file, the race car "knows" that it came from CorelDRAW and from a file called RACE_CAR.CDR that resides in a particular subdirectory of a specific drive. In other words, it knows precisely its roots. Therefore, when you double-click on the car in PageMaker, the OLE engine can go out and find RACE_CAR.CDR and load it into Corel.

This link remains active as long as the original RACE_CAR.CDR file exists.

An *embedded object* is different—it no longer needs its source file. When you choose the Paste command instead of Paste Special, the Clipboard delivers to PageMaker not only the graphic, but also all of the original data required by CorelDRAW to edit the graphic. This embedded object is completely self-contained—it can be printed and edited without regard for its original file.

Think of it this way: The linked graphic in PageMaker is still owned by CorelDRAW. The fate of that graphic depends solely on the condition of RACE_CAR.CDR. But when you paste a graphic as an embedded object, it becomes the property of PageMaker. *All of the data necessary to edit the graphic in Corel is contained in the object.* So if you were to double-click on the object, Corel would start (or return from the background if already running) and the graphic would appear there, ready to be edited. Corel won't display RACE_CAR.CDR on its title bar, as it's not editing the original file. It's editing the object delivered to it by PageMaker. The title bar simply reads SPORTS.PM5, the name of the PageMaker publication.

The important thing to know about embedded objects is that they don't need the original source file. Everything needed to edit the file is contained in the embedded object.

Suppose you open a publication that you created some time ago, and you can't remember the source of its graphics. Are they embedded objects, files linked through OLE, or files linked through the Place command? The Links dialog box can provide you with this information. Figure 11.32 shows how how the three types of imported graphics are listed in the Links dialog box. Here is how to interpret this list:

➤ When the graphic is *imported* with the Place command, the file name is listed, and the Kind column lists the type of import filter used (Excel Chart).

➤ When the graphic is *linked* with the Paste Special command, the file name is listed, and the Kind column indicates the source program to which the file is linked (Linked Microsoft Excel Chart).

FIGURE 11.32: *By studying the Links dialog box, you can determine how your graphics were imported.*

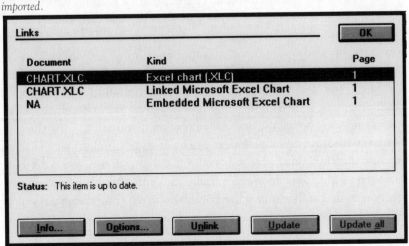

453

➤ When the graphic is *embedded* with the Paste command, no file name is given, but the source program is listed (Embedded Microsoft Excel Chart).

Using the Insert Object Command

Embedded objects can make their way into PageMaker in one of two ways: The typical way, outlined above, begins with the server program (Corel-DRAW in this case) delivering the object to the client over the Clipboard with the Copy and Paste commands. A second way is to use PageMaker's Edit ➤ Insert Object command, which allows the server to be launched by the client. This method is used when you haven't yet created the graphic in the server program.

Let's say you began work on your publication when you concluded that you wanted to add the race car as an embedded object. Instead of launching CorelDRAW and creating the car, you could use PageMaker's Insert Object command, choose CorelDRAW as the server, and Windows would automatically launch Corel, at which point you could create or import the car. When you close down Corel, the image would magically appear in PageMaker. The result is the same—PageMaker now owns an embedded object created in Corel—but the procedure is different.

When to Use Linked Files or Embedded Objects

Use linked files if you are using several copies of a graphic in one or more publications and you want to make sure they all look the same. Pasted as links, you could ensure that editing the original RACE_CAR.CDR would automatically update all copies of it that appear in PageMaker.

In general, use linked files whenever you want the control of an original file. Most of us are used to the concept of an original file driving copies in other programs, so linked files might be easier to understand.

On the other hand, use embedded objects if you are sharing the publication with someone else and/or you want to be efficient with disk space. Because the embedded object doesn't have a source file, you don't have to drag it along. You can archive it and move it off your disk completely should you desire. If sending the publication to a coworker, you could make the embedded object part of the file and not have to worry about any source files. "Do you have CorelDRAW?" you would ask. "Yes? Good, here take this." As long as your co-workers have Corel on their systems, they will be able to edit the race car. Windows and OLE will see to it.

Other OLE Features

Here are a few other features of OLE:

- ➤ PageMaker will only show changes in linked OLE graphics without any prompting if you turn on the Update Automatically switch that is hidden in the Links dialog box, under Options.

- ➤ The program that created the original data does not have to be running when you double-click on an OLE object in Page-Maker. Windows checks to see if it is running; if it's not, then Windows automatically launches it.

- ➤ If the server program is running and has an unsaved file opened, then you will be given a chance to save it before the graphic is opened. Or Windows may open a second instance of the server program, leaving the first instance and its unsaved file undisturbed.

- ➤ If you are sharing publications with other users, their programs do not need to be in the same locations as yours. For instance, if you keep CorelDRAW in C:\CORELDRW, but co-worker Dave keeps his on D:\COREL, you two will still be able to work on the race car. When Dave double-clicks on the car in PageMaker, Windows goes out and finds his copy of Corel, wherever it may be.

We have found that OLE objects print with exceptionally high quality and accuracy. They finish a close second to EPS files, but in many cases, the differences between the two are virtually indistinguishable. This is welcome relief for users of non-PostScript printers who have felt left out not being able to use EPS files, and generally good news for anyone who wants to enjoy the unprecedented convenience of hot-linked graphics and data.

SUMMARY

If a picture really is worth a thousand words, then PageMaker's ability to include graphic images in a document is an electronic gold mine. PageMaker recognizes the format of a variety of graphic file formats, enabling it to do business with programs ranging from CorelDRAW to Harvard Graphics.

HANDS-ON PRACTICE: IMPORTING GRAPHICS INTO THE NEWSLETTER AND BROCHURE

To demonstrate the use of external graphics, you will import graphic files into two of the publications you have seen in other chapters: the PC users' group newsletter and the Blue Chip Realty brochure.

For the exercise, you will need the following files:

- → NWSLTR11.PM5 (the newsletter publication)
- → COVER.WMF (the artwork for the newsletter cover page)
- → CARTOON.WMF (the cartoon graphic for a newsletter article)
- → BROCH11.PM5 (the brochure publication)
- → KEYS.WMF (the set of keys for the brochure)

These files are in the C:\PM5PUBS directory.

IMPORTING THE COVER ART

Figure 11.33 shows the cover page for the newsletter. The series of cartoon graphics and the circular text are part of a single graphic file created in CorelDRAW.

To import the cover artwork, follow these steps:

1. Open the NWSLTR11.PM5 file, located in the C:\PM5PUBS directory.
2. Press Ctrl+D to display the Place Document dialog box.

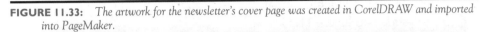

FIGURE 11.33: *The artwork for the newsletter's cover page was created in CorelDRAW and imported into PageMaker.*

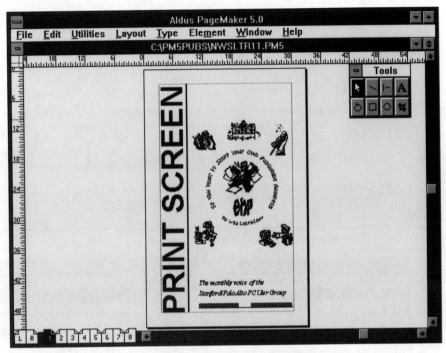

3. Double-click on the file name, COVER.WMF.

4. Click the graphic gun on the page, roughly where you want the artwork to go.

This graphic is so large that it doesn't fit on the screen. The easiest view in which to size this graphic is Show Pasteboard.

5. Choose the Show Pasteboard option on the Layout ➤ View menu.

6. Proportionally size the graphic until it fits within the right column guide: Hold down Shift as you drag the lower-right handle.

7. Switch to Fit in Window view.

8. Move the graphic so that it is vertically centered on the page, as shown in Figure 11.33.

9. Save the publication.

WRAPPING TEXT AROUND THE CARTOON GRAPHIC

Figure 11.34 shows a cartoon graphic that has been placed on page 7 of the newsletter. Notice that text flows around all four sides of the graphic.

1. Go to page 7.

2. Press Ctrl+D to display the Place Document dialog box.

3. Double-click on the file name, CARTOON.WMF.

FIGURE 11.34: *Text flows around all four sides of the cartoon graphic.*

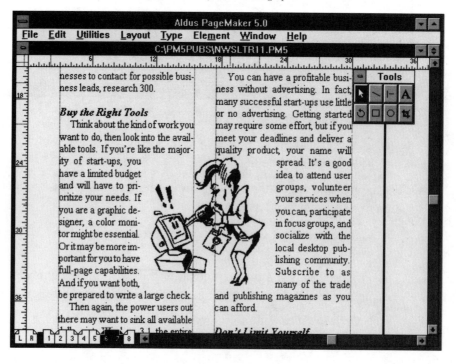

4. Click the graphic gun on the page, roughly where you want the graphic to go (refer to Figure 11.34).

The text currently flows behind the graphic—you need to turn on the text wrap feature. Text wrap is an option you apply to a selected graphic, not to the text, so make sure that the graphic is selected before continuing.

5. From the Element menu, choose Text Wrap.

6. Click on the second text wrap icon to turn on the text wrap feature. The third text flow icon—the one that wraps the text on all sides—is already selected.

7. Change the standoff values for Top and Bottom to 0.

8. Choose OK.

The text now flows around the cartoon, as shown in Figure 11.34. Reposition the graphic if necessary, and then save and close the file.

WRAPPING TEXT AROUND THE KEYS GRAPHIC

The Blue Chip Realty brochure you've worked on in earlier chapters has room for a graphic on page 2, next to the bulleted list. In the following steps, you'll place the graphic and turn on text wrap.

1. Open the BROCH11.PM5 publication.

2. Press Ctrl+D and choose KEYS.WMF in your C:\PM5PUBS directory. Choose OK and place the keys graphic on the pasteboard.

3. Proportionally size the graphic until it is approximately the final size. (See Figure 11.35.)

4. Move the graphic so that it is near the right side of the bulleted list item *We hand you the house keys*. Refer to Figure 11.35 for the exact location. Text flows behind the graphic because text wrap is turned off by default.

FIGURE 11.35: *The keys graphic placed in the brochure*

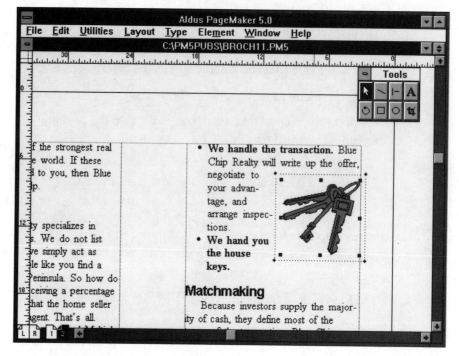

5. Choose Element ➤ Text Wrap.

6. Click on the second text wrap icon to turn on the text wrap feature.

7. Change the standoff values to 0.5 picas and choose OK.

8. If necessary, adjust the size of the graphic using the square graphic handles and reposition the graphic.

To bring the text closer to the graphic, decrease the standoff.

9. Display the Text Wrap dialog box.

10. Specify a 0 standoff on all sides of the graphic.

11. Choose OK. The text now comes closer to the graphic.

! **W**ARNING

Don't specify a zero standoff until the graphic is the perfect size because you will not be able to resize the graphic.

CREATING A CUSTOM WRAP AROUND THE KEYS

Try your hand at customizing the text wrap around the keys. Figure 11.36 shows the keys with a custom boundary.

1. Click on the boundary to create new handles.

2. Drag the diamond-shaped handles so that they lie against the graphic.

3. Save and close the file.

FIGURE 11.36: *The set of keys with a custom text wrap*

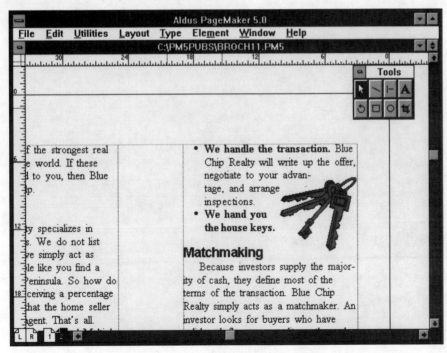

Working with Color

*f*ast tracks

To add a color to your palette: **469**

Choose Element ➤ Define Colors and click on the New button. Select the type of color (Spot or Process). Choose the library from the Libraries list. In the Library dialog box, select the desired color and choose OK. Edit the color name, if desired.

To create a tint: **473**

Choose Element ➤ Define Colors and click on the base color for your tint. Choose the New button. Type a name for the tint, making sure to include the base color and tint percentage. Click on Tint. Enter the tint percentage in the Tint text box.

To apply color to rectangles and ellipses: **475**

Select the object with the pointer tool, and choose Element ➤ Fill and Line. Choose a fill color, and if you like, specify a different color for the outline.

To apply color to text: **476**

Select the text with the text tool. Choose the color in the color palette or in the Type Specifications dialog box.

To remove a color: **478**

Display the Define Colors dialog box. Select the color to be removed and click on Remove. Choose OK to confirm the deletion.

To replace one color with another: **478**

Display the Define Colors dialog box. Click on the color to be replaced and choose the Edit button. Choose a Library and select the replacement color. Choose OK. Edit the color name in the Name field, if desired.

To print a composite on your desktop printer: **480**

Press Ctrl+P to display the Print Document dialog box. Choose your desktop printer in the Print To field. Click on the Color button and make sure the Composite option is turned on. Choose the Print button.

To print color separations in a print file: **482**

In the Page Setup dialog box, make sure your service bureau's output device is listed in the Compose to Printer field. In the Print Document dialog box, make sure this same device is specified in the Print To and Type fields. Click on the Options button and turn on the Printer's Marks and Page Information checkboxes. Click on the Color button and turn on the Separations option. Select which inks you want to print.

ESIGNING YOUR DOCUMENT IN color has many benefits. Color gets more attention, especially if the document is well designed and maximizes the use of color as a design element. Your audience will retain more information if color is used to correctly emphasize or aid the eye in reading the most important parts. You can also use color to create a sense of continuity and cohesiveness throughout your document. Color gives your document power, can stimulate the senses, and evoke emotions in your audience that will make them more receptive to your message. In this chapter, we will assume that you will use a commercial printer to print your final document. (It is possible to print your color document on a desktop color printer, but it is usually not possible in this way to get sufficient quality for a finished professional piece; it is adequate for proofing purposes.)

There are also some disadvantages to working with color. Your publication size is increased, the screen redraw is slightly slower, and color printing is much more expensive. Also, you can't trust the colors on your monitor to correspond to the final printed color; you must discipline yourself to use the percentages or codes on the color guides.

Finally, color simply takes more time. It's more complicated, and includes more variables and things that can go wrong. It is generally wise to estimate how much time you think it will take and then double it, at least. Don't be discouraged if the process is less than smooth. If you have established a good relationship with your service bureau and you let them know that this is your first time, they may give you a break if there's a problem. The good news is that almost every problem can be solved. If you are careful to remember the steps you went through, you can usually track down the problem.

You really need to develop a close relationship and good communication with both your service bureau and your printer so that the whole process will run smoothly and you will know what they need from you. Take the time to shop around and find service providers who are willing to answer your questions, who help you to design your document to avoid problems, and who will show you samples of their work. A little extra time up front to discuss potential printing problems and to identify prepress tasks and who's responsible for what may save a lot in the end.

DEFINING COLORS

There are three types of color you can use in your publications: spot colors, process colors, or a combination of both. A *spot color* is a premixed ink and requires a different plate for each spot color used. It is printed as a solid or semi-opaque ink on the press.

Process color is made up of varying percentages of cyan (C), magenta (M), yellow (Y), or black (K); thus it is referred to as the CMYK model. These inks are translucent and absorb some colors and reflect others. Different colors are obtained on the printing press by varying the dot size and distance. Each process color requires its own plate, which also contains tints or shades of that color. The four process color plates ultimately combine to form the desired final colors.

When you use a combination of spot and process colors, you can have as many as six or seven different plates, the spot colors printing the solid inks and the process colors being superimposed. Some very high-end publications use this method.

You would use spot color when:

➤ You have fewer than three colors in your document and each of those three colors can be specified from a spot color library (such as Pantone).

➤ You have to match exactly a color from a logo or other graphic that you or the client already has.

➤ You have a limited budget.

➤ You want to use special inks such as metallic or fluorescent colors.

You would use process color when:

➤ You are printing more than three colors.

➤ You have a big budget.

➤ You have color photographs in your publication.

You would use the combination of spot and process colors when:

➤ You have a huge budget.

➤ You need to print five or more colors.

➤ You want to use process colors for most of the publication, but you also must match a color on a logo.

➤ You want to use process color but also add a metallic or fluorescent color.

In addition to the CMYK model, PageMaker offers two other ways of defining colors: RGB (Red-Green-Blue) and HLS (Hue-Lightness-Saturation). Both of these models are used to define colors on your monitor; they are not to be used for creating color separations.

SELECTING A COLOR-MATCHING SYSTEM

PageMaker includes several different *color libraries* or color-matching systems. Some of the libraries are for spot colors, some are for process colors, and some are for both. The spot color libraries include Dainippon (DIC), Pantone, and Toyo. The process color libraries are Focoltone, Pantone, and Trumatch. The Greys library is made up of shades of gray in both spot and process colors. The library called Crayon is used as a starting point for creating your own libraries (see "Creating Custom Color Libraries," later in the chapter). To ensure the best possible color match, ask your commercial printer which color system he or she prefers to use and then select the color library to match that system. You can then be assured that the colors you pick will print predictably in the final printed piece.

ADDING A COLOR TO YOUR PALETTE

The default color palette (shown in Figure 12.1) contains only a handful of colors. [Paper] refers to the color of the paper (currently white). If you want your screen to simulate the color of paper you will be using in the final publication, you can change this color. The paper color has absolutely no effect on the printing process.

[Black] is the default color of all text and drawn objects. [Registration] refers to the color of the registration marks that are printed in color separations, as explained later in the chapter. The only other colors listed in the palette are Blue, Green, and Red. To add additional colors to the palette, you need to define them.

FIGURE 12.1:   *The color palette*

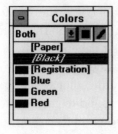

To define a color, choose Define Colors from the Element menu and then click on the New button. This brings up the Edit Color dialog box, shown in Figure 12.2. In this dialog box, decide whether the color will be Spot or Process, and make sure the CMYK model is selected. Your next task is to choose a color-matching system; to do this, display the Libraries drop-down list and click on the desired library.

FIGURE 12.2:   *The Edit Color dialog box*

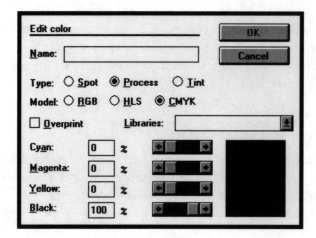

There are four choices for Pantone: Pantone (spot colors), Pantone Euro (spot colors, European version), Pantone Process (process colors), and Pantone Process Euro (process colors, European version).

After you choose a library, PageMaker will display a dialog box of color swatches in that library. Figure 12.3 shows a window of color swatches for the Pantone library. Use the horizontal scroll bar until you find the desired color, and then click on the swatch. Because you can't depend on the screen color to match the printed output color, you should purchase a swatch book from your commercial printer to match the color system you are using. These swatch books have codes that correspond to each swatch color. Instead of scrolling through the library until you find the color, you can simply enter the code in the text box at the top of the dialog box; the swatch with this code will automatically be selected.

FIGURE 12.3: *Some of the color swatches in the Pantone library*

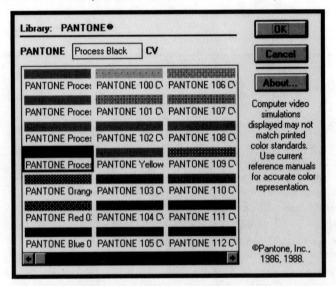

When you are in the Library dialog box, you can select multiple color swatches by holding down Ctrl as you click on each one.

Choose OK once you have selected the color(s) you want. You are then returned to the Edit Color dialog box. In the Name field, the library name as well as the color code is automatically entered (for example, *Pantone 110 CV*). You can edit this name if you like. You may want to make it more descriptive because the name listed here is what appears in the color palette. (However, using the assigned color names helps you keep track of information you'll need to give to your commercial printer.)

The Edit Color dialog box also lists the appropriate percentages of Cyan, Magenta, Yellow, and Black for the color you selected (assuming you are using the CMYK model). Another way to define the color is to enter the percentages yourself.

To help you decide whether you want to turn on the Overprint option, see the sidebar below.

OVERPRINTING VERSUS KNOCKING OUT COLORS

If all the colored text and objects were to print on top of one another, you would not only have too much ink in one place, but the layers of different colored inks would create unwanted (and probably ugly) new colors. PageMaker takes this into account and by default, colors and objects (such as the lines and fills of rectangles and ellipses) *knock out* the colors and objects beneath them. In other words, when there are overlapping colors, the top color will print, but the colors positioned behind it will not. This also applies to imported TIFF and EPS images, which knock out the colors or objects positioned behind them.

Knockouts help solve some problems, but create others. When the color or object underneath is simply knocked out, the color on top must print in exactly the correct position (printers call it a "kiss fit"), or small, white edges will appear around the objects underneath. Most presses cannot register the paper that accurately.

Usually this problem is prevented by what printers call *trapping*. Trapping is a process in which either the knockout is *choked* (the edges are shrunk inward) or the object on top is *spread* (the edges are expanded outward). Chokes are typically used to trap a dark element to a light background. Spreads are used to trap a light object to a dark background. PageMaker does not perform trapping. You can simulate it in some cases by specifying a color or object to *overprint*. As a rule, you would always overprint black text. Overprinting is also used when you want to intentionally create an additional color.

You can create an overprinting color by choosing an existing color, creating a 100% tint of it, and checking the Overprint option in the Edit Color dialog box. You can then apply that color to the objects, lines, and fills that you want to overprint. You can also specify object-level overprinting by specifying that the lines or fills of an individual element overprint. (Overprint is an option in the Fill and Line dialog box.) Object-level overprinting overrides the color-level defaults. This means that an object set to overprint will do so even if the color is set to knock out. This procedure may simulate a spread, but it will frequently create a third color, or a colored border, around the edges of the overprinted object. In essence, you've simply moved the problem from one place to another.

It is possible to use an illustration program such as Aldus Freehand to perform trapping on your graphics before you import them into PageMaker. Alternatively, your service bureau might have Aldus TrapWise to trap your PageMaker pages and any art they contain.

In your color palette, all process colors you add are italicized and spot colors are in normal type.

CREATING A TINT

Version
5.0

Tints are lightened shades of a particular color, expressed as a percentage of the base color. For example, if your base color is Process Blue, you could produce a tint named 20% Process Blue. If precise predictability is needed in specifying a lighter shade of a spot color, it is best to stick to the shades shown in the color library you are using; your printer can then mix the ink precisely according to the swatch book. To see the available related shades for a spot color, scroll through the color swatches and notice that different numeric codes are assigned to lighter (and darker) versions of the same base color.

If you do want to specify a tint of a spot color (so you can use both tint and solid color for the price of one plate), be aware that there is no simple way to get a precise idea of what your tint will look like. Most swatch books don't include tint examples, and if they do it's only a few specific percentages.

To create your own tint from a process color, you must have already added the base color using the procedure described in the previous section. Then, in the Define Colors dialog box click on the base color and choose the New button. Type a name for the new tint, preferably one that shows the base color name with the appropriate percentage for the new tint. When you click on the Tint option, the dialog box changes to the one shown in Figure 12.4. To specify the tint percentage, enter a value (in 1 percent increments) in the Tint text box. You can also specify the percentage by adjusting the slider bar; as you click on the scroll arrows or drag the scroll box, the dialog box shows you what the tint looks like, as compared to the base color (these colors are pointed out in Figure 12.4). Decide whether you want the tint to overprint (see the sidebar above), and then click on OK to close the dialog box.

FIGURE 12.4:   *A tint is being created in this dialog box.*

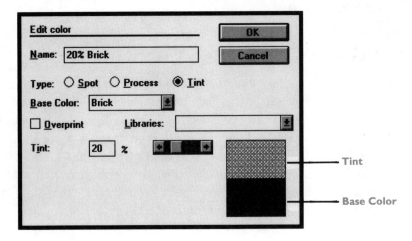

!ℓ𝒲ARNiNG

Be careful about specifying tints lighter than 20%. With many high-resolution imagesetters, a tint that light would not show up. Also, consider the line weight when applying a tint to a line or an outline; hairlines and .5-point lines may not be visible.

After you create your tint, you can apply it to text, lines, and fills just as with any other color. The tint will show up in your color palette, as well as in the Define Colors and the Fill and Line dialog boxes. In the color palette, all tints will have a % sign in front of them.

ASSIGNING COLOR

After you have defined the colors that you wish to include on the color palette, you can apply those colors to text, monochrome or grayscale imported images, and objects drawn in PageMaker, such as rectangles and lines. The colors can be applied to lines, outlines, and fills (the area within a rectangle or ellipse).

APPLYING COLORS

To apply colors, you'll want to display the color palette by choosing Color Palette on the Window menu (or pressing Ctrl+K). Then, select the text or graphic you want to add color to and click on the color in the color palette. You must select text with the text tool and graphic elements with the pointer tool.

Applying color to rectangles and ellipses involves a slightly different procedure because these objects can use different colors for their outlines and fills. If the object has a percentage fill, any color you apply will be shaded to this percentage. Or, if the object has a pattern fill, the design will have the color you choose. You can specify the fill on the Fill menu or in the Fill and Line dialog box, shown in Figure 12.5. This dialog box not only lets you choose the type of fill, but it also lets you choose colors for lines and fills—one-stop shopping.

FIGURE 12.5:   *Use the Fill and Line dialog box to apply colors to outlines and fills of rectangles and ellipses.*

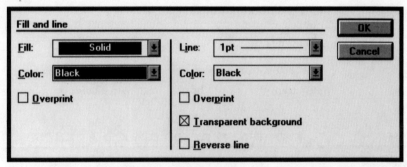

It is also possible to use the color palette to apply or change the colors of the outlines and fills of objects. By default, when you click on the color, it is applied to both the outline and the fill. (Note the word *Both* at the top of the color palette.) To apply the color to just the fill or just the line, display the drop-down list in the color palette, and choose Fill or Line. You can also click on the filled-in square (to choose Fill) or diagonal line (to choose Line) at the top of the palette. Figure 12.6 points out these areas. Once you have selected Fill or Line, you can click on the color you want.

FIGURE 12.6: *When changing the color of an object, you can choose whether to apply the color to the fill, line, or both.*

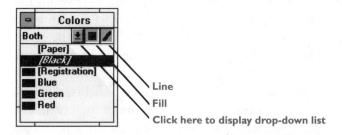

To remove the color inside a rectangle or ellipse, select the object and choose None on the Fill menu.

To apply color to text, first select it with the text tool. Then, make sure the top of the color palette says Both or Fill, and click on the desired color. Another way to assign color to text is to press Ctrl+T to display the Type Specifications dialog box and choose the color from the Color drop-down list.

If the top of the color palette says Line when text is selected, you will not be able to choose a color.

APPLYING COLOR TO IMPORTED GRAPHICS

Version
5.0

When you import a color EPS graphic, the colors are automatically imported and will show on your color palette. (Colors from other types of graphics are not imported.) Imported colors are differentiated from other colors by an EPS symbol next to the name. You can apply these colors to other objects and to text, and you can convert spot colors to process. Note that you cannot edit colors imported from an EPS graphic.

PageMaker allows you to apply color to certain kinds of imported images: grayscale and monochrome bitmapped TIFF images, EPS graphics,

PICT and PICT2 files (from the Macintosh), and Windows metafiles graphics. You can apply both process and spot colors to these types of images. You will be able to see the applied color in TIFF, PICT, and Windows metafile images on your screen; you will not be able to see the color applied on-screen in EPS or PICT2 images. All images will print with the applied color, which can be separated if you so desire.

You cannot apply color to RGB TIFF, CMYK TIFF, or DCS types of images. If you try, it will have no effect and those images will retain their original colors.

When you apply color to a graphic, you are applying one color to the whole image. If the image contains shades, they will become shades of the new applied color. You cannot select out certain colors and apply new colors to them individually.

If you change your mind about a color you have applied to an imported graphic, you can remove it. To do this, select the graphic and choose Restore Original Color from the Element menu. The image will revert back to its original color.

MANAGING YOUR COLORS

Once you have added colors to your color palette, your need for these colors may change. You may no longer need a color or maybe you want to replace one color with another. You also may discover that you want to use the same set of colors in your current publication that you defined in another publication. All these color management tasks can be handled in the Define Colors dialog box.

REMOVING A COLOR

If you no longer need a color in your palette, or if you want to get rid of the default Red, Green, and Blue colors that are included in every publication's color palette, use the Remove button in the Define Colors dialog box. First, click on the color name you want to remove. When you click on the Remove button, you'll see a message similar to the one shown in Figure 12.7. If you choose OK, the color (Blue, in this case) will be removed from your color palette. Any text or objects that used this color will then be colored black.

FIGURE 12.7:   *When you click on the Remove button in the Define Colors dialog box, you'll see a message like this one.*

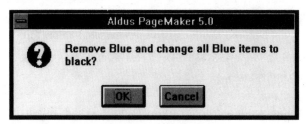

If your palette contains a tint based on the color you removed, its base color will change to black, i.e., the tint will change to gray.

REPLACING ONE COLOR WITH ANOTHER

It's easy to replace one color with another and when you do, PageMaker will automatically remove the old color and apply the new color to all the items that used the original color. The replacement color can even be from a different color library. To replace one color with another, follow these steps:

1. Choose Element ➤ Define Colors.

2. Click on the color that you want to replace and then choose the Edit button.

3. Choose a color-matching system from the Libraries list, and select the replacement color from the Library dialog box. Choose OK.

4. Edit the color name in the Name field, if desired.

5. Close all dialog boxes.

PageMaker will then substitute the replacement color for the original color in all text, graphics, and objects that used the color. The new color will replace the old color in the color palette, and in the Define Colors and Fill and Line dialog boxes.

COPYING COLORS FROM ANOTHER PUBLICATION

If you added or created new colors in one publication and want to use them in another, you can copy them. The Copy button in the Define Colors dialog box copies all the colors in the publication you indicate; you can't select which colors to copy.

If the current publication has a color with the same name but with different color specifications, PageMaker will ask if you want to replace the existing color with the imported color. If you decide to keep the color in the current publication, just click on Cancel—PageMaker will not copy the new color. If you want to replace the original color, click on OK when PageMaker asks. All the new colors will be placed in the color palette as well as in the Define Colors and Fill and Line dialog boxes.

Instead of copying colors into a new publication, you can use a different approach: Open a template that already contains the colors you frequently use. Chapter 14 describes how to create a template. Your color template should be an empty publication in which you have defined the set of colors you frequently use. When you open this template, the publication will already have the desired color palette in place.

COLOR PRINTING

Even though you have created a color document, you may not have color printers available on site. But you will still need to do as much on-site proofing as possible to best ensure that you will get positive results when you take your final files to your service bureau for color separation on the imagesetter. Fortunately, PageMaker will allow you to use a black-and-white laser printer or a desktop color printer for your proofs. Obviously, the resolution will be lower on these printers and if you use a color printer, the colors will probably not accurately match those on the screen or in the final printed output. However, you will be able to see that the colors are similar to the ones you have selected and that they appear in the correct locations. You will also have the opportunity to pick out places where you might want to change things such as overprinting versus knockouts. And you would use this proof for all the other normal proofing tasks as well, such as looking for typing mistakes, layout problems, and improper spacing.

PRINTING A COMPOSITE

A *composite* is simply a printout of all colors on a single page on either a color or a black-and-white printer. Before you print to your desktop printer for proofing purposes, remember that you must first select the printer in the

Print To field of the Print Document dialog box. When you select a low-resolution printer, PageMaker will use the appropriate settings for that printer and use color if you check the Color option in the Color print dialog box.

Version
5.0

You can print the composite in color, in grayscale, or in shades of black. These options are in the Color dialog box shown in Figure 12.8; to display this dialog box, press Ctrl+P and choose the Color button. Note that the Color dialog box options vary according to the printer driver you are using; your dialog box may look different from Figure 12.8. When you select Grayscale, PageMaker prints colors as grays, and it will simulate the different intensities of the actual colors. For instance, if you have a 20% tint of blue and a 20% tint of sky blue, the black-and-white printer will print the tint of blue slightly darker than the tint of sky blue. If your printer is a desktop color printer, the Grayscale option in the Color dialog box will be replaced with an option for Color. If you are using a PCL printer, such as the HP LaserJet, the option is listed as Color/Grayscale.

With the Print Colors in Black option, all the colors in your document will be printed as shades of black on your black-and-white printer. This is different from shades of gray. For example, if you are printing a 20% tint of blue and 20% tint of sky blue, they will look the same instead of being of different gray shades. If one were a 40% color, it would print darker than either of the 20% colors even if it was 40% of a lighter color than blue

FIGURE 12.8:   *The Color dialog box is accessed through the Print Document dialog box.*

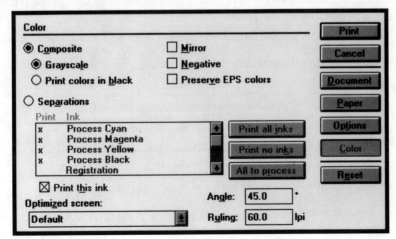

(such as pink). This option prints imported images in shades of black also. It is difficult to think of a situation when using this command would be beneficial.

The Composite, Color/Grayscale, and Print Colors in Black options are available and work the same way on both PostScript and PCL desktop printers. However, it would not be wise to attempt to do color separations on a PCL printer.

PRINTING COLOR SEPARATIONS

Version
5.0

Before printing color separations, you should have developed a good working relationship with your service bureau and commercial printer. You should know what your service bureau needs from you in the way of files and media, and you should know which services the bureau can provide, such as trapping, stripping, and impositions.

You should also know what kinds of images to include within your document to maximize PageMaker's separation abilities. For best results, do not include RGB TIFF images or PICT files. PageMaker cannot separate RGB TIFF images, so you would need to use an image enhancement program to convert them to CMYK TIFF before importing them into your publication. PICT files do not separate reliably, so you should convert them to EPS or Windows metafile for best results.

Check your proofs carefully and make all your corrections before you print your separations. Service bureau time is expensive and film negatives are hard to read. All the money you save by doing separations from your desktop can be lost if you need to make corrections after the film has been made.

PageMaker gives you a number of printing options for color separations:

➤ You can have PageMaker do all of the separations, including TIFF images.

➤ You can have PageMaker prepare the separation files for another post-processing separation program such as Aldus PrePrint or Publishers Prism. These programs can use your PageMaker-created OPI (Open Prepress Interface) files.

➤ You can print process or spot color separations.

➤ You can print some or all colors.

➤ You can specify if you want certain inks to knock out or overprint.

➤ You can change the screen angles and ruling for your colors.

Before printing your color separations, go to the Page Setup dialog box and make sure your service bureau's output device is specified in the Compose to Printer field. You will most likely be printing your separations to a high-resolution PostScript device such as a Linotronic 330 or Agfa 9400 image-setter with resolutions of 1270 to 3386 dpi. If you change the printer after creating the publication, it's a good idea to go through your publication for one final check to be sure that the recomposition didn't move or change anything in a way you don't want. This rarely happens, but it's better to check and correct it now if it does. Once your publication is composed for the correct final output device, you are ready to begin the separations.

For details on creating files for remote printing, see Appendix C.

To make process-color separations, you should:

1. Choose File ➤ Print. In the Print To field, select the printer for the device you want to print to. In the Type field, choose the corresponding PPD file. The PPD (PostScript Printer Description) file describes your printer's standard features, including information on paper sizes and printing color separations.

2. Click on the Paper button, display the Size drop-down list, and choose the correct paper size for your publication.

3. Click on the Options button and turn on the Printer's Marks and Page Information checkboxes.

4. Click on the Color button, and turn on the Separations option. Notice that when you choose Separations, the Composite option deselects and the Ink list is now available (see Figure 12.9).

FIGURE 12.9:   *When you select the Separations option, you can choose which inks to print.*

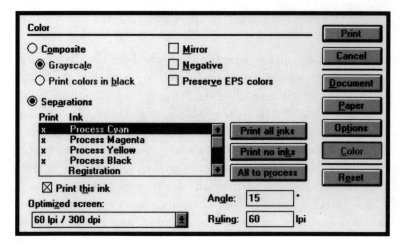

Selecting Inks

PageMaker defaults to printing all four process inks (there is an X next to each ink color). You can leave this the way it is, remove one or more colors, or add other ink colors to the list. To print another color separation, highlight the desired ink color and turn on the Print This Ink checkbox. If you don't want a color printed, highlight it, and turn off the Print This Ink checkbox. Two buttons are provided as shortcuts for choosing or deselecting inks: Print All Inks and Print No Inks. When you have several ink colors selected, PageMaker will print all the colors in one file. If your publication is very large and you print all the pages, your print file will be *huge*.

Although creating all your color separations in one large print file is convenient, it is much more difficult to determine which page or color has a problem should you encounter one when trying to process the file at the service bureau. Furthermore, once the problem is pinpointed, the entire job must be redone, increasing your costs dramatically. To maximize your ability to find the problems quickly and to avoid extra charges at your service bureau, create a separate print file for each color on each page. Granted, this technique requires a lot more work and print jobs than creating one large print file, but it will likely save you time and money in the long run. For your first several attempts at printing color separations, we suggest that you use a relatively short publication.

In order to print this way, type in a single page number in the Ranges field of the Print Document dialog box, and then click on the Colors button. Select Separations and uncheck all but one ink. When you choose the Print button, a box displays for you to type in the path and file name of the print file. To help keep track of all these files, you might want to use the page number for the file name and the color for the file extension, such as Page1.cya, Page1.mag, Page1.yel, Page1.bla, and so on with the subsequent pages. If your publication contains spot colors that you have not converted to process, you will need to select them separately and print individual plates for your spot colors, too.

> Because of the nature of imagesetters and film, it is best for your service bureau to print all the colors on a page in the same pass. Film can stretch and the density of imagesetters can sometimes change, so if color separations for a page are created on different days or at different times of the day, you will likely experience registration problems—the colors will not line up properly.

If you do choose to print several pages and all of the colors in one file, you would simply specify the desired range of pages and turn on the Print This Ink option for the desired inks. For the name of the print file, type something like 1-3.SEP (for pages 1 through 3).

You may have a publication that uses only two or three spot colors. If you are using all spot colors and want to separate them as spot colors, follow the same steps as described for separating process colors.

CONVERTING SPOT COLORS TO PROCESS

Version
5.0
You can use spot colors while constructing your publication, and then convert them to process colors at the time you print your separations. The All to Process button is in the Colors dialog box. The conversion applies to all the spot colors you have used in your publication as well as any that were

imported with graphics. PageMaker will attempt to simulate the spot color as closely as possible, but it will not be exact. Unlike most other print settings, the All to Process option is not saved as part of your publication.

Although the All to Process print option is a fast way to convert spot colors to process, you cannot be confident of what colors will actually print. Therefore, we advise against using the All to Process option. A more accurate way to do the conversion is to redefine each spot color as a process color in the Define Colors dialog box.

SCREEN RULING AND ANGLES

Version
5.0

Each color has Ruling and Angle values assigned to it. PageMaker picks up these values from the PPD file for your specified printer. You can change either of them by typing in new values. Printers can produce a wide variety of colors by varying dot sizes of the four process color inks. The pattern that results from those dots is called a *halftone screen*. The two factors, *screen ruling* (also called lines per inch or lpi) and the *screen angle* (the pattern of dots), are used by the press to determine how these dots relate to each other and to determine the quality of your final printed piece.

The Ruling also relates to the type of paper on which your final output will be printed. This paper can range from newsprint to high-quality coated stock run on very accurate presses. For newsprint, the screen ruling is 65 to 85 lpi; for inexpensive coated stock, it is 90 to 133 lpi; for medium and high-quality coated stock printed on fast presses, it is between 133 and 150 lpi; and for high-quality coated stock on accurate presses, it is 150 to 200 lpi. When you select an ink, PageMaker will show you the ruling that it reads from the PPD file for that output device. You may wish to change this ruling based on the advice of your commercial printer as to the stock you are using and the press on which your job will be printed.

The other factor is screen angle. Again, you should accept PageMaker's default setting specified by your output device's PPD file unless you have very good reasons to change it. Traditionally, printers have used screen angles of 45 degrees for black, 75 degrees for magenta, 90 degrees for yellow, and 105 degrees for cyan. PageMaker's default settings for process colors will usually be the same as the traditional screen angles unless the PPD file for a specific output device dictates otherwise. Spot colors default to 45 degree angles. You may want to change your spot color angles to achieve special effects. You will definitely want to change the spot color default angle if a screened spot overprints another or a black screen or halftone. If you specify the wrong screen angles, you will get an undesirable moire pattern in the final printed piece.

MIRROR AND NEGATIVE

Version
5.0

There are several other options you can change in the Color dialog box: Mirror and Negative. Mirror works with Negative to determine whether your file will print positive, negative, emulsion up, or emulsion down. (*Emulsion* is the light-sensitive coating on the film.) You should consult with your service bureau to determine how it would like to receive your files. Most service bureaus prefer to control these settings on their imagesetters and will have you print your file as positive, right-reading, emulsion up so that they can do the reversal process themselves on the hardware. For example, to print your file as positive, right-reading, emulsion up, you leave the Mirror and Negative options unchecked. That allows your service bureau to simply reverse your file in order to print negative, wrong-reading, emulsion down on the final film.

You can use the following chart to determine the correct setting for Mirror for positives.

	RIGHT-READING		**WRONG-READING**	
Emulsion	Up	Down	Up	Down
Set Mirror to	Off	On	On	Off

CREATING CUSTOM COLOR LIBRARIES

Version
5.0

PageMaker 5.0 lets you create your own color libraries. You might create a custom color library if you want to use a limited number of colors consistently in multiple publications (perhaps for a certain project). There are two ways to do this. By far the easiest way is to use the Create Color Library Addition. Before you run this Addition, you should define all the colors and tints you want to include in the custom color library; the new library will contain all the colors in the current color palette.

The Create Color Library dialog box is shown in Figure 12.10. In the Library Name field, type in a description for your new library; this description will appear in the Libraries drop-down list in the Edit Color dialog box. The Rows and Columns fields refer to the number of rows and columns of color swatches in the Library dialog box; the more rows and columns you have, the smaller the color swatches. In the Notes field, enter any comments that will help you remember what this custom library is for or how you created it. Your notes will appear when you click on the About button in the Library dialog box. When you are done, click on the Save button. This library can now be used in any publication.

FIGURE 12.10: *The Create Color Library dialog box*

Create color library

Library name:

File name: CUSTOM.BCF

Rows: 5

Columns: 3

Notes:

Save

Cancel

Browse...

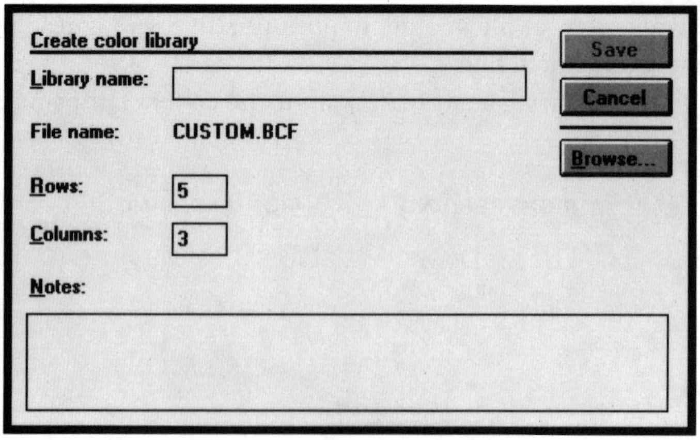

By default, the custom color library file has the name CUSTOM.BCF. To change the name, or to create multiple custom color libraries, you must click on the Browse button in the Create Custom Library dialog box and then type in the desired file name (it will automatically be assigned a BCF extension.) When you choose OK, the new name will display in the dialog box.

You can also create a custom color library by editing an existing color library and assigning it a new name. To do this, use a text editor (such as Windows Notepad) and open the file named CRAYON.ACF located in the \ALDUS\USENGLSH\COLOR directory. Edit the file as described in Aldus' Commercial Printing Guide. When you are done, save the file with a new name, with the .ACF extension.

SUMMARY

Version 5.0 truly expands PageMaker's color capabilities. Using the Define Colors dialog box, you can access colors from several standard color-matching systems (such as Pantone and Trumatch) and add these colors to your palette. Once done, you can apply these colors to text, graphics drawn from within PageMaker, and some imported graphics. To print composites and color separations, you will use the Print Document and Color dialog boxes.

HANDS-ON PRACTICE: DEFINING AND APPLYING COLORS

In this hands-on practice, you'll get an opportunity to play a bit with color. You will remove colors, define new colors, create a tint, apply colors to text and graphic objects, and then replace one color with another.

This exercise uses the file COLOR12.PM5 in the C:\PM5PUBS directory. Open this file before you begin. Your screen should look similar to Figure 12.11.

FIGURE 12.11: *You will apply colors to the text and objects in this drawing.*

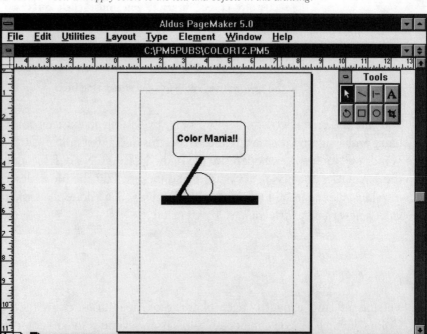

REMOVING THE DEFAULT COLORS

Every color palette contains four colors: black (the default color applied to all objects), blue, green, and red. You cannot delete black, but you can remove the other three colors. Follow these steps:

1. In COLOR12.PM5, display the color palette by choosing Window ➤ Color Palette. Note the default colors in this palette.

2. Choose Element ➤ Define Colors.

3. Click on Blue and then the Remove button. Choose OK to confirm the removal of this color.

4. Repeat step 3 for Green and Red.

5. Choose OK to close the dialog box.

Note that the three colors are removed from the color palette. Also, the red rectangle is now filled with black.

DEFINING PANTONE COLORS

Let's suppose you have the Pantone Color Formula Guide and you have selected two colors you wish to use in this publication. The color swatches you have chosen are numbered 284 (a shade of reflex blue) and 203 (a pink). You will need to reference these numbers when defining the colors in PageMaker.

1. Choose Element ➤ Define Colors.

2. Click on the New button.

3. In the Libraries list, choose Pantone. You will then see the Library dialog box, full of color swatches. To locate the desired color, you can use the scroll bar, or since you know the color number, you can enter the number in the Pantone field at the top of the dialog box. We'll use the latter method here.

4. Select the text currently in the Pantone field (probably *Process Black*) and type **284**. The color swatch numbered 284 is then selected in the dialog box. Choose OK.

5. In the Edit Color dialog box, select the text in the Name field (PANTONE 284 CV) and type **Periwinkle 284**. This name is more descriptive of the color and is more recognizable in the color palette.

6. Choose OK.

The new color, Periwinkle, is now listed in the Define Colors dialog box. Now, let's create another color (Pantone 203) and name it Rose 203.

7. Click on the New button.

8. In the Libraries list, choose Pantone.

9. Select the text currently in the Pantone field and type **203**. The color swatch numbered 203 is then selected in the dialog box. Choose OK.

10. In the Edit Color dialog box, select the text in the Name field (PANTONE 203 CV) and type **Rose 203**.

11. Close the dialog boxes.

Your two new colors, Periwinkle and Rose, are now listed in the color palette.

CREATING A TINT

Let's create a tint that is a 30% shade of our Periwinkle color.

1. Display the Define Colors dialog box and click on Periwinkle 284.

2. Choose the New button.

3. Click on Tint. The Edit Color dialog box changes, and now has an option to specify a tint percentage.

4. In the Tint text box, type **30** for the percentage.

5. In the Name field, type **30% Peri**. Your dialog box should look like Figure 12.12.

6. Close the dialog boxes.

FIGURE 12.12: *Defining a 30% tint for the Periwinkle base color*

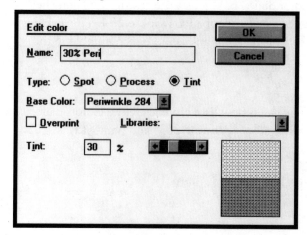

Your color palette should now look like the one in Figure 12.13. (So that all the names fit, we enlarged our color palette; you can do this by dragging the palette borders.)

FIGURE 12.13: *The color palette with three new colors*

APPLYING COLOR TO TEXT

Follow these steps to apply Periwinkle to the *Color Mania!!* text:

1. Choose the text tool.

2. Select the text *Color Mania!!*.

3. Press Ctrl+T to display the Type Specifications dialog box.

4. Display the Color drop-down list and choose Periwinkle 284.

5. Choose OK to close the dialog box.

6. Click off to deselect the text so that you can see the color.

The text is now colored Periwinkle. You also could have assigned the color by choosing Periwinkle in the color palette.

APPLYING COLOR TO LINES

Choose Periwinkle for the diagonal line that connects the two rectangles:

1. Select the pointer tool.

2. Click on the diagonal line.

3. In the color palette, choose Periwinkle 284.

APPLYING COLOR TO RECTANGLES AND CIRCLES

The rectangle at the bottom of the graphic already has a solid fill (black). Use the color palette to change both its outline and fill to Rose:

1. Select the solid rectangle with the pointer tool.

2. Check the top of the color palette and make sure it says Both (referring to both the line and the fill). If it doesn't, display the drop-down list and choose Both.

3. In the color palette, choose Rose 203.

Use the Fill and Line dialog box to fill the circle with 30% Peri:

4. Select the circle with the pointer tool.

5. Choose Element ➤ Fill and Line.

6. For the Fill, choose Solid.

7. For the fill color, choose 30% Peri.

8. Choose OK.

Notice that the outline of the circle is black because we did not specify a line color in the Fill and Line dialog box, so PageMaker used the default (black).

Fill the rounded rectangle with solid black and choose a 6-point Rose-colored line:

9. Select the rounded rectangle.

10. Display the Fill and Line dialog box.

11. For the Fill, choose Solid. Leave the fill color at Black.

12. For the Line, choose 6pt.

13. For the line color, select Rose 203.

14. Choose OK.

15. Press Ctrl-B to send the rectangle to the back.

REPLACING THE ROSE COLOR WITH GREEN

Let's suppose that we don't like the rose color—we want green (Pantone 3395) instead. The easiest way to make this replacement is to edit the color in the Define Colors dialog box.

1. Display the Define Colors dialog box.

2. Click on the color to be replaced—Rose 203.

3. Choose the Edit button.

4. In the Libraries list, choose Pantone.

5. Select the text currently in the Pantone field and type **3395**. The color swatch numbered 3395 is then selected in the dialog box. Choose OK.

6. In the Edit Color dialog box, select the text in the Name field (PANTONE 3395 CV) and type **Green 3395**.

7. Close the dialog boxes.

Now all items that were formerly Rose (the rectangle and the outline of the rounded rectangle) are now Green. If you like, you can save the file before closing it.

Using the Table Editor

fast tracks

To load the Table Editor: **501**

From the Program Manager, double-click on the Table Editor icon in the
Aldus program group.

To set up a table: **501**

Choose New on the File menu. Specify the number of columns and
rows, as well as the table dimensions. Choose OK.

To spread text across multiple cells: **505**

With the pointer tool, drag across the cells to be grouped together.
Choose Group on the Cell menu. Switch to the text tool, and type
the text.

To import a Lotus 1-2-3 spreadsheet: **505**

Pull down the File menu and choose Import. Select the .WK? file to be
imported. Enter the range of cells you wish to import, or select the range
name from the list. Choose OK.

To remove borders: **510**

Press Ctrl+A to select the entire table. Choose Borders on the Element
menu. Turn on the checkbox options for which you wish to remove borders. Display the Line drop-down list and choose None. Choose OK.

To adjust column widths: 514

Place the mouse pointer in the column grid-label area, on the vertical line between columns. (The mouse pointer turns into a double-headed arrow.) Click and drag to the left to narrow the column or to the right to widen.

**To decrease the row gutter
(which decreases the row height):** 516

From the File menu, choose Table Setup. Enter a smaller value for the row gutter.

To calculate totals: 518

With the pointer tool, select the range of cells to be summed. Choose Sum from the Cell menu. Click where you want to paste the total.

To import a table into Pagemaker: 520

Choose Place on the File menu, and select the .TBL file. Click on the page where you want to place the table.

To modify a table after it's been placed in PageMaker: 522

Select the table with the pointer tool, hold down the Alt key and double-click on the table. The table will automatically load into the Table Editor. Modify the table as necessary and save the changes. Exit from the Table Editor. In PageMaker, display the Links dialog box, highlight the table name and choose the Update button.

HE TABLE EDITOR INCLUDED WITH
PageMaker is an alternative way of creating columnar data for your publications. Instead of setting tabs and entering the data with PageMaker's text tool, you can create the table in the external Table Editor program and then import it into your publication.

ADVANTAGES OF THE TABLE EDITOR

Why would you want to use an external program when you can create the table right in PageMaker? Here are a few advantages of the Table Editor:

- → You enter the data in a spreadsheet grid of rows and columns.
- → You don't have to type commas, dollar signs, and percent signs; numeric punctuation is added with a command.
- → You don't have to manually draw horizontal and vertical lines— the borders are there automatically.
- → Rather than resetting tab stops, you can change the space between columns by dragging a column boundary.
- → The Table Editor can add and subtract numbers.

As you can deduce from the above list, the Table Editor has the look and feel of a spreadsheet program. In fact, if you have used an electronic spreadsheet program, such as Excel, you will find the Table Editor easy to use. It doesn't have the powerful calculating capabilities of a full-blown spreadsheet, but it offers more formatting options. Figure 13.1 shows an example of a table created and formatted in the Table Editor.

CREATING A TABLE

The process of creating a table in the Table Editor consists of three basic steps: specifying the table's dimensions, entering the data, and saving the file.

LOADING THE TABLE EDITOR

The Table Editor is a stand-alone program that has the file name TE.EXE. It is copied to your PageMaker directory when you run the Aldus Setup program. To load the Table Editor, go to Program Manager and double-click on the Table Editor icon in the Aldus program group.

SETTING UP A TABLE

Before you create a new file in the Table Editor, you need to have a good idea of the table's dimensions. The Table Setup dialog box, shown in Figure 13.2, requires you to enter the total number of rows and columns in the table, in addition to its width and length. Sometimes you'll know the exact size of your table because you need it to fit into a certain area of a PageMaker publication; other times the size may be more flexible. If you are unsure of a table's final size, make your best guess. Fortunately, you can change the settings later, or scale the table once it's in PageMaker.

The *gutter* refers to the space between rows and columns. We'll talk more about the gutter later when we get into a discussion on changing row heights.

FIGURE 13.1: *This table is a product of the Table Editor.*

Santa Clara County Residential Real Estate Sales					
Area	**# of Sales**	**Lowest Price**	**Highest Price**	**Median Price**	**Average Price**
Cupertino	9	$215,500	$512,200	$330,000	$320,022
Los Altos	10	420,000	870,000	529,900	582,215
Los Altos Hills	0	0	0	0	0
Los Gatos	11	82,000	755,500	350,000	369,918
Mountain View	12	135,500	447,750	270,000	275,520
Palo Alto	15	165,500	1,200,000	385,500	441,136
Santa Clara	17	86,500	325,500	212,200	219,938
Saratoga	7	278,800	580,000	509,900	469,907
Sunnyvale	16	170,000	440,000	253,300	276,687

This information, recorded in September 1993, is from deeds after the close of escrow. Average housing figure includes single-family homes, condos, townhouses, and mobile homes.

FIGURE 13.2:   *The Table Setup dialog box*

```
Table setup                          OK

Number of columns:    4              Cancel

Number of rows:       4

Table size:    5.91    x  3.15     inches

Gutter in inches    Column:  0.1

                    Row:     0.1

Target printer: HP LaserJet Series II on LPT1:
```

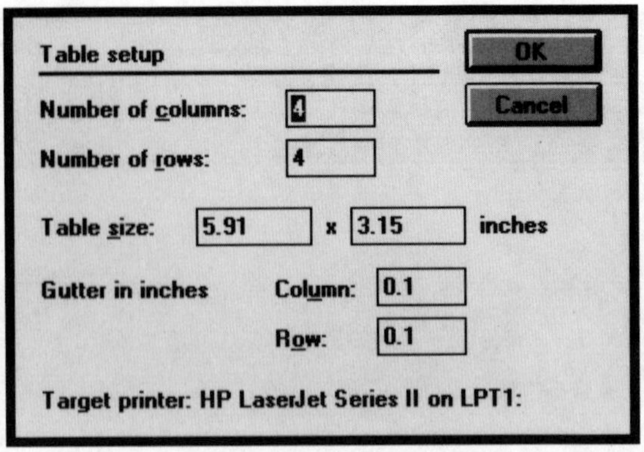

NOTE

You can see in Figure 13.2 that measurement is in inches. To choose a different measurement system, select Edit ➤ Preferences.

After you close the Table Setup dialog box, an empty spreadsheet grid appears, as shown in Figure 13.3. The rows are numbered and the columns are labeled with letters. (If you don't see these labels, turn on the Grid Labels option on the Options menu.) The intersection of a row and a column is called a *cell*. You refer to a specific cell by its column and row coordinates (for example, A1 or C3). A cell is where you enter your data.

Notice the two tools in the toolbox in the upper-right corner of the screen. Use the text tool to type or edit data and the pointer tool to select cells for formatting.

ENTERING DATA

To enter data, choose the text tool, click the I-beam in a cell, and start typing. If the text exceeds the cell width, it will automatically word wrap within the cell, and the height of the row will increase to accommodate the extra lines of text.

FIGURE 13.3: *An empty table grid*

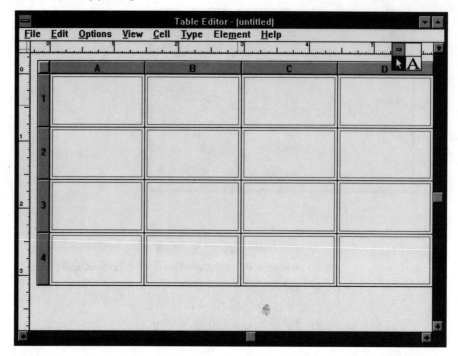

To move the text cursor to another cell, you can use any of the following methods:

➤ Press Enter to move down to the next cell.

➤ Press Tab to move to the cell to the right.

➤ Press Shift+Tab to move to the cell to the left.

➤ Click on any cell.

**If the text cursor is at the bottom of a column when
you press Enter, it moves to the top of the next column.
If the cursor is at the end of a row when you press Tab, it
moves to the beginning of the next row. By using Tab to
enter data a row at a time, or the Enter key to type data
a column at a time, you can fill in your table quickly and
efficiently.**

Whenever you want text to appear across multiple cells, use the Group
command on the Cell menu. This command creates one long cell from a
range of consecutive cells. Figure 13.1 contains two sets of grouped cells:
the title at the top and the sentences at the bottom. To group cells together, select the range with the pointer tool and choose the Group command, or press Ctrl+G.

Importing Data

If the data for a table already exists in another file, such as in a spreadsheet
or database, you don't need to retype it. The Import option on the File
menu will bring in the following types of files:

- Excel spreadsheet files
- Lotus 1-2-3 spreadsheet files (actually, any file in 1-2-3 format
  that has the extension .WKS, .WK1, or .WK3)
- Symphony spreadsheet files
- Comma- or tab-delimited text files (a file in which each piece of
  data is separated by a comma or tab)

Before importing a delimited text file, you must create a new table with
dimensions appropriate for the imported data. For example, if the text file
contains 30 lines with 6 items of data in each line, you should create a

table that has 6 columns by 30 rows. If you don't want to import the entire file, you can import the first so many rows and columns by making your table this size.

This step is unnecessary when you are importing a spreadsheet file because you indicate the range of cells you wish to import. Figure 13.4 shows the Place a 1-2-3 or Symphony Range dialog box. You can either type the range coordinates in the Range field or select the range name from the list of names.

FIGURE 13.4:   *The Place a 1-2-3 or Symphony Range dialog box*

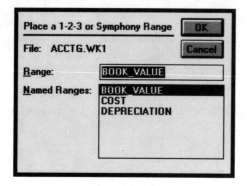

ARNiNG

When typing the range coordinates in the Range field, you must enter a valid range specifier. For Excel, the range specifier is a colon, for example A1:J25. For 1-2-3 or Symphony, you must use two periods, for example A1..J25. Although the Lotus programs themselves will accept a single period for a range specifier, the Table Editor will not. For Lotus 1-2-3 Release 3.x, a valid range specification must include the sheet letter, e.g., B:A1..B:J25. You may import from only one sheet at a time. (This refers only to .WK3 files.)

The Define Flow option on the Edit menu offers a couple of settings that apply to imported or pasted data. The Define Flow dialog box, shown in Figure 13.5, lets you specify the direction in which cells are pasted: horizontally (from left to right) or vertically (from top to bottom). The primary reason for changing the flow direction is to transpose data. Suppose you set up a table and then decide you want the table laid out differently—you want the rows to become columns and the columns to be rows. You can easily accomplish this by selecting the table, cutting it to the Clipboard, changing the flow direction to *Top to Bottom*, and then pasting. Or, if you are importing a text file that contains data you want to transpose, just choose *Top to Bottom* before you import.

FIGURE 13.5:   *Before importing or pasting data, check the settings in the Define Flow dialog box.*

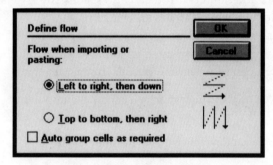

The Auto Group checkbox will automatically group the cells of a long label, such as a title. This feature saves you the time and trouble of grouping the cells yourself. It is necessary to use this option only when importing text files; long labels in spreadsheet files are automatically grouped, regardless of the status of the Auto Group checkbox.

SAVING A TABLE

As in all Windows applications, the Save and Save As options on the File menu save your file to disk. Table files are saved with the extension .TBL.

You may notice that the Table Editor's Save dialog box is different from the one in PageMaker 5.0. The Table Editor has a single list called Files/Directories where you select names, switch drives, and change directories.

(PageMaker 5.0 has separate fields for files, directories, and drives.) Drive letters and directory names are at the bottom of the list, so you may need to use the list's scroll bar to select them.

You may be wondering why Aldus wasn't consistent in its products' Save dialog boxes. The Table Editor's Save box actually matches the previous version of PageMaker—Aldus did not update the dialog boxes when it came out with Version 5.0.

FORMATTING A TABLE

The Table Editor's Type, Cell, and Element pull-down menus offer numerous ways to format your tables. You can change the font, size, leading, type style, and alignment of text and numbers. You can also specify the style and weight of the lines and add a variety of shades and patterns.

Before issuing a formatting command, you'll first want to select a cell or range of cells. To select a single cell to format, click on the cell with either the text or pointer tool. You can select groups of cells in several ways:

➤ With the pointer tool, click and drag to select any rectangular range.

➤ To select an entire row, click on the row number in the grid-label area.

➤ To select multiple rows that are adjacent to one another, click and drag on the row numbers.

➤ To select an entire column, click on the column letter in the grid-label area.

➤ To select multiple columns, click and drag across the column letters.

➤ To select the entire table, click in the upper-left corner of the grid-label area, or press Ctrl+A.

Another way to select multiple rows or columns is to click on the first one, and then hold down Shift as you click on the last one.

CHANGING THE TYPE SPECIFICATIONS

The Table Editor does not offer all the typographical controls that Page-Maker does, nor can you format part of a cell. However, you can change the font, size, leading, and type style of a single cell or a range of cells. Figure 13.6 shows the Type Specifications dialog box that the Table Editor offers.

FIGURE 13.6: *The Table Editor Type Specifications dialog box*

Type specifications		
Font: Times New Roman		OK
Size: 12 points		Cancel
Leading: Auto points ☒ **Autoleading**		
Type style: ☒ **Normal** ☐ **Italic** ☐ **Strikethrough**		
☐ **Bold** ☐ **Underline** ☐ **Reverse**		

Alignment is the only paragraph specification that is available in the Table Editor. Either use the Alignment cascading menu or the keyboard shortcut, such as Ctrl+Shift+C to center. Text is aligned with respect to the cell's right and left boundaries. The boundaries are cyan on a color monitor, or light gray on a black-and-white screen.

In addition to left, right, centered, and justified horizontal alignment, the Table Editor offers top, middle, and bottom vertical alignment. For these options, the text is aligned with respect to the cell's upper and lower boundaries. By default, text is aligned with the top of the cell boundary.

SPECIFYING BORDERS

Borders are horizontal and vertical lines in a table. By default, each cell is outlined with 1-point lines on all four sides. But a complete border is not always appropriate. When the columns are widely spaced, you don't need vertical rules; in a small table with only a few rows, horizontal lines are not really necessary. The Table Editor gives you free reign over where the borders are placed and what line style is used for the borders.

Changing the Line Style

The Line option on the Element menu lets you change the style of existing lines. Most of the line styles offered in PageMaker are available here. The weight of your borders can range from hairline to 12 points, and you can select from several styles of double- and triple-lines.

If you want the line style change to apply to the entire table, press Ctrl+A (or choose Select All on the Edit menu) before choosing a new line style.

Specifying Interior and Perimeter Lines

Through the Borders dialog box, shown in Figure 13.7, you can apply different line styles to the perimeter and the interior of the table. The perimeter refers to the top, bottom, left, and right sides of the selected range while the interior refers to the horizontal and vertical lines inside the range.

FIGURE 13.7: *The Borders dialog box*

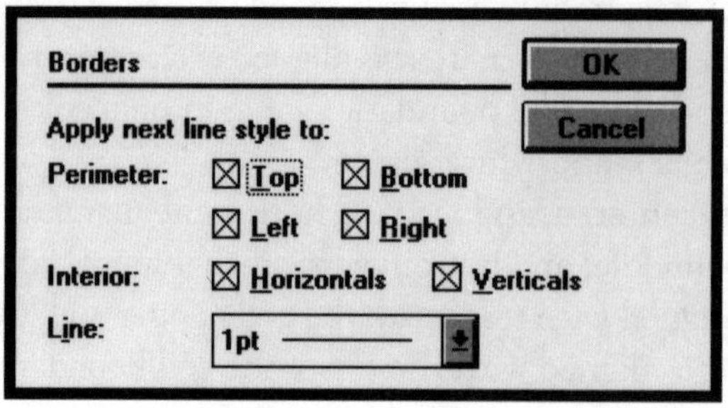

If the entire table is selected, the perimeter refers to the top, bottom, and sides of the table. To change a line style for one of these elements:

1. Select the table.

2. Pull down the Element menu and choose Borders (or press Ctrl+B). As you can see in Figure 13.7, all border areas are turned on by default.

3. Turn off all the border areas except for the ones for which you want to change the line style.

4. Display the Line drop-down list and choose the desired line style.

5. Choose OK.

Let's look at a couple of examples. Suppose you want to choose a heavier line style for the outside borders of the table. In the Borders dialog box, you would turn off Horizontals and Verticals (making sure that Top, Bottom, Left, and Right were all turned on) and choose the style (such as 2pt) from the Line list. Or, suppose you want the interior lines of the table to be a different style. In this case you would turn off all the perimeter lines (Top, Bottom, Left, and Right) so that the only checked options were Horizontals and Verticals. You would then choose the desired line style from the Line list.

To see the borders more clearly, you can turn off the Grid Lines option. (Choose Grid Lines on the Options menu, or press Ctrl+9.)

> To remove all border lines, you must first select the en-
> tire table, then make sure all the border area options
> (perimeter and interior) are turned on and then specify
> None for the line style.

ADDING SHADES

You can shade or fill a cell with a pattern by choosing the Fill option from the Element menu. Figure 13.8 shows the fill patterns that can be applied to selected cells. As in PageMaker, the percentages refer to gray shades, and the solid fill can be used in conjunction with the reverse type style to create reversed text, such as the title in Figure 13.1.

FIGURE 13.8:   *The Fill menu*

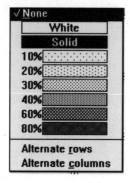

Shading Every Other Row or Column

At the bottom of the Fill menu are two options not available in Page-Maker: Alternate Rows and Alternate Columns. When these options are turned on, the shade is applied to every other row or column, as shown in Figure 13.9. Alternating shades help differentiate rows and columns in a large table, making it easier to read. To create alternating shades, follow these general steps:

1. Select the entire range in which you want to alternate shades. The shading will begin in the first row or column of the selected range.

2. From the Fill menu, choose Alternate Rows or Alternate Columns.

3. Display the Fill menu again and choose the desired shade.

FIGURE 13.9: *Alternating rows of shading*

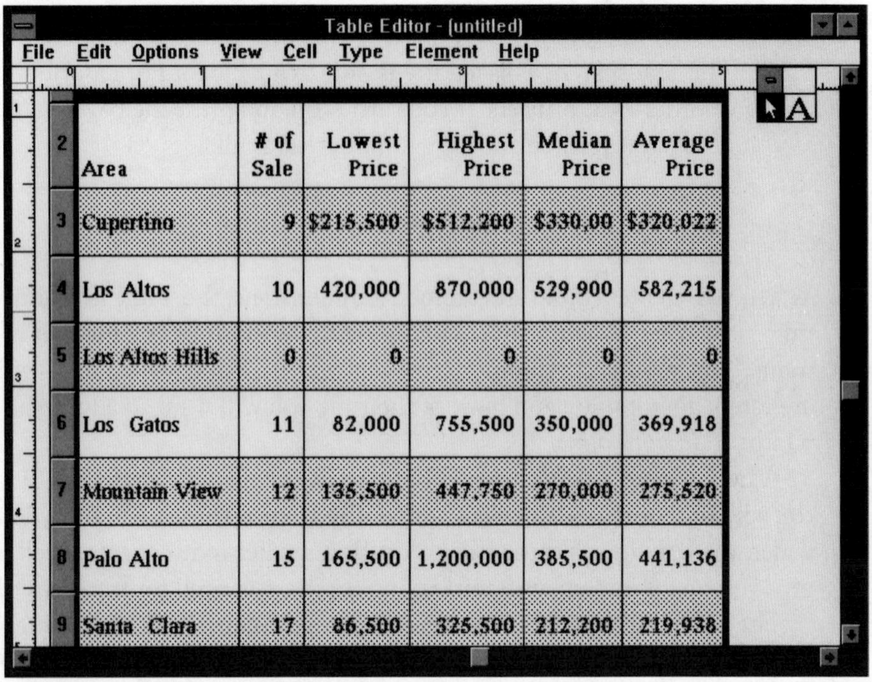

	Area	# of Sale	Lowest Price	Highest Price	Median Price	Average Price
3	Cupertino	9	$215,500	$512,200	$330,00	$320,022
4	Los Altos	10	420,000	870,000	529,900	582,215
5	Los Altos Hills	0	0	0	0	0
6	Los Gatos	11	82,000	755,500	350,000	369,918
7	Mountain View	12	135,500	447,750	270,000	275,520
8	Palo Alto	15	165,500	1,200,000	385,500	441,136
9	Santa Clara	17	86,500	325,500	212,200	219,938

Creating Transparent Fills

The Transparent Fills toggle on the Options menu controls whether your shades are transparent or opaque when the table is placed in PageMaker. If Transparent Fills is turned on, any text and graphics on the PageMaker page that are underneath the shaded portions of a placed table will show through. If Transparent Fills is turned off (as it is by default) the shaded cells will block out any underlying PageMaker elements. This feature is typically used when you have a graphic that you want to include in a table or as a backdrop to the table.

Note the following points:

→ Only percentage fills (10-80%) can be transparent—not solid fills.

➤ By default, all cells have no fill. Thus, unless you assign a fill, the cells will automatically be transparent when the table is imported into PageMaker.

➤ The Transparent Fills feature is only available for HP LaserJet or other PCL printers. If you turn it on and print the page on a PostScript printer, the fill will not print at all.

ADJUSTING COLUMN WIDTHS

When you create a table and define its dimensions, the Table Editor determines the column widths by dividing the table width by the number of columns. This produces columns with equal widths. But equal column widths are rarely appropriate, and most of the time you will want to adjust the widths to fit your data.

When a column is not wide enough to fit the data, it word wraps within the cell, or if only one word is entered, the word is truncated until you widen the column. Because this truncation applies to numbers as well as letters, you might end up with misleading results, so watch for truncated data.

The Table Editor offers two ways to change column widths: by dragging the column boundary with the mouse, or by typing a value in the Column Width dialog box. (Column Width is an option on the Cell menu.) When you use the latter technique, the width of the entire table is altered. For example, if you widen a column by 1 inch, the width of the table increases by 1 inch.

To change the column width with the mouse, place the mouse pointer in the column grid-label area, on the vertical line between columns. For example, if you want to adjust the width of column C, place the mouse pointer between columns C and D. The pointer turns into a double-headed arrow when it is in the proper location. Once you see the double-headed arrow, click and drag to the right (to widen the column) or to the left (to narrow it). You may want to refer to the horizontal ruler for precise measuring. When you change the width with the mouse, the Table Editor adjusts the column to the right so that the width of the table doesn't change. For instance, if you widen column B by $1/2$ inch, column C decreases by $1/2$ inch. However, when you change the width of the last column in a table, you do alter the table width. If you were to drag the last column's boundary, the table size would increase or decrease by the amount of the change.

Changing column widths with the mouse has a couple of advantages. First, you can eyeball the width. You can keep dragging the column borders until the widths are just right, without having to make repeated trips to the Column Width dialog box. The second advantage to using the mouse is that the table size remains constant when you adjust column widths. This is useful when the table must fit in a fixed area.

If you prefer using the mouse to resize columns but you don't want the adjacent column's width to change, you can hold down Alt as you drag the column border. Keep in mind that this technique *will* change the width of the table.

ADJUSTING ROW HEIGHT

Just as you can adjust the width of columns, you can change the height of the rows. Row height is not a simple issue, and it is determined by a number of factors:

- ➤ Largest type size and leading used in the row
- ➤ Number of lines of text typed in a cell
- ➤ Row gutters specified in the Table Setup dialog box
- ➤ Value specified in the Row Height dialog box

Increasing the Row Height

Increasing the height of a row is straightforward, so we'll attack this subject first. There are two ways to increase the row height: by dragging the row boundary with the mouse or by typing a value in the Row Height dialog box (Row Height is an option on the Cell menu). Either way, the total length of the table is increased. Unlike with column width, there is no way to automatically keep the table size constant when you change the row height.

Decreasing Row Height

To decrease a row's height, you have the same techniques available to you: dragging the row boundary with the mouse or filling in the Row Height dialog box. However, the leading and the row gutter limit how short you can make the rows. If you try to reduce the row height too much, you'll get an error message. To decrease the row height significantly, you must specify a smaller row gutter in the Table Setup dialog box. To change the row gutter, choose Table Setup from the File menu.

WORKING WITH NUMBERS

The Table Editor provides some additional formatting options that are specific to numbers. And when your table includes numbers, you can use the Sum option on the Cell menu to total them.

FORMATTING NUMBERS

You can enter numeric punctuation (dollar signs, commas, decimal places and percent signs) yourself, but the Table Editor provides an easier way: choose the format in the Number Format dialog box, shown in Figure 13.10.

Table 13.1 explains and provides an example of each of the numeric formats. Notice that formatting rounds off the numbers.

Once a number is rounded off with a formatting command, it is permanently rounded off. For instance, suppose a cell contained 123.45 and you chose a format that didn't have any decimal places; *123* would display in the cell. If you then change to a format with two decimal places, *123.00* would display—you have permanently lost the original number (123.45). Also note that the percent formats multiply the numbers by 100; this is also a permanent change.

FIGURE 13.10: *The Number Format dialog box*

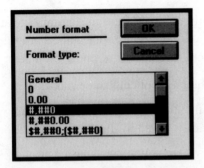

TABLE 13.1: *Number Formats*

Format	Description	Example
General	No punctuation, variable decimal places	1200.647
0	No punctuation, no decimal places	1201
0.00	No punctuation, two decimal places	1200.65
#,##0	Commas, no decimal places	1,201
#,##0.00	Commas, two decimal places	1,200.65
$#,##0	Dollar sign, commas, no decimal places	$1,201
$#,##0.00	Dollar sign, commas, two decimal places	$1,200.65
0%	Percent sign, no decimal places	34%
0.00%	Percent sign, two decimal places	34.25%

 ! **W**ARNiNG

Because formatting often increases the number of characters in a cell, make sure that the numbers aren't truncated; if they are, adjust the column widths.

CALCULATING TOTALS

The Table Editor has one built-in mathematical function: summing a range of cells. If the range contains any negative values, those numbers are subtracted from the total. Here are the general steps for summing numbers:

1. With the pointer tool, select the range of cells to be summed.

2. Choose Sum from the Cell menu. You will see a small icon that says SUM. The total is temporarily stored in this icon.

3. Place the sum icon on the cell where you want to paste the total, and then click.

The total appears, overwriting anything that may be in the cell.

MODIFYING A TABLE

Once a table is created, it is inevitable that you will want to make changes to it. You might need to insert rows or columns, move text to other cells, erase data, or remove rows or columns. This section describes how to make these types of modifications.

INSERTING ROWS AND COLUMNS

How you insert rows and columns depends on where you want them to go. To insert additional rows at the bottom of the table, change the number of rows in the Table Setup dialog box. For example, to add another row to the bottom of a six-row table, enter **7** for Number of Rows in the dialog box. Use a similar approach to add columns to the right side of the table. When you choose OK in the Table Setup dialog box, the Table Editor warns you that the table size must be increased to accommodate the new rows or columns. Choose OK to accept the increased table size.

To insert rows and columns anywhere else in the table, use the Insert command on the Cell menu. Before you issue this command, however, position the cursor in the proper position, keeping in mind that rows are inserted above the current row and columns are inserted to the left of the current column. The Insert dialog box, shown in Figure 13.11, requires two responses: whether you want to insert a row or a column, and how many you want to insert. The Row button is chosen unless you selected an entire column before displaying the dialog box.

FIGURE 13.11:   *The Insert dialog box*

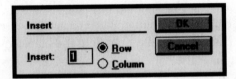

DELETING CELLS

Before deleting a row or column, make sure this is really what you want to do. All the data, in addition to the actual cells in the column or row, will be removed. If all you want to do is clear the data so that the cells are blank, don't delete the row or column. Instead, use the Clear command on the Edit menu or press the Del key. You are then presented with the Clear dialog box, where you can select what you want to erase: the text, the lines, the fill, or all of the above. When you want to clear the contents of a range of cells and not the borders, do not accept the default selection (All); choose Text instead. The cells will be emptied, and you can enter new data or leave them blank.

If you want to eliminate the data without leaving empty cells, use the Delete command on the Cell menu. Make sure that the correct button is selected (Row or Column) before you OK the dialog box.

The Table Editor does not offer an Undo feature, so be careful with the Delete and Clear commands.

MOVING CELL CONTENTS

To move the contents of a range of cells to another area in the table, you can use the cut-and-paste method you have already learned. However, moving cell contents in the Table Editor is not quite as easy as moving text in PageMaker.

Because the Table Editor does not automatically insert when it pastes, the range that you paste into should be blank. If it's not, you will overwrite the data that was previously there. Therefore, you will need to insert a row or a column that you will paste into, and then delete the blank row or column which originally contained the data. Thus, the cut-and-paste procedure is actually more of an insert-cut-paste-and-delete routine. Note that cut and paste also affects cell borders—they may have to be redone afterwards.

Another tricky part about moving cells is that the selected range you paste into must be the same size as the range that was cut. You can't get away with pasting into the first cell in the range—you must select the entire range.

Follow these general steps to move a row:

1. Insert a row in the new location.

2. Select the row to be moved and cut it to the Clipboard.

3. Select the newly inserted row, and paste the data from the Clipboard.

4. Select the blank row (the one that previously held the data you moved) and delete it.

IMPORTING A TABLE INTO PAGEMAKER

To bring a table you created in the Table Editor into PageMaker, you follow the same procedure as you do for importing a graphic: Choose the file in the Place dialog box and indicate where you want to place it. Before you can import a table, you must have previously installed the Table Editor import filter in the Aldus Setup program (see Appendix A for details).

The table will come into PageMaker in its Table Editor size. Once the table is placed, you can drag the handles to size it, but be sure to hold down the Shift key as you drag so that the table is sized proportionally. When you change the size of an imported table, the type sizes are scaled accordingly. For example, if you make a table smaller than its original size, 12-point type might become 11 points.

PRINTING A TABLE

If the Table Editor offered a Print command, you wouldn't even need Page-Maker to produce a final product. Since there is no way to print in the Table Editor, you must import it into PageMaker.

Once the table is in PageMaker, you can print it in its original size or scale it. There are three ways to scale in PageMaker: proportionally stretch the graphic's bounding box, enter a scaling percentage in the control palette, or enter a scaling percentage when printing. The first two methods were discussed in Chapter 11. The scaling print option is located in the Options sub-dialog box for HP LaserJet printers or in the Paper sub-dialog box for PostScript devices. When using the scaling option, place the table in the center of the page so that it has room to grow.

IMPORTING TABLES INTO OTHER PACKAGES

You can import tables into other software packages by exporting the file from the Table Editor to Windows Metafile Format. When you do so, the table looks just as it does in the Table Editor. It has the same borders, shades, fonts, alignment, and so on.

Another export option is Text Only format. A text file does not have any of the formatting you specified in the Table Editor, except for tabs between columns.

Why would you want to use the Text Only format if it doesn't include any formatting? Text Only offers one major advantage: the table can be edited. If you discover an error in the data, you can fix it on the spot. A table in Windows Metafile Format, on the other hand, is a graphic that cannot be edited.

MODIFYING THE TABLE

The imported table is like an imported graphic, so you cannot directly modify the data. However, as with all imported files, the imported table is linked to its external file, allowing you to easily update the internal copy when you change the original file.

One way to update the table is to load the Table Editor, open the table, make and save the changes, and then use the Update button in the Page-Maker Links dialog box. However, a less circuitous route is available: Select the table with the pointer tool, then hold down the Alt key while double-clicking on the imported table. This combination loads the Table Editor (if it's not already in memory) and opens the table file. You can then make your change to the table and resave the file. After exiting the Table Editor and switching back into PageMaker, you will need to update the link in the Links dialog box (unless you have turned on the Update Automatically option).

SUMMARY

The Table Editor offers an alternative way of producing columnar data for your PageMaker publications. Financial reports, forms, calendars, schedules, and price lists are a few types of tables that the Table Editor can produce with ease.

You will find that data entry into a spreadsheet grid is easier than typing a table with the text tool in PageMaker. More important, the Table Editor specifically addresses the formatting requirements of columnar data. The program's main drawback is that the formatted tables cannot be directly edited in PageMaker.

HANDS-ON PRACTICE: CREATING A CALENDAR

For our example, we will create the calendar shown in Figure 13.12. This calendar will be formatted before being placed in a newsletter. The table has three columns and eight rows and will be 4½ by 3 inches; the dimensions of the table are determined by the allotted space in the newsletter. (Note: Even though the text at the bottom of the calendar appears on two lines, it's considered one row because it is typed in a single paragraph.)

FIGURE 13.12: *The calendar is 3 columns by 8 rows, and 4.5 by 3 inches*

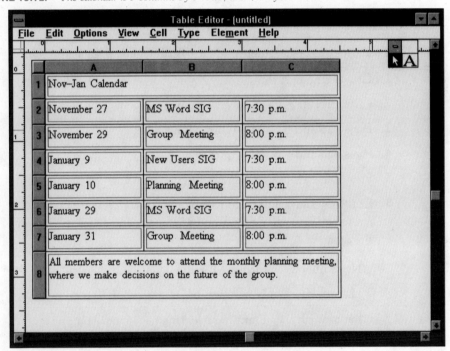

CREATING THE CALENDAR TABLE

Follow these steps to create the table grid for the calendar:

1. Load the Table Editor by double-clicking on the icon in the Aldus program group.

2. Choose New on the File menu. The Table Setup dialog box appears.

3. Specify **3** columns and **8** rows.

4. For the table size, enter **4.5** inches by **3** inches.

5. We will keep the default gutter, 0.1 inch—choose OK. A spread-sheet grid with 3 columns and 8 rows appears.

6. If you don't see the row numbers and column letters, turn on the Grid Labels option on the Options menu.

ENTERING DATA INTO THE CALENDAR

Let's use the row-by-row method first to enter some data in the table.

1. Choose the text tool.

2. Click on cell A2 and type **November 27**.

3. Press Tab and type **MS Word SIG**.

4. Press Tab and type **7:30 p.m.**

5. Press Tab to move to cell A3.

6. Continue using Tab to go row by row, or try pressing Enter after each entry to go column by column, and enter the rest of the data:

November 29	Group Meeting	8:00 p.m.
January 9	New Users SIG	7:30 p.m.
January 10	Planning Meeting	8:00 p.m.
January 29	MS Word SIG	7:30 p.m.
January 31	Group Meeting	8:00 p.m.

At this point, your table should look like Figure 13.13.

The first and last rows of the calendar have text that spans more than one column. Follow these steps to create a set of grouped cells at the top of the table and another at the bottom:

7. Switch to the pointer tool.

8. Click and drag across row 1, from cell A1 to cell C1. The range is blackened except for the first cell, which is outlined in black.

FIGURE 13.13: *The calendar data*

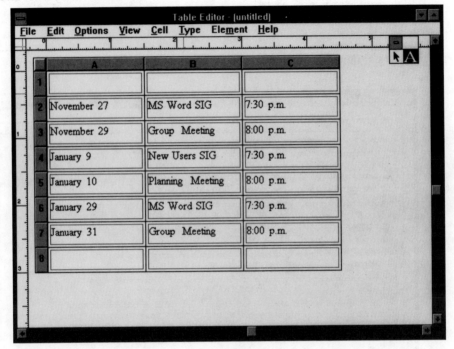

9. Choose Group from the Cell menu, or press Ctrl+G. The three cells are now one long cell.

10. Follow the same procedure to group the cells in row 8.

11. To enter the data, switch to the text tool.

12. Click in row 1 and type **Nov–Jan Calendar**. (Note: To create an en-dash between *Nov* and *Jan*, press Alt+0150 on the numeric keypad.)

The title currently fits within column A, but later on you will be enlarging the text and centering it across all three columns—that's why you grouped the cells.

13. Click in row 8 and type **All members are welcome to attend the monthly planning meeting, where we make decisions on the future of the group.**

The text automatically word wraps within the cell. Your calendar should look similar to Figure 13.14.

FIGURE 13.14: *The Group command was used on rows 1 and 8 so that data appears across multiple columns.*

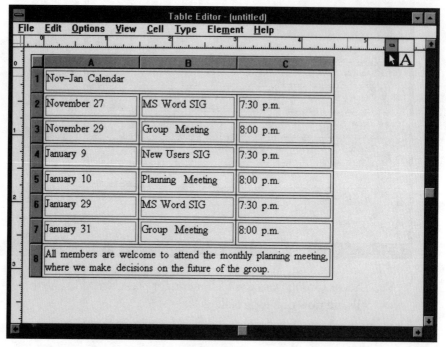

Now, save your calendar:

14. Choose Save from the File menu.

15. Navigate to the C:\PM5PUBS directory.

16. Enter **CALENDAR** in the Name field and choose OK.

FORMATTING THE CALENDAR

The calendar in Figure 13.15 has been formatted as follows:

- ➤ Most of the text is 14-point Times New Roman.

- ➤ The title is 22-point Arial bold.

- ➤ The paragraph at the bottom is 12-point Times New Roman italic.

- ➤ The title and the paragraph are centered.

Follow these steps to format the table:

1. Click on row 1 with either the text or pointer tool.

2. Press Ctrl+T to display the Table Editor's Type Specifications dialog box.

FIGURE 13.15: *The formatted calendar*

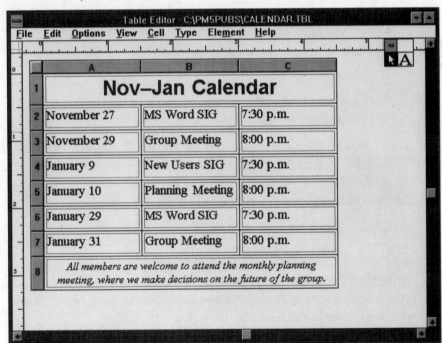

3. Format the title as 22-point Arial bold.

4. Choose OK.

5. Press Ctrl+Shift+C to center the title.

6. With the pointer tool, click and drag from cell A2 through cell C7.

7. Format the text in the table as 14-point Times New Roman.

8. Click on row 8 with either tool.

9. Format the paragraph at the bottom as 12-point Times New Roman italic.

10. Press Ctrl+Shift+C to center the paragraph.

CHANGING AND REMOVING BORDERS ON THE CALENDAR

Try a different line style for your calendar:

1. Press Ctrl+A to select the entire table.

2. Choose Line on the Element menu.

3. Select 2pt.

4. Click outside the table to remove the selection highlighting so that you can see the new line weight.

The cell outlines are now twice as thick and much too heavy for this particular table. A nicer effect might be to specify 2-point lines for the perimeter of the table and 1-point lines for the interior. Now you will specify different line styles for the interior and perimeter of a range.

5. Select the entire table.

6. Choose Borders on the Element menu, or press Ctrl+B.

Since both the perimeter and interior are already set to 2 points, you only need to change the horizontal and vertical lines in the interior. Therefore, you need to uncheck the perimeter boxes.

7. Click on Top, Bottom, Left, and Right to uncheck these options. Horizontals and Verticals should remain checked.

8. Display the Line drop-down list and choose 1pt.

9. Choose OK.

Your table now has a 2-point border on its perimeter and 1-point lines in the interior. To see the borders more clearly, turn off the Grid Lines option, as in Figure 13.16. (Choose Grid Lines on the Options menu, or press Ctrl+9.)

After changing the borders, you come to the conclusion that the calendar doesn't really need any borders because it doesn't have many rows or columns. Follow these steps to remove the calendar's borders:

10. Press Ctrl+A to select the entire table.

11. Press Ctrl+B to display the Borders dialog box.

12. Turn on *all* check-box options.

FIGURE 13.16: *The table has a 2-point border on the perimeter and a 1-point border in the interior.*

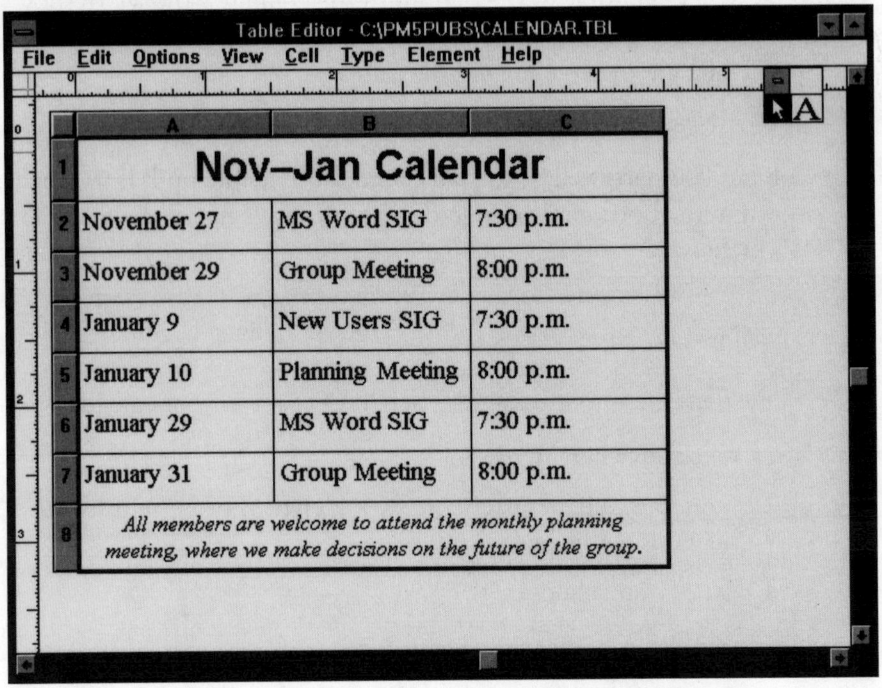

13. Display the Line drop-down list and choose None (it's at the top of the list).

14. Choose OK.

The lines are now removed from the table. The thin gray line that surrounds the table is a nonprinting border.

ADJUSTING THE CALENDAR'S COLUMN WIDTHS

While the current column widths in the calendar are adequate and don't cut off any text, the column spacing is not ideal because columns B and C are too close together. Let's use the mouse to change the width of column B in the calendar. Follow these steps:

1. Place the mouse pointer in the column grid-label area, on the vertical line between the letters B and C. The mouse pointer turns into a double-headed arrow when it is in the proper location.

2. Click-and-drag to the right until the column is the width shown in Figure 13.17, about 2 inches wide. Use the horizontal ruler to measure the column width exactly.

3. Release the mouse button.

Column C is narrowed by the same amount that column B is widened. As shown in the horizontal ruler guide, the net result is that the table remains $4\frac{1}{2}$ inches wide.

CHANGING THE TABLE'S ROW HEIGHTS

Follow these steps to increase the height of row 1 in your calendar:

1. Click anywhere in row 1.

2. From the Cell menu, choose Row Height. The current row height is .47 inches.

3. Type **.7** and choose OK.

FIGURE 13.17: *The calendar with its new column widths*

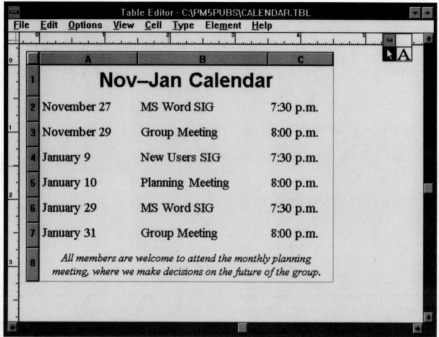

The extra space is added below the title since text is vertically aligned at the top of the cell. As the vertical ruler shows, the table is now more than 3 inches long. When you increased the row height, the table itself grew taller.

To keep the table 3 inches high, you need to decrease the height of other rows. As discussed earlier in the chapter, the row gutter limits how short you can make the rows. Let's try to reduce the row height from 0.38 to 0.30 inches:

4. Select rows 2 through 7.

5. Choose Row Height on the Cell menu.

6. Enter **.30** and choose OK. A window appears with the message

```
Can't reduce one or more row height(s) to specified
value given the amount of text in selected row(s).
Reduce row height(s) as much as text allows?
```

This means that, given the current row gutters, a row height of 0.30 is insufficient.

7. Choose OK.

Now decrease the row gutters to further decrease the row height:

8. From the File menu, choose Table Setup.

9. Change the row gutter to .05, which is half of its current size.

10. Choose OK.

The rows are now closer together and consume less space. The table height is very close to 3 inches, as shown in Figure 13.18.

FIGURE 13.18: *The calendar, after reducing the row heights and decreasing the row gutter*

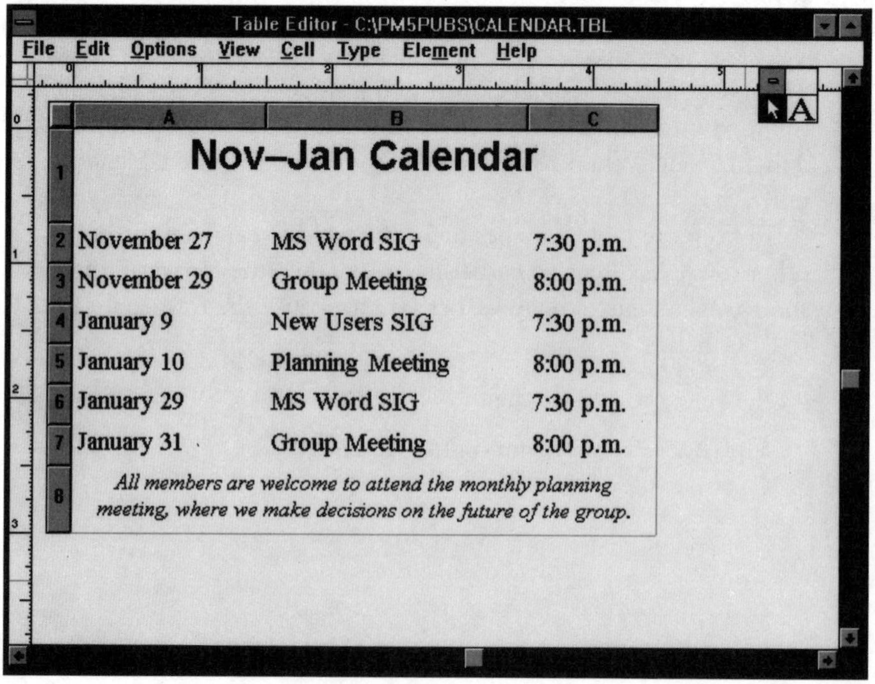

Notice how close the paragraph in row 8 is to the text in row 7. To get a little extra space between the rows without increasing the table length, align the text with the bottom of the cell.

11. Select row 8, and choose Alignment on the Type menu.

12. Select Align Bottom.

13. Save and close the CALENDAR file.

IMPORTING THE CALENDAR INTO THE NEWSLETTER

Follow these steps to import the calendar table into the newsletter publication you worked on in Chapters 10 and 11:

1. Exit from the Table Editor.

2. Load or switch into PageMaker.

3. Open the NWSLTR13.PM5 publication in your C:\PM5PUBS directory and go to page 2.

4. Press Ctrl+D to display the Place File dialog box.

5. Double-click on CALENDAR.TBL. You will see an icon with a pencil, which is the object-oriented graphic gun.

6. Place the graphic gun in the upper-left corner of the shadow box and click.

Your imported calendar should look similar to Figure 13.19. You may need to move the table a little so that it is centered in the box.

MODIFYING THE CALENDAR

In the following exercise, you will go through the steps that are required when you make a change to the calendar:

1. Select the calendar with the pointer tool.

2. Hold down the Alt key and double-click on the calendar. This combination loads the Table Editor (if it's not already in memory) and opens CALENDAR.TBL.

533

FIGURE 13.19: *The imported calendar*

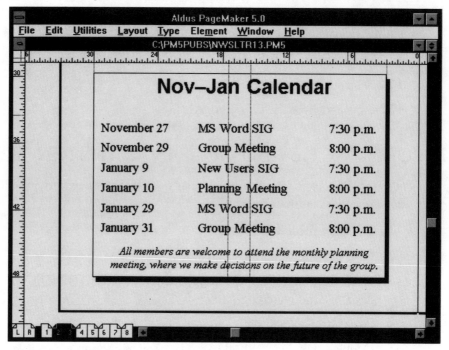

3. Change the meeting time of the New Users SIG to 8:00.

4. Press Ctrl+S to save this change in the table file.

5. Exit from the Table Editor. You are automatically brought back into PageMaker.

6. Choose Links on the File menu to display the Links dialog box.

7. Highlight CALENDAR.TBL and choose the Update button.

8. Close the Links dialog box. The internal calendar graphic now matches the external calendar file.

9. Save and close the NWSLTR13.PM5 publication.

part

f o u r

IV

This final section of the book provides you with strategies for managing your publishing projects. Read Chapter 14 to find out how to clone a publication that you will be using over and over again, such as a monthly newsletter. If you are going to be creating a long publication, such as a book, Chapter 15 shows you how to create a table of contents and an index. The last chapter explains how to approach a variety of projects, from menus and invitations to business cards and directories.

MANAGING YOUR PROJECTS

Cloning Your Publications

*f*ast tracks

To repeat elements on every page in a publication: **540**

Create the elements on the master pages. To display the master pages, click on the L and R page icons at the bottom of the window.

To include the page number in a header or footer: **542**

Press Ctrl+Shift+#.

To turn off the display of master page items on a page or page spread: **549**

Display the page or page spread. Choose Display Master Items on the Layout menu.

To create a template: **549**

Create a publication that contains the elements that remain standard (headers, footers, styles, logos, other graphics, and so forth). When finished, turn on the Template option in the Save As dialog box and give the template a name.

To modify an existing template: **551**

In the Open File dialog box, click on the template name and then turn
on the Original option.

To use templates for a multichapter project: **556**

Design a template that contains the book's margins, styles, headers, and
footers. For each chapter in the book, open this template and import the
appropriate text file(s). Apply styles, if necessary.

To use PageMaker's templates: **559**

Choose Utilities ➤ Aldus Additions ➤ Open Template. To preview the
template, click on the file name. To load the template, double-click on
the name.

OU FINALLY DID IT. YOU GENER-
ated an issue of your monthly newsletter with PageMaker. You crashed
a few times, went through four variations of margins and column widths,
and generated enough style names to publish the Bill of Rights. But you
did it—all four pages. You're happy and proud, but you can't face the
prospect of doing it all over again next month. How do you spell relief?
R-E-T-I-R-E-M-E-N-T.

For frustrated PageMaker hackers, there is hope. With a small amount of
file management, you can create your newsletter (or any other publication)
just once and use it from one issue to the next. When you are through with
this chapter, cloning a publication you already created will be as easy as
starting PageMaker, opening a file, and making a few modifications. This
strategy relies on three PageMaker features: master pages, templates, and
file linking.

SETTING UP MASTER PAGES

Consider the text and graphic elements that might appear on every page in
a publication. Here are a few that immediately come to mind: page numbers, dates, titles, revision numbers, logos, and horizontal and vertical rules.
While you can manually place them on every page, it would be better to
put these repeating elements on *master pages*. Figure 14.1 shows a left

FIGURE 14.1: *By placing column guides and other repeating elements on the master page, you will avoid having to create these items manually on every page*

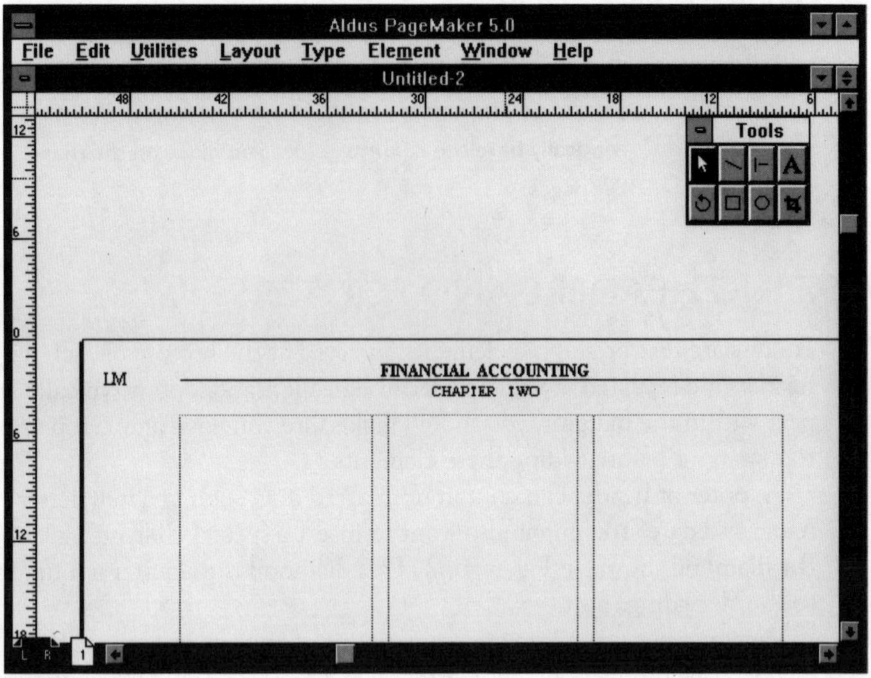

master page with three columns, and a horizontal rule between a title and chapter number, and a page number in the left margin. (LM is the page number code—more on that later.)

The master pages are accessed by clicking on the L and R page icons at the bottom of your publication window. Whatever text and graphics you place on these pages appear on all pages in the publication. In a double-sided publication, the items on the left master page are repeated on even-numbered pages; the items on the right master page are repeated on the odd-numbered pages. A single-sided publication has only a right master page.

Master pages can also contain nonprinting elements, such as column and ruler guides. Can you imagine manually specifying column guides for a 50-page publication? Not much fun. But when you set up the column guides on the master pages, you only have to issue the Column Guides command once.

Column guides on existing pages will override the guides
you set on the master pages, but any new pages will automatically have the column guides you place on the master pages.

ADDING HEADERS AND FOOTERS

Footers are text or graphic elements repeated at the bottom of each page;
headers are repeated at the top. Because headers and footers typically appear within the margins, you should make sure you have ample top or bottom margins before adding these elements.

A footer or header can contain formatted text, such as a newsletter
name and date. You might also want to insert a special character, such as
the diamond shown in Figure 14.2. This diamond is the letter u formatted
to the Wingdings font.

Page numbers are a frequent component of headers or footers. To include a page number on your master page, press Ctrl+Shift+# wherever you
want the page number to print (usually in the top or bottom margin). You
will see either LM or RM, depending on whether you pressed Ctrl+Shift+#
on the left or right master page. This code is replaced with the actual page
number when you leave the master pages.

The publication's starting page number is 1 by default. To
start with a different page number, choose File ➤ Page
Setup and enter the desired value in the Start Page #
field. You might want to change the starting page number
if the current publication is a continuation from another.
(Alternatively, you can have the page numbers updated
automatically using the book feature. See Chapter 15.)

FIGURE 14.2: *The diamond in the footer was created with the Wingdings font*

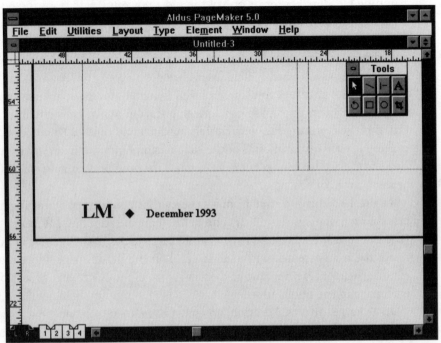

CHANGING THE PAGE NUMBERING STYLE

PageMaker offers five different styles of page numbering:

- ➤ Arabic numerals (1, 2, 3,...)

- ➤ Uppercase Roman numerals (I, II, III,...)

- ➤ Lowercase Roman numerals (i, ii, iii,...)

- ➤ Uppercase alphabetic (A, B, C,...)

- ➤ Lowercase alphabetic (a, b, c,...)

Arabic numerals are the default; to choose a different style (for example, if the publication contained a book's title page and table of contents, and you wanted to number the pages with lowercase Roman numerals), click on the Numbers button in the Page Setup dialog box.

RUNNING HEADERS/FOOTERS ADDITION

Version
5.0

Running Headers/Footers is one of the most powerful Additions included with Version 5.0. This Addition allows you to get context-sensitive headers and footers on each page. For example, dictionaries, glossaries, and thesauruses have headers that indicate the first and last word on each page, while a telephone book's header includes information about the first and last surnames on the page. As you can very well imagine, having to manually place this data on each page of a long publication would be incredibly tedious. But the Running Headers/Footers Addition automates the process, making it virtually painless. For the sake of simplicity, we will refer only to headers in this discussion but bear in mind that the text can also be placed at the bottom of the page.

Figure 14.3 shows a page from a glossary that contains two running headers, *Program Manager* (the first term defined on the page) and *Windows 3.1* (the last term). Each one is in a separate text block. The solid line underneath them was created with the rule tool on the master page. Note that running headers are not part of the master page—they are text blocks on each page of the publication.

In order to use this Addition, you must have assigned styles to your paragraphs. It looks for the first or last occurrence of a particular style and takes part of the text in that paragraph and places it in a header or footer. In Figure 14.3, each paragraph was assigned a style named Glossary. Thus, the *Program Manager* paragraph was the first instance of the Glossary style on the page and *Windows 3.1* was the last.

PageMaker lets you decide how much text in the paragraph to include in the header. We chose to include the first two words, but there are many other options available. Here is a complete list:

First word

First two words

Entire paragraph

First word, no articles

First character, no articles

First two characters

FIGURE 14.3: *Running headers*

PROGRAM MANAGER   WINDOWS 3.1

Program Manager   A launching pad for all
your software programs.

Task list   The list of open applications.

Title bar   A horizontal bar at the top of a
window that indicates the name of the application and/or the name of the document.

Windows 3.1   A graphical operating environment for the IBM PC and compatible computers.
With Windows you can   load your programs
by clicking on pictures on the screen, run more
than one software program at a time, easily
transfer data between files and other programs,
and manage your files.

First three characters

Swap first two words

Swap first two words + space

Second word of paragraph

Your text plus paragraph

The "no articles" option will eliminate words such as "the" and "A."
The "Swap first two words" option was designed for people's names. For

example, if the paragraph begins with *John Jones* you can use this option to display *Jones, John* in the header. Or if you want just the last name in the header, choose the "Second word of paragraph" option. The "Entire paragraph" option only makes sense if the key words or name is on a line by itself. "Your text plus paragraph" lets you insert any text you want in front of the paragraph; you enter your text by clicking on the Edit button.

Creating Running Headers

Before you run this Addition, use the pointer tool to select the first text block for which you want to create the running header. (The Addition will create running headers for all following pages that are part of the threaded story.) You can then display the Running Headers/Footers dialog box. Figure 14.4 is the dialog box for the First Instance header shown in Figure 14.3. You can choose whether you want the Addition to find the First Instance or Last Instance of a particular style, and then select the style. Over in the Insert section of the dialog box, select the appropriate amount of text from the paragraph to be included in the header.

FIGURE 14.4: *These are the settings used to create the First Instance running header.*

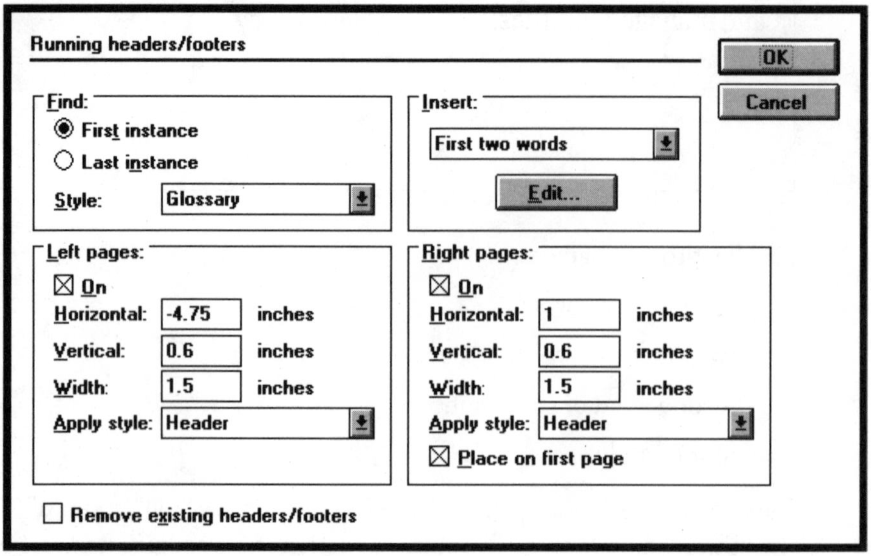

In the bottom half of the dialog box you indicate exactly where you want the header placed. In a double-sided publication, you can place the header in a different spot on left and right pages. For example, you may want the header text to always be near the outside margin—on the left on a left-hand page and on the right on a right-hand page. Be sure the On checkbox is turned on for both sides, if this is what you want.

The Horizontal and Vertical measurements are calculated from the publication's zero point. Unless you have moved it, the zero point is at the top-left edge of the right page. (The horizontal and vertical rulers will indicate where the zero point is.) For the horizontal value, use the ruler to calculate where you want the header to begin. This will be a positive value for the right-hand page and a negative value for the left-hand page. To determine the vertical value, measure from the top of the page to where you want the baseline of the text to rest. For headers, this will be within the top margin. To create a footer, just enter a vertical value that places the text in the bottom margin (such as 10.5 inches).

Carefully calculate your Horizontal and Vertical measurements. The process of generating the running headers is slow—you wouldn't want to have to go through the process more than once, especially in a long publication.

In the Width field, specify the width of the header's text block. Make sure the value you specify will accommodate the longest amount of text that will be in any header. If you are doing both a First Instance and Last Instance header, be careful not to make the Width value so large that the two text blocks overlap. If the blocks do overlap, you will get an error message and only the Last Instance text block will display (the First Instance will be deleted).

Before you produce the running headers, it's a good idea to create a style for them, and then you can use the Apply Style field to automatically assign the style to each of the header text blocks. If you create the style after you've produced the headers, you'll have to assign the style manually to each header text block. You can assign different styles to left page and right page headers as well as to First Instance and Last Instance headers. This is useful when you want one of the headers aligned at the right margin. For example, the Last Instance header in Figure 14.3 has a style that is identical to the one used for the First Instance header except that it is right aligned.

Specifying the proper Width value is the trick to getting a header aligned at the right margin. Your Width should be the distance from the Horizontal value to the right margin.

If you want both First Instance and Last Instance headers, fill in the dialog box for First Instance and then click on the Last Instance button. The settings for First Instance temporarily disappear so that you can fill in the values for Last Instance. However, they will reappear when you click on First Instance again. When you choose OK, PageMaker will generate the headers for both instances.

Removing Running Headers and Footers

The Running Headers/Footers dialog box has an option that automates the process of deleting headers and footers, saving you from going to each page and deleting them manually. To remove a running header, select the first text block from which the header was made. Run the Addition, and choose either First Instance or Last Instance, depending on which header you want to remove. Turn on the Remove Existing Headers/Footers field and choose OK.

The next time you run the Addition, the Remove Existing Headers/ Footers field will still be checked, and several of the options in the dialog box will be dimmed. Remember to turn off the Remove field if you ever want to generate headers again.

TURNING OFF MASTER ITEMS

While elements on your master pages belong on most pages, they are not appropriate for every page. For example, in a newsletter, the footer does not belong on the cover page. The Display Master Items option on the Layout menu lets you turn off the repeating elements for individual pages (in a single-sided publication) or page spreads (in a publication with double-sided facing pages). The Display Master Items option is a toggle, and it is automatically turned on (checked) for each page or page spread in the publication. All master items, except for the guides, will disappear when it is turned off.

COPYING MASTER GUIDES

When you create, move, or remove ruler guides or set different column guides or gutters for a particular page, that page uses *custom guides* that override the guides on the master pages.

If you decide that you want to replace the custom guides with the column and ruler guides on the master pages, display the page or page spread and choose the Copy Master Guides option on the Layout menu. All the custom guides will be removed, and the page or spread will use the master guides.

ADVANTAGES OF USING TEMPLATES

A *template* is a reusable publication that defines the structure and layout of a specific type of document. Templates save you from having to recreate the wheel whenever you need to use the same design for multiple projects. You can create templates for any kind of publication, such as brochures, newsletters, letterheads, memos, and manuals.

Templates can contain any of the following:

- ➤ Margin, column, and ruler guides
- ➤ Master pages
- ➤ Custom formatted pages

➤ Style sheets

➤ Logos

➤ Headings

➤ Stories

➤ Graphics (PageMaker-drawn or imported)

Let's look at a simple example. If you did the hands-on practice exercise in Chapter 4 you created a letterhead in a publication called LETHEAD2. The letterhead is essentially a template because it is designed to be used over and over again.

While LETHEAD2.PM5 is a reusable publication, it is not technically a template. To create a template, you turn on the Template option in the Save Publication As dialog box. This option is indicated in Figure 14.5. The file will then be saved with a .PT5 extension.

How does a .PT5 file differ from a .PM5 file, and what do you actually gain from saving a publication as a template? The difference between the two file types is subtle and mainly one of convenience. When you open a .PT5 file, PageMaker opens an *untitled copy* of the publication, and the original template remains on disk. Because the publication is untitled, you will be prompted for a file name when you save it.

FIGURE 14.5: *Turn on the Template option to save the file as a template*

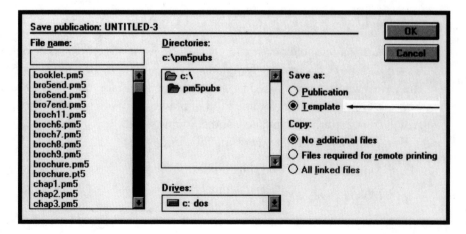

The problem with using a .PM5 file as a template is that you may forget to change the file name when you save your publication, inadvertently altering your template. This is not a concern when you open .PT5 files. Think of .PT5 files as untitled publications that give you a running start.

Because you will be using the template over and over again, it should be as perfect as possible. But mistakes are inevitable, and as you use a template, you might decide to change part of the design. Keep in mind that changes in your .PM5 publication do not affect the .PT5 template file, and changes to the template do not affect existing publications.

To make changes to an existing template, turn on the Original option in the Open File dialog box when you open the template.

ADDING STYLES TO A TEMPLATE

As you learned in Chapter 7, paragraph styles allow you to automate the formatting process, and they ensure that your publication is formatted consistently. A style sheet, therefore, is an integral part of a template. With the style sheet in place, you don't have to manually format the imported text. You can assign style names to the paragraphs after you bring in the text. An even easier way is to tag the paragraphs in your word processor, so that the text will be formatted automatically when you import the file.

OPENING A TEMPLATE

To open a template you have created, use the same command you use to open your publications: File ➤ Open. In the Open Publication dialog box, PageMaker lists both .PM5 files and .PT5 files. Click once on the template name and you'll see the Copy button turned on. When you click on OK, an untitled copy of the template will be opened.

CREATING A NEWSLETTER TEMPLATE

Templates are particularly handy for newsletters. When deciding which elements belong in a template, think of the items that are standard from one issue to the next.

For example, the nameplate on the cover page of a newsletter is a constant and should be a part of the template. While the date and volume will change with each issue, you should keep this line in the template as a placeholder. When you use the template, you replace the placeholder with the new text.

Any standard headings and graphic elements within a newsletter should also remain in the template. For example, the logo shown in Figure 14.6 always appears on page 4 of this newsletter, so it should be part of the template.

Even graphics and stories that will change in each publication are good candidates for a template, because they act as placeholders. For example, we edit and lay out a monthly newsletter for our tennis club. The front page always has a file called FRONT.DOC, page 2 holds AROUND.DOC, page 3 has TENNIS.DOC, and page 4 has SPORTS.DOC. The contents of each file change from month to month, but the file name remains constant. Your newsletter may not be as straightforward as ours, but most newsletters will have at least some consistency in file placement.

FIGURE 14.6: *The logo should be included in the template because it always appears at the top of page 4.*

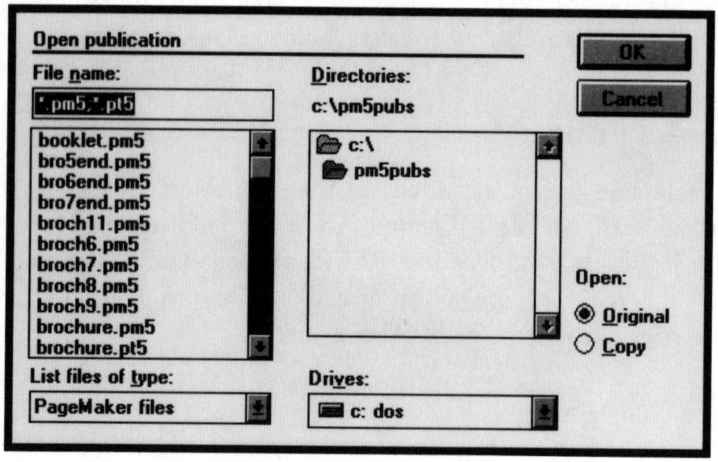

USING A NEWSLETTER TEMPLATE

To use a newsletter template on a regular basis, follow this basic procedure:

1. Type the new stories and locate the clip art graphic files you want to use.

2. Open the template.

3. Replace the placeholders with the new stories and graphics.

4. Import any new text or graphic files.

Now let's look at these steps in more detail. After you've typed the stories for the next newsletter, open the template and replace each of the stories or graphics with its updated file. One way to do this is to import the file again with the Place command. You don't need to delete the original file. Just click on the story or graphic before displaying the Place File dialog box, choose the file name, and turn on the Replacing Entire Story (or Graphic) option. For text files, turn on the Read Tags option as well.

Alternatively, you can use the file linking feature, as described in the next section.

In a perfect world, the imported stories are the same length as the placeholders. Realistically, you will need to do some *copyfitting*, which is the process of adjusting the length of your stories so they fit in their allotted space. When a story is too long, read through the text and look for sentences or paragraphs that can be cut. (Your writers may scream, but cutting is an inevitable part of the publishing process.) When a story is too short, use pull-quotes, graphics, or *fillers* (short paragraphs to fill space). But don't feel that you must fill every blank spot on the page. A little white space gives your publication a feeling of openness that readers appreciate, even if only subconsciously.

The next step is an easy one to overlook: Replace the remaining placeholders with the current text. For example, you may need to type new headlines and pull-quotes for a feature story, as well as change the date in your footer on the master pages and under the nameplate on the cover page. Select the old text with the text tool and type right over it. The new text will automatically be formatted like the original.

The final step is to import text and graphics specific to the current newsletter.

LINKING FILES TO YOUR TEMPLATE

True automation of your template occurs when your stories and graphics are linked to their external files. As you know from Chapter 8, files are automatically linked when you import them with the Place command. When files are linked to their external files, you do not need to use the Place command to replace the existing files; you just tell PageMaker to update the files in the publication. Actually, the updating can even occur automatically, as explained in the next section.

If you imported your publication's original stories from text files, the files are automatically linked to the publication. But if you typed the text in the Story Editor, you must export each of the files and reimport them to establish a link. If necessary, follow these steps to create an external file for each story:

1. Place the text cursor in the story.

2. Use the Export command, and turn on the Export Tags option. Choose any of the word processor export filters.

3. Import the newly created external file using the Place command. Be sure to turn on the Read Tags and Replacing Entire Story options.

ULTIMATE AUTOMATION

Here is the ultimate in automation: Open a copy of the template, and all the new stories and graphics are automatically in place. There are two keys to making this system work:

➤ The new files must have the same names as the ones that are linked to the template. For example, if the template is linked to AEROBICS.DOC, CLUBNEWS.DOC, and HOURS.DOC, your new files should have these same names. They must also be stored in the same subdirectory as the original files.

→ Turn on the Update Automatically link option for each of the files. That way, when you open the template, each of the files is automatically imported. To turn on this option, press Ctrl+Shift+D to display the Links dialog box, click on the file name, and choose the Options button. Figure 14.7 shows a list of files in the Links dialog box.

File management is an important part of cloning a publication. Because each issue's files should have the same names as those in the previous issue, you need to decide what to do with the original files. If you don't want to keep the outdated files, you can simply overwrite the existing files for each issue. On the other hand, if you want to preserve the data, you should develop a system for archiving the files. Either copy the files to another subdirectory or floppy disk, or use an archiving software program, such as LHARC or PKZIP.

UPDATING THE FILES MANUALLY

If you want more control over linked files, you can turn on the Alert Before Updating option in the Link Options dialog box. When this option is on, PageMaker will ask if you want to import each modified file when you open the template or publication. For even more control, don't use the automatic updating feature at all. Instead, choose the Update command button in the Links dialog box whenever you want to update a linked file.

FIGURE 14.7: *Turn on the Update Automatically option for each of the files linked to the template.*

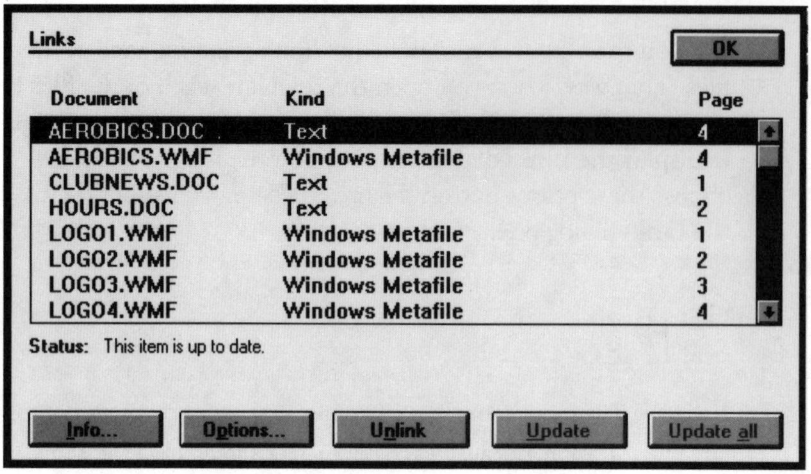

LINKING TO A DIFFERENT FILE

What if the new files have different names from the ones linked to the publication? One solution is to rename them in DOS or in Windows' File Manager. Alternatively, you can tell PageMaker to link to a different file, as follows:

1. Display the Links dialog box and click on the original file name.

2. Choose the Link Info command button.

3. If necessary, navigate the Drives and Directories lists until you find the new file name.

4. Click on the new name, choose Link, and choose OK to update the file.

USING TEMPLATES FOR LARGE PROJECTS

Large projects, such as multichapter books and manuals, can really benefit from templates. By using a standard template, you can be assured that each chapter is formatted consistently, and at the same time save yourself a lot of repetitive work. After you have created a template, you can just open it up for each chapter and import the appropriate text file.

DESIGNING A TEMPLATE FOR A BOOK

Your template should contain the appropriate margins, styles, headers, and footers for your book. If the book is double-sided and will be bound, make sure your inside margins are larger than the outside margins. (If you forget to do this, your margins will look uneven, or worse yet, the beginning or endings of lines will be cut off when the book is bound. Check with your printing house or bindery for exact dimensions.) You may want to import sample text so that you have something to format when designing your styles. After creating the styles, you can then delete the text.

On the master pages, place any repeating elements such as rules, graphics, headers, and footers. You'll probably want to create placeholders for the chapter number and title. Because most large publications are double-sided, you'll need different headers and footers for odd- and even-numbered pages. Always place the page number on the outside of the header or footer so that your readers can easily find it while thumbing through the book. In other words, the page number should go on the left side of an even-numbered page and on the right side of an odd-numbered page. Figures 14.8 and 14.9 respectively show a set of master pages in which the left footer has a left-aligned page number and chapter number and the right footer has the chapter title and page number aligned on the right.

USING THE TEMPLATE TO CREATE EACH CHAPTER

The template can now be used to produce all chapters in a book. Follow this general procedure to create a book:

1. In your word processor, create a separate file for each chapter. If you like, insert paragraph tags, using the same names that are in the template's style sheet. For example, tag each of your subheadings with <Subhead>.

2. In PageMaker, open the template.

FIGURE 14.8: *On the left master page, the page number and chapter number are left-aligned.*

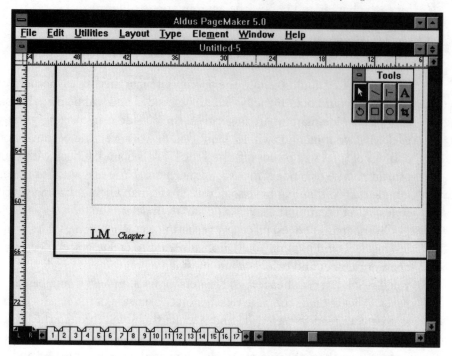

3. Replace any placeholders with the actual text. For example, if you have placeholders for the chapter number and title in the headers, replace these with the actual chapter number and title.

4. Import text files and any graphics.

5. Format the text with the style sheet. This step is not necessary if you tagged the text in your word processor.

6. Save the publication with a unique name.

7. Repeat steps 2 through 6 for each chapter in the book.

Chapter 15 explains how to print the chapters of a book with continuous page numbering, create a table of contents, and produce an index.

FIGURE 14.9: *On the right master page, the chapter title and page number are right-aligned.*

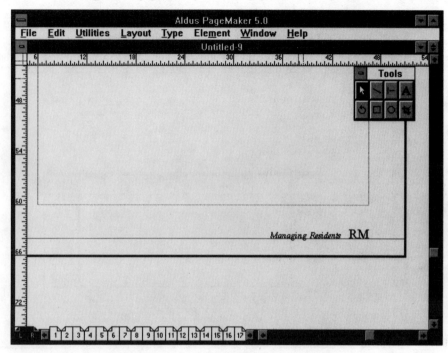

USING PAGEMAKER'S TEMPLATES

PageMaker comes with a set of ready-made templates for a variety of publications, including brochures, calendars, envelopes, invoices, labels, manuals, newsletters, and purchase orders. Like the templates you create, the PageMaker templates contain column grids, style sheets, and placeholders. Figure 14.10 shows a template for an invoice.

Version
5.0

The templates that come with PageMaker are stored in a special type of file format called a *script*, and in order to open up these templates you must run an Addition called Open Template. There are two reasons why Aldus didn't just give you the .PT5 files. First, template files consume much more disk space than script files. For example, the Invoice script is 8K while its template file is 12K. Second, the Open Template Addition lets you view the template before you load it—just by clicking on the template name. Figure 14.11 shows this latter feature in action.

FIGURE 14.10: *PageMaker's invoice template*

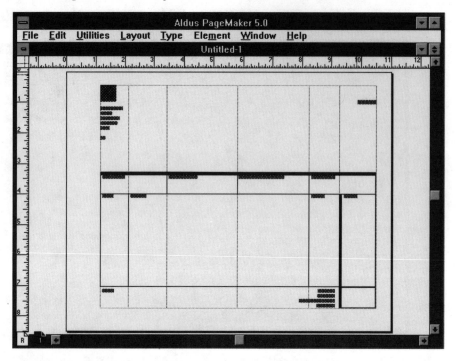

FIGURE 14.11: *To see what a template looks like before you load it, just click on its name.*

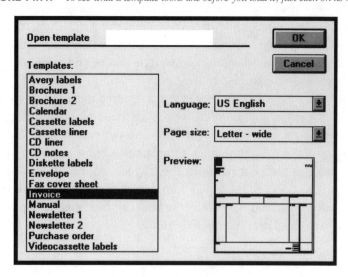

14

Once you open one of these scripts, you can save it as a template in the usual way. PageMaker's templates, like the ones you create, contain text and graphic placeholders that you can replace. However, none of the templates are linked to external files, so the Place command is the only way you can import text and graphics.

You may want to use these templates to give you ideas on how to design a certain type of publication. For example, if you are going to be creating a newsletter, open the newsletter templates to see the page layout, styles, and graphic elements that the folks at Aldus used to design their newsletters.

SUMMARY

In this chapter, you saw several ways that templates can eliminate repetitive work for similar publications. Templates are ideal for newsletters and other publications that you publish on a regular basis. They work equally well for large projects, such as books, that are divided into multiple files. By creating templates, you can be confident that each clone has the same page layout, style sheet, and graphic elements as the original. Well-designed templates automate the publishing process and save you a tremendous amount of time.

HANDS-ON PRACTICE: CREATING A BOOK TEMPLATE

In the following steps, you will begin to create a handbook on managing rental properties. Each chapter in the book is contained in its own publication. Because each chapter will have the same layout and style sheet, you will design a template for the book, and then create each chapter by opening the template. The final handbook will have 12 chapters, but you will create only three chapters here.

Create a new file and specify the following page setup:

Size: 45 by 54 picas ($7\frac{1}{2}$ by 9 inches)

Double-sided, no facing pages

Inside margin: 6p

Outside margin: 4p6

Top margin: 6p

Bottom margin: 6p

INSERTING PAGE NUMBERS

For our example, we're going to place a page number within the bottom margin of the left and right pages. The placement of the left-hand page number is shown in Figure 14.12.

1. Click on the left master page icon at the bottom of the document window.

FIGURE 14.12:   *On the left master page, the page number is within the left and bottom margins.*

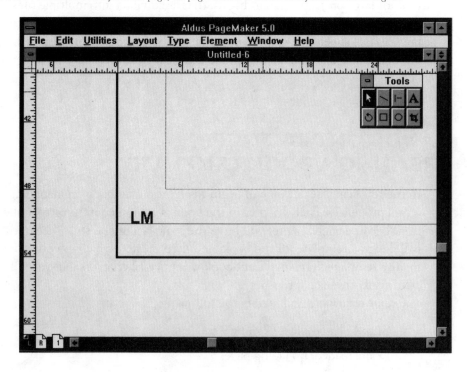

2. Position the screen so that you see the bottom of the master page, in Actual Size view.

3. Pull down a ruler guide at the 51-pica ($8\frac{1}{2}$-inch) mark.

4. With the text tool, click on the ruler guide. Don't worry about exact placement.

5. Specify the type as 18-point Arial bold.

6. Press Ctrl+Shift+# to insert a page number code. LM appears on the left master page.

7. With the pointer tool, align the baseline of the page number code on the ruler guide, and move the code to the position shown in Figure 14.12.

8. Remove the ruler guide.

9. Click on the right master page icon.

10. Repeat steps 2 through 8 to insert a page number on the right side of the page. RM appears as the right page number code.

CREATING THE HEADERS

The left- and right-hand pages will have different headers. The left-hand header will contain a placeholder for the name of the book while the right-hand header will have the chapter number. Refer to Figures 14.13 and 14.14 as you create these headers.

Follow these steps to create a header for the left-hand page:

1. Click on the left master page icon.

2. Position the screen so that you see the top of the left master page, in Actual Size view.

3. Pull down a ruler guide at the 3-pica ($\frac{1}{2}$-inch) mark.

4. With the text tool, click on the ruler guide, at the left margin.

5. Specify the type as 14-point Arial bold with small caps.

6. Type **Managing Rental Properties** and press Ctrl+Shift+C to center the line.

FIGURE 14.13:   *The header for the left master page*

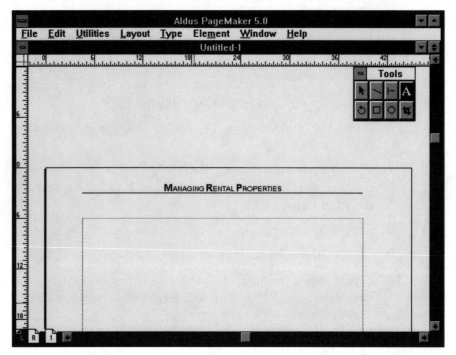

7. With the pointer tool, align the baseline of the text just above the ruler guide.

8. Draw a 1-point line on top of the ruler guide (refer to Figure 14.13 for the length of this line). Note that you won't be able to see this line until you move the ruler guide.

9. Remove the ruler guide.

10. Click on the right master page icon.

11. Repeat steps 3 through 9 for the header on the right master page, referring to Figure 14.14. The header text is **Chapter #**.

12. Click on the page 1 icon.

On page 1, you will now see the right-hand header (Chapter #) and the page number at the bottom.

FIGURE 14.14: *The header for the right master page*

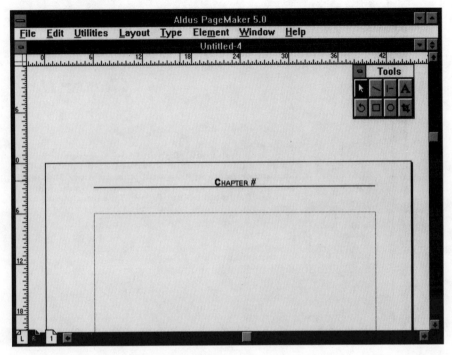

CREATING THE BOOK STYLES

The book template will have three styles: Chapter Head, Subhead, and Body Text. Figure 14.15 shows examples of these styles.

Display the style palette, and notice that the style sheet contains the six default style names. These styles should be removed before you create the new styles.

1. Pull down the Type menu and choose Define Styles.

2. Remove each of the styles and close the dialog box.

FIGURE 14.15: *These three styles are used in the book template.*

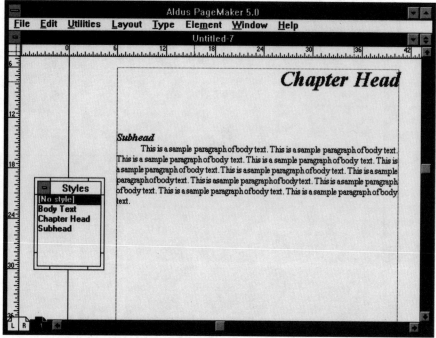

Creating the Chapter Head Style

Follow these steps to create the style that will format the chapter title and number:

1. Pull down the Type menu and choose Define Styles.

2. Click on the New button and type **Chapter Head** for the style name.

3. Click on the Type button and specify the following type specifications:

   Font: Times New Roman
   Size: 30 points
   Leading: 30 points
   Type Styles: Bold, Italic

4. Choose OK and click on the Para button. Specify the following paragraph formats:

> After: 3p9
> Alignment: Right

5. Close the dialog boxes.

Creating the Subhead Style

Now create the style for subheadings:

1. Display the Define Styles dialog box.

2. Click on the New button and type **Subhead** for the style name.

3. Click on the Type button and specify the following type specifications:

> Font: Times New Roman
> Size: 15 points
> Leading: 15 points
> Type Styles: Bold, Italic

4. Choose OK and click on the Para button. Specify the following paragraph formats:

> Before: 1p3
> Alignment: Left
> Keep with Next

5. Close the dialog boxes.

Creating the Body Text Style

Finally, create the style for body text:

1. Display the Define Styles dialog box.

2. Click on the New button and type **Body Text** for the style name.

3. Click on the Type button and specify the following type specifications:

> Font: Times New Roman
> Size: 12 points
> Leading: 15 points
> Type Style: Normal

4. Choose OK and click on the Para button. Specify the following paragraph formats:

> First indent: 3p
> Alignment: Justify
> Widow Control (1 line)
> Orphan Control (1 line)

5. Close the dialog boxes.

The style palette now lists three styles: Body Text, Chapter Head, and Subhead.

SAVING THE BOOK TEMPLATE

The book template now contains all the elements that are consistent from one chapter to the next: margins, headers, footers, and styles. You are ready to save the publication as a template:

1. Display the Save As dialog box.

2. Type **RENTAL** for the name.

3. Change to the C:\PM5PUBS directory.

4. Turn on the Template option.

5. Choose OK. The template is saved with the name RENTAL.PT5.

6. Close the file.

PRODUCING THE CHAPTERS

Creating the template was the hard part; producing the chapters is now a simple matter of importing the appropriate text files. Since the text files have been tagged with the same style names that were used in the template, the text will automatically be formatted. Follow these steps to create the first chapter:

1. Choose File ➤ Open. Double-click on RENTAL.PT5. The title bar of the window displays Untitled until you save the file.

2. Display the Place Document dialog box and click once on CHAP1.DOC in the C:\PM5PUBS directory—do not close the dialog box yet.

3. Turn off the Retain Format option and turn on the Read Tags option and choose OK. (If you don't turn on Read Tags, the text will not be formatted with your paragraph styles—instead, you will see the style names enclosed in angle brackets.)

4. If necessary, turn on the Autoflow option on the Layout menu.

5. Place the text gun at the top-left corner of page 1 (inside the margin guides) and click. PageMaker will create four additional pages for the imported text.

6. Switch to Actual Size view and scroll through the chapter. Notice how all the text is formatted with the appropriate styles. (No, the body text is not full of typos—this text is actually dummy text, called *greeked text*.)

Don't forget that the template has a placeholder in the right-hand header for the chapter number. Our final step in creating this chapter is to update this number.

7. Display the right master page.

8. Click and drag across the # sign in the header, and type **One**. Your header should look similar to Figure 14.16.

9. Display page 1 and notice that the header is updated.

FIGURE 14.16: *The chapter number placeholder has been replaced with the actual number.*

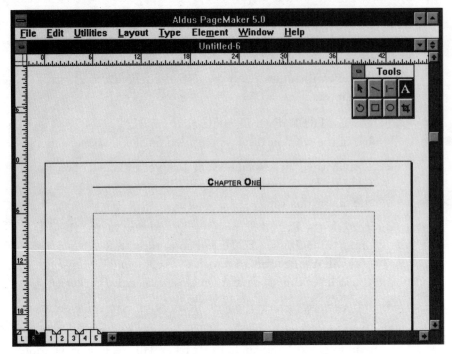

10. Save the file with the name **RENTAL01**.

11. Close the file.

You can now repeat the above steps for chapters two and three. The text files are named CHAP2.DOC and CHAP3.DOC. We are only creating three sample chapters here, but additional chapters could be cloned in the same fashion.

C H a P T e R 15

Working with Monster Projects

*f*ast tracks

To define a book list: 578

Go to the first publication in the project and choose File ➤ Book. One by one, click on the file names to be included in the book and choose the Insert button. The files should be listed in the same order they will appear in the book. To automatically renumber the pages across all publications, choose one of the Auto Renumbering options (Next Page, Next Odd Page, or Next Even Page). Close the dialog box.

To print all publications in a book: 580

Open the first publication in the project—the one that contains the book list. Display the Print dialog box and turn on the Print All Publications in Book option. Change other options as necessary and choose OK.

To mark a table of contents entry: 582

With the text tool, click on the entry, and turn on the Include in Table of Contents option in the Paragraph Specifications dialog box. If this option is set as part of your head and subhead style formats, all your headings will be marked automatically.

To generate a table of contents: 583

If the TOC spans multiple documents, you must be in the publication that contains the book list. Choose Utilities ➤ Create TOC. Change any options and choose OK. Place the text gun where you want the TOC to go and click.

To format a table of contents: 585

Edit the TOC styles.

To mark an index entry: 590

Select the word or phrase and press Ctrl+;. Choose the appropriate page range (for example, Current Page or To Next Style Change), change any other index options, and close the dialog box.

To create a cross-reference: 595

Press Ctrl+; (it doesn't matter where the cursor is) and make sure the Cross-Reference option is turned on. Type in a topic name and choose the appropriate Denoted By option (such as *See [also]* or *See herein*). Click on the X-Ref button and choose the topic to which you want to cross-reference. Close the dialog boxes.

To generate an index: 597

If the index spans multiple documents, you must be in the publication that contains the book list. Choose Utilities ➤ Create Index. Change any options and choose OK. Place the text gun where you want the index to go and click.

OST OF THE PUBLISHING PROJECTS
we have dealt with so far have been small projects: letterheads, brochures, and newsletters. But what if you have to produce a 70-page document, or a monster-sized 700-page publication? The rules change as the page count increases. Even if PageMaker could handle 700 pages in one publication, you couldn't. Just the amount of time you spend scrolling would be overwhelming. Large documents need to be divided into several smaller publications, for the sake of PageMaker's processing speed, not to mention your own sanity.

THE APPROACH TO LARGE PROJECTS

When approaching longer jobs, let the content determine the form. If you are producing a book about birds, with discussions of six species, each species could be discussed in its own chapter and stored in its own publication. If you are embarking on a sociological examination of the impact of being left-handed, perhaps each case study would be a separate publication.

PageMaker provides tools for grouping and controlling several publications as a single project. As you might already have guessed, a template is an important part of creating a large project. A template eliminates repetitious work and ensures consistent formatting across all publications. The master template for the project will specify the appropriate page setup, footers, styles, and placeholders. Then, to create each publication, open the template, place text and graphic files, and replace the placeholders.

The collection of publications related to a single project is called a *book*. With PageMaker's book feature, you can create a table of contents and an index that spans all the publications in the book. You can also print the entire book with a single Print command.

Monster projects are made up of many files. Each chapter is in its own publication file, and each publication is made up of at least one text file and any number of graphic files. Consequently, file management is extremely important. We recommend creating a subdirectory for the large project and storing all related files in it.

CREATING A BOOK

After creating the individual chapters of your monster project, you need to tell PageMaker that these chapters are part of a larger, single document: a *book*. You define a book by creating a list of the related publications in the Book dialog box.

After you have created a book, you can issue commands that will be carried out across all the publications in the book: page numbering, printing, table of contents generation, and index generation.

The book list is created in the first publication in the project. Although this could be in the book's first chapter, a better place for it is in a separate introductory publication. This publication might contain a title page, acknowledgments, a preface, and a table of contents. The introductory material, or *front matter*, belongs in a separate publication so that these pages do not affect the pagination of the first chapter.

Unfortunately, PageMaker does not let you have more than one page numbering sequence in a publication. This is surprising since even some word processors, such as Word for Windows, have this capability. Therefore, when you have two or more page numbering sequences, you must place each set of pages in its own separate publication. This is true even when you have a single page at the beginning of the document (such as a title page) that you don't want numbered and you want the second page to begin numbering with one—you would have to place the title page in its own publication.

DEFINING A BOOK LIST

To define the publications that are part of the book, pull down the File menu and choose Book. The Book Publication List dialog box is shown in Figure 15.1.

FIGURE 15.1: *The Book Publication List dialog box*

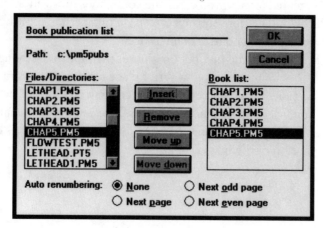

The book list is on the right, and the current publication is automatically at the top of the list. If this publication is the one containing the front matter, you will not want this file in the book list because it will affect the pagination of the book (more on this later). Click on the Remove button if you want to eliminate the current publication from the book list.

To add a publication to the list, select the name from the Files list and click on the Insert command button. The files in your book list should be listed in the same order they will appear in the book. If they aren't, the table of contents will be out of order, and the page numbering may be off.

Because the order of the files on the book list is so important, Page-Maker offers two command buttons for rearranging the order of the files: Move Up and Move Down. For instance, to move a file higher up on the list, click on the name and click on the Move Up button until the file is in its correct position.

NUMBERING PAGES ACROSS PUBLICATIONS

If you were to print the publications in your book individually, the pages in each of these documents would be numbered beginning with 1. To number pages consecutively across publications, you could go into each of the documents and change the starting page number in the Page Setup dialog box. This requires that you know the ending page number of the preceding publication. For example, if chapter one is numbered 1 through 25, you would enter 26 as the starting page number in chapter two. You would repeat this process down the line for each publication in the book.

If you have grouped your publications into a book, however, you can have PageMaker number the pages when the book is printed. The Auto Renumbering options in the Book Publication List dialog box (see Figure 15.1) are the key to consecutive page numbering across publications.

By default, PageMaker does not renumber the pages when it prints the book (the None option). Instead, it uses the page numbers in each publication. To turn on auto-renumbering, choose one of the three remaining options: Next Page, Next Odd Page, or Next Even Page.

The Next Odd Page option is probably the most common. It makes sure each publication begins on an odd-page number—the right-hand page. If the publication would naturally start on an even page, a blank page is inserted. The Next Even Page option ensures that each publication begins on an even-numbered (left-hand) page. The Next Page option allows the publication to begin naturally, with no regard to whether the page is odd or even.

In the previous section, we recommended that you remove the front-matter publication from the book list. Although it would be nice to have the front matter automatically print before the book chapters, you can't have your cake and eat it, too. If you turn on one of the Auto Renumbering options, every page in every publication is renumbered. Thus, if your front matter document had three pages, the first page in chapter one would be numbered 4. To exclude the front matter from the page count, do not include that publication in the book list.

Version
5.0

After you choose an Auto Renumbering option, PageMaker will ask if you want to update the page numbers of all publications in the book now. If you choose Yes, the page numbers are updated in each of the book's publications (it doesn't matter whether the publications are open or not). If you choose No, the publications aren't renumbered. However, the pages will be properly numbered when you print the book.

PRINTING A BOOK

To automatically print all the publications in a book, you must open the file that contains the book list, bring up the Print dialog box, and turn on the Print All Publications in Book option. Then PageMaker would print one chapter after the other, with consecutive page numbering. If you turned on the Next Odd Page or Next Even Page option, a blank page may be inserted between chapters to ensure that the next chapter begins on an odd or even page number; you do not need to turn on the Print Blank Pages option for this to work.

! ARNiNG

Before you tell PageMaker to print all the publications in a book, make sure you have either selected an Auto Re-numbering option in the Book dialog box or manually set the starting page number in each publication. If the page numbers aren't correct, you will have to reprint the entire publication.

After the book is printed, the page icons in each of the publications reflect the new page numbering. Figure 15.2 shows that CHAP2.PM5 contains pages numbered 26 through 42.

Version
5.0

If one or more of the publications in your book has a unique paper size, you may want to turn on the option Use Paper Settings of Each Publication.

FIGURE 15.2: *The CHAP2 publication contains pages numbered 26 through 42.*

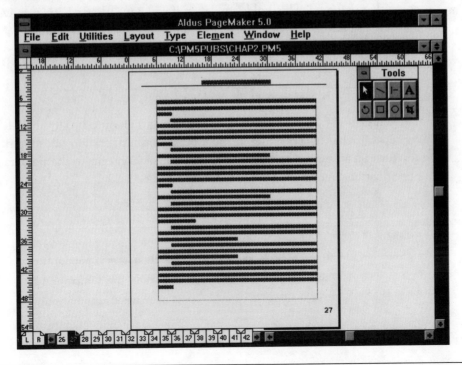

With this option turned on, PageMaker will obey the paper settings (size and source) that are specified in each publication's printer setup dialog box. Otherwise, the paper settings of the current publication are used.

CREATING A TABLE OF CONTENTS

Creating a table of contents requires these basic steps:

1. Tag each title to be included in the table of contents.

2. For a book that spans multiple publications, you will need to create a book list as previously described.

3. Make sure the pages in each publication are accurately numbered.

4. Open the publication that contains your book list.

5. Tell PageMaker to generate the table of contents.

If you turned on auto-renumbering, step 3 is taken care of—the pages are correctly numbered. This holds true even if you have inserted and removed pages. If you haven't turned on auto-renumbering, you must manually change the starting page number in each publication.

MARKING A TABLE OF CONTENTS ENTRY

The template-designing stage is the time to begin planning your table of contents. Including a heading in the table of contents couldn't be easier: You turn on an option called Include in Table of Contents in the Paragraph Specifications dialog box (indicated in Figure 15.3).

If the Include in Table of Contents option is part of the style format and the style is part of the template, all the headings in your book will be marked automatically.

FIGURE 15.3: *Turn on the Include in Table of Contents option for each heading you want in your table of contents.*

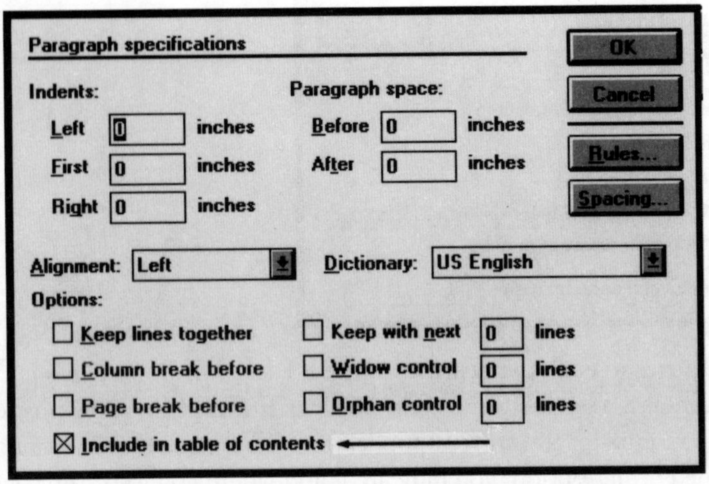

If you forgot to plan ahead for your table of contents and you created your styles without turning on the TOC option, you'll need to edit the styles in each publication. A way to speed up this process is to modify the styles in one file and then copy the styles to each of the other publications. (The Hands-On Practice exercise at the end of this chapter has an example of this procedure.)

GENERATING A TABLE OF CONTENTS

Before you generate the table of contents, make sure you are in the file that contains the book list. When you choose the Create TOC command from the Utilities menu, PageMaker searches for paragraphs that are tagged for inclusion in the table of contents and makes a note of what page each one is on. You are then presented with a loaded text gun that contains the newly generated table of contents. Click on a page, and you have your table of contents.

The Create Table of Contents dialog box is shown in Figure 15.4. Next to Title is the heading that appears above the table of contents. *Contents* is the default title, but you can change it to *Table of Contents* or any other single line of text. The Include Book Publications option looks for table of

FIGURE 15.4:   *The Create Table of Contents dialog box*

Create table of contents

Title: Contents

OK

Cancel

☐ Replace existing table of contents

☐ Include book publications

Format: ○ No page number

○ Page number before entry

◉ Page number after entry

Between entry and page number: ^t

contents entries in each publication on the book list. If you are in a publication that contains a book list, the option is automatically turned on. To create a table of contents for the current publication only, turn off this option.

With the Format option, you indicate if and where you want the page number placed with relation to its entry in the table of contents—before or after the text. Page Number After Entry is the most common and is therefore the default.

**The No Page Number choice for the Format option is
useful for creating an outline that displays the structure
of a publication or a book.**

The ^t at the bottom of the dialog box indicates that the table of contents entry and the page number will be separated by a tab—by default, a right-aligned tab stop is set at the right margin. The tab also contains leader dots—a series of periods that appear in the space between the end of the entry and the page number. The leader can be removed or changed, as you will see later.

Although a tab is the most common way to separate the entry and page number, you can replace it with something else, such as a comma and a space. Figure 15.5 shows a table of contents that uses commas as separators.

FIGURE 15.5: *Instead of leader dots, a comma appears between the entry and the page number.*

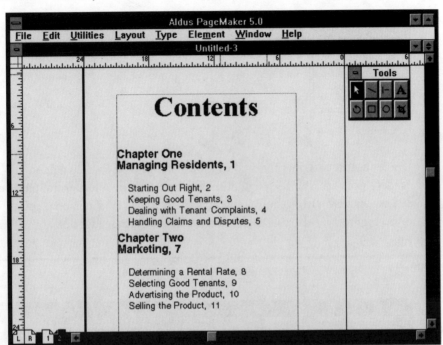

FORMATTING THE TABLE OF CONTENTS

When PageMaker generates a table of contents, each entry has the same type specifications as the text in the original publication. Thus, if the chapter heads were 30-point Times New Roman bold, the table of contents entries for these heads would also have this font. However, these "borrowed" formats are not always appropriate.

PageMaker simplifies the process of formatting a table of contents by creating and assigning styles to the entries. Figure 15.6 shows a style palette that contains these style names. The styles actually have the same names as the original styles, except the name is preceded by *TOC*, for example, *TOC Subhead*. Therefore, to change the type or paragraph specifications of the table of contents entries, you can simply edit the TOC styles. Remember, to edit a style, hold down Ctrl as you click on the name in the style palette. You can then choose the Type and/or Para buttons and make your desired changes.

FIGURE 15.6:   *The style palette, with styles for the table of contents*

CHANGING THE LEADERS

Leader dots are frequently used in tables of contents to help guide the reader's eye across to the page numbers, but some people feel the page tends to get too busy with so many dots. It's really a matter of personal preference. Figure 15.7 shows a table of contents without leader dots.

FIGURE 15.7:   *The leader dots have been removed from this table of contents by editing the TOC styles.*

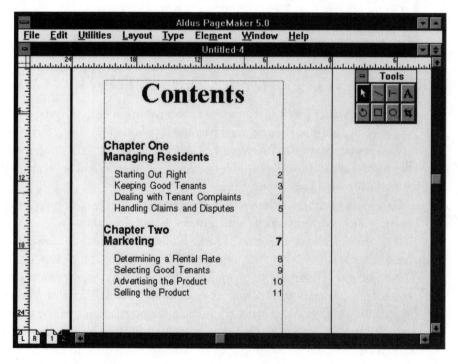

To remove leader dots, you need to edit the TOC styles; in particular, you need to adjust the tab stop that right-aligns the page numbers. Here are the general steps for eliminating leader dots for a style:

1. Hold down Ctrl and click on the TOC style name in the style palette.

2. Choose the Tabs button. You cannot see the tab symbol in the ruler because it is directly on top of the right indent symbol.

3. Click on the right indent symbol. The field next to Leader displays the current leader setting.

4. Click on the Leader button. A drop-down list of types of leaders is displayed.

5. Choose None to turn off the leaders.

6. Close all dialog boxes.

REGENERATING THE TABLE OF CONTENTS

The table of contents is about as undynamic as you can get. After Page-Maker generates a table of contents, it is nothing more than an unintelligent story that has no knowledge whatsoever of its roots. If your page numbering were to change, or if you were to change the wording of one of your subheads, your table of contents would not be updated.

 **Note**

The only way to update the table of contents is to regenerate it or manually edit the text. Generally, you shouldn't have to do this more than once or twice because the table of contents (and index) should be one of the very last things that you create, to guarantee that page numbering and content are correct.

Regenerating a table of contents is not difficult. First of all, the new table of contents automatically replaces the existing one; the Replace Existing

Table of Contents option is turned on automatically when the current publication already contains a table of contents. Also, PageMaker respects the changes you have made to the styles for the table of contents entries, so you will not need to modify the styles again.

CREATING A TABLE OF CONTENTS FOR A SINGLE PUBLICATION

Theoretically, you do not need to create a book if all you want to do is create a table of contents for a single publication. Just mark your table of contents entries as described earlier, and then create the table of contents.

Your only problem is where to put the table of contents. If you place it at the beginning of the publication, you change the pagination of the document; but placing it at the end of the document doesn't make any sense.

The best place for the table of contents is in its own publication. Although you have to create an additional file, your pagination is safe. And perhaps most important, you can ignore the table of contents until the end, instead of having to pay attention to it when you would rather be focusing on the document itself.

We started out this section by saying you don't have to create a book if you are creating a table of contents for a single publication. However, if you want to place the TOC in a separate publication (as we recommend), the easiest way to accomplish this is to create a book. The book feature lets you be in one publication and generate a TOC for another. Here's how this works:

1. Create a new publication to hold your table of contents.

2. Create a book list that contains the publication(s) for which you want to generate a table of contents. Be sure to remove the current publication (the one that will hold the TOC) from the list.

3. Generate the table of contents and place it on the page.

It's that simple.

You might want to include other front matter, such as a title page, in this file.

CREATING AN INDEX

Creating an index can be a time-consuming activity, and PageMaker allevi-ates it only to a small degree. PageMaker will search an entire publication for index markers and generate an index with all entries in place, including the correct page numbers. It does this in the same manner in which it cre-ates a table of contents, except for one very unfortunate exception: you have to tell PageMaker where to embed every single index marker. Mark-ing table of contents entries is easy because you can set it up as part of a style. However, there is no similar shortcut for marking index entries.

Until PageMaker can read your mind, the task of indexing will remain only slightly more comfortable than root canal work. This section explains how the indexing function works. The hard part is still up to you!

Before we go into the how-to's of indexing, you need to understand PageMaker's indexing terms. Take a look at the index shown in Figure 15.8. An index is divided into *sections* titled with a letter of the alphabet. Page-Maker automatically groups your index entries alphabetically and inserts the appropriate letter above the section.

There are two types of index entries:

➤ A *page reference* lists the page number after the entry.

➤ A *cross-reference* refers the reader to another topic.

A particular topic can have up to three *levels*. Each level gets increasingly more specific. For instance, the topics *Abandonment* and *Accounting* in Fig-ure 15.8 have only one level each. But the topic *Advertising* has three lev-els; *Advertising* is the general topic, and its second-level headings, *apartment rental agencies* and *types of*, are subtopics. The *types of* subtopic has three

FIGURE 15.8: *A sample index*

Index

A

Abandonment, 137-139
Accounting, 7, 220
Advertising, 115
   apartment rental agencies, 32-35
   types of
      fliers, 34
      newspapers, 33-36
      signs, 34, 36

B

Bookkeeping, 210
Break-even formula, 21-22

C

Certificate of error, 109
Cleaning, 120, *see also* Maintenance
COE, *see* Certificate of error

third-level topics: *fliers*, *newspapers*, and *signs*. Each level is indented from
the previous level.

MARKING AN INDEX ENTRY

To create an index entry, select the word or phrase you want to mark, and
then press Ctrl+; (Ctrl+semicolon) or choose Utilities ➤ Index Entry to
display the Add Index Entry dialog box. This dialog box is shown in Figure 15.9. If you want the index entry to have significantly different wording
from the text in the publication, don't select the text. Instead, click the
text cursor in front of the phrase. You can then manually type the topic in
the Add Index Entry dialog box.

FIGURE 15.9: *The Add Index Entry dialog box*

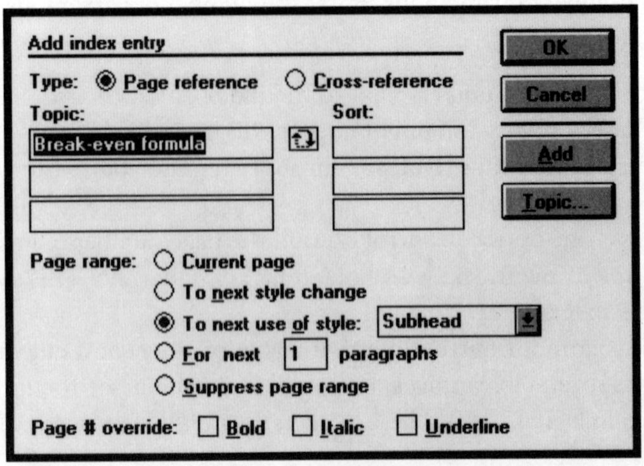

If you selected the index entry before displaying the dialog box, this text will be entered into the Topic section, as a first-level topic (as is *Break-even formula* in Figure 15.9). The two empty text boxes underneath are for specifying second- and third-level topics. As mentioned previously, these additional levels allow you to get more specific in the index. The next section describes multilevel topics in more detail.

The Page Reference option is selected as the default type; the other type of index entry, cross-reference, is discussed in the "Creating Cross-References" section.

The various Page Range options let PageMaker know where the topic ends. (The location of your text cursor indicates where the topic begins.) By default, the page reference includes the current page only. To have PageMaker specify a page range (such as 5–9), choose one of the following options:

- ➤ **To Next Style Change**—use this option when a topic is covered in consecutive paragraphs having the same style. The end of the topic is triggered when a different style is used.

- ➤ **To Next Use of Style**—use this option if the topic is discussed for the remainder of a section. You can then display the drop-down list and select which style triggers the end of the topic—usually a heading style.

➤ **For Next __ Paragraphs**—use this option when the topic spans a certain number of paragraphs. Enter the number of paragraphs in the text box.

If you don't want any page numbers next to the index entry, choose the Suppress Page Range option. You might choose this option if you are revising an index and you want to create entries to remind yourself to index later.

The Page # Override options control how all the page number references are formatted in the index: with bold, italic, or underline. This setting overrides the index styles.

You can mark your index entries in either layout or story view, but the Story Editor offers several advantages. First, you can actually see the index markers, as shown in Figure 15.10. These markers are invisible in layout view.

FIGURE 15.10: *The Story Editor shows index markers*

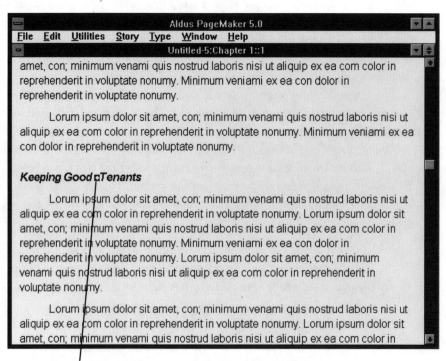

Index Marker

Another advantage to marking index entries in story view is that you can use the Change command to mark the entries. This offers an easy way to mark a word or phrase that occurs many times throughout the publication. Instead of manually marking each occurrence, display the Change dialog box in the Story Editor, enter the term to be indexed in the Find What box, and type ^; in the Change To box. When you click on the Change All button, the text will be marked throughout the publication.

CREATING TWO- AND THREE-LEVEL INDEX ENTRIES

The first-level topic goes in the box under *Topics* in the Index dialog box— it is filled in automatically if you selected the text before issuing the Index Entry command. To enter a subtopic of this main topic, you type the word or phrase in the second Topic field in the dialog box. And to enter a subtopic of the subtopic, enter the text in the last Topic field. All indexes have at least some second-level topics, but some people don't include third-level topics, either because the subject matter doesn't warrant that much detail or because the additional entries would require extra time and effort.

The circular arrow button next to the first-level topic rotates the topics to subsequent levels. The first time you click on this button, the first-level topic becomes a second-level topic. If the entry already had a second-level topic, this topic would be pushed down to the third-level. And if the entry had a third-level topic, it would move to the first-level.

CHOOSING A TOPIC FROM A LIST

The Topic command button in the Add Index Entry dialog box lets you choose an existing topic from a list instead of typing the topic yourself. The main advantage to this method is that you can be sure the topic is always entered the same way—with the same spelling, capitalization, verb tense, and so on. Otherwise, each variation, no matter how minor, will be listed as a separate topic in the index.

To select a topic from a list, you do not select the text before displaying the Add Index Entry dialog box. Just click before the word and press Ctrl+;. Choose the Topic button and the Select Topic dialog box, shown in Figure 15.11, appears. A list of entries in the first topic section is then displayed. Figure 15.11 shows section T. To display the entries for a different section letter, click on the Next Section button until the section is displayed, or type the section letter next to Topic Section. You can also display the drop-down list next to Topic Section and select the letter that way. When you find the appropriate entry, click on it, and the text will fill in next to the Level 1, Level 2, and Level 3 fields. You can delete or modify the subtopics, if necessary. When you're finished, click on OK.

FIGURE 15.11:   *The Select Topic dialog box*

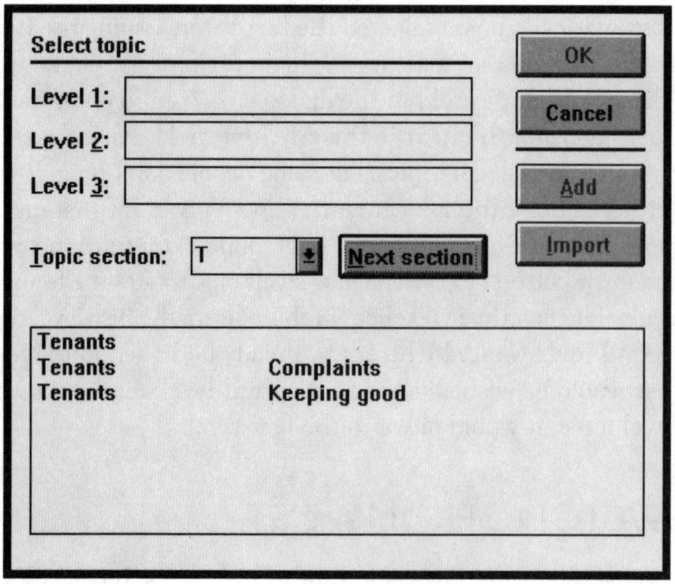

CREATING CROSS-REFERENCES

A cross-reference lists a related topic instead of a specific page number. You see these all the time in indexes; for example, _Actual size, see Page views._ Sometimes an index entry has both a page reference and a cross-reference; for example, _Soft fonts, 125–129, see also Fonts._ Since cross-references do not refer to a specific page in the publication, you do not need to select text or insert a text cursor to include them in the index.

When you are creating a cross-reference, it doesn't matter where the text cursor is or whether the text tool or pointer tool is selected. If the pointer tool is active, PageMaker automatically knows that you are creating a cross-reference. To create a cross-reference, press Ctrl+; and choose the Cross-Reference option, if necessary. When Cross-Reference is selected, the dialog box changes, as shown in Figure 15.12. Since page numbers are not applicable to cross-references, the Page Range options are replaced with a list of cross-reference options.

The See [also] option, the default, is the most versatile because the cross-reference displays either _See_ or _See also_, depending on whether the topic has page references; for example, _Page spread, See Facing pages_ or _Page spread, 26, 119, See also Facing pages._ You can force it to choose either _See_ or _See also_ by turning on the appropriate option. The _See Herein_ and _See_

FIGURE 15.12:   _The Add Index Entry dialog box for cross-references_

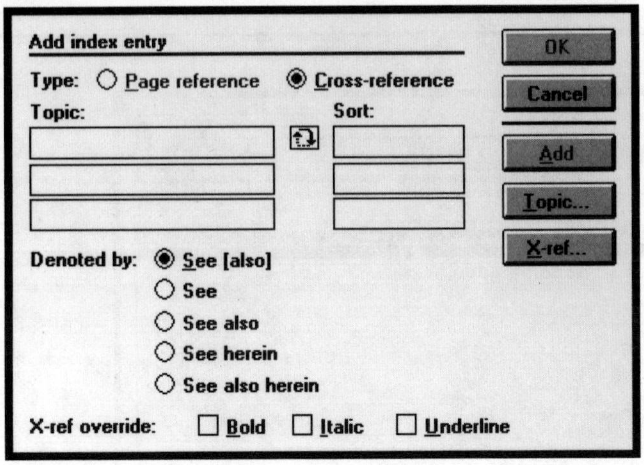

Also Herein options refer the reader to other levels within the same index entry; for example, *Double-sided pages, See herein Page spread.*

You can either type the topic name yourself, or use the Topic button to select it from a list of current entries. To enter the topic to which you are cross-referencing, click on the X-Ref command button, and the Select Cross-Reference Topic dialog box appears. This box is identical to the Select Topic dialog box because your goal is the same: to choose a topic. You can then navigate to the appropriate section and click on the entry. Alternatively, you can type the cross-reference yourself in the Level 1 field.

LOOKING AT THE INDEX

The Show Index command on the Utilities menu allows you to peruse the entries before you generate the index. While browsing, you can edit the entries if you discover a mistake or remove unnecessary or duplicate entries. You view the index section by section. In other words, each letter of the alphabet has a separate list. Click on the Next Section button to view other sections of the index.

The page references are listed next to each topic, as you can see in Figure 15.13. To delete an entry, click on the topic in the list and choose the Remove button. The Edit button takes you to the Edit Index Entry dialog box, where you can modify the name of the topic or change the Page Range option.

FIGURE 15.13:   *The Show Index dialog box for section T*

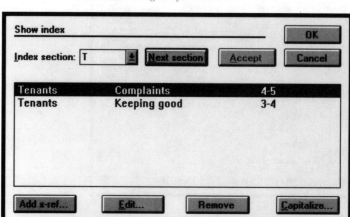

Version
5.0

The Capitalize button lets you automate the process of capitalizing the first letter of a selected topic, all Level 1 entries, or all entries. The option is available only in the individual publications that actually contain the marked text; the Capitalize button is dimmed if you are in the publication that contains your book list (assuming this document doesn't have any marked index entries).

CREATING THE INDEX

Marking the index entries is the grueling part of indexing; generating the index is the easy part. The process of creating an index is the same as creating a table of contents. When you issue the Create Index command, Page-Maker compiles all your index entries and their references into a single story. You are then presented with a loaded text gun that contains the newly generated index. Click on a page, and you have your index.

To create an index that spans multiple publications, you must have previously created a book list of these publications, and you must be in the publication that contains this list.

The Create Index dialog box is shown in Figure 15.14. Next to Title is the heading that appears above the index. If you are in a publication that contains a book list, the option Include Book Publications is turned on. This option compiles index entries for each publication on the book list. The

FIGURE 15.14: *The Create Index dialog box*

Create index

Title: [Index]

□ Replace existing index
☒ Include book publications
☒ Remove unreferenced topics

[OK]
[Cancel]
[Format...]

CUSTOMIZING YOUR INDEX

The Format button in the Create Index dialog box lets you customize your index—for instance, you can specify the characters and spacing between the different parts of an index entry. Clicking on this button displays the dialog box shown in Figure 15.15.

If you don't want the single, large capital letters preceding each section of the index, you can turn off the Include Index Section Headings checkbox. To reserve space for each section, even when there aren't any index entries for it, turn on the Include Empty Index Sections checkbox. When you do this, the phrase *no entries* will appear in the section.

Two format layouts are available: Nested and Run-In. With Nested (the default), each entry is on a separate line and Level 2 and Level 3 entries are indented. With Run-In, all levels of an entry are combined into a single paragraph—the levels are run together. To see an example of each layout, click on the format and look at the example at the bottom of the dialog box.

The remaining options control the characters and spacing of the different parts of an index entry. You may notice that some of the text boxes contain *metacharacters*, special characters that cannot be directly entered into the dialog box. For example, the ^> combination is a code that represents an en space, and ^= represents an en dash. To see a complete list of metacharacters, choose Help ➤ Shortcuts and click on the Meta icon at the bottom of the Help window.

The list below describes each of the options:

Following topic	Characters between the entry text and the page number; the default is two spaces.
Between page #s	Characters between multiple page references; the default is a comma and an en space.
Between entries	Characters between Level 2 and 3 entries in a run-in format, or the characters between cross-references in any index entry; the default is a semicolon and an en space.
Page range	Characters that separate the first and last numbers in a page range; the default is an en dash.
Before x-ref	Characters before a cross-reference; the default is a period and an en space.
Entry end	Characters at the end of every referenced entry in nested format, or characters that follow the last cross-reference in the topic in run-in format; the default is no character.

FIGURE 15.15:   *The Index Format dialog box lets you customize the format of your index.*

Index format

☒ Include index section **h**eadings

☐ Include empty index **s**ections

Format: ⦿ **Nested**   ○ **R**un-in

Following topic:		**P**age range:	`^=`
Between page #s:	`.^>`	Before **x**-ref:	`.^>`
Be**t**ween entries:	`;^>`	**E**ntry end:	

OK

Cancel

Example: Index commands 1-4
      Index entry 1, 3. See also Index mark-up
      Show index 2-4

Remove Unreferenced Topics option eliminates entries that do not have page references or cross-references.

When PageMaker finishes generating the index, you will see a loaded text gun. If you don't have a blank page ready to receive your index, you can create it at this point. Before placing the text, you'll probably want to turn on the autoflow option so that PageMaker will automatically create as many pages as necessary for your index.

As the style palette in Figure 15.16 shows, several new styles are created for index entries. The Index Level 1 and Index Level 2 styles control the format of the first- and second-level topics. Both levels are 10-point, but the second-level topics are indented. The Index Section style formats the capital letters preceding each section. By default, the letters are 12-point bold with extra space above and below the paragraph. The Index Title style formats the heading at the top of the index. It is 30-point bold by default. To change the format of the index, edit the appropriate style.

FIGURE 15.16:   *The style palette, with styles for index entries*

Styles
[No style]
Index level 1
Index level 2
Index section
Index title

Note

The typeface of the index text is determined by your default typeface (probably Times New Roman). To see what font is your default, choose Type ➤ Font, with the pointer tool active. The default font has a checkmark next to it. If you want your index text to be formatted with a different font, you can save yourself some time by changing the default font *before* generating the index. If you've already generated the index, you'll have to edit each style to change the font.

Like a table of contents, an index is not dynamically linked to its entries and must be manually edited or regenerated whenever you add new entries or make any changes that affect pagination. You do not need to delete the outdated index—just go directly to the Create Index dialog box; the Replace Existing Index option is automatically checked.

As always, a bit of experimentation goes a long way toward understanding the intricacies of this function. PageMaker's indexing tools can make the job of creating an index a bit easier.

SUMMARY

With the tools discussed in this chapter, you can tame your monster projects. Just design a template, clone it for each chapter, and create a book list. Once you have laid out the pages in each publication, you can use a few PageMaker commands to generate a table of contents and an index that reference all the publications in the book.

HANDS-ON PRACTICE: COMPLETING THE RENTAL HANDBOOK

This exercise continues with the rental property handbook that you worked on in Chapter 14. To complete the exercise, you will need the publications created in Chapter 14—RENTAL01.PM5, RENTAL02.PM5, and RENTAL03.PM5. (Therefore, you will need to do Chapter 14's Hands-On Practice exercise if you haven't done so already.) In the following steps, you will print the book with continuous page numbering, create a table of contents, and produce an index.

CREATING A PUBLICATION FOR THE FRONT MATTER

The handbook needs a publication that will hold the book's front matter: a title page and the table of contents. This publication will also contain the book list—the list of publications that are part of the complete project. We could use the template we created in Chapter 14, but you would have to delete the headers and footers. Therefore, we'll create a publication from scratch, using the same page setup as the template.

1. Create a new file.

2. Specify the following page setup:

   Size: 45 by 54 picas ($7\frac{1}{2}$ by 9 inches)
   Number of pages: 2
   Inside margin: 6p
   Outside margin: 4p6
   Top margin: 6p
   Bottom margin: 6p

3. On page 1, create a title page for the book. Recreate the simple one shown in Figure 15.17, or be creative and design your own.

4. Save the file with the name RENTBOOK.PM5.

FIGURE 15.17: *The title page*

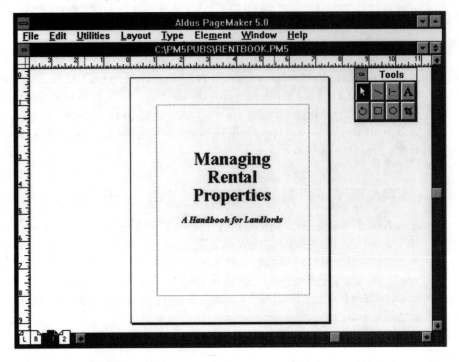

DEFINING A BOOK LIST

Follow these steps to define the publications that are part of the book:

1. Pull down the File menu and choose Book to display the Book
Publication List dialog box.

RENTBOOK.PM5, the current publication, is already at the top of the list.
We don't want this file in the book list because it will affect the pagination
of the book. Let's remove it.

2. Click on the Remove button.

3. To add the first file, click on RENTAL01.PM5 in the list on the
left and then on the Insert button in the dialog box. The file
name is added to the book list.

4. Repeat step 3 for RENTAL02.PM5 and RENTAL03.PM5.

5. To automatically renumber the pages in the book and begin each chapter on a right-hand page, choose the Next Odd Page option.

6. Choose OK.

7. Click on Yes to renumber the pages now.

8. Once the page numbers have been processed, save the file.

The book list now contains three publications: RENTAL01.PM5, RENTAL02.PM5, and RENTAL03.PM5, in that order.

PRINTING THE RENTAL PROPERTY BOOK

Now, print the chapters:

1. Display the Print dialog box.

2. Click on the Options button and turn on the Printer's Marks option (because the pages are smaller than the paper size).

3. Click on the Document button to return to the main Print dialog box.

4. Turn on the Print All Publications in Book option.

5. Choose Print.

All three chapters will be printed. Chapter one is numbered 1 through 5. Because you instructed PageMaker to begin each publication on an odd-numbered page, page 6 is blank, and chapter two begins on page 7.

If you open the second chapter, you will see that the page icons reflect the new page numbering. Figure 15.18 shows that RENTAL02.PM5 contains pages numbered 7 through 12.

FIGURE 15.18: *The RENTAL02 publication contains pages numbered 7 through 12.*

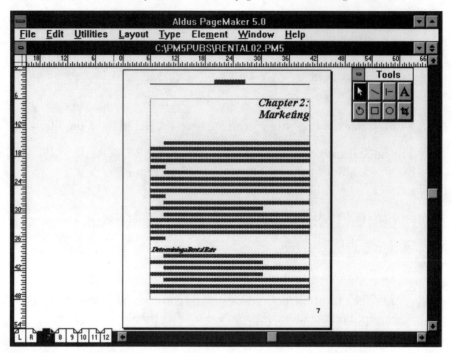

INCLUDING A HEADING
IN THE TABLE OF CONTENTS

To create a table of contents, you need to mark which headings are to be included in the table of contents. In the rental book, two headings will be included: the chapter heads and the subheadings. Styles were created for these headings, but the Include in Table of Contents option was not turned on. Therefore, you need to modify the styles in the three chapters so that the headings will be included in the table of contents.

1. Save and close RENTBOOK.

2. Open RENTAL01.PM5.

3. If necessary, display the style palette.

4. Hold down Ctrl and click on Chapter Head in the style palette. The Edit Style dialog box appears.

5. Click on the Para command button.

6. Turn on Include in Table of Contents.

7. Press Alt and choose OK to close the dialog boxes.

8. Hold down Ctrl and click on Subhead in the style palette.

9. Repeat steps 5 through 7 to modify the Subhead style.

10. Save and close RENTAL01.PM5.

Now, copy the styles from RENTAL01.PM5 to the other chapters of the rental book:

11. Open RENTAL02.PM5.

12. Pull down the Type menu and choose Define Styles.

13. Click on the Copy button. Then double-click on RENTAL01.PM5 —the file you want to copy styles from.

14. Choose OK to copy over the existing styles, and then close the dialog box.

15. Save and close RENTAL02.PM5.

16. Open RENTAL03.PM5 and repeat steps 12 through 14 to copy the styles into this publication.

17. Save and close RENTAL03.PM5.

GENERATING THE RENTAL BOOK'S TABLE OF CONTENTS

The table of contents for our handbook should go in the publication that contains the book list. Follow these steps to create it:

1. Open RENTBOOK.PM5.

2. Pull down the Utilities menu and choose Create TOC.

3. The default settings will work fine for our purposes, so choose OK.

When PageMaker finishes generating the TOC, you will see a loaded text gun.

4. Go to page 2 and click on the upper-left corner of the page.

5. Switch to Actual Size view so that you can see the entries and page numbers.

Your table of contents should look similar to the one shown in Figure 15.19. The entries are formatted just like the text in the publication, which is not appropriate for a table of contents. Also, notice that each chapter title is broken into two lines. This is because there is a line break code (Shift+Enter) between the chapter number and title, and PageMaker duplicates this in the table of contents. The second line of the chapter head is indented because, by default, PageMaker creates a hanging indent for multiple-line entries. We will eliminate the indent in the next section.

FIGURE 15.19: *The generated table of contents*

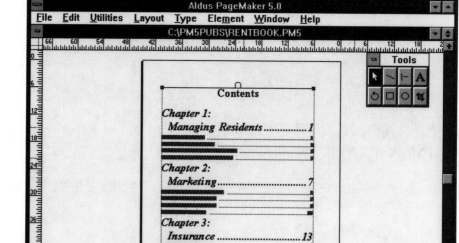

15

FORMATTING THE RENTAL BOOK'S TABLE OF CONTENTS

In the following steps, you will edit the TOC styles to remove the indents and change the type specifications.

1. If necessary, display the style palette.

The three TOC style names are shown in Figure 15.20. Notice that we widened the palette so that the longest style name fits. We also removed the six default style names. The TOC Title style controls the format of the heading at the top of the table of contents.

2. Hold down Ctrl and click on TOC Chapter Head in the style palette. The Edit Style dialog box appears.

3. Choose the Para command button.

4. Change the left and first-line indents to zero.

5. Specify 1 pica before and 0.5 pica after the paragraph.

6. Choose OK.

7. Choose the Type command button.

8. Change the size to 12 points, with 12-point leading, and turn off italic.

9. Press Alt, and then choose OK to close all dialog boxes.

Figure 15.21 shows the revised TOC with the new chapter title formatting. Next, we will modify the TOC Subhead style.

FIGURE 15.20: *The style palette, with the TOC style names*

FIGURE 15.21: *The table of contents with reformatted chapter titles*

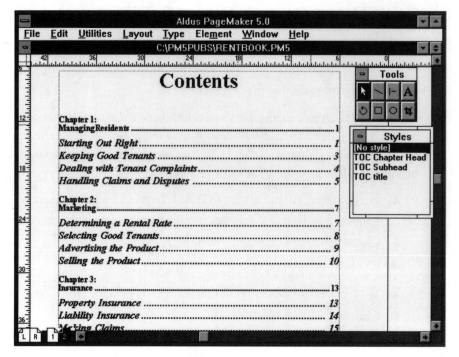

10. Hold down Ctrl and click on TOC Subhead in the style palette.

11. Choose the Para command button in the Edit Style dialog box.

12. Change the left indent to 1 pica and the first-line indent to zero.

13. Choose OK.

14. Choose the Type command button.

15. Change the size to 10 points.

16. Choose the Normal type style.

17. Press Alt and choose OK to close all dialog boxes.

The subheadings are more clearly defined when they are indented from the chapter headings. Also, the chapter titles stand out more when they are the only bold entries. Your table of contents should look similar to the one shown in Figure 15.22.

FIGURE 15.22: *The table of contents with reformatted subheadings*

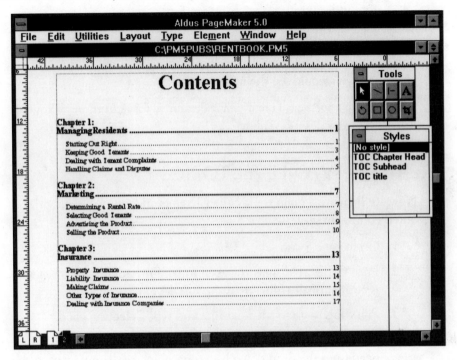

MARKING INDEX ENTRIES IN THE RENTAL BOOK

Let's mark an index entry in the RENTAL02.PM5 publication:

1. Save and close the RENTBOOK publication and then open RENTAL02.PM5.

2. Go to page 7 (actually the first physical page in the publication) and select *Rental Rate* in the subhead.

3. Press Ctrl+; to display the Add Index Entry dialog box.

Rental Rate is automatically entered into the Topic section, as a first-level topic. The two empty text boxes underneath are for specifying second- and third-level topics. The Page Reference option is selected as the type.

4. Turn on the To Next Use of Style option, and select Subhead from the drop-down list. This will specify a page range from the

index mark until the next subhead (in other words, the rental rate is discussed in the entire section).

5. Choose OK.

You don't see the index marker in layout view, but if you were to switch to story view, you would see the index code.

6. Go to page 9 and create an index entry for *Advertising* following the steps described above.

CREATING TWO-LEVEL TOPICS

Now, we'll create a main topic called *Tenants* and define a second-level entry. Follow these steps:

1. Go to page 8 and select *Tenants*.

2. Press Ctrl+; to display the Add Index Entry dialog box. *Tenants* is automatically filled in as the first-level topic.

3. Press Tab to go to the next line and type **Selecting good**.

4. Turn on the To Next Use of Style option, and then select Subhead from the drop-down list. Your dialog box should match the one in Figure 15.23.

FIGURE 15.23: *A two-level topic*

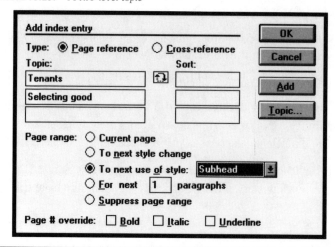

5. Choose OK.

6. Save and close the publication.

Let's move back to chapter one and mark a two-level index entry in that publication.

7. Open RENTAL01.PM5.

8. Go to page 3 and select *Tenants*.

9. Press Ctrl+;, press Tab to go to the next line, and type **Keeping good**.

10. Turn on the To Next Use of Style option and select Subhead from the drop-down list.

11. Choose OK.

CHOOSING A TOPIC FROM A LIST

Page 4 also has a reference to the word *tenant*. Since this word already exists as a topic, let's use the Topic button, as follows:

1. Go to page 4 and place the text cursor right before the word *Tenant*. Because we will be choosing the topic from a list, you don't need to select the word.

2. Press Ctrl+; and click on the Topic button.

The Select Topic dialog box, shown in Figure 15.24, displays the existing topics for section T.

3. Click on Tenants. The topic fills in next to Level 1, and the subtopic, *Keeping good*, fills in next to Level 2.

4. Press Tab to go to Level 2, and then type **Complaints**.

5. Choose OK.

6. Turn on the To Next Use of Style option and select Subhead from the drop-down list.

7. Close the dialog box.

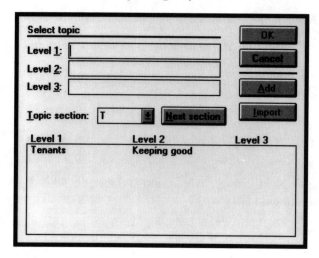

CREATING
CROSS-REFERENCES FOR THE RENTAL BOOK

Let's create a cross-reference for the topic *Residents* that refers the reader to the topic *Tenants*. Because you are creating a cross-reference, it doesn't matter where the text cursor is or whether the text tool or pointer tool is selected. Follow these steps:

I. Press Ctrl+; and choose the Cross-Reference option.

When you select Cross-Reference, the dialog box changes. Since page numbers are not applicable to cross-references, the Page Range options are replaced with a list of cross-reference options.

2. For the topic name, type **Residents**.

3. Leave the default Denoted By option (See [also]) on and click on the X-Ref command button.

The Select Cross-Reference Topic dialog box appears. This box is identical to the Select Topic dialog box because your goal is the same: to choose a topic.

4. Choose either *Tenants* item.

5. Delete the text next to Level 2.

6. Close all dialog boxes.

7. Save and close the publication.

MARKING INDEX ENTRIES IN RENTAL03

You haven't marked any index entries in RENTAL03.PM5 yet. Open this publication and mark the following two-level entries (for each one, be sure to turn on the To Next Use of Style option and choose Subhead):

FIRST LEVEL	SECOND LEVEL	PAGE #
Insurance	Property	13
Insurance	Liability	14
Insurance	Other	16

Save and close the file when you are finished.

SHOWING THE RENTAL BOOK'S INDEX

Show the index for the RENTAL01.PM5 publication:

1. Open RENTAL01.PM5.

2. Choose Show Index from the Utilities menu.

The Show Index dialog box displays the first section in this publication, R. There is just one entry in section R (Residents) and it has a cross-reference instead of a page number.

3. Click on the Next Section button to see section T. The entries are listed with their page number references, as shown in Figure 15.25.

4. Click on Next Section. There are no more sections, so the first section reappears.

5. Choose OK.

6. Save and close the RENTAL01.PM5 publication.

FIGURE 15.25: *The index for section T in RENTAL01.PM5*

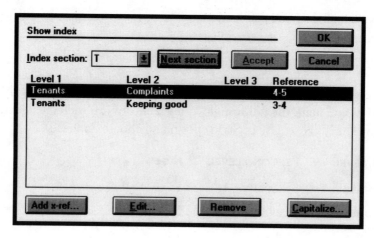

If you like, open RENTAL02.PM5 and/or RENTAL03.PM5 and browse through their indexes. Use the Edit button to correct any mistakes if necessary, and then close the files.

GENERATING THE RENTAL BOOK'S INDEX

Follow these steps to generate the index for RENTBOOK.PM5:

1. Open RENTBOOK.PM5.

2. Insert a page after page 2 for the index.

3. Pull down the Utilities menu and choose Create Index.

4. Choose OK to generate the index.

When PageMaker finishes generating the index, you will see a loaded text gun.

5. Click in the upper-left corner of page 3 and switch to Actual Size view so that you can see the entries and page numbers. Your index should look similar to Figure 15.26.

6. Save and close the file.

FIGURE 15.26: *The generated index*

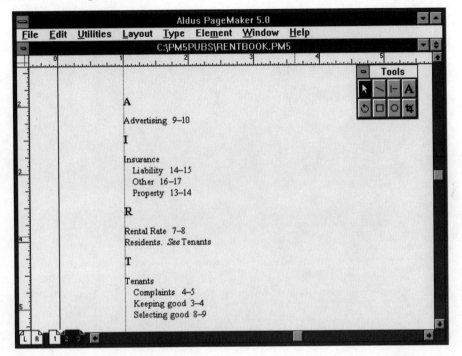

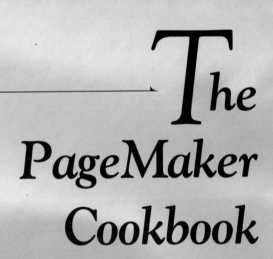

The
PageMaker
Cookbook

fast tracks

If you want to run a resume production business: **621**

Create a resume template with the appropriate margins and styles. For each of your clients, type their resume text in your word processor, inserting the appropriate style tags (for example, <Objective>) in front of each paragraph. Open the resume template and place the text file; the resume is done except for some copyfitting, perhaps. The text will be formatted automatically since you entered style tags in the text file.

To create camera-ready business cards: **623**

There are two ways you can create business cards. One way is to create a publication that contains a single card; the page dimensions will be the actual, final size of your business card. You should then print out the card with crop marks. The second way is to create an $8\frac{1}{2}$-by-11-inch page of business cards, all positioned and ready to be cut. You'll want to design one card and copy it seven times to fill out the page. Use ruler guides and hand-drawn crop marks to help you position the cards.

To create a three-panel brochure: 627

Create a two-page publication with Wide (landscape) orientation.
Use the Layout ➤ Column Guides command to create three column
guides; the gutters should be double the size of the outer margins. Typically, the brochure text begins on the first column of the second page
and flows across all three columns. You can continue the story onto the
first column of the first page, if you like, or you can place a separate story
on this panel. The brochure cover goes on the third column of the first
page. To create a self-mailing brochure, put your return address (rotated
90-degrees) on the middle column of page 1.

To create a directory of names and addresses: 630

In dBASE, Lotus 1-2-3, or Excel, use string functions to insert style
tags. Create an ASCII file of this data. Import this ASCII file into a
PageMaker publication, using the Autoflow option to create as many
pages as necessary.

Ways you can use PageMaker in your personal life: 642

To create menus, wedding invitations, wedding programs, and birth
announcements.

T'S TIME TO PUT ON YOUR CHEF'S hat again. In this chapter, you will find a variety of recipes for producing different types of projects in PageMaker. We'll start with the publications for business applications, and then move on to ones that are fun (menus, birth announcements, invitations, and wedding programs).

INSTANT RESUMES

At the risk of insulting an entire industry of resume-makers, producing resumes does not require state-of-the-art design brilliance. Resumes need to be neat, well-conceived, and readable. Those who receive resumes do not judge them on their aesthetic qualities, but rather on the professionalism and sense of priority that they convey.

If there is any project that calls for recycling, it is the production of a resume. A resume usually follows the same basic structure: it is one page, begins with a name and address, and then describes the applicant's qualifications (objective, education, experience, and so on). Furthermore, there is nothing wrong with making resumes that look the same—they go to different customers and different employers. Aside from the obvious benefit of making production easier, it gives you a visual trademark as a resume-maker. Figure 16.1 shows an example of a resume design.

FIGURE 16.1: *A resume assembly line*

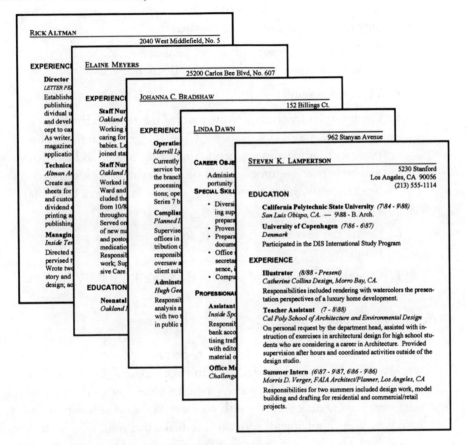

MAKING THE PERFECT RESUME

If you're going into the cloning business, your original should be the best you can produce. If you have been producing resumes long enough to recognize a pattern, use it as a guide for your master resume. If you're new to resume-making, don't worry—your "perfect resume" will evolve over time. Pick an existing, typical resume and do the following:

1. For organizational purposes, create a subdirectory that will hold all the files pertaining to resumes. You will store your text files, resume template, and publications in this subdirectory.

2. In your word processor, type the text for the resume. Give this file any name you like (usually the person's last name), making sure to save it in the resume subdirectory.

3. In PageMaker, create a one-page publication and specify the resume's margins, typically 1 inch all around.

4. Place the resume text file.

5. Create styles for the following parts of the resume: the name, address, headings (for example, Objective, Education, and Experience), subheadings (such as university names and job titles), and body text. Resumes should be conservative looking, so don't be extreme with your formatting, and use just one or two different fonts.

6. Delete the text block because it doesn't need to be part of the template.

7. Save the file as a template, with the name RESUME.

CLONING THE PERFECT RESUME

Ideally, a resume-maker should spend 90 percent of his or her time writing a resume and 10 percent producing it in PageMaker. For example, let's say a customer hires you to produce a resume. She gives you all the pertinent data, and you create a text file with your word processor. It is here that you earn your keep, applying all your skills to make this resume as professional as possible. Also, you recognize that this resume fits the typical structure, so you should be able to pour it right into your template.

Depending on your preferences, tag the text in your word processor or in PageMaker. The fastest way is to create macros in your word processor and tag the text there. If you decide to wait until you're in PageMaker, you can assign styles with the style or control palette.

Suppose that you name the file JONES.WP5 (after the customer's name). When the file is ready, here are the steps to take:

1. Start PageMaker and open your resume template, RESUME.PT5.

2. Place the JONES.WP5 text file.

3. Assign style names if necessary.

4. Save the file with the name JONES.PM5.

5. Print. You're done.

With this system, you can actually meet the prescribed 90–10 proportion of time spent editing the resume to time spent producing it. The production work is freeze-dried in the template; all you do is add text.

CAMERA-READY BUSINESS CARDS

Business cards may be your simplest PageMaker project. The only tricky part is ensuring that your final product is truly camera-ready; that is the focus of this section.

Business cards typically have no borders around them. Therefore, you must furnish crop marks to ensure that the type is positioned correctly on the card. By creating a page that is the exact size of your business card and using the Printer's Marks option, you can let your print shop know where the type should be placed on the card.

SETTING UP A CUSTOM PAGE SIZE

Let's say you intend to produce a standard 2-by-3½-inch business card. Here's how you do it:

1. Create a new file with the following page setup:

   Page dimensions: 12p by 21p (or 2i by 3.5i)
   Orientation: Landscape (unless you want a vertical business card)
   Margins: 1p all the way around

Even though the page size is very small, the page still takes up most of the publication window. It doesn't look like it, but you are in Fit in Window view. You will even be able to read small point sizes without having to switch to Actual Size view. In fact, Fit in Window view is larger than the actual size of the pages.

2. Type and format the text for your business card.

3. Add graphic elements if desired. Extend rules past the edge of the page to create a bleed, as shown in Figure 16.2.

4. Display the Print dialog box, choose the Options button, turn on the Printer's Marks option, and print the page.

FIGURE 16.2: *Rules extended past the edge of the page create a bleeding effect.*

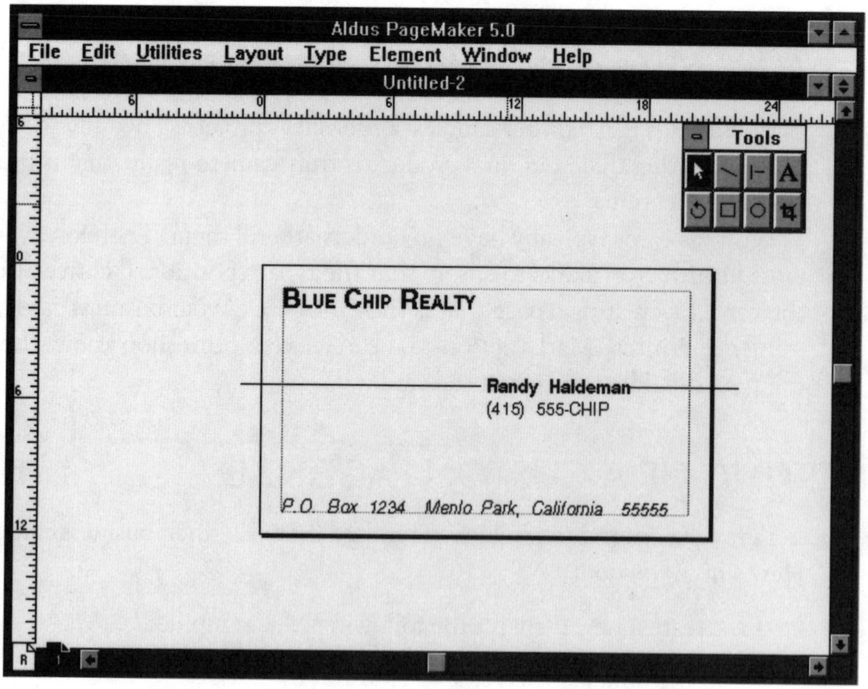

If you want higher quality than your 300-dpi laser printer can produce, print a master business card on a high-resolution typesetting machine (see Appendix C for details).

CREATING A SHEET OF CARDS

Depending on your print shop, you may save time and expense by providing a full page of business cards, all positioned and ready to be cut. That way, your printer does not have to print as many pages, and each pass under the blade cuts up to four cards.

In this scenario, you create one business card and copy it seven times to fill out a normal 8½-by-11-inch page. Spacing is critical because each card must be the same exact size. The easiest way to do this is to use the business card template that comes with PageMaker. This file is called BIZCARDS, and can be opened with the Open Template addition (see Chapter 14 for information on this addition).

The template, shown in Figure 16.3, has placeholders for eight business cards. Each card is delineated with column, margin, and ruler guides, creating eight 2-by-3½-inch boxes. Since these boxes represent the final card size, you need to build margins into the business card text. For example, if you want a 1-pica left margin, set 1-pica left indents. Also, be sure to leave extra space above the first element and below the last element on the card.

If you switch to a magnified view, you can see that this template contains eight different styles of business cards. Choose your favorite style and replace the placeholders with your name, address, and phone number. If you prefer a different layout, create your own design in a separate file, copy it to the Clipboard, and paste it in the BIZCARDS template.

FIGURE 16.3: *The business card template*

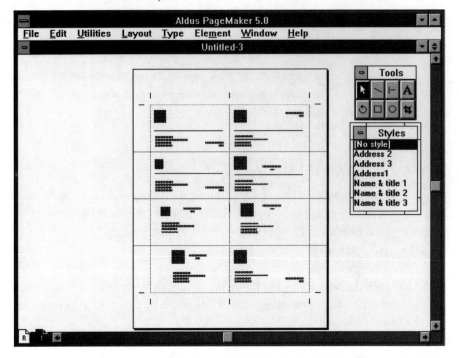

Once your master card is as perfect as you can make it, you need to make seven copies of it. Follow these steps:

1. Delete all the sample business cards except for your master card.

2. Press Ctrl+A to select all the elements in your card.

3. Copy the selected elements to the Clipboard.

4. Switch to Actual Size view and position the screen so that you can see one of the empty boxes.

5. Press Ctrl+V to paste the business card.

6. Move the card into position (see the sidebar, "Tips for Moving a Group of Objects.")

7. Repeat steps 5 and 6 until you have placed a copy of the business card in all eight boxes.

> ## TIPS FOR MOVING A GROUP OF OBJECTS
>
> Moving a group of selected objects can be a little tricky. Here are a few pointers:
>
> ➤ If the original object you copied to the Clipboard is on the screen when you paste, the copy is pasted on top of the original, creating confusing text over text. Whenever possible, position the screen so that the original does not show. That way, the copy is pasted on the middle of the screen.
>
> ➤ Make sure you do not click on any of the text or graphic handles; otherwise, you will end up moving or sizing this one object. If this happens, issue the Undo command immediately.
>
> ➤ To make sure you move the entire group of selected objects, click inside one of the text blocks and hold the mouse button for a moment before you begin dragging. That way, you drag the actual card instead of a box representing its size, and it will be immediately apparent whether or not you are moving all the elements on the card.

The Printer's Marks print option won't work for the sheet of business cards because you need marks at the corners of each card, not just at the corners of the page. Therefore, the marks must be drawn manually with the rule tool. Fortunately, these crop marks are part of the BIZCARDS template. These lines were drawn on the master page. You cannot see all of them because they are drawn on top of the guides. Figure 16.4 shows the master page with the guides turned off so that the crop marks are visible.

EFFECTIVE BROCHURES

Keep in mind that the cover of a brochure is the first thing the reader sees, so you want it to entice your audience to open the brochure and read the important information inside. *Do not* call attention to your brochure by using five different fonts in bold and italic—commonly referred to as the ransom-note method of desktop publishing. The most effective front covers contain just a few words and perhaps a photograph. Frequently, as in the

FIGURE 16.4: *The crop marks on the master page indicate where each business card is to be cut.*

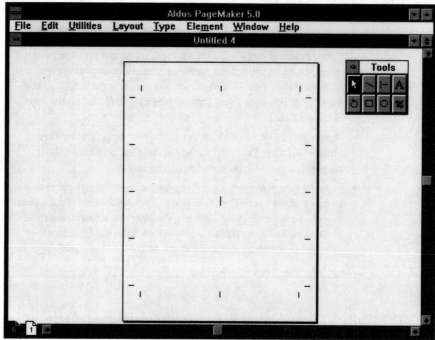

brochure you created for Blue Chip Realty, the cover lures the reader with a short, catchy question or statement, or perhaps a graphic.

Make the entire brochure light and airy. Don't try to cram too much information on each page. Usually, the purpose of a brochure is to give readers just enough information to spark their interest and encourage them to call for details. If the brochure has too much text, readers might feel overwhelmed or get bored before they finish reading. Allow plenty of white space and use graphic elements to provide visual interest.

A common format is the three-panel landscape brochure on 8½-by-11-inch paper. In the brochure shown in Figure 16.5, the panels are laid out as follows:

- → The brochure text starts on the first column of page 2 and continues across all three columns.

- → The first column on page 1 is a separate story. However, it can also be a continuation of the main brochure story.

FIGURE 16.5: *A three-panel brochure*

Seminars & Lunch

Hosted by Rick Altman

Featuring David Brickley,
Grand Prize Winner,
Annual CorelDraw
Design Contest, 1990

San Mateo: March 9 & 10
The Dunfey Hotel

Santa Clara: March 16 & 17
The Westin

Concord: March 23 & 24
Sheraton Hotel and
Conference Center

Day One: Beginning/Intermediate $129
Day Two: Intermediate/Advanced $129
Both Days $229

Call (408) 252-5448

The Northern
California

COREL
DRAW

Seminar Series

March, 1993

Why is CorelDraw No. 1?

Because designers and illustrators use it for a wide array of projects, and because even after years of operation, its users continue to discover new features and techniques. That is why over 500 CorelDraw users attended Rick Altman's seminars in 1992.

Whether you have broken speed records with CorelDraw, or have just broken the seal, this seminar series is your best stop for vital information, education, and discovery. Join efficiency expert Rick Altman and award-winning designer David Brickley for one or two enlightening and entertaining days.

Day One: Beginning to Intermediate

If you are a new or occasional user, this day of practical, concise instruction is for you. Altman and Brickley cover both the left and right sides of the brain with clear visuals and uncomplicated language.

You'll learn to get started with the program, how to advance an idea to completion, how to ensure tasteful and effective typographic effects, and how to incorporate your illustrations into projects on other programs.

Day Two: Intermediate to Advanced

Regular CorelDraw users, quick learners, and Day One "graduates" will revel in a wealth of tips, tricks, techniques, secrets, and insights.

You'll discover the most efficient and productive steps to power drawing. You'll go inside the head of an artist as he builds and unbuilds his illustrations for you. You'll explore the joy, and the frustration, of advanced font management. And you'll take an in-depth tour of logos and graphics making their way into and out of CorelDraw.

Whether you sign up for one day or both days, you'll find stimulating topics, relevant discussion, and ample time for questions and answers. You'll get a nice lunch, and as with all Altman seminars, a chance at winning one of several awesome prizes.

Your Registration Includes:

■ Entry to all seminars

■ Morning coffee and danish, and lunch

■ Seminar booklet, complimentary gifts, and a disk of fonts, art, and utilities

■ A chance to win one of the following prizes (to be given away each day):

– Adobe typeface packages

– Font management software

– Clip art packages

– Certificates for CorelDraw upgrades

– And the grand prize of a LaserMaster WinJet high-speed printer controller card.

Day One		Day Two	
9:00	Registration / Coffee & Danish	9:00	Registration / Coffee & Danish
10:00	**SETTING UP SHOP:** So you've installed the software—now what?? This hour offers tips for surviving your first few projects and for establishing good drawing habits.	10:00	**APPETIZERS:** We start the day with a stroll down Productivity Lane, for a collection of tips, tricks, and tidy time-savers covering a variety of topics.
11:00	**THE ESSENCE OF EFFECTIVE DRAWING:** Where does creative ability leave off and the software tools begin? Learn easy-to-understand fundamentals about how to design and create original work.	11:00	**DRAWING SECRETS:** How much of CorelDraw is inspiration and how much is perspiration? David Brickley demonstrates quick and effective techniques to help improve your drawing skills.
12:00	Lunch	12:00	Lunch
1:00	**TYPE TIPS FOR TYROS:** What to do with all those typefaces? If you're new to type and design, the answer might be: Nothing! Details and more during this hour.	1:00	**FONT AND FUNCTION:** How come your text draws slowly? How come you ask for Palatino and get Courier? This hour helps you cope—and thrive—with CorelDraw's abundant and often ill-behaved typefaces.
2:00	**LOGOMANIA, PART 1:** Statistics show that CorelDraw users turn to the program to produce logos more than any other project. Our expert shows why…and how.	2:00	**LOGOMANIA, PART 2:** Blends, fills, rotations, traps—this hour offers a little of everything.
3:00	**GRAPHICS AWAY!** Moving images in and out of CorelDraw is the essential feature for many users. Sometimes, though, there is more to it than meets the mouse.	3:00	**GRAPHICS AWAY, OLE!** With today's tools, your CorelDraw images can travel between applications farther and faster than ever before.
4:00	Conclusion / Prizes	4:00	Conclusion / Prizes

The Northern
California

COREL
DRAW

Seminar Series

One Day
$129 in advance
$149 at the door

Two Days
$229 in advance

CALL (408) 252-5448

➤ The brochure cover is on the third column of page 1.

➤ The return address is placed on the middle column of page 1.

**Remember to follow the rule of thumb for brochure de-
sign: The gutters must be double the size of the outer
margins. That way, when the inner panels are folded and
the inner margins halved, they equal the outer margins.
For example, set .35-inch left and right margins and
.70-inch gutters between the columns.**

If you have more information than can fit in a three-panel brochure, you can use four panels on legal-size paper ($8\frac{1}{2}$ by 14 inches) in landscape orientation.

DIRECTORY ASSISTANCE

Let's say you have a database of names, addresses, and phone numbers, and you want to produce a directory, such as the one shown in Figure 16.6. Can you create this directory in your database or spreadsheet program? Probably not. Database software is designed for sorting, manipulating, and managing information, but report formatting is not its forte; however, this type of formatting is PageMaker's strength.

PageMaker includes filters for importing data from databases (such as dBASE) and spreadsheet programs (such as Excel and Lotus 1-2-3). The dBASE filter even offers a directory format option and lets you choose which fields you want to import. While these filters sound ideal for import-ing a database, you may find that they don't offer enough flexibility in the layout of your data. A case in point is the directory in Figure 16.6—you would not be able to produce this format using the dBASE, Excel, or 1-2-3 filters. So how did we import the data with this layout? We used Page-Maker's ASCII import filter.

FIGURE 16.6: *A club membership directory*

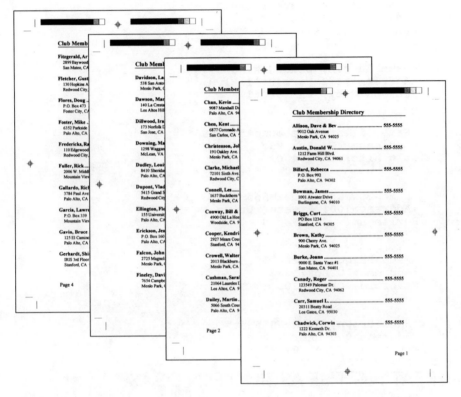

The data in the directory shown in Figure 16.6 was originally entered in dBASE III Plus, but it was exported to an ASCII file before being placed in PageMaker. Part of the ASCII file appears in Figure 16.7. Notice the two style tags, <Name> and <Address>, embedded in the ASCII file. Because the paragraphs are tagged, the text will automatically be formatted when it is imported. The asterisk between the name and phone number is a place-holder for a tab that you will find and replace in PageMaker's Story Editor. The Text-Only import filter will eliminate the extra blank lines.

Later in the chapter, we'll describe how to create properly formatted ASCII files in Lotus 1-2-3 and Excel.

FIGURE 16.7: *An ASCII file that was exported from dBASE III Plus*

```
<Name>Allison, Dave & Bev*555-5555
<Address>9012 Oak Avenue
Menlo Park, CA   94025


<Name>Austin, Donald W.*555-5555
<Address>1212 Farm Hill Blvd.
Redwood City, CA   94061


<Name>Billard, Rebecca*555-5555
<Address>P.O. Box 992
Palo Alto, CA   94302


<Name>Bowman, James*555-5555
<Address>1001 Atwater Drive
Burlingame, CA   94010


<Name>Briggs, Curt*555-5555
<Address>PO Box 1234
Stanford, CA   94305


<Name>Brown, Kathy*555-5555
<Address>900 Cherry Ave.
Menlo Park, CA   94025
```

CREATING THE ASCII FILE IN DBASE

The easiest way to design the layout of each directory entry is to use
dBASE's Create Label command. The mailing label generator allows up to
four lines of text per label. The database in our example has three lines:

- ➤ The name and phone number

- ➤ The street address

- ➤ The city, state, and zip code

Because you want multiple fields on a line, you need to use *string formulas*
to place the fields and text together on a single line. A plus sign goes
between each item, and text is enclosed in quotation marks. Here are the
three string formulas for our phone directory:

```
"<Name>"+trim(LNAME)+", "+trim(FNAME)+"*"+PHONE
```

```
"<Address>"+ADDRESS

Trim(CITY)+", "+STATE+"   "+ZIP
```

The field names are in capital letters; the style names are enclosed in brackets. To produce the ASCII file, issue the Label Form command, as follows:

```
LABEL FORM list TO list.txt
```

In the above command, *list* is the name of the existing label format, and *list.txt* is the name of the ASCII file that will be created with this command (the file shown in Figure 16.7).

CREATING THE DIRECTORY PUBLICATION

The most efficient page size to work with is the standard half-size page of $5\frac{1}{2}$ by $8\frac{1}{2}$ inches. This size doesn't require extra cutting, and you can easily make full-scale proofs and mock-ups on your laser printer. If you prefer a full-size page of $8\frac{1}{2}$ by 11 inches, you can fit two or more columns on a page, depending on the type size you use. Figure 16.8 shows an example of a two-column directory with a vertical rule between columns.

Follow these steps to create a directory publication:

1. Create a new file and specify the page dimensions and margins of your directory. Decide whether the publication is going to be single- or double-sided. Don't worry about the number of pages because extra pages will be inserted automatically when you place the file.

2. Go to the master pages and set up column guides and vertical rules if necessary.

3. Specify headers and footers on your master pages. Be sure to include a page number.

4. Create the styles for the directory. Our directory has the following two styles:

   Name: 12-point Times Roman, bold, right-aligned tab at 18p7 with leader dots, 1-pica before, keep with next 2 lines
   Address: 10-point Times Roman, 1-pica left indent

FIGURE 16.8: *One page of a two-column directory*

Club Membership Directory

Allison, Dave & Bev 555-5555
9012 Oak Avenue
Menlo Park, CA 94025

Austin, Donald W. 555-5555
1212 Farm Hill Blvd.
Redwood City, CA 94061

Billard, Rebecca 555-5555
P.O. Box 992
Palo Alto, CA 94302

Bowman, James 555-5555
1001 Atwater Drive
Burlingame, CA 94010

Briggs, Curt 555-5555
PO Box 1234
Stanford, CA 94305

Brown, Kathy 555-5555
900 Cherry Ave.
Menlo Park, CA 94025

Burke, Joann 555-5555
9000 E. Santa Ynez #1
San Mateo, CA 94401

Canady, Roger 555-5555
123549 Palomar Dr.
Redwood City, CA 94062

Carr, Samuel L. 555-5555
20311 Beatty Road
Los Gatos, CA 95030

Chadwick, Corwin 555-5555
1222 Kenneth Dr.
Palo Alto, CA 94303

Chan, Kevin 555-5555
9087 Marshall Drive
Palo Alto, CA 94303

Chen, Kent 555-5555
6877 Coronado Ave.
San Carlos, CA 94070

Christenson, John 555-5555
191 Oakley Ave.
Menlo Park, CA 94025

Clarke, Michael 555-5555
72101 Sixth Ave.
Redwood City, CA 94063

Connell, Les 555-5555
1637 Buckthorn Way
Menlo Park, CA 94025

Conway, Bill & Jane 555-5555
4900 Old La Honda Road
Woodside, CA 94062

Cooper, Kendric C. 555-5555
2927 Mears Court
Stanford, CA 94305

Crowell, Walter 555-5555
2013 Blackburn Ave.
Menlo Park, CA 94025

Cushman, Sarah 555-5555
21064 Laureles Drive
Los Altos, CA 94022

Dailey, Martin 555-5555
5066 South Court
Palo Alto, CA 94306

Davidson, Larry 555-5555
538 San Antonio Ave.
Menlo Park, CA 94025

Dawson, Martin E. 555-5555
140 La Cresta Drive
Los Altos Hills, CA 94022

Dillwood, Ira S. 555-5555
173 Norfolk Drive
San Jose, CA 95129

Downing, Mark 555-5555
1298 Waggaman Circle
McLean, VA 22101

Dudley, Louise 555-5555
8410 Sheridan
Palo Alto, CA 94306

Dupont, Vladimir 555-5555
5415 Grand St.
Redwood City, CA 94062

With these styles, there will be 1 pica of empty space between each listing in the directory, and the address lines will be indented 1 pica from the left. A series of dots will fill the space between the name and phone number because a tab with leader dots is specified as part of the Name style. Turning on the Keep with Next option ensures that a person's name and address will not be split between columns or pages.

IMPORTING THE ASCII FILE

When you place the ASCII file that contains the directory file, turn on the Read Tags option. Then, in the Text-Only Import Filter dialog box, turn on the Between Paragraphs option to remove the extra carriage returns in the file.

To flow the text, turn on the Autoflow option. PageMaker will automatically create extra pages for the imported text.

The imported text will already be formatted for three reasons: The file contained style names, you turned on the Read Tags option, and these styles were previously defined in PageMaker.

CLEANING UP THE IMPORTED TEXT

The amount of clean-up work you will have to do in the Story Editor depends on which program you used to create the data file. Lotus 1-2-3 and Excel files require a bit more work because the data is imported in a columnar format, so you must use the Story Editor's Change command to replace the tabs with carriage returns, as explained in the next section.

Because dBASE allows you to set up the data in a format that is similar to the final directory layout, all you need to do in the Story Editor is use the Change command to replace the asterisk placeholder (*) with a tab (^t is the tab code).

In a long directory, you might want to group together names that begin with the same letter and place the appropriate letter above each section. Figure 16.9 illustrates this layout.

FIGURE 16.9: *In this directory, names that begin with the same letter are grouped together.*

Club Membership Directory

A

Allison, Dave & Bev 555-5555
9012 Oak Avenue
Menlo Park, CA 94025

Austin, Donald W. 555-5555
1212 Farm Hill Blvd.
Redwood City, CA 94061

B

Billard, Rebecca 555-5555
P.O. Box 992
Palo Alto, CA 94302

Bowman, James 555-5555
1001 Atwater Drive
Burlingame, CA 94010

Briggs, Curt 555-5555
PO Box 1234
Stanford, CA 94305

Brown, Kathy 555-5555
900 Cherry Ave.
Menlo Park, CA 94025

Burke, Joann 555-5555
9000 E. Santa Ynez #1
San Mateo, CA 94401

C

Canady, Roger 555-5555
123549 Palomar Dr.
Redwood City, CA 94062

Carr, Samuel L. 555-5555
20311 Beatty Road
Los Gatos, CA 95030

Chadwick, Corwin 555-5555
1222 Kenneth Dr.
Palo Alto, CA 94303

Chan, Kevin 555-5555
9087 Marshall Drive
Palo Alto, CA 94303

Chen, Kent 555-5555
6877 Coronado Ave.
San Carlos, CA 94070

Christenson, John 555-5555
191 Oakley Ave.
Menlo Park, CA 94025

Clarke, Michael 555-5555
72101 Sixth Ave.
Redwood City, CA 94063

Connell, Les 555-5555
1637 Buckthorn Way
Menlo Park, CA 94025

Conway, Bill & Jane 555-5555
4900 Old La Honda Road
Woodside, CA 94062

Cooper, Kendric C. 555-5555
2927 Mears Court
Stanford, CA 94305

Crowell, Walter 555-5555
2013 Blackburn Ave.
Menlo Park, CA 94025

Cushman, Sarah 555-5555
21064 Laureles Drive
Los Altos, CA 94022

D

Dailey, Martin 555-5555
5066 South Court
Palo Alto, CA 94306

Davidson, Larry 555-5555
538 San Antonio Ave.
Menlo Park, CA 94025

Dawson, Martin E. 555-5555
140 La Cresta Drive
Los Altos Hills, CA 94022

IMPORTING SPREADSHEET DATA

Directory information can also be imported from a spreadsheet database. The procedure is similar to the one used to bring in dBASE data:

1. Create string formulas that combine the tag names, fields, and text.

2. Produce an ASCII file.

3. Use your word processor or PageMaker's Story Editor to clean up the ASCII file.

4. Create a publication in PageMaker.

5. Place the file.

In an Excel or Lotus 1-2-3 database, each field is in a separate column, and each record is in a separate row. Figures 16.10 and 16.11 show examples of

FIGURE 16.10: *An Excel database*

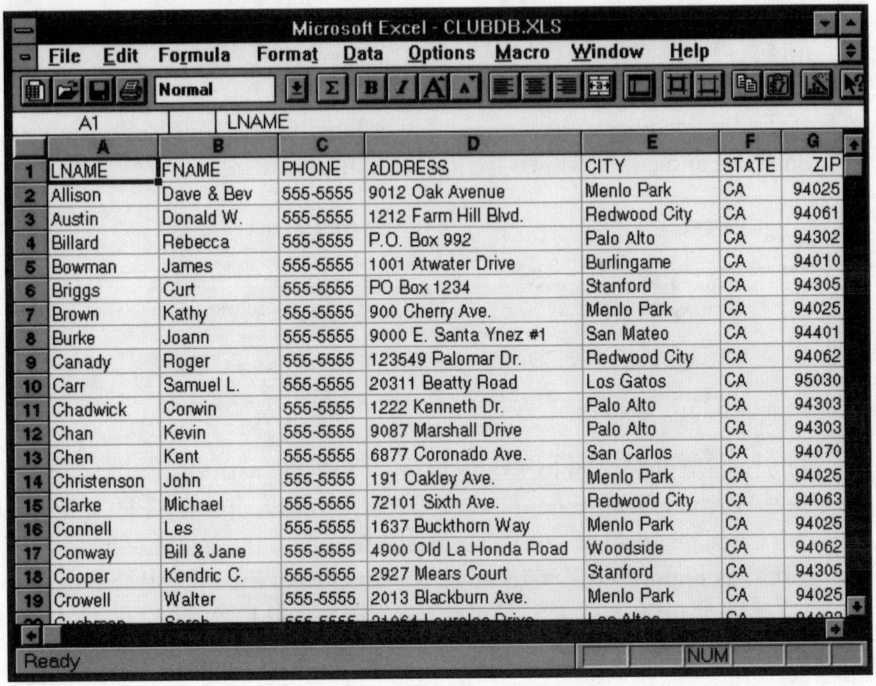

FIGURE 16.11: *A Lotus 1-2-3 database*

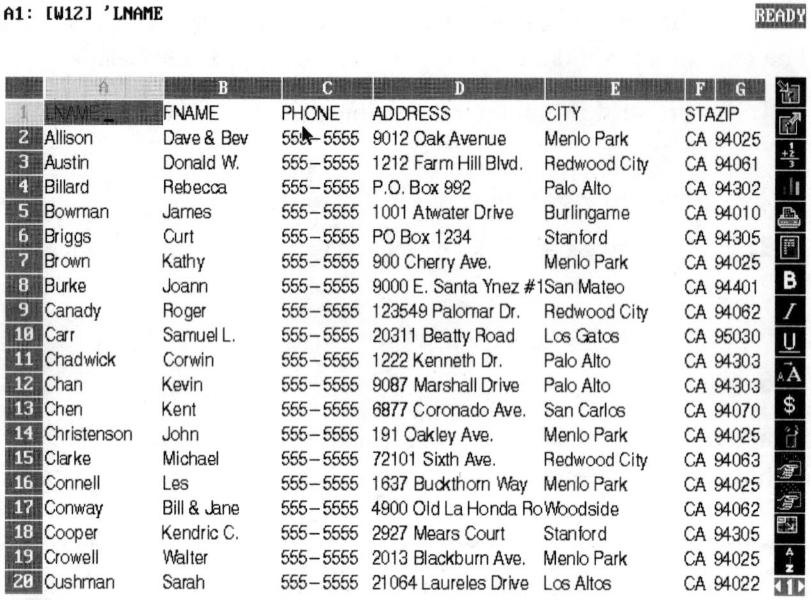

A1: [W12] 'LNAME   READY

	A	B	C	D	E	F	G
1	LNAME	FNAME	PHONE	ADDRESS	CITY	STA	ZIP
2	Allison	Dave & Bev	555-5555	9012 Oak Avenue	Menlo Park	CA	94025
3	Austin	Donald W.	555-5555	1212 Farm Hill Blvd.	Redwood City	CA	94061
4	Billard	Rebecca	555-5555	P.O. Box 992	Palo Alto	CA	94302
5	Bowman	James	555-5555	1001 Atwater Drive	Burlingame	CA	94010
6	Briggs	Curt	555-5555	PO Box 1234	Stanford	CA	94305
7	Brown	Kathy	555-5555	900 Cherry Ave.	Menlo Park	CA	94025
8	Burke	Joann	555-5555	9000 E. Santa Ynez #1	San Mateo	CA	94401
9	Canady	Roger	555-5555	123549 Palomar Dr.	Redwood City	CA	94062
10	Carr	Samuel L.	555-5555	20311 Beatty Road	Los Gatos	CA	95030
11	Chadwick	Corwin	555-5555	1222 Kenneth Dr.	Palo Alto	CA	94303
12	Chan	Kevin	555-5555	9087 Marshall Drive	Palo Alto	CA	94303
13	Chen	Kent	555-5555	6877 Coronado Ave.	San Carlos	CA	94070
14	Christenson	John	555-5555	191 Oakley Ave.	Menlo Park	CA	94025
15	Clarke	Michael	555-5555	72101 Sixth Ave.	Redwood City	CA	94063
16	Connell	Les	555-5555	1637 Buckthorn Way	Menlo Park	CA	94025
17	Conway	Bill & Jane	555-5555	4900 Old La Honda Ro	Woodside	CA	94062
18	Cooper	Kendric C.	555-5555	2927 Mears Court	Stanford	CA	94305
19	Crowell	Walter	555-5555	2013 Blackburn Ave.	Menlo Park	CA	94025
20	Cushman	Sarah	555-5555	21064 Laureles Drive	Los Altos	CA	94022

an Excel and a Lotus 1-2-3 database, respectively. You must create string formulas to combine the appropriate fields with tag names and text.

The following string formulas are entered in the cells to the right of the database and copied down the rows for all records:

EXCEL	LOTUS 1-2-3
="<Name>"&A2&"," &B2&"*"&C2	+"<Name>"&A2&"," &B2&"*"&C2
="<Address>"&D2	+"<Address>"&D2
=E2&","&F2&" "&G2	+E2&","&F2&" "&G2

The first formula combines the <Name> style tag with the LNAME field in cell A2, the FNAME field in cell B2, an asterisk, and the PHONE field in cell C2. The asterisk will be replaced with a tab in PageMaker. The second formula combines the <Address> style tag with the ADDRESS field in cell D2. The third formula combines the CITY (cell E2), STATE (cell F2), and

ZIP (cell G2) fields, inserts a comma between the city and state, and places two blank spaces before the zip code.

Creating an ASCII File in Excel

Figure 16.12 shows the results of the formulas after they have been copied in Excel. Follow these steps to create the ASCII file:

1. Copy the range of formulas to the Clipboard.

2. Paste the range into a new spreadsheet with the Paste Special command, using the Values option to convert the formulas to text.

3. Save the new spreadsheet as a text file (in the Save Worksheet As dialog box, display the Save File As Type drop-down list and choose Text).

FIGURE 16.12: *After copying the string formulas*

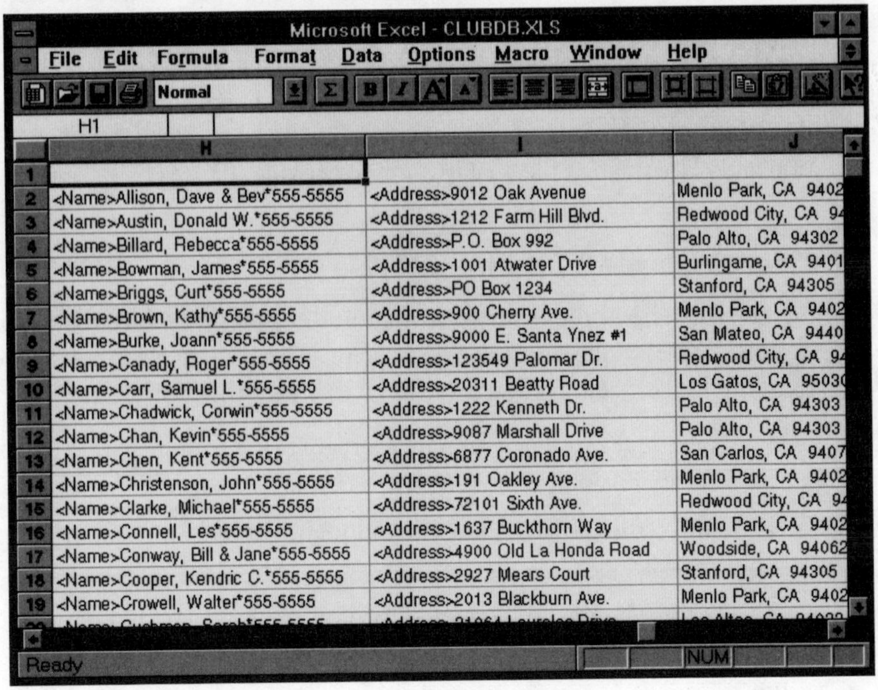

This text file, shown in Figure 16.13, has tabs between each column and quotation marks around the fields that contain commas. The tabs need to be replaced with carriage returns, the quotation marks need to be deleted, and the asterisk placeholders should be replaced with tabs. You can make these changes in your word processor or in the Story Editor.

FIGURE 16.13: *The ASCII file that was exported from Excel*

```
"<Name>Allison, Dave & Bev*555-5555"   <Address>9012 Oak Avenue       "Menlo Park, CA  94025"
"<Name>Austin, Donald W.*555-5555"     <Address>1212 Farm Hill Blvd. "Redwood City, CA  94061"
"<Name>Billard, Rebecca*555-5555"      <Address>P.O. Box 992 "Palo Alto, CA  94302"
"<Name>Bowman, James*555-5555"         <Address>1001 Atwater Drive    "Burlingame, CA  94010"
"<Name>Briggs, Curt*555-5555" <Address>PO Box 1234   "Stanford, CA  94305"
"<Name>Brown, Kathy*555-5555" <Address>900 Cherry Ave.       "Menlo Park, CA  94025"
"<Name>Burke, Joann*555-5555" <Address>9000 E. Santa Ynez #1      "San Mateo, CA  94401"
"<Name>Canady, Roger*555-5555"         <Address>123549 Palomar Dr.   "Redwood City, CA  94062"
"<Name>Carr, Samuel L.*555-5555"       <Address>20311 Beatty Road    "Los Gatos, CA  95030"
"<Name>Chadwick, Corwin*555-5555"      <Address>1222 Kenneth Dr.    "Palo Alto, CA  94303"
"<Name>Chan, Kevin*555-5555"  <Address>9087 Marshall Drive  "Palo Alto, CA  94303"
"<Name>Chen, Kent*555-5555"   <Address>6877 Coronado Ave.    "San Carlos, CA  94070"
```

If you didn't use your word processor to clean up the ASCII file, load the Story Editor and place the text file with the Convert Quotes and Read Tags options turned off. (You don't want the tags read just yet because you are editing the file first.) Use the Change command to replace the tabs (^t) with carriage returns (^p), eliminate all the quotation marks by replacing them with nothing, and replace the asterisks with tabs. Then export the text to an ASCII file and exit from the Story Editor. Finally, turn on the Autoflow option and place the text file, making sure to activate the Read Tags option.

Creating an ASCII File in 1-2-3

Figure 16.14 shows the first two string formulas after they have been copied in Lotus 1-2-3. Make sure the columns are at least three characters wider than the longest cell. Follow these steps to create the ASCII file:

1. Issue the /Print File command and enter a file name with a TXT extension.

2. Choose the Range command and highlight the range of formulas.

3. Set the Margins to None and turn on the Unformatted option.

4. Choose Go to create the ASCII file.

FIGURE 16.14: *After the string formulas have been copied*

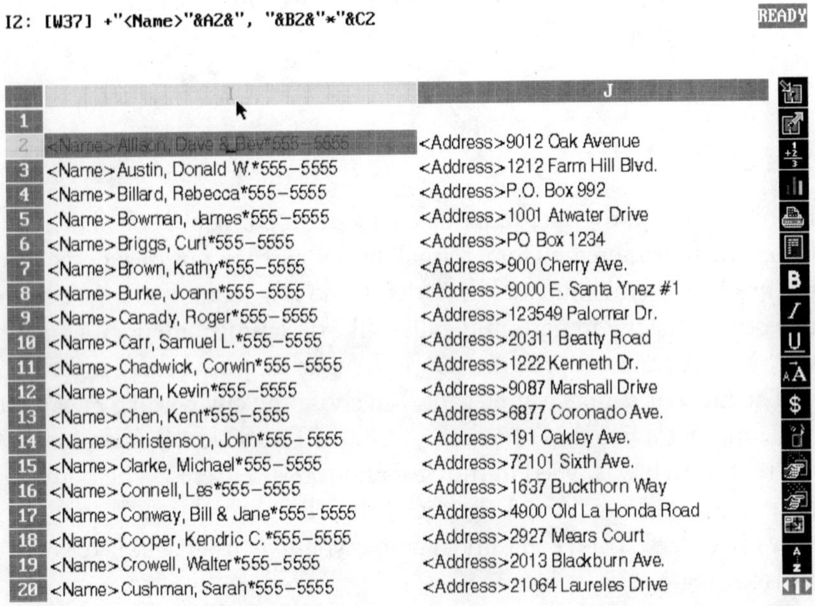

I2: [W37] +"<Name>"&A2&", "&B2&"*"&C2   `READY`

	J
<Name>Allison, Dave & Bev*555-5555	<Address>9012 Oak Avenue
<Name>Austin, Donald W.*555-5555	<Address>1212 Farm Hill Blvd.
<Name>Billard, Rebecca*555-5555	<Address>P.O. Box 992
<Name>Bowman, James*555-5555	<Address>1001 Atwater Drive
<Name>Briggs, Curt*555-5555	<Address>PO Box 1234
<Name>Brown, Kathy*555-5555	<Address>900 Cherry Ave.
<Name>Burke, Joann*555-5555	<Address>9000 E. Santa Ynez #1
<Name>Canady, Roger*555-5555	<Address>123549 Palomar Dr.
<Name>Carr, Samuel L.*555-5555	<Address>20311 Beatty Road
<Name>Chadwick, Corwin*555-5555	<Address>1222 Kenneth Dr.
<Name>Chan, Kevin*555-5555	<Address>9087 Marshall Drive
<Name>Chen, Kent*555-5555	<Address>6877 Coronado Ave.
<Name>Christenson, John*555-5555	<Address>191 Oakley Ave.
<Name>Clarke, Michael*555-5555	<Address>72101 Sixth Ave.
<Name>Connell, Les*555-5555	<Address>1637 Buckthorn Way
<Name>Conway, Bill & Jane*555-5555	<Address>4900 Old La Honda Road
<Name>Cooper, Kendric C.*555-5555	<Address>2927 Mears Court
<Name>Crowell, Walter*555-5555	<Address>2013 Blackburn Ave.
<Name>Cushman, Sarah*555-5555	<Address>21064 Laureles Drive

This text file, shown in Figure 16.15, has spaces between each column. The spaces need to be replaced with carriage returns, so that each field is on a separate line.

Load the Story Editor and import the text file with the Read Tags option turned off. In the Text-Only Import Filter dialog box, turn on the Replace 3 or More Spaces with Tab option. (This is why you should make sure that there are at least three spaces between the columns in 1-2-3.)

Then use the Story Editor's Change command to replace the tabs (^t) with carriage returns (^p), and replace the asterisks with tabs. Export the

FIGURE 16.15: *The ASCII file exported from 1-2-3*

```
<Name>Allison, Dave & Bev*555-5555    <Address>9012 Oak Avenue        Menlo Park, CA  94025
<Name>Austin, Donald W.*555-5555      <Address>1212 Farm Hill Blvd.   Redwood City, CA  94061
<Name>Billard, Rebecca*555-5555       <Address>P.O. Box 992           Palo Alto, CA  94302
<Name>Bowman, James*555-5555          <Address>1001 Atwater Drive     Burlingame, CA  94010
<Name>Briggs, Curt*555-5555           <Address>PO Box 1234            Stanford, CA  94305
<Name>Brown, Kathy*555-5555           <Address>900 Cherry Ave.        Menlo Park, CA  94025
<Name>Burke, Joann*555-5555           <Address>9000 E. Santa Ynez #1  San Mateo, CA  94401
<Name>Canady, Roger*555-5555          <Address>123549 Palomar Dr.     Redwood City, CA  94062
<Name>Carr, Samuel L.*555-5555        <Address>20311 Beatty Road      Los Gatos, CA  950303
<Name>Chadwick, Corwin*555-5555       <Address>1222 Kenneth Dr.       Palo Alto, CA  94303
<Name>Chan, Kevin*555-5555            <Address>9087 Marshall Drive    Palo Alto, CA  94303
<Name>Chen, Kent*555-5555             <Address>6877 Coronado Ave.     San Carlos, CA  94070
```

text to an ASCII file and exit from the Story Editor. Your last step is to turn on the Autoflow option and place the text file, with the Read Tags option turned on.

THE MENU, PLEASE

It only seems appropriate to include a menu in our cookbook. The menu in Figure 16.16 was created for a formal dinner party in our new home. Since the meal was being prepared by a friend who is a gourmet chef, we had time to worry about the important details—like designing a menu. Our guests were so delighted with the menu, we thought we would share it with others.

The menu is simple, yet elegant. We chose the cursive-like Zapf Chancery font, but if you don't have this font, try Times New Roman italic. All the text, which was typed in the Story Editor, is centered. The border is a piece of clip art from Arts & Letters. Most clip-art collections contain a variety of borders. If you can't find a border you like, use PageMaker's drawing tools to create one.

We created the menu on a landscape $8\frac{1}{2}$-by-11-inch page, with $\frac{1}{2}$-inch margins all the way around. As Figure 16.17 shows, we made a copy of the perfected menu and placed the two menus side by side. We also drew hairline crop marks with the rule tool to indicate the final menu size. The menus were printed on an ivory-colored card stock and trimmed to $5\frac{1}{2}$ by 7 inches with two swoops of the paper cutter.

If you are creating a restaurant menu, be sure to take the room's lighting and the customers' eyesight into consideration when selecting a typeface, size, and ink color. Eight-point Zapf Chancery in pale rose ink would not be easy to read in candle light. In general, you shouldn't choose a very small typeface.

FIGURE 16.16: *A simple menu for a not-so-simple dinner*

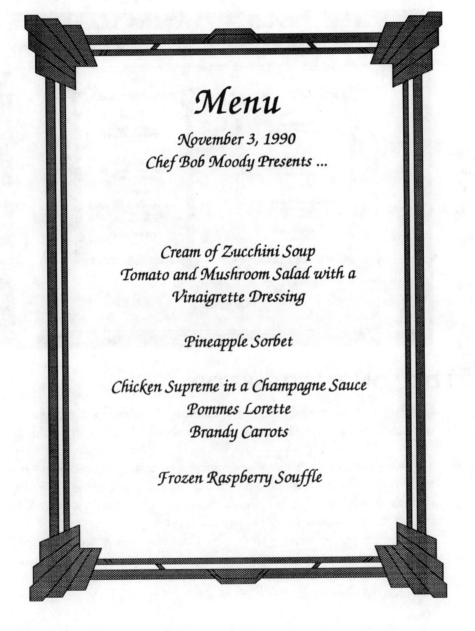

Menu

November 3, 1990
Chef Bob Moody Presents ...

Cream of Zucchini Soup
Tomato and Mushroom Salad with a
Vinaigrette Dressing

Pineapple Sorbet

Chicken Supreme in a Champagne Sauce
Pommes Lorette
Brandy Carrots

Frozen Raspberry Souffle

FIGURE 16.17: *Two menus are placed side-by-side with crop marks.*

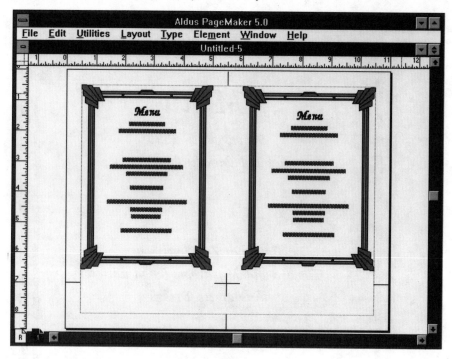

"I DO" ON THE DESKTOP

Contrary to claims made by those who know us, we did not exchange our wedding vows via fax machine, nor did the proposal take place on the Aldus Forum on CompuServe. On all other counts of electronic romance during our 1989 wedding, we plead guilty. Our computers, especially our desktop-publishing software, played a prominent role in the wedding plans. In fact, amid the frustrations and headaches of planning the event, self-publishing our wedding invitations and program proved to be a relaxing experience.

When you are designing your own wedding materials, you can take advantage of the fact that you'll have a sympathetic and forgiving audience. Feel free to create a document that reflects your personalities and have some fun in the process.

CREATING AN INVITATION

Our wedding invitation, shown in Figures 16.18 (the cover) and 16.19 (the inside), has a simple design. The cover was created in CorelDRAW and exported to an EPS file. The rose came from the Arts & Letters clip-art collection. The font used for the invitation text is Park Avenue, a light, cursive typeface.

When determining the dimensions of your invitation, keep in mind that it must fit inside a standard-size envelope. Our invitation's dimensions were 6 by 4$^1/_2$ inches.

In addition to the invitation, we designed return envelopes and reply cards, all set in Park Avenue. The master copies were printed on a 1270-dpi Linotronic imagesetter (see Appendix C), and a print shop printed the invitations on a white, textured card stock.

PRODUCING A PROGRAM

Another item you can produce for a wedding is a program to hand out at the ceremony.

FIGURE 16.18:   *The front cover of the wedding invitation*

FIGURE 16.19:   *The inside text of the wedding invitation*

*Your friendship and love have touched their lives and
you are invited to share in the wedding celebration for*

Rebecca Ruth   &   Frederick Ronald
daughter of   son of
Edwin and Marjorie Bridges   David and Beverly Altman

*The huppah will be raised at five o'clock on
Sunday, August 27, 1989.*

*Congregation Beth Am
26790 Arastradero Road
Los Altos Hills, California*

The cover of our program contained our names and wedding date in addition to the arched type and rose that we used on the wedding invitation.
The text on the two inside pages, shown in Figure 16.20, uses only three
paragraph styles. The Head style (*The Ceremony* and *The Supporting Cast*)
is 20-point University Roman with a 1-point rule below. The Subhead style
(*The Processional, Candle Lighting,* and so on) is 13-point University Roman. It is indented on the left and has extra space above. The Body Text
style is 9-point Helvetica Light, indented on the left.

Because there wasn't a PostScript Hebrew typeface available at the time,
we used a greeting card with the word *Shalom* printed on it to create the
background on the inside pages. Using a hand-held scanner, we produced a
TIFF file and brought it into CorelDRAW. After tracing each letter, we
grouped them together as a word and assigned it a 20% shade. This was too
dark, so we switched to a 12% shade. When creating background art such

FIGURE 16.20:   *The inside pages of the wedding program*

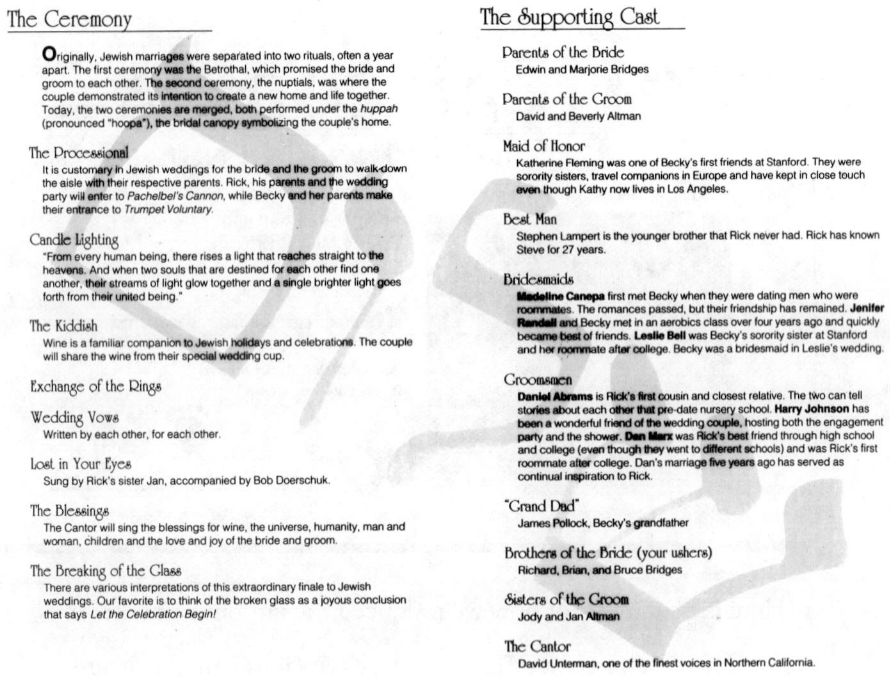

The Ceremony

Originally, Jewish marriages were separated into two rituals, often a year apart. The first ceremony was the Betrothal, which promised the bride and groom to each other. The second ceremony, the nuptials, was where the couple demonstrated its intention to create a new home and life together. Today, the two ceremonies are merged, both performed under the *huppah* (pronounced "hoopa"), the bridal canopy symbolizing the couple's home.

The Processional
It is customary in Jewish weddings for the bride and the groom to walk down the aisle with their respective parents. Rick, his parents and the wedding party will enter to *Pachelbel's Cannon*, while Becky and her parents make their entrance to *Trumpet Voluntary*.

Candle Lighting
"From every human being, there rises a light that reaches straight to the heavens. And when two souls that are destined for each other find one another, their streams of light glow together and a single brighter light goes forth from their united being."

The Kiddish
Wine is a familiar companion to Jewish holidays and celebrations. The couple will share the wine from their special wedding cup.

Exchange of the Rings

Wedding Vows
Written by each other, for each other.

Lost in Your Eyes
Sung by Rick's sister Jan, accompanied by Bob Doerschuk.

The Blessings
The Cantor will sing the blessings for wine, the universe, humanity, man and woman, children and the love and joy of the bride and groom.

The Breaking of the Glass
There are various interpretations of this extraordinary finale to Jewish weddings. Our favorite is to think of the broken glass as a joyous conclusion that says *Let the Celebration Begin!*

The Supporting Cast

Parents of the Bride
Edwin and Marjorie Bridges

Parents of the Groom
David and Beverly Altman

Maid of Honor
Katherine Fleming was one of Becky's first friends at Stanford. They were sorority sisters, travel companions in Europe and have kept in close touch even though Kathy now lives in Los Angeles.

Best Man
Stephen Lampert is the younger brother that Rick never had. Rick has known Steve for 27 years.

Bridesmaids
Madeline Canepa first met Becky when they were dating men who were roommates. The romances passed, but their friendship has remained. **Jenifer Randall** and Becky met in an aerobics class over four years ago and quickly became best of friends. **Leslie Bell** was Becky's sorority sister at Stanford and her roommate after college. Becky was a bridesmaid in Leslie's wedding.

Groomsmen
Daniel Abrams is Rick's first cousin and closest relative. The two can tell stories about each other that pre-date nursery school. **Harry Johnson** has been a wonderful friend of the wedding couple, hosting both the engagement party and the shower. **Dan Marx** was Rick's best friend through high school and college (even though they went to different schools) and was Rick's first roommate after college. Dan's marriage five years ago has served as continual inspiration to Rick.

"Grand Dad"
James Pollock, Becky's grandfather

Brothers of the Bride (your ushers)
Richard, Brian, and Bruce Bridges

Sisters of the Groom
Jody and Jan Altman

The Cantor
David Unterman, one of the finest voices in Northern California.

as this, it's better to err on the side of too light than to have the artwork overshadow the text.

Again, the masters were printed on a high-resolution typesetting machine. We even matched the ink to the color of the bridesmaid's dresses: teal. We took a swatch of material over to the print shop and matched it to a PMS color. The paper was the color of the bride's ivory wedding dress. How's that for color coordination?

BIRTH ANNOUNCEMENTS

One week after we received the long-awaited 5.0 beta version of Page-Maker, we received another much-anticipated bundle—our daughter Erica. Computer-nerds that we are, we thought it only appropriate that we design our birth announcement on a PC. The result is shown in Figure 16.21.

FIGURE 16.21: *The authors' birth announcement for their baby who was born during the writing of this book*

Here is a summary of how we produced the announcement:

➤ The announcement uses the TrueType font called Brittanic.

➤ The series of lines at the top were created with the rectangle tool, using a horizontal-line fill pattern; the lines were set to None.

➤ The "X" next to the signature line was pasted in from the Windows Character Map accessory; this character is from the Zapf Dingbats font.

➤ The photograph and footprints were scanned into the computer using Logitech's ScanMan 256 hand-held scanner. The photograph was touched up in CorelPAINT and exported to a TIFF file. The footprints were traced in CorelDRAW and exported to a WMF file. The quality of the photo isn't great, but we didn't have many photographs to choose from and we were in a hurry to get the announcements out. Because this announcement was for the eyes of family and friends, perfection wasn't an issue. For a more professional look, we would have used a higher-grade scanner, or perhaps stripped in the photo rather than scanning it.

➤ We printed the announcements directly onto card stock at 800 dpi. There were two reasons why we chose this route rather than produce an original and have a copy or print shop make copies: quality and time. A photocopy machine at a local copy center would have murdered the scanned image, turning it into mud. We could have taken our original to a commercial printer, but then we would have lost a week, not to mention a few hundred dollars.

SUMMARY

In this book's final chapter, you saw samples of a variety of publications that can be produced in PageMaker. All these projects follow the basic DTP recipe you learned back in Chapter 1:

➤ Create a file.

➤ Add your basic ingredients: text and graphics.

➤ Spice it up with up some formatting.

➤ Save and print it.

Most of the publication ingredients come from other software packages. For example, the resume text was imported from a word processing file, the data in the membership directory came from dBASE, and the cover of the wedding invitation was created in CorelDRAW. PageMaker is simply the kitchen where your publications are prepared.

αPPENDICES

A   B   C   D

*I*nstalling
*P*ageMaker 5.0

NSTALLING PAGEMAKER ON YOUR
computer is not difficult; Aldus provides a guided installation that essentially holds your hand through the process of copying the program floppy
disks to your hard disk. Installation takes approximately 30 minutes.

HARDWARE AND SOFTWARE REQUIREMENTS

To run PageMaker on your computer, you need the following hardware and
software setup:

- An IBM PC or compatible computer with an 80286, 80386, or
  80486 processor

- At least 4 megabytes (MB) of memory (RAM); 8 MB is
  recommended

- Windows 3.1

- Depending on how much of the package you install, 7 to 15 MB
  of free hard disk space

- A VGA or Super VGA video card

- A Windows 3.1-compatible mouse

- A printer supported by Windows 3.1 (for example, PostScript or
  Hewlett-Packard LaserJet)

RUNNING THE ALDUS SETUP PROGRAM

The PageMaker disk labeled Disk 1 includes an installation program, called ALDSETUP, which takes you through the complete process of copying PageMaker to your hard disk.

To speed up the installation process, close any open applications.

Follow these steps to run the Setup program:

1. If necessary, load Windows. The Windows Program Manager should be displayed.

2. Insert Disk 1 into your floppy disk drive.

3. Pull down the File menu and choose Run.

4. Type **A:\ALDSETUP** or **B:\ALDSETUP**, depending on which floppy disk drive you are using.

5. Click on OK.

CHOOSING INSTALLATION OPTIONS

When the Setup program is loaded, you see the window shown in Figure A.1. Here, you choose which parts of the program you want to install. The Install Everything option copies all the options on the list: the PageMaker 5.0 program, the tutorial, all the import and export filters, all the Additions, and the printer files you select. The advantage to choosing this option is that you needn't make any decisions as to which filters and Additions to install. On the down side, this installation will clutter your hard disk with files you'll never need.

FIGURE A.1: *The Aldus Setup Main window*

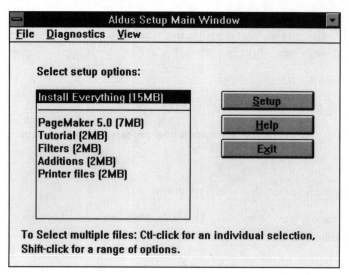

An alternative to installing everything is a custom installation in which you select one or more of the following options:

PageMaker 5.0   The main program and the Table Editor. It includes several Additions (Open Template and the Library palette), import filters (MacPaint, PC Paintbrush, Rich Text Format, ASCII import, TIFF, and Windows bitmap), and the ASCII export filter.

Tutorial   An online tutorial to help you learn PageMaker.

Filters   *Filters* allow you to import and export files to and from other programs such as word processors, spreadsheets, graphics packages, and so on. You choose which filters to install.

Additions   *Additions* either automate a PageMaker task or offer a capability not otherwise available in PageMaker.

Printer files These files contain specific information about a variety of PostScript printers and Hewlett-Packard printers with PostScript cartridges. You do not need to choose this option if you don't have a PostScript device, or if you won't be using a service bureau to print PostScript files.

At the very minimum, you should select the PageMaker 5.0 and Filters options. To select or deselect multiple options, hold down Ctrl as you click on the item. When you are done selecting options, click on the Setup button.

You will then have a chance to change the default paths for the Page-Maker program. C:\ALDUS is the default path for files that can be used with other Aldus products. C:\PM5 is the default path for PageMaker-specific files. Type a new path if necessary, making sure you include the drive and subdirectory name, and then click on OK.

If you selected the Filters, Additions, or Printer Files options, you will be asked to choose specific files to install. If you chose the Install Everything option, you will only be prompted to select printer files. See "Selecting Printer Files" later in this appendix.

SELECTING FILTERS

Filter selection is one of the most important parts of installation. It determines which types of files can be imported into and exported from Page-Maker. The available filters are listed on the left side of the Select Filters dialog box, shown in Figure A.2.

If you have enough disk space, you can choose the Select All button to install all the filters. However, the complete set of filters consumes about 2 MB of hard disk space, so we suggest that you install only the ones you are likely to use. Also, the more filters you install, the longer it will take to load PageMaker. You should begin by installing a filter for your word processing program (for example, WordPerfect or Word for Windows), and for your spreadsheet program (such as Excel or Lotus 1-2-3). Be sure to select the appropriate version number.

FIGURE A.2: *The Select Filters dialog box*

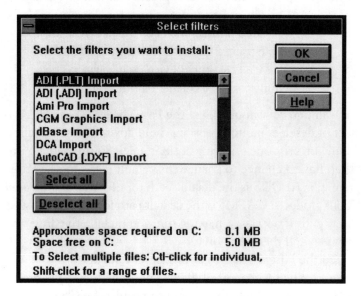

In addition, we recommend that you install these filters:

- Text-Only Import
- PageMaker Pub (.PM5) Import
- PageMaker Template (.PT5) Import
- Table Editor Import
- Windows Metafile Import
- EPS Import
- ASCII Text Export
- One of the other export filters, such as WordPerfect or Microsoft Word

Follow these steps to select filters:

1. To select all filters, click on the Select All button. Or, to select certain filters, hold down Ctrl and click on each filter you want to install.

The bottom of the dialog box lets you know how much space is required for the items you have selected, and the amount of space that is free on the drive on which you are installing PageMaker. Keep your eye on these figures to make sure you have adequate disk space.

2. To display additional filters, use the scroll bar.

3. When you are finished selecting filters, click on OK.

SELECTING ADDITIONS

If you selected the Additions option in the Aldus Setup Main Window, you will be prompted to select which Additions you want to install. The procedure for selecting Additions is just like the one for selecting filters. For a description of the Additions, see Appendix D in this book.

SELECTING PRINTER FILES

The Select Printer Devices dialog box, shown in Figure A.3, lets you select the manufacturer and model number of your PostScript device. If you will be giving a service bureau PostScript files to print on a high-quality imagesetter, you should also select the appropriate device from the list. To select multiple devices, hold down Ctrl as you click on the item. When you're finished, click on OK.

PERSONALIZING YOUR PROGRAM

The next dialog box you are presented with is called Personalize Your Program. In this box, you need to fill in your name and company name, along with the serial number of your PageMaker program. You can find this number on Disk 2 if you are a new PageMaker user. If you are upgrading to Version 5.0, use the serial number from your previous version; the number is located on the bottom of the PageMaker 3.0 or 4.0 product box, in the startup screen of 4.0, or inside the front cover of the 3.0 manual.

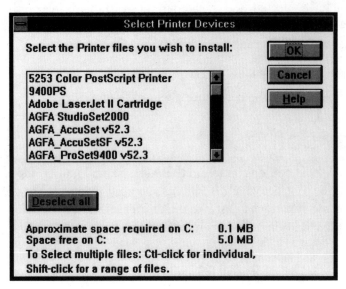

The information you enter here will appear each time you load Page-
Maker. Follow these steps to personalize your program:

1. Type your name in the box underneath Name. You can enter
   your whole name or just your first or last name. If several people
   will be using the same copy of PageMaker on the same computer, enter a department name. The name can be from 1 to 63
   characters long.

2. Press Tab to move the cursor to the box underneath Company.

3. Type your company name. You can use up to 63 characters.

4. Press Tab.

5. Type your complete serial number, including hyphens.

6. Click on OK.

If you made a mistake in typing your serial number, you will see a message
indicating that you entered an invalid serial number. If this happens, click
on Continue and repeat steps 5 and 6 above. You cannot install PageMaker
until you enter a valid serial number.

COMPLETING INSTALLATION

If your drive has insufficient space to install PageMaker with all the options you specified, you will see the dialog box shown in Figure A.4. As the box indicates, you can delete files to make room for PageMaker. Calculate how much additional space you need by subtracting the space required from the space available. Then load the Windows File Manager, and delete files you no longer need. If you still don't have enough space, an alternative is to install fewer options; for example, don't install the tutorial or select fewer filters. To do this, you would have to choose the Cancel option and repeat the installation procedure.

Assuming you have sufficient disk space, the Setup program will then install the files from the floppy disks to the path you specified. It will prompt you when you need to switch disks. The horizontal bar that you see on your screen indicates how much of the program has been installed. For example, when the bar is halfway across the box, you are halfway through the installation process.

When installation is complete, you will see a window that informs you that a program group has been created for PageMaker and related programs. Click on Continue.

FIGURE A.4:   *The warning dialog box that appears when you have insufficient disk space*

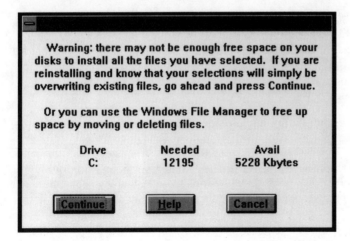

If you aren't installing printer drivers, installation is over and you can exit the Aldus Setup program. Otherwise, proceed to the next section.

INSTALLING A PRINTER IN WINDOWS' CONTROL PANEL

In some cases you may need to install a printer driver. If it's necessary, the Aldus Setup program will take you right into Windows' Control Panel:

1. Click on the Add button in the Printers control panel.

2. Make sure Install Unlisted or Updated Printer is selected and click on the Install button.

3. Place your last PageMaker disk in your floppy drive and enter this drive when prompted (**A:** or **B:**) and choose OK.

4. Select PostScript Printer, or select one of the other printers on the list.

5. Choose OK, and follow the instructions on-screen.

STARTING PAGEMAKER

When you install PageMaker, a program group called Aldus is created in your Windows Program Manager. This group, shown in Figure A.5, contains the icons for loading PageMaker, the Setup program, the Table Editor, and the Tutorial. Follow these steps to load PageMaker:

1. Load Windows.

The Aldus program group may already be open, as in Figure A.5. If it is, skip to step 3.

2. Move the mouse pointer to the Aldus group icon and double-click.

FIGURE A.5: *The Aldus group window*

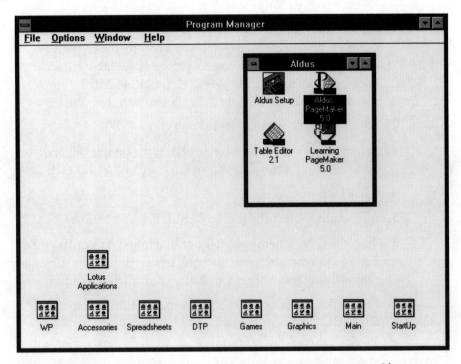

A window appears containing the Aldus group's program icons. If you see a menu instead of the window, you didn't click the button correctly. Press Esc and try again.

   3. Move the mouse pointer to the PageMaker 5.0 icon, and double-click the left mouse button. The PageMaker program will be loaded, and after 30 seconds or so, you will see the menu bar at the top of the screen.

MODIFYING YOUR PAGEMAKER SETUP

After you begin using PageMaker, you might discover that you need to install some of the items you skipped over in the initial installation, or perhaps you need to install additional import/export filters. To install additional items, follow these general steps:

1. In the Aldus group, double-click on the Aldus Setup icon. After a moment, you will be asked to choose a control file (PM5_144.CTL or PM5_12M.CTL). The control file lets PageMaker know the size of disk you are using (PM5_144.CTL is for 1.44 MB 3$\frac{1}{2}$-inch disks; PM5_12M.CTL is for 1.2 MB 5$\frac{1}{4}$-inch disks).

2. Select the CTL file on your list and choose OK.

3. Select the item(s) you wish to install (for example, Filters). To select multiple items, hold down Ctrl as you click on each one.

4. Click on Setup.

5. If prompted, select the files to be installed and choose OK.

6. Type the drive where you are installing from (**A:** or **B:**). Before you choose OK, make sure you have a disk in the drive (any disk will do); you will get a disk error if the drive is empty.

7. Follow the instructions on the screen, inserting the specified floppy disks when prompted.

8. The Setup program may ask you to install printer drivers. If you have already done this, click on the Close button.

9. Exit the Setup program.

Working with Fonts

NE OF THE MOST WELCOME aspects of PageMaker 5.0 is its unconditional support for Windows 3.1's TrueType faces. We choose the word "unconditional" deliberately, as Version 4.0 offered support for this new typeface format seemingly according to the roll of the dice. About half of the approximately 500 users we have encountered say that they can use TrueType fonts with PageMaker 4.0; about half say they can't. The percentage should change to 100 percent success with Version 5.0.

Users of PostScript typefaces should enjoy equal levels of support. In fact, the entire landscape of typeface use and management has changed significantly since the last release of PageMaker, mostly for the better.

BYE-BYE, BITMAPS

There is no doubt what the best change is: the widespread acceptance of outline typeface formats, ushered in by Adobe Type Manager (ATM) and TrueType. We don't want to give complexes to those who still use fixed-size, bitmapped fonts on older laser printers, but we have to be honest here—it's time to make a change.

While Windows applications still support the use of bitmapped fonts, the present and the future of electronic typefaces lie with typeface outlines, like the ones generated by ATM and TrueType. An outline typeface creates fonts of any size for both the screen and the printer. In other words, with the outline of, say, Helvetica or Swiss Black installed on your system, you can set type in PageMaker in any size, any color, and any angle, and see the type on your screen and print it on your printer.

ATM is Adobe's type management system, designed to support the vast supply of Type 1 PostScript faces on the market today. Adobe Type 1 faces are thought by many to be the highest quality typefaces, and they are the de facto language of the high-resolution service bureau industry.

The TrueType format was brought to Windows in 1992 in an attempt to integrate into Windows a single font-imaging engine for all users. (Many will say the attempt was really to bring Adobe down a notch or two from its position of authority in the typeface industry, but that's another story.) TrueType is both a typeface format and a font management tool, offering convenience, speed, and potentially high-quality typefaces to many hundreds of thousands of LaserJet users. TrueType faces also work with Post-Script printers—as you might imagine, this has not been particularly happy news at Adobe. Ultimately, though, the competition has been good for all, as Adobe's latest release, ATM 2.5, offers markedly better support for non-PostScript printers, while TrueType developers know that they must hold to a very high standard of typeface quality established by Adobe. Users win either way.

We paint with a broad brush here, but in general, TrueType faces perform better at the printer, while Type 1 faces tend to look better. TrueType faces are quicker to spool and quicker to print, thanks to a very efficient character-downloading scheme that sends only those characters needed; this is in contrast to ATM's method of downloading the entire character set to the printer, without regard for which characters are actually being called into service.

Type 1 faces, on the other hand, have a tradition of excellence, while TrueType faces have yet to earn such stripes. Kerning pairs…professional hinting…expert sets…small capitals…ligatures—these features (available almost exclusively in Type 1) are the domain of professional typesetters, who would not entrust their publications to anything but the best.

In short, ATM is the gateway to Adobe's library of high-quality, professionally-rendered typefaces, while TrueType is the road to many hundreds of low-cost, speedy, and convenient typefaces.

INSTALLING AND USING TYPEFACES

We look back on our last edition of this book and we laugh. This section was one of the most lengthy ones in the book, so complex and varied were the ways to get fonts into Windows. But today, we can practically skip this section—installing ATM or TrueType faces is a breeze.

ADDING ATM TYPEFACES

ATM adds its own icon to Program Manager when installed, and it provides a clean, friendly set of tools for adding or removing typefaces. Run the ATM control panel, click on the Add button, navigate to the drive containing your font disk, and double-click on the desired typefaces. Done.

As of Version 2.5, you do not need to exit and reenter Windows in order to see newly-added typefaces, but applications open during a font installation will need to be closed and reopened before they can make use of the new faces.

ADDING TRUETYPE FACES

Adding a TrueType face to your system is just as easy—maybe even easier, as you don't have to use any third-party tools at all. Since TrueType support is built into Windows, all you need to do is run Control Panel, located in your Main program group, unless you moved it. Click on Fonts, click on Add, find the typeface(s) and click on OK.

By default, Windows places all TrueType outlines in the SYSTEM directory under Windows, a very crowded piece of real estate. We suggest you create a special subdirectory for your TrueType faces. Manually copy your new TrueType font files to this subdirectory. Then, in the Add Fonts dialog box, instruct Windows not to "Copy Fonts to Windows Directory" when adding typefaces.

The other caveat with TrueType faces has to do with removing them. Windows, in its finite wisdom, displays the system fonts in the same list that shows TTF faces, and the unsuspecting user could easily remove them. If you do this, you might end up with Courier or a hideous stick-figure font when you pull down menus and open dialog boxes. Make sure that when you remove typefaces with Control Panel, you pick only those that display "TrueType" in parentheses after them.

With ATM or TrueType faces, you don't need to worry about screen fonts—they are produced on the fly, for all practical sizes. The only thing you might want to concern yourself with is the number of typefaces you have installed. There was a time when the standard set of 35 PostScript typefaces was considered an embarrassment of riches. And those who were introduced to outline type by TrueType practically swooned over having Arial, Times New Roman, and Wingdings. But today, programs like Corel-DRAW, offering 250 typefaces with the software, and companies like Bit-stream, offering type packages at $19, have given new meaning to the term "typeface library."

Have you become one of the type mongers? Are you not satisfied until you have 500 typefaces at your beck and call? Do you yearn to watch Page-Maker fill the screen when you choose the Type ➤ Font command? That's all fine and well, but know the consequences of your new-found addiction: Your system will run slower with all of those typefaces in memory. Windows will take longer to load, most programs will require more time to display their font dialog boxes, and PageMaker will take significantly longer to load.

Test this for yourself by removing some of your typefaces and checking performance. You might find that you may be able to do without your 20 billion typefaces after all.

A QUESTION OF RESIDENCY

If you are using TrueType faces, you need not worry about whether you remembered to download your typeface to the printer before sending that 250-page document. To date, TrueType doesn't reside in your printer; it resides in your computer, and Windows sees to it that the required face is sent with every job. Like we said before—TrueType is quintessentially convenient.

If you are using ATM with a non-PostScript printer, you don't have to worry either, as ATM automatically creates renditions of its Type 1 outlines and sends them off to the printer.

If you are using ATM with a PostScript printer, you have the opportunity to use what many consider the finest electronic typefaces in the world today, but that luxury comes with a price tag. If you venture past the 35 typefaces that live in most PostScript printers, you must deal with the dreaded downloading issue. You must figure out how you are going to get your nice Type 1 font to the printer.

You have two choices: You can tell Windows to send the typeface to the printer as a print job begins, or you can send it to the printer yourself beforehand. When you add a typeface with ATM, you can designate which way you want a typeface to be handled. Let's say you have just added Garamond-Light to your system, a typeface that is not part of the standard set of 35 faces etched into printer ROM. ATM automatically places a line in your WIN.INI file that makes the typeface available to all Windows programs. This line will appear under a heading in WIN.INI that refers to the printer and its port connection, such as [PostScript, LPT1]. WIN.INI refers to the face by its actual file names, in this case GAL_____.PFM and GAL_____.PFB. The first file is the one that contains all character spacing and kerning information (PFM=Printer Font Metric), while the second one is the actual typeface outline (Printer Font Binary). If you ask ATM to automatically download the face for you, then it must keep references to both the PFM and PFB files—the first so that programs like PageMaker can determine correct spacing, and the second so that the typeface can be sent to the printer. The line that ATM adds to WIN.INI would look something like this:

```
softfont=c:\psfonts\gal_____.pfm;c:\psfonts\gal_____.pfb
```

The subdirectories would vary from system to system, but this lengthy entry in WIN.INI (of which PostScript printer users will find many) is what tells Windows to download the typeface automatically.

If you intend to download Garamond-Light to your printer yourself, then you would need to do two things: 1) Use Adobe's PCSEND program to make the typeface resident (PCSEND comes with every Adobe typeface, and instructions for use are available just by running the program); and 2) indicate via the line in WIN.INI that the typeface should be treated as resident. If you make this decision as you add the face, you can have ATM create the line in WIN.INI for you, and it would look like this:

```
softfont=c:\psfonts\gal_____.pfm
```

Notice how only the PFM file is referenced—Windows is no longer concerned with the typeface outline, as it expects it to already be resident in the printer. If you decide to have the typeface be treated as resident after adding it, then you will need to edit WIN.INI yourself. This is easily done with Notepad, or better yet, the SYSEDIT program that launches Notepad and WIN.INI together. As always, back up WIN.INI before editing it, just to be safe.

AUTOMATIC VERSUS MANUAL DOWNLOADING

Having Windows download your typefaces is easier, but it adds significantly to your printing times, and the typeface is sent to an area of printer memory known as "volatile memory." In other words, your printer disposes of the typeface as soon as it is done with it. If you set a line of type in Garamond-Italic, Windows will download all of Garamond-Italic (remember, bold and italic variations of a type design are their own typefaces), and the printer will use it for that line and then discard it, oblivious to the fact that you might call for it again in the very next paragraph.

On the other hand, if you download the face manually, it will generally stay in printer memory for as long as there is power to the printer. This can cut down considerably on print times and sizes of print files, as PageMaker expects to find the typeface resident, thereby declining to send any typeface information. If you forget to perform the download after telling Page-Maker that you have done it, you'll get Courier.

Some printers, such as the HP LaserJet 4M, clear memory whenever you change their status, like going from PCL to PostScript, or going from 300 dpi resolution to 600 dpi. If this happens, you will need to download your typeface once again in order to make it resident.

So here are our rules of thumb. Download the typeface ahead of time if:

➤ You expect to be printing many proofs of a publication that has just one or two typefaces.

➤ You have a publication that involves many incidental typeface changes, like lines of type set in bold or italic.

➤ Simply put, you print with one typeface a lot

Have Windows download the typeface if:

➤ You only use it occasionally.

➤ You are not bothered by the time Windows requires to send typeface information during printing.

➤ You just don't want to hassle with downloading.

If you regularly create PostScript print files to send to your service bureau, there is more to this discussion, and it picks up in Appendix C.

Creating Print Files for Remote Printing

F THIS WERE A PERFECT WORLD,
printing your PageMaker publications at your service bureau on high-
resolution paper or film would be easy: You would copy your publication
onto a disk, go to your service bureau, and hand over your disk. They
would open it, print it, and deliver beautiful, crisp artwork for you to take
back to work. You would show it to your boss, and promptly get a raise.

Okay, time to wake up now. What's wrong with this picture? Easy—
most service bureaus don't know a dime about PC applications. We know
that's changing, and we know we just insulted many service bureaus who
have worked hard to get up to speed with Windows. But the fact remains
that most people who run service bureaus hook their imagesetters up to
Macintosh computers, cringe when faced with a PC-formatted disk, and
would probably faint dead away if confronted with a $5\frac{1}{4}$-inch disk.

All is not lost for PageMaker users intent on sending out for film—not
by a long shot. There is a universal language that links imagesetters, Macs,
and PCs: the language of PostScript. That wonderfully unintelligible collection of ASCII printer instructions is the key to this puzzle and turning that
key is easy: Instead of sending PostScript data to a printer, you capture it in
a file. This appendix shows how.

BECOMING POSTSCRIPT CAPABLE

You don't need to own a PostScript printer to create a PostScript file; you just need to tell PageMaker that you have one. If you have a PostScript laser printer, you can use it to create proof copies of your publication before sending the file to the service bureau.

If you do not own a PostScript laser printer and therefore have not added a PostScript printer driver to Windows, you will need to do so now. Open the Windows Control Panel and choose Printers. Click on Add, and choose the first item on the list, "Install Unlisted or Updated Printer." When prompted for a disk, insert the last disk from the original PageMaker disks and choose PostScript Printer from the list of printers. Windows will add it to your existing list of printers, at which point you could use the Connect button to connect the printer to FILE for the purposes of creating PostScript files.

Next, you will need to start Aldus Setup to install the PostScript Printer Description (.PPD) file specific to the PostScript printer or imagesetter on which your file will ultimately be printed. For details, refer to "Selecting Printer Files" in Appendix A.

Once you have installed the printer, you must designate it as your target printer—display the Page Setup dialog box and select the PostScript printer in the Compose to Printer field. When you are ready to create your PostScript printer file, choose Print on the File menu. If the PostScript printer is not your Windows default printer, you will need to select it in the Print To drop-down list box. Then click on the Options button, and choose Write PostScript to File. Choose the Normal option and type the path and file name for your file. You can create the file on your floppy disk directly but it is faster to create it on your hard drive and then copy it to your floppy. Either way, this file, called a PostScript file, is ready to be taken to your service bureau.

WHAT ABOUT TYPEFACES?

In Appendix B, we discussed the factors surrounding resident typefaces and your options for managing typefaces that are not resident in your printer. If your service bureau is worth its salt, you should expect it to have virtually all typefaces in the Adobe Type 1 library and the means to download them to the raster image processors that drive the imagesetters. In other words, when going to a service bureau, all PostScript typefaces should be treated as resident, the only exception being any obscure or custom-made faces that you know your service bureau wouldn't own.

Treating typefaces as resident is easy to establish with a bit of WIN.INI editing, as discussed in Appendix B, but what if you want those same typefaces to be automatically downloaded to your laser printer? How do you have them handled one way for your laser, and another way for your service bureau? Windows allows for this, as it keeps separate typeface listings for each printer connection. It has one set of listings for "PostScript printer on LPT1," and another for "PostScript printer on FILE." Therefore, to continue the example from Appendix B, you could designate Garamond-Light and its related weights to be downloaded to your laser printer on LPT1, and you could have them treated as resident typefaces when being sent to FILE.

The burden is on you to manage your WIN.INI listings, and those frequently troubled with this task should consider picking up FontMinder, the handy utility from Ares Software (415-578-9090). For about $50, this utility will manage all of these typeface shenanigans from a friendly dialog box, instead of requiring you to go ten rounds with WIN.INI. Furthermore, users of fast computers and HP LaserJet II, III, and IV printers should look closely at LaserMaster's line of WinJet printer controller cards (612-944-9457). In addition to offering very good resolution at high speeds, the WinJet treats all Type 1 faces on your hard drive as resident. When you use the WinJet for your PostScript printing, you never need to worry about downloading typefaces.

TRUETYPE AND SERVICE BUREAUS

Despite frequent rumors to the contrary, you can use any valid TrueType face in a publication that is bound for your service bureau. The TrueType engine renders its characters as curves and places them right into the PostScript stream. Your service bureau need not worry about owning the typeface—to the imagesetter, TrueType characters are treated like other curves.

The problem that fuels these reports of incompatibility occurs when unsuspecting users try to substitute TrueType for Type 1 faces. Unless the faces match exactly—a rare occurrence—such a substitution usually produces unsatisfactory results at small sizes, and at worst, returns Courier.

Windows provides for this substitution in the Advanced section of its Printer Setup Options dialog box. Unless you really mean to assign such a substitution, make sure that the "Use Substitution Table" field remains unchecked. Once done, TrueType faces have no choice but to work correctly. The only conceivable problem would be if you used a very complex typeface—like an exceptionally frilly script face—that proves too taxing for the imagesetter. This is an unlikely, but perhaps not impossible, event.

CREATING EPS FILES

If you understand the concept of a PostScript file, you should have no problem with its cousin, the Encapsulated PostScript file. While a PostScript file's mission is to describe a publication to an imagesetter, an EPS file's purpose in life is to represent an individual page inside of another document.

The two files are almost identical in nature, but when you click on the EPS button in the print Options dialog box, you instruct PageMaker to add a few critical lines of code to the file. With this code, the file can be placed inside of another document, be it one from PageMaker, Ventura Publisher, FrameMaker, CorelDRAW, or one of dozens of other programs that support the EPS format. You have essentially "encapsulated" the page inside of another—hence the name—and can size or shape it to suit your purpose. When printed to a PostScript device, the program whose document contains the EPS file sends everything down to the printer, no questions asked.

There is one requirement of EPS files: They can only represent one page. Multiple-page EPS files are a contradiction in terms, because only one image can be represented. Think of an EPS file as just another type of graphic imported into another program.

Finally, EPS files are subject to all of the same rules of typeface handling as regular PostScript files. They will download a typeface or treat it as resident, according to the instructions in WIN.INI.

Aldus Additions

HIS APPENDIX BRIEFLY DESCRIBES
the Aldus Additions included with PageMaker 5.0 at the time of this writing. Aldus, as well as third-party vendors, will be creating more of these Additions as time goes by; you can use the Aldus Setup program to install Additions. For each Addition that is discussed in more detail in the body of this book, the appropriate chapter numbers are referenced.

To access the Additions, choose Utilities ➤ Aldus Additions.

BALANCE COLUMNS

The Balance Columns Addition evens out columns so that they are the same length. You can choose to align the columns at the top or the bottom. See Chapter 8.

BUILD BOOKLET

If you create $5\frac{1}{2}$-by-$8\frac{1}{2}$-inch booklets on $8\frac{1}{2}$-by-11-inch paper or $8\frac{1}{2}$-by-11-inch newsletters on 11-by-17-inch paper, the Build Booklet Addition will save you time and money. The Addition repaginates a publication so that the pages are in the proper order for printing signatures. See Chapter 3.

BULLETS AND NUMBERING

The Bullets and Numbering Addition numbers a list or inserts bullets in front of each paragraph in a list. See Chapter 4.

CONTINUATION

When a story continues onto another page, you can use the Continuation Addition to create the "Continued on page" and "Continued from page" lines. The Addition will figure out and insert the correct page numbers. See Chapter 8.

CREATE COLOR LIBRARY

The Create Color Library Addition creates a color library file out of the current publication's color palette. This library can then be used in any publication. See Chapter 12.

CREATE KEYLINE

The Create Keyline Addition draws a box around any selected object (text blocks or graphics). See Chapter 10.

DISPLAY PUB INFO

The Display Pub Info Addition shows font information, status of linked files, and styles used. By clicking on the Save button, you can save all of this information to a file for future reference or comparison. See Chapters 7, 8, and 11.

DROP CAP

A drop cap is the first character of a paragraph that has been enlarged and hangs down into the body of the paragraph. The Drop Cap Addition automates its creation. See Chapter 9.

EDIT ALL STORIES

The Edit All Stories Addition creates a cascade of windows for all the stories in the current publication. See Chapter 5.

EDIT TRACKS

The Edit Tracks Addition lets you edit tracking information for any typeface. Use this to customize the letter spacing associated with PageMaker's built-in tracks (Very Loose, Loose, Normal, Tight, and Very Tight) for individual typefaces.

EXPERT KERNING

The Expert Kerning Addition automates the kerning process, and provides more precise kerning control. Use this Addition to fine-tune the kerning of large text, such as headlines and posters. See Chapter 9.

FIND OVERSET TEXT

The Find Overset Text Addition will find text that has not yet been placed on the page; it will display the last text block in a story that contains unplaced text. See Chapter 8.

GROUP IT

Use the Group It Addition to combine several objects so that you can move, size, rotate, or crop the objects as one unit.

LIBRARY PALETTE

The Library Palette Addition is an option on the Window menu. Use the Library Palette to store and retrieve frequently-used text and graphics.

LIST STYLES USED

The List Styles Used Addition displays the styles used in a particular story. The list indicates the number of paragraphs that are tagged with each name. This Addition is useful for finding out if paragraphs are tagged incorrectly. See Chapter 7.

OPEN TEMPLATE

Use the Open Template Addition to open the templates included with PageMaker. You can preview the template before opening it. See Chapter 14.

PRINTER STYLES

The Printer Styles Addition offers a variety of printing-related functions. For example, you can use it to batch-print several publications, and to create and apply style sheets that define particular printer dialog box settings.

RUN SCRIPT

The Run Script Addition allows you to automate PageMaker tasks by running a script file. The script, which is similar to a macro, is a text file that contains instructions written in the PageMaker scripting language.

RUNNING HEADERS/FOOTERS

The Running Headers/Footers Addition allows you to get context-sensitive headers and footers on each page, such as those found in dictionaries and thesauruses. It looks for the first or last occurrence of a particular style and takes part of the text in that paragraph and places it in a header or footer. See Chapter 14.

SORT PAGES

The Sort Pages Addition provides you with on-screen thumbnails of all the pages in your publication. Use it to quickly move pages to different places in a publication. See Chapter 3.

STORY INFO

The Story Info Addition provides information about the selected story: the name of the linked file (if any), number of text blocks in the story, the number of characters and column inches in the story, the pages the story spans, and whether there is any overset text (text that is not placed). See Chapter 8.

TEXTBLOCK INFO

The Textblock Info Addition is similar to Story Info, except it returns information about a single text block. Textblock Info tells how a text block fits into the whole of the story, how much space it consumes, and how many characters are contained in it. See Chapter 8.

TRAVERSE TEXTBLOCKS

The Traverse Textblocks Addition allows you to quickly move through a story that spans multiple, and possibly noncontiguous, pages. It provides options for going to the first, last, next, or previous text block in the story. See Chapter 8.

Note to the Reader: Boldfaced page numbers indicate pages containing definitions of terms and principal discussions of topics. Italic page numbers indicate illustrations.

B

Backspace key
  Alt + Backspace,
    undoing deletions, 132
    undoing guide moves, 382
  deleting with, 131
Balance Columns Addition, 318–319,
    319, 320, 684
baseline alignment, 219–220, *219,*
    220
baseline leading, **223**
baseline offset option, control palette,
    427–428, *428*
.BCF extension, 489
birth announcements, **647–649,** *648*
bitmap graphics. *See also* graphics,
    imported; TIFF images
  controlling lightness and contrast,
    439–441
  printer memory for, 98
  screen resolutions for, *438,*
    438–439, *439, 440, 441*
  sizing, 419
  versus vector graphics, **412–415,**
    414
bitmapped fonts. *See also* ATM fonts;
    fonts; TrueType fonts
  versus ATM and TrueType fonts,
    668–670
  print orientation and, 74–76
  printer memory for, 98
  printers and, 90
bleeds, 379–380, *379*
body text
  assigning styles to, 258, 272
  creating styles for, 269–270
  editing styles for, 273–274, *275*
  paragraph formatting for, 52
bold type style, *119,* 122, 124–125
book feature, **574–615.** *See also* Build
    Booklet Addition; master pages;
    templates
  creating books, **577–582**
    creating publication for front
      matter, 577–578
    defining book list, 574, **578–579,**
      602–603

numbering pages across
  publications, 574, **578,**
  579–580
handbook exercises, **601–615**
  choosing topics from a list, 611
  creating cross-references, 612–613
  creating publication for front
    matter, 601, *602*
  creating sub-entries in index,
    610–611
  defining book list, 602–603
  formatting table of contents,
    607–608, *608, 609*
  generating index, 614, *615*
  generating table of contents,
    605–606, *606*
  marking index entries, 609–610,
    613
  marking table of contents entries,
    604–605
  printing, 603, *604*
  viewing index, 613–614
indexes, **589–600,** *590, 615. See
    also* Add Index Entry dialog box
  choosing topics from a list,
    593–594, 611
  Create Index dialog box,
    597–599, *597*
  creating multiple levels in, **593,**
    610–611
  cross-references, 575, **595–596,**
    612–613
  formatting, 599
  generating, 575, **597–600,**
    605–606, *606, 615*
  Index Format dialog box, 598, *599*
  marking index entries, 575,
    590–593, *592,* 609–610, *613*
  overview of, **589–590**
  Select Topic dialog box, 594, *594,*
    611, *612*
  Show Index dialog box, 596–596,
    596, 613, 614
  styles for, 599–600, *599*
  viewing, **596–597,** 613–614
overview of, **576–577**
printing all publications, 574,
    580–582, *581,* 603, *604*
table of contents, **582–589**

changing leaders, 585, 586–587,
  586
Create Table of Contents dialog
  box, 583–584, *584*
creating for a single publication,
  588–589
formatting, 575, **585,** 607–608,
  608, 609
generating, 575, **583–584,**
  587–588
leader characters for, 584, *585,*
  586, **586–587**
marking entries for, 574,
  582–583, 604–605
regenerating, 587–588
styles for, **582–583,** 585, *586,*
  607, *607*
Book option, File menu, 574
Book options, Print Document dialog
  box, **95**
Book Publication List dialog box
  Auto Renumbering options, 574,
    578–579
  defining book list in, 578–579, *578*
book template exercises, **561–570.**
    See also master pages; templates
  creating book styles, **565–568,** *566*
    body text style, 566, 567–568
    chapter head style, 566–567, *566*
    subhead style, 566, *567*
  creating chapters, 569–570, *570*
  creating headers, 563–564, *564, 565*
  inserting page numbers, 562–563,
    562
  master pages in, 562–564, *562, 564,*
    565
  saving book template, 568
book templates, **557–558,** *559. See
    also* book feature; Build Booklet
    Addition; master pages;
    templates
  creating chapters, **557–558,** *559,*
    569–570, *570*
  designing, 557
  master pages in, **557,** 558, *559,*
    562–564, *562, 564, 565*
booklets, Build Booklet Addition, 71,
  86–89, *87, 89,* 684

693

Help Yourself with Another Quality Sybex Book

Understanding Presentation Graphics
Michael Talman

A must for anyone using a computer to produce business graphics, reports, and presentations, whether on a Macintosh or a PC, and regardless of software used. It's an in-depth guide to effective communication, with guidelines for planning and organization; graphic design do's and don't's; ways to use color to best advantage; and proven techniques for conveying a clear message.

382pp; 7 1/2" x 9"
ISBN: 0-7821-1023-1

Available
at Better
Bookstores
Everywhere

Sybex Inc.
2021 Challenger Drive
Alameda, CA 94501
Telephone (800) 227-2346
Fax (510) 523-2373

SYBEX

Sybex. Help Yourself.

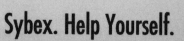

SYBEX

FREE BROCHURE!

Complete this form today, and we'll send you a full-color brochure of Sybex bestsellers.

Please supply the name of the Sybex book purchased.

_____

How would you rate it?

_____ Excellent   _____ Very Good   _____ Average   _____ Poor

Why did you select this particular book?

_____ Recommended to me by a friend
_____ Recommended to me by store personnel
_____ Saw an advertisement in _____
_____ Author's reputation
_____ Saw in Sybex catalog
_____ Required textbook
_____ Sybex reputation
_____ Read book review in _____
_____ In-store display
_____ Other _____

Where did you buy it?

_____ Bookstore
_____ Computer Store or Software Store
_____ Catalog (name: _____)
_____ Direct from Sybex
_____ Other: _____

Did you buy this book with your personal funds?

_____ Yes   _____ No

About how many computer books do you buy each year?

_____ 1-3   _____ 3-5   _____ 5-7   _____ 7-9   _____ 10+

About how many Sybex books do you own?

_____ 1-3   _____ 3-5   _____ 5-7   _____ 7-9   _____ 10+

Please indicate your level of experience with the software covered in this book:

_____ Beginner   _____ Intermediate   _____ Advanced

Which types of software packages do you use regularly?

_____ Accounting	_____ Databases	_____ Networks
_____ Amiga	_____ Desktop Publishing	_____ Operating Systems
_____ Apple/Mac	_____ File Utilities	_____ Spreadsheets
_____ CAD	_____ Money Management	_____ Word Processing
_____ Communications	_____ Languages	_____ Other _____

(please specify)

Which of the following best describes your job title?

_____ Administrative/Secretarial   _____ President/CEO

_____ Director   _____ Manager/Supervisor

_____ Engineer/Technician   _____ Other _____

                                                   (please specify)

Comments on the weaknesses/strengths of this book: _____

_____

_____

_____

_____

Name _____

Street _____

City/State/Zip _____

Phone _____

PLEASE FOLD, SEAL, AND MAIL TO SYBEX

-- -- -- -- -- -- -- -- -- -- -- -- -- -- -- -- -- -- --

SYBEX INC.
Department M
2021 CHALLENGER DR.
ALAMEDA, CALIFORNIA USA
94501

SYBEX

SEAL

DISK CONTENTS

The companion disk contains the files for the Hands-On Practice exercises at the end of the chapters. These files are PageMaker 5.0 publication files, text files (in Word for Windows 2.0 format), and graphic files (in Windows metafile format). If you install this disk, you will be able to open existing publications and do all the exercises without having to type a lot of text.

INSTALLATION

Before you install the disk, you should be aware of a few things. The companion disk contains a file called INSTALL.EXE. When you run this program, the exercise files will be extracted from this file and placed in the current directory. The files consume about 920K of disk space.

To install the disk, follow these simple instructions:

1. Create a subdirectory called PM5PUBS on one of your hard drives.

2. Copy INSTALL.EXE from the companion disk to that subdirectory.

3. Change to the PM5PUBS directory.

4. Type INSTALL and press Enter.

In order to use your companion disk's text and graphic files in PageMaker, you must install the following filters: Word for Windows 2.0 Import and Windows Metafile Import. See Appendix A for information on installing PageMaker filters.

Note: Upon opening some of the publication files, you may get a message about font-mapping. If this happens, just click on OK.

IF YOU NEED A 3½-INCH DISK...

To receive a 3½-inch disk, please return the original 5¼-inch disk with a written request to:

SYBEX Inc.
Customer Service Department
2021 Challenger Drive
Alameda, CA 94501
(800) 227-2346

Be sure to include your name, complete mailing address, and the reference number 1182-3; otherwise, your request cannot be processed. Allow six weeks for delivery.